W9-ADU-984

Dimensions of Storytelling in German Literature and Beyond

Studies in German Literature, Linguistics, and Culture

Dimensions of Storytelling in German Literature and Beyond

"For once, telling it all from the beginning"

Edited by

Kristy R. Boney and Jennifer Marston William

CAMDEN HOUSE

Rochester, New York

First published 2018
by Camden House

Camden House is an imprint of Boydell & Brewer Inc.
668 Mt. Hope Avenue, Rochester, NY 14620, USA
www.camden-house.com
and of Boydell & Brewer Limited
PO Box 9, Woodbridge, Suffolk IP12 3DF, UK
www.boydellandbrewer.com

ISBN-13: 978-1-64014-040-0
ISBN-10: 978-1-64014-040-9

Library of Congress Cataloging-in-Publication Data

CIP data is available from the Library of Congress.

This publication is printed on acid-free paper.
Printed in the United States of America.

Contents

Part II. Expressions of Modernity: Using Storytelling Unconventionally

Part III. The Personal Narrative: Storytelling in Acute Historical Moments

Acknowledgments

THE EDITORS EXPRESS their sincere appreciation to the following sources of financial support for this volume: The School of Languages and Cultures, the College of Liberal Arts, and the Office of the Executive Vice President for Research and Partnerships at Purdue University; and the College of Arts, Humanities, and Social Sciences, as well as the Department of Government, International Studies, and Languages at the University of Central Missouri.

We are also appreciative of {X, Y, and Z museums / archives / foundations} for their permission to use the images that have been reprinted in this book and on its cover.

Jim Walker, the editorial director at Camden House, has provided invaluable help and support of this project from its beginnings. We are most grateful to him and to Sue Martin for her careful copyediting.

Finally, we take this opportunity to recognize Dr. Helen Fehervary, whose literary scholarship informs and inspires many of the essays in this volume. This book attests to the far-reaching effect that her passion for, and extensive knowledge about, the art of narrative have had on the editors and each of the contributors in our varied scholarly pursuits.

Introduction: The Social, Political, and Personal Dimensions of Storytelling

Kristy R. Boney and Jennifer Marston William

THIS VOLUME'S TITLE QUOTATION, ". . . for once, telling it all from the beginning" (einmal alles von Anfang an erzählen), stems from Anna Seghers's exile novel *Transit*, in which the author told not only her own story but that of countless others who faced political, personal, and bureaucratic obstacles in their attempts to escape peril during the Nazi era. While sitting in a café in the old harbor of Marseilles, the unnamed narrator of *Transit* spins the quintessential tale of exile in 1940s France: "Which view do you prefer? The *pizza* baking over the open fire? Then you'll have to sit beside me. The Old Harbor? Then you'd better sit opposite. You can see the sun go down behind Fort Saint-Nicolas. That won't bore you, I'm sure."[1] *Transit*, completed by the prolific Seghers in 1942 and first published in English in 1944, and in German in 1948, is a political novel that shows the author's acute awareness of human compassion. It also makes clear that without the vitality of storytelling, the experience of exile becomes more of a fleeting historical moment, too easily left in the past. Storytelling forms the basis of a lasting and powerful historical chronicle.

In *Transit* and so many other literary works in the twentieth century, storytelling is thematized and put forth not only as a way to chronicle events but also as a means of processing the dire situation in which the exiles found themselves—indeed, as a means of psychological survival. Michel de Certeau, in his *The Practice of Everyday Life*, argues that the practice of storytelling defines our society, and that without stories, societies break down.[2] This is pertinent when considering how fiction can define a society, or help in redefining one. Writers such as Seghers, who experienced the harsh and alienating effects of exile and persecution first-hand, created characters with similar backgrounds who also engage in various forms of storytelling about their trials and triumphs. The resulting *mise-en-abyme*, story-in-a-story structure highlights the enduring tenacity of both oral and written narrative through the ages.

Certeau is not alone in his view of stories as the backbone of our contemporary existence. Jonathan Gottschall, for instance, finds a connection between storytelling and biology, suggesting that our penchant to tell stories is a compulsive evolutionary—and thus universal—function.[3] Storytelling is clearly a constant in human social life, and a perennial topic for scholarly examination as well. A recent notable monograph on the topic is Martin Puchner's ambitious and compelling *The Written World: The Power of Stories to Shape People, History, and Civilization* (2017),[4] which details how stories have influenced the course of humankind. Also of note is Marco Caracciolo's *The Experientiality of Narrative* (2014),[5] which focuses on the receptive aspect of fictional stories that often contradict the "rules" of reality, but to which readers nonetheless tend to respond based on their own, real experiential background—an exploration with distinct implications for the study of autobiographical narratives such as those discussed in the pages that follow. With the current volume, we continue this contemporary scholarly trend of exploring the various facets of storytelling with a focus on the ways in which narrative has documented sociopolitical developments and left its mark on cultural history, particularly but not exclusively within the twentieth-century German literary tradition.

This essay compilation is at its heart a tribute to the work of German Studies scholar Helen Fehervary. Her expertise in East German literature and particularly the prose of Anna Seghers continues to inspire many researchers who examine the facets of narrative and storytelling in a number of sociohistorical contexts. While Walter Benjamin, in his famous essay "The Storyteller" (1936), lamented the decline of the storytelling tradition in the age of the modern novel, Seghers and other writers went on to record—in many forms, including novels—the darkest days of the twentieth century in creative and compelling ways. This volume examines a number of those writers and places particular emphasis on the themes of exile, the Holocaust and its aftermath, modernism (and its precursors, for example, Heine), and East German literature. Many contributors explore, either implicitly or explicitly, the tensions between aesthetics and politically conscious writing, as well as individual struggles involving conformity and resistance in a totalitarian state. Writing about storytelling and understanding those documents of the past opens a lens to historical truths. In an increasingly interconnected world of commerce and communication, the stories that chronicle world history play a crucial role in reminding us of our shared humanity.

In the twenty-first century, the humanities have increasingly come under assault. The future of many humanities programs is uncertain at best. Essentially, this amounts to an assault on the right and ability to tell stories about personal and political obstacles. As the above passage from Seghers's *Transit* intimates—with its narrator's choice of view as he settles in for a story, either being lulled by a fire or focusing on a historical site that was a center of the French resistance—storytelling frames our daily lives and, as such, is so much more than an object of scholarly analysis.

Further, while German literature gives us many examples for such a project, this essay compilation reminds us that the implications go far beyond a limited national boundary. One of our goals with this volume is to provide a larger understanding of the dimensions of storytelling as a cross-cultural and social phenomenon, especially pertinent in times of crisis.

A number of essays in this book pay homage to one of the most inventive and productive German-language storytellers of the twentieth century. Anna Seghers (1900–1983), born Netty Reiling, grew up in Mainz and was raised in an Orthodox Jewish family. A student of art history at the University of Heidelberg, she received her doctorate with a dissertation on Jews and Judaism in the work of Rembrandt. Seghers treasured legends, myths, fables, and fairytales from many cultures, and their deep influence on her work is unmistakable. Her stories and novels often gesture toward the storytellers she enjoyed reading most. Coming from a variety of cultural traditions, they included Jean Racine, Honoré de Balzac, Heinrich von Kleist, Georg Büchner, Fyodor Dostoyevsky, Leo Tolstoy, and Franz Kafka.[6] Seghers, in turn, left her own mark on the writing of many younger generation East German writers, most notably Christa Wolf, Heiner Müller, and Franz Fühmann (see Brockmann, this volume). As Fehervary has asserted in her influential book *The Mythic Dimension*, "Seghers's prose invokes the form of the chronicle and legend," and, rather than evoking readers' identification with her characters, Seghers instead was concerned in her writing with "the truth as related by the storyteller, the credibility and skill of the witness."[7]

We assert, as the title of part 1 stresses, that Seghers has been unduly neglected in the study of German literary history. She is sometimes dismissed unjustly as a Communist writer who did little more than toe the party line, or she is known solely as the author of the acclaimed antifascist novel *Das siebte Kreuz* (The Seventh Cross, 1942). The essays featured here work to remedy that misconception, continuing the tireless efforts of the past few decades by Seghers experts such as Ute Brandes, Helen Fehervary, Sonja Hilzinger, Christiane Zehl Romero, Silvia Schlenstedt, Alexander Stephan, as they demonstrate the far-reaching, multifaceted richness of her storytelling, which spans seven decades and chronicles some of the most crucial, watershed events of the twentieth century. One way to understand Seghers's commitment to storytelling—and to differentiate her from a more typical socialist-realist stance—can be found in her 1938/39 correspondence with the Hungarian literary historian Georg Lukács. Lukács asserted in a 1938 essay entitled "Realism in the Balance" that while new modernist writers were nuanced and important, they were not "true" realist writers and lacked revolutionary power. Seghers disagreed and emphasized to the theorist that the "present reality, with its crises, wars, etc. must . . . first be endured, it must be looked in the face, and secondly it must be portrayed."[8] Seghers was ever aware of the larger context of art in a political world, and her attempt to connect with the "immediacy of basic experience,"[9] sometimes through aesthetically and stylistically experimental ways in her writing, aptly illustrates the importance of storytelling in moments of political crisis.

While this volume's nineteen contributions are diverse and quite wide-ranging, there is considerable thematic overlap among them. The essays explore themes that confront traditional understandings of German history within the twentieth century. Further, they reimagine how storytelling can be used to grasp and process moments of political crisis, but above all, they explore unique topics related to (and related through) storytelling. With these areas of common ground in mind, the book is divided into three parts. Part 1, "Anna Seghers: A Missing Piece in the Canon of Modernist Storytellers," begins with Christiane Zehl Romero's close look at Anna Seghers's formative intellectual time as a student in Heidelberg. Romero argues that, given the available archival material, a rethinking of this period in Seghers's life is a worthwhile pursuit, and indeed is essential to the process of forming a more complete life narrative of this prolific writer. Seghers's novel *Die Gefährten* (The Comrades, 1932) reflects on this crucial time in its content and its motifs. Romero attributes the lack of dogmatism in Seghers's storytelling largely to the influence of Heidelberg's stimulating intellectual community in the 1920s, which encouraged open interdisciplinary discourse and debate on history, politics, and philosophy.

Peter Beicken discusses the complex narrative structure of Anna Seghers's 1943 novella *Der Ausflug der toten Mädchen* (The Excursion of the Dead Girls, 1946) by reviewing previous analyses of this masterful piece of Holocaust literature and discussing its visual and cinematic mode of narration. Differentiating this work from the *Erinnerungs-Novelle* (memory-work) tradition, Beicken shows not only how some autobiographical details are fictionalized in the narrative but also how Seghers uses her first-person narrator in the cinematic function of a documentary-style voiceover commentary, thereby exposing the memories of the childhood idyll retrospectively as dystopic in the aftermath of the Holocaust.

Ute Brandes considers Seghers's immediate postwar stories in the context of *Trümmerliteratur* (rubble literature), a movement that focused on the return home of soldiers and prisoners of war via a terse writing style that signified the utter devastation of postwar Germany. Brandes points out the stylistic and thematic connections between Seghers's stories and rubble literature, while also considering the sociopolitical implications surrounding them. She explores, for example, how passages that were censored by East German authorities undermined the narrative integrity of some of Seghers's texts, and she investigates through archival records Seghers's opinions on the GDR's socialist-realist doctrine and related issues.

Stephen Brockmann covers the topics of reeducation, "denazification," and ideological transformations in post-Nazi society, and elucidates how these processes played out in East Germany, as reflected in such works as Seghers's novella *Der Mann und sein Name* (The Man and His Name, 1952), and her novels *Die Entscheidung* (The Decision, 1959) and *Das Vertrauen* (Trust, 1968). Brockmann expounds on the notion of Seghers's "subdued optimism" (also alluded to by Jennifer Marston William later in this section with her discussion of the hopeful ambivalence apparent in Seghers's work). He also elaborates on Seghers's mentorship of younger-generation GDR writers, such as Franz Fühmann, who wrote about his experiences with being seduced by Nazism. Seghers saw such revelations as "essential for the future of Germany, and of German literature."

Hunter Bivens also examines Seghers's novels *Die Entscheidung* and *Das Vertrauen* as chronicles of the GDR's formative years and as depictions of individual engagement with the developing socialist project there. In particular, Bivens considers the dissonance between form and content of these novels with a focus on the tropes of trust (*Vertrauen*) and contingency/coincidence (*Zufall*), and the tensions between the idealized, aspired dynamic time of building up (*Aufbauzeit*) and the realities of the young GDR's "flaue Zeit" (time of stagnation). Seghers's epic style of storytelling and the form of her novels in the socialist context, Bivens argues, reflect the particular conditions under which the GDR came to exist, in a way that was distinct from most other socialist-realist writing of that time.

Benjamin Robinson provides yet another insightful critical perspective on Seghers's 1959 novel *Die Entscheidung*. As Robinson points out, the novel was criticized by West German critics for its adherence to official socialist doctrine, but he argues that the work in fact can be "read as a bleak depiction of a socialist state." Robinson examines the aesthetic development that is evidenced in the different expressions of temporality and chronotope in this and Seghers's earlier novels; *Die Entscheidung* highlights real socialist principles through the use of allegory and its depiction of the characters' "busy efforts tending toward the riddle of history's final resolution."

Using elements of the cognitive approach that has been evolving within literary scholarship in recent years, Jennifer Marston William explores language in Anna Seghers's works. She discusses how Seghers's use of conceptual-metaphorical language reflects the situations that her characters experience. William stresses how Seghers's writing is also political, in that she takes a critical stance toward political events and their ramifications. In particular, William analyzes the use of the conceptual metaphor of emptiness (*die Leere*) that surfaces in much of Seghers's writing. It is a concept that corresponds with ambivalence, characterizing a simultaneous sense of optimism and pessimism, both on an individual and a collective level. Ultimately William argues that Seghers's texts, while focusing on the horrors of both nature and modern civilization, suggest that existential feelings of emptiness are mutable and that the human spirit will prevail.

Part 2, "Expressions of Modernity: Using Storytelling Unconventionally," starts farther back in time with a focus on a major forebear to literary modernism, as Robert Holub explores the poet Heinrich Heine's various—and mostly less than successful—attempts at novelistic fiction, with particular concentration on *Buch Le Grand* (1827), in which stories are told and the process of storytelling is self-reflexively thematized. Holub argues that *Buch Le Grand* is successful because Heine does not concern himself with narrative convention but rather highlights the stories and reflects on his own storytelling style. Holub speculates on Heine's reasons for experimenting with forms outside of poetry and provides a balanced account of the celebrated poet's strengths and weaknesses in writing narrative prose.

Kristy Boney brings us back into the early twentieth century as she explores the modernist topographies of writer Franz Kafka and painter Paul Klee and discusses how through different mediums each artist depicted the individual in a fragmented but dynamic existence. Modernist space was shaped by the new perceptions of temporality, and this reality was reflected in the stories told both in words and in pictures. For these two artists in particular, Boney argues that "approaching an external landscape was not a matter for interpretation, but it was a matrix of experience." Kafka and Klee expressed through their work how physical topography becomes inextricably enmeshed with the modern individual's experience.

Weijia Li discusses the "transtextuality" of German-Jewish writer W. Tonn, who infused his stories with a blend of both Western and Eastern mythical and folkloric elements after spending years as an exiled émigré in China. Li details the author's biography and closely analyzes some of Tonn's wartime stories. Despite heavy borrowing in the texts, Li rejects any notion of plagiarism in Tonn's work, arguing instead in favor of "a playful experiment with intertextuality, a type of transtextual relationship between texts," resulting in writing that anticipates postmodernism and "challenges the conventional mode of reading."

Elizabeth Loentz takes us on a different kind of storytelling exploration as she examines student writing of various genres that was published by the Sholem Aleichem Yiddish schools in Chicago in the twentieth century. Her readings of these texts focus not on their literary, rhetorical, or linguistic merits, but on their topics, themes, and content, and how these reflect the interplay of the children and teenagers' own concerns with the pedagogical agendas of the Sholem Aleichem schools in Chicago. Loentz shows how these agendas and the schools' missions varied over time in response to historical, political, and social changes (the Holocaust, McCarthyism and the Cold War, the founding of the State of Israel, assimilation and Americanization, and so on).

Michaela Peroutková examines the postwar representation of Czech and East German Jews in Jurek Becker's 1976 novel *Der Boxer* and in the 1969 autobiographical story *Alle Farben der Sonne und der Nacht* (All the Colors of the Sun and the Night) by Lenka Reinerová. After summarizing the sociopolitical situation for Jews in Czechoslovakia and in the German Democratic Republic—including the many problems and crises surrounding citizenship, anti-Semitism, and persecution—Peroutková explores the portrayal of how the exiled Jewish protagonists in these literary works experienced their return home after the war, and how they came to grips with their Jewish identity in their respective postwar Communist societies.

The comparative view taken by most of the essays in this section culminates in the essay by Kristen Hetrick, who looks at how the stories of human physical maladies are told in two works of literature published half a century apart and in different parts of the world. While the "quest narrative" that portrays illness as a journey toward enlightenment or self-improvement has been common since the early nineteenth century, Hetrick explores some contrasting twentieth-century literary approaches to depicting cancer patients. The two texts under examination in this essay, Thomas Mann's *Die Betrogene* (1954) and Nadine Gordimer's *Get a Life* (2005), present alternative views of the transformative nature of a cancer experience. Hetrick argues, "While Mann's work is essentially an indictment of the very concept of transformative change through his portrayal of the afflicted protagonist, Gordimer's offers a more nuanced depiction of it than the traditionally dramatic one."

Part 3, "The Personal Narrative: Storytelling in Acute Historical Moments," begins with a fitting opening about storytelling and autobiography, as Jost Hermand presents a self-reflexive piece examining his own writing from the 1990s about his experiences in the youth evacuation camps for children in Germany during the Nazi period, a program that has not had a great deal of publicity and has often been misunderstood as a positive initiative of the Nazi regime. Hermand relates his traumatic experiences and memories of the camps where "the master race for the future Europe" was to be trained. In the process of writing and reflecting on his own writing across two languages, Hermand addresses the crucial issues of translation, intention, and effect of autobiographical narration, and the mistrust of the faculty of memory when telling one's own story.

Andy Spencer uses filmmaker Konrad Wolf's wartime diaries as well as an analysis of the 1968 autobiographical film *Ich war neunzehn* (I Was Nineteen) to point out the contradictions between Wolf's public and private utterances regarding enemies of the socialist state (namely of the

Soviet Union), and his expression of these issues in his filmmaking. Spencer illustrates this tension by delineating Wolf's relationship to dissident writer Lev Kopelev, whose shadow, as Spencer argues, hangs over *Ich war neunzehn* and informs Wolf's problematizing of the image of the heroic Red Army soldier. Spencer concludes that the film can be seen not as resolving this tension but as a "playing out of Wolf's dilemma" on screen for the East German public.

In sharing his own scholarly journey, particularly his academic engagement with the German Democratic Republic, Marc Silberman simultaneously tells the story of a nation and a culture. In an "intellectual autobiography of sorts," Silberman gives an overview of the study of East German culture, literature, and history as it has been conducted both in the past and currently. In addition, he ponders the future of East German Studies, particularly how this field fits in with the broader areas of German and European modernism, technology, socialism, and contemporary politics. The transnational perspective, Silberman argues, becomes increasingly important as we move further away from the end of the GDR era but still strive to keep its memory alive.

Luke Springman's essay investigates the mnemonic function of auditory signs and symbols in Christa Wolf's autobiographical novel *Kindheitsmuster*. He looks at how Wolf uses the processes of forgetting and remembering as both an individual and communal way of dealing with the past. Springman argues that by writing her childhood while simultaneously recording the process of doing so, Wolf connects lifeless forms with emotions and is able to attach moral judgments to her memories. Ultimately, she not only indicts herself in terms of the German guilt regarding the Holocaust but also blames the contemporary public sphere, thus placing *Kindheitsmuster* into the canon of cultural memory.

Amy Kepple Strawser's meticulous and smooth English translation of a chapter from Ursula Krechel's 2012 novel *Landgericht* (District Court) touches on themes directly related to those covered in other essays of this volume: the plight of "displaced persons" after the Second World War; expatriation; and storytelling as a means of confronting the personal and collective past. The story is told mostly through the point of view of Kornitzer, a former judge who has found his wife after the war and is trying to come to grips with the postwar present. With narrative techniques such as flashbacks and free indirect discourse, the style is reminiscent of that of Anna Seghers, the storyteller who is most celebrated in this volume. Krechel's text exemplifies *Heimkehrerliteratur* (literature written from the perspective of those returning from war), while also being a touching story of love reunited.

Sylvia Fischer's piece provides a fitting conclusion both to part 3 and to this volume, as it touches on many themes that are addressed throughout. For the first time in print, she shares her interview with Eberhard

Aurich, a freelance writer who was the last leader of the Free German Youth in the GDR, and his partner Christa Streiber, a television editor. Their discussion sheds light on the social and educational functions of literature for youth under Communism, as Fischer and her interviewees discuss what kinds of stories were told to and read by East German youth, and why, and they consider the intended and actual effects of some of this literature. The interview also addresses current trends in storytelling about the GDR, ending with Aurich and Streiber's striking opinion that the literature written between 1949 and 1989 is becoming largely irrelevant for everyone besides scholars of German culture.

* * *

Relying on various analytical lenses, the contributors to this volume conceptualize storytelling as a vital and indispensable way for the modern individual to chronicle lived human experience. Committed to addressing the present, the past, and prospects for the future, the literary writers represented here call attention to the concentric circles of human relationships—to the self and one's beliefs, to the family and one's upbringing, to the community and its expectations, and to the world and its imperatives. By collecting these diverse studies in one volume, we seek to create a collage that celebrates these social, political, and personal dimensions of storytelling and opens up new perspectives on our understanding of history, memory, and humanity. In the digital age, when communication is often reduced to texting, tweeting, and other truncated forms, storytelling may start to seem like a lost art. Yet with every historical turning point, with every crisis and every recovery period, come renewed opportunities to step back and tell it all "from the beginning." The cautious, grounded optimism of Anna Seghers and others like her who have lived and written through times of autocracy and perilous nationalism should inspire us as readers, writers, artists, and scholars to continue to turn to narrative, not only as an escape from the "real world" in troubled times, but as a way of reconnecting with it. Through it all, storytelling remains. It is a perennial art form, always at humanity's disposal as a tool for helping us to reevaluate where we came from and where we might be—or should be—headed.

Notes

1 Anna Seghers, *Transit*, trans. James A. Galston (Boston: Little Brown, 1944), 3.
2 Michel de Certeau, *The Practice of Everyday Life*, trans. Steven F. Rendall (Berkeley: University of California Press, 1984).
3 Jonathan Gottschall, *The Storytelling Animal: How Stories Make Us Human* (Boston: Houghton Mifflin Harcourt, 2012).
4 Martin Puchner, *The Written World: The Power of Stories to Shape People, History, and Civilization* (New York: Random House, 2017).

[5] Marco Caracciolo, *The Experientiality of Narrative: An Enactivist Approach* (Berlin: De Gruyter, 2014).

[6] Christiane Zehl Romero, "Anna Seghers," *Jewish Women: A Comprehensive Historical Encyclopedia*, 1 March 2009, Jewish Women's Archive, https://jwa.org/encyclopedia/article/seghers-anna.

[7] Helen Fehervary, *Anna Seghers: The Mythic Dimension* (Ann Arbor: University of Michigan Press, 2001), 3.

[8] Georg Lukács and Anna Seghers, "Correspondence," in *Essays über Realismus* (Berlin: Aufbau, 1948), 171.

[9] Ibid., 177.

Part I.

Anna Seghers: A Missing Piece in the Canon of Modernist Storytellers

1: Anna Seghers in Heidelberg: The Formative Years

Christiane Zehl Romero

NETTY REILING, as Anna Seghers was called by her maiden name, matriculated at the University of Heidelberg on April 20, 1920. (In this essay I will refer to the student as Netty Reiling, to the writer as Anna Seghers.) She published her first story, which she wrote while still a student, under the name Seghers, and as Anna Seghers she would become one of the most if not the most important German woman writer of the twentieth century. At the time Heidelberg was considered "the secret capital of intellectual Germany." Among the professoriate many were liberal to left, which was not the norm among German professors either before or after the First World War. They included Max and Alfred Weber, Emil Julius Gumbel, Gustav Radbruch, and Netty Reiling's teachers Emil Lederer, Carl Neumann, Hermann Oncken, and Karl Jaspers. Among the students there were many who later made a name for themselves, veterans of the First World War like Carl Zuckmayer, Carlo Mierendorff, and Leo Löwenthal, and of course younger ones, like Hannah Arendt (she came after Netty Reiling) and Jürgen Kuczynski, as well as émigrés from Eastern Europe, some of whom would become her friends. Many of them, not only Zuckmayer, left vivid descriptions of the intellectual atmosphere in Heidelberg during their time. He is the only one, however, who gave us his well-known recollections of the young, pretty, and somewhat shy Netty Reiling and his speculations about how she chose the pen-name Seghers— from the Dutch painter and Rembrandt contemporary Hercules Segers (or Seghers), who was being rediscovered and interpreted by an instructor and his students in Heidelberg.[1] Other young intellectuals, most notably Georg Lukács and Walter Benjamin, whom Seghers would get to know later on, came to town at different times, one for a few years, the other briefly in search of the all-important *Habilitation* (the next step after a doctorate and the prerequisite for a university career) and the academic employment it promised. Neither received the chance, Benjamin finding Karl Mannheim already in place. The difficulties of securing an academic or other appropriate position loomed as a dark cloud over the young people and their heady intellectual enterprises, especially over those of Jewish descent, who made up a sizeable contingent.

Through László Radványi, the fellow student whom she early on decided to make her life's partner, Netty Reiling was more affected by this insecurity than Seghers would later acknowledge. After finishing his dissertation on chiliasm with Karl Jaspers in 1923, Radványi longed for an academic career to do with philosophy or religion but could not find any work at all to support himself, let alone the wife Netty Reiling hoped to become.[2] Unpublished letters she wrote to him between 1921 and 1925 show how much this concerned her.[3] The marriage she wanted and her parents' at best reluctant consent were impossible without employment. When he finally found something, albeit unsatisfactory, in Berlin (at the Russian Trading Company) and was looking forward to their wedding she reminded him "My dear beloved life . . . do you remember . . . how I once wept in the Frankfurt railroad station, so many people and all with employment?"[4] What Seghers recalled later and publicly—in a "Talk to Students" from 1952—were contemporary events and revolutions "and while we shared in them, discussing them passionately, we pursued our studies. We loved the arts and scholarship."[5] This love was genuine, but for many of the young intellectuals it was also refuge and defiance in the face of the harsh realities of looming un- or underemployed. Heidelberg's great reputation rested on the study of the humanities, arts, and social sciences but, as one student, Jürgen Kuczynski, soberly put it in his remembrances, "the knowledge offered us was of relatively little economic value."[6]

Netty Reiling studied in Heidelberg from 1920 to 1924, with a two-semester break for an internship in Cologne, and graduated with a doctorate in Art History. Thus in US academic parlance one could call her a "product of Heidelberg." Yet, apart from scholars specializing in Seghers, who have done careful research on certain aspects of her time there, there is still little awareness of how important Heidelberg was for her and how much she belonged among the German and immigrant intellectuals who made up the vibrant atmosphere of the town at the time.[7] Her roots lie there along with those of many others of her generation. In the following I propose to pull together and highlight facets of Netty Reiling's Heidelberg experience, which on rethinking the available material warrant more attention and contribute to a more inclusive view of Anna Seghers, whose image and reputation have been and to a certain degree continue to be colored and somewhat distorted by post–Second World War political events.

Netty Reiling was almost twenty years old when she came to Heidelberg. She had just graduated from a girls' prep school in February 1920, and was in a hurry: "I only wanted to study because I was terribly afraid of getting stuck in this backwater Mainz," was Seghers's offhanded comment much later.[8] She had grown up in Mainz as the only child of a religious and well-established Jewish family. Her father, together with his older brother, owned a respected antiquarian and art dealership; her mother came from a very wealthy Frankfurt family. By the 1920s, it had become possible for young women from the middle and upper classes to go to university, but it was not yet as much a matter of course as Seghers later presented it. Heidelberg was situated in the province of Baden, where university study became open to women in 1900, earlier than elsewhere in Germany. Women constituted a small minority that grew slightly after the First World War, rising from 12 to 15 percent between 1919 and 1925.

Nor can it have been quite so easy to receive her traditional family's permission. Her female cousins did not go on to university, nor did most of her classmates in Mainz. Perhaps the fact that there were no male heirs to take over the family business helped her. University training and a doctorate might make it easier to carry on what the Reilings had built up over generations, after starting as itinerant traders. Neither her father nor his brother had gone to university.

Seghers never talked about such matters, nor did she explain why she chose Heidelberg or why she studied what she did. She was notoriously reticent about her own biography. The few remarks she later made about her student days came in specific contexts and often had a pedagogical purpose. In general, she did not care to speak about personal matters for public consumption, and famously put off her would-be biographer Christa Wolf with the words: "As far as the biographical questions are concerned: I believe that a writer's experiences and views emerge most clearly from his work, even without a particular biography."[9]

Thus, to understand the role the student years in Heidelberg played for Anna Seghers we must glean as much as we can from her occasional, sometimes mystifying, sometimes educational remarks, various other sources, and above all her future life and writings. It was certainly a larger and more varied role than she later thought important or consciously remembered. Thus, the frivolous-sounding remark about wanting to get away from provincial Mainz, a hometown she otherwise remembered fondly, can be read as masking and revealing a profound truth about Seghers's younger self, namely the overwhelming need to find an environment where she could learn and find a purpose beyond the vague wish to write and to do good. She sought the life of the mind, not the life of society as she knew it in her well-to-do Jewish family circle. At the end of her studies, Netty Reiling, still with her parents and vacationing in fashionable Scheveningen in the summer of 1924, expressed her longing and her existential angst most strikingly in a letter to László Radványi, who had become and was to remain the love of her life: "The place itself is full of tourists, and in the evenings, seen from the beach, is a large bundle of lights with many coffeehouses, something [which] makes me desolately miserable . . . The people here irritate me more than the sea pleases me. Dear heart, do you know the pain of losing consciousness? Here it is more terrible for me than ever. . . . My loneliness is probably to blame for all of this, I too need surroundings, i.e. an earth that supports me, for I am useless in this society and need human beings to receive and give myself to."[10]

There surely were practical reasons to choose Heidelberg: not quite as close to home as Frankfurt and its new university, but still in the region she loved, it had a great reputation and attracted many Jews, among whom her father had connections. Netty Reiling would also find and befriend some in the sizable group of international, mostly Eastern European, students. Looking back, Anna Seghers remembered her student days as joyous ones: "We were carefree and openhearted then. How ready we were to be happy! We always found something to enjoy, despite the threatening times, despite the problems."[11] The pronoun "we" is important.

Netty Reiling came to Heidelberg to find community and answers to the questions that plagued her in a time of crisis which she, despite her comfortable home, clearly perceived as such. In her novel *Die Gefährten* (1932; The Wayfarers) which draws on her time in Heidelberg, Seghers has one of the characters, Steiner, reflect on his communality with the other students there: "They too are looking for answers. A foothold in these stormy times, the meaning of their path 'between life and death.'"[12] Through him Seghers is speaking for herself as well as for many she knew. The sociologist Karl Mannheim, who became a good friend, characterized the atmosphere in Heidelberg in even more clearly religious terms as one of "waiting for prophets," an "incredible . . . readiness . . . for some kind of redemption."[13] Both Reiling and Mannheim realized that not only they themselves but also so many around them were seekers, which created a common bond between them. When Netty Reiling began to see Mannheim's career building critically—she had met him through Radványi and later modeled her character Steiner on him—she still felt this bond very strongly, "as if we had spent an unextinguishable common youth in *one* house . . . and would once be buried in *one* graveyard, however differently we passed through the trial of life," she reminded Radványi in early 1925.[14]

A large part of the student body in the Heidelberg of that time had also been seekers, but had already found or were in the process of finding their path, they were "völkisch national" (right-wing nationalist). While Netty Reiling had little to do with them, she could not avoid them altogether because the town and the classrooms were full of people of all stripes and persuasions. She gave an example in a letter to Radványi and could still joke about it: "the whole seminar [which she had invited to her home, i.e. her Jewish parents' home in Mainz] really came. On the farthest left there was a woman student of Korsch / very nice / as center a chaplain (in a cowl), on the right Hitlergorpins [?], who probably only noticed during dinner that they were at the home of Jews und who now will suffer all their lives from the indelible shame of having been the guests of Jews. It was all very funny."[15]

Retrospectively, and in the context of later times, Seghers presents a more particular and limited experience than she really had. Then the encounter with exiles from failed revolutions in the East becomes the one unforgettable experience. As she says in a post–Second World War foreword to *Die Gefährten*, they struck "us" as "wirkliche, nicht beschriebene Helden" (real, not fictional heroes).[16] By then she had made a clear political choice, but at the time she was like many of the young people around her, who eventually went in very diverse directions, searching for community, answers, and "real heroes" among the large variety on offer. Things were still open and fluid, and the budding Nazis in their midst were only one group, which could be seen with derision.

Netty Reiling was a good student and took her work very seriously: "My studies interested me so much that they occupied me totally. Still, my imagination never stopped working, but did not produce anything. Then one day, when I started to write, it poured from me like a torrent: I wrote, studied, wrote, studied—like a crazy woman, until exhaustion. Then I realized that I could not keep up with both for any length of time: I decided upon writing."[17] Letters to Radványi, her brief diary, and posthumously discovered stories show that Netty Reiling did indeed experience a creative rush towards the end of her studies and spent the following years experimenting with stories.[18] Writing fiction, she realized, would be her priority, but she concluded her studies with a doctorate and never ceased to be the intellectual she became in Heidelberg, nor even the idea of working as an academic, an idea to which she returned in exile. There was no real break. As soon as she had established herself as a writer of fiction she stepped out as a public intellectual, one who spoke out on important cultural issues, and relied on the considerable knowledge she had acquired in Heidelberg, but did so quietly and unobtrusively.

Already in her academic work as a student—her dissertation *Jude und Judentum im Werke Rembrandts* (Jew and Jewry in the Work of Rembrandt) and two still existing handwritten seminar papers, titled "Römische Soldatengräber im Rheingebiet" (Roman Soldiers' Graves in the Rhine Area) and "Anfang und Entwicklung der frühromanischen Grabplastik" (Beginning and Development of Early Romanesque Grave Sculpture)—she avoided overly abstract and theoretical language, an avoidance in which some of her professors such as Carl Neumann, her dissertation advisor, may have confirmed her. Perhaps Seghers's much-admired ability to speak freely, in well-formulated, clear sentences, was also something she picked up from her best teachers. There is no question, though, that she absorbed ideas and theories and transformed them as she saw fit much later for her talks and essays. Even if she did not call herself an intellectual in the narrower sense and used her academic title only at the very beginning of her writing career, she became one in Heidelberg and counted on the interests, ideas, and knowledge she acquired there for the rest of her life.

Netty Reiling received—or better, gave herself—an excellent education in Heidelberg. As many in her cohort, but probably more diligently than most, she chose a large variety of courses. She also internalized the spirit of interdisciplinarity that was in the air in Heidelberg "als geistiges Fluidum" (as spiritual aura), as one of her teachers, Ludwig Curtius, put it.[19] Her approach to art and literature would continue to draw on the synergies between the many subjects she pursued, such as German, Russian, and French literatures, art from diverse periods and regions—East-Asian, Egyptian, and European—and different epochs of history.[20] Her studies in art history led her to develop the conviction that art was specific to a time and place and that periods of crisis and war, such as her own, demanded new ways of expression, imperfect and splintered as they might still be. This would become her argument in defense of literary modernism in the famous "Expressionism debate" with George Lukács, but is already present in her student papers.[21]

There are many more aspects in Seghers's thinking that can be traced to her studies in Heidelberg, such as her global interests and the "long view" she took on historical developments.[22] As a counterbalance, she very early formulated her concept of "Gedenksteine" (memorial stones), which she developed as a student in her analysis of the reliefs on Roman soldiers' graves. She found that these achieved "die Wiedergabe des Menschen als Realität und zwar auf dem höchsten Punkte seiner irdischen Lebensentfaltung" (the representation of the human being as reality, namely at the apex of his development in life).[23] The wish to create such "Gedenksteine" would inform her storytelling as well as her exile project begun in 1935, the so-called "Heldenbuch" (Book of Heroes), in the context of which she uses the term again. The plans for this "Heldenbuch," which was to unite antifascist writers from many countries, shows the international stature as an intellectual she had achieved by that time. Unfortunately, and through no fault of her own, this project did not come to fruition: it never saw publication and has been lost.[24]

There was another model of interdisciplinarity available in Heidelberg at the time, and many students demanded and some professors provided it: the infusion of contemporary issues and of politics into the classroom. As yet the atmosphere was one of debate and discussion, certainly among the socially critical and left-wing faculty whom Netty Reiling sought out from the very beginning of her studies, such as Emil Lederer (1882–1939) and Hermann Oncken (1869–1945), who were considered "political professors." In her first semester she took Lederer's "Sozialtheorie des Marxismus" (Social theory of Marxism) and Oncken's "Allgemeine Geschichte im 19. Jahrhundert" (General history of the nineteenth century), and continued studying with both in coming semesters. She was looking for the relevance they offered and later used the models they provided. It would take her many more years to make a clear political commitment herself, but both relevance and debate would become central to her writing and inform her dream of what political discourse could and should be.

Of course, life outside the classroom and personal encounters also played a very large role, and boundaries were quite blurry. We know that Netty Reiling became friends with Philipp Shaffer,[25] the Mannheims, György Káldor,[26] and Heinz Pflaum,[27] that she knew Carl Zuckmayer and met Ernst Toller when he passed through. She may have had contact with Jürgen Kuczynski already in Heidelberg, also perhaps with Walter Benjamin and maybe with Carlo Mierendorff.[28] There surely were others. Her most important and transformative encounter was with Laszlo Radványi, who has been mentioned before, but must be introduced here. He was a Hungarian Jew, an "Ostausländer" ("eastern foreigner," a derogatory term used in the Weimar Republic, e.g., in the debates about Mannheim and his Habilitation, the prerequisite for a university appointment for him). Radványi was a member of the Budapest Sunday Circle around Georg Lukács, and like the others had to flee Hungary in 1919 when Miklós Horthy ousted the revolutionary government in which they had participated and took over the country. She met him in her second semester and they quickly grew close. They exchanged presents, mostly in the form of books such as Kierkegaard's *Die Krankheit zum Tode*, and Dostoyevsky's *Crime and Punishment* (in Russian) and Buber's *Die Legende des Baalschem*, all of which contain tender dedications. These were authors who moved many people of their generation and who impacted Seghers considerably. In their relationship she sometimes called herself his "Mutterkind" (motherchild) and soon came to depend on him for emotional and intellectual support but cared for him in practical matters, a dynamic that lasted a lifetime. Her choice of the penniless intellectual who did not pay back his debts with friends, took little care of his clothes and appearance, and had other faults she noticed even then was quite conscious. Apropos of Heinz Pflaum, who was much more suitable in her parents' and family's eyes, she notes in her diary: "Lieber Mensch. Aber jetzt habe ich gewählt, weit weg das schreckliche geliebte, andre Leben." (Nice guy. But now I have chosen, far away, the terrible, beloved, other life.)[29]

Radványi was attractive and was one of the "heroes," but what really captivated Netty Reiling was the heady intellectual baggage he brought with him from the Budapest Sunday Circle where he had been one of the youngest members. She was drawn to the intransigence with which he— and the others—rejected the superficial, rationalistic, and individualistic culture of the West and to the radicalness with which they searched for a profound cultural and moral revolution. For his part, Radványi paid loving attention to her, taking her imagination and intellect seriously. The Sunday Circle had quite a few remarkable women among its members—

among them Júlia Láng, Mannheim's wife, Anna Lesznai, and Edit Gyömröi—and the young man had learned to recognize and respect them. Radványi made Netty Reiling feel his appreciation for her talent then and throughout their life together, whatever else would happen between them.

Seghers met Georg Lukács, the center of the Budapest Sunday Circle, only later in Berlin, and would become friends with him and still later thank him for all he had taught her. Yet, as Helen Fehervary has argued, it was the early Lukács, to whose pre-Communist writing she was exposed in Heidelberg, probably by Karl Mannheim as well as Radványi, who left a lasting imprint on her imagination with his idea that "there is a standard attached to correct and incorrect action. This standard we call sacrifice."[30] It became the "gold standard" for Seghers in all her work.

In conclusion, throughout her long and difficult life, Seghers remained true to her Heidelberg roots, even if later on she only mentioned them selectively. During these few years she stored nourishment for a lifetime and laid the foundations that transformed Netty Reiling into Anna Seghers, a major writer and intellectual. She shared the experience of Heidelberg with other German and European intellectuals during a period of extraordinary flowering and should be seen in this larger context. Like her, many others went forward from Heidelberg to remarkable lives of writing, thinking, political action—and suffering under the Nazis. Seghers's eventual choice of Socialism/Communism sprang from her Heidelberg experiences and her search for community and purpose as well, albeit slowly and through her time in Berlin. However, if she never became dogmatic, it was, I believe, because she was first steeped in the "Geist von Heidelberg" (spirit of Heidelberg) as it was called nostalgically: its openness to quests and questions.

Notes

[1] Carl Zuckmayer, "Grußwort," in *Anna Seghers aus Mainz*, ed. Walter Heist (Mainz: Krach, 1973), 10ff.

[2] See Helen Fehervary, *Anna Seghers: The Mythic Dimension* (Ann Arbor: University of Michigan Press 2001), 91. She refers to letters in Hungarian from as late as 1926.

[3] Archive Pierre Radvanyi, Orsay, France.

[4] "Mein teures geliebtes Leben . . . erinnerst du dich . . . wie ich mal im Bahnhof von Frankfurt weinte, so viele Menschen u alle mit Stellung?" June 13, 1925 to Radványi in Berlin (Archive Pierre Radvanyi, Orsay, France.

[5] "und während wir daran teilnahmen, leidenschaftlich diskutierend, folgten wir unserem Studium. Wir liebten Kunst und Wissenschaft." Anna Seghers, *Aufsätze, Ansprachen, Essays 1923–1953* (Berlin: Aufbau, 1980), 391.

[6] Jürgen Kuczynski (1904–97), an economist and later a prominent intellectual in the GDR, briefly overlapped with Netty Reiling in Heidelberg and later became a good friend, but we do not know if they actually met in Heidelberg. "das dargebotene Wissen war von relativ geringem ökonomischen Wert," Jürgen Kuczinsky, *Memoiren: Die Erziehung des J. K. zum Kommunisten und Wissenschaftler* (Berlin: Aufbau, 1973), quoted from *Intellektuelle in Heidelberg*, ed. Markus Bitterolf, Oliver Schlaudt and Stefan Schöbel (Heidelberg: edition Schöbel, 2014), 159–60.

[7] Helen Fehervary, *Anna Seghers: The Mythic Dimension*, especially on the Budapest Sunday Circle and its impact; Sigrid Bock, *Der Weg führt nach St. Barbara* (Berlin: Karl Dietz Verlag 2008), on the political development; Christiane Zehl Romero, *Anna Seghers: Eine Biographie 1900–1947* (Berlin: Aufbau, 2000).

[8] "Ich wollte überhaupt nur studieren, weil ich fürchterliche Angst hatte, in dem Nest Mainz hängenzubleiben." Quoted in Achim Roscher, *Positionen I: Wortmeldungen zur DDR Literatur*, ed. Eberhard Günther (Halle, Leipzig: Mitteldeutscher Verlag, 1984), April 28, 1973.

[9] "Was die biographischen Fragen anbelangt, die Erlebnisse und die Anschauungen eines Schriftstellers, glaube ich, werden am allerklarsten aus seinem Werk, auch ohne spezielle Biographie." Anna Seghers, *Aufsätze, Ansprachen, Essays 1954–1979* (Berlin und Weimar: Aufbau, 1980), 411.

[10] "Der Ort selbst voll Kurgäste u abends vom Strand aus gesehen ein großes Lichterbündel mit vielen Kaffeehäusern etwas [sic] mich trostlos elend macht. . . . Die Menschen hier irritieren mich mehr als mich das Meer freut. Liebstes Herz, kennst du die Qual des Bewußtseinsverlierens? Hier ist es mir schrecklicher denn je. . . . Schuld an allem ist wohl meine Einsamkeit, ich brauche halt auch eine Umgebung, d. h. eine Erde, die mich trägt, denn in dieser Gesellschaft bin ich unnütz u ich brauche Menschen um zu empfangen u mich zu geben." To L. Radványi, July 7, 1924 (Archive Pierre Radvanyi, Orsay, France).

[11] "Sorglos, offenherzig waren wir damals. Wie waren wir bereit, uns zu freuen! Wir fanden immer etwas zum Freuen, trotz der bedrohlichen Zeit, trotz aller Bedrängungen." Anna Seghers, *Aufsätze 1953–1979*, 388.

[12] "Auch sie suchen Antworten. Halt in den Stürmen der Zeit, fragen nach dem Sinn ihres Weges zwischen Leben und Sterben." Anna Seghers, *Die Gefährten* (Berlin: Aufbau, 1959), 34.

[13] Karl Mannheim, "Heidelberger Briefe" in *Georg Lukács, Karl Mannheim und der Sonntagskreis*, ed. Eva Karády und Erzsébet Vezér (Frankfurt am Main: Sendler, 1985), 81.

[14] "als ob wir eine gemeinsame unauslöschbare Jugend verlebt hätten in einem Hause . . . u einstmals auf einem Friedhof begraben würden, wie verschieden wir auch die Probe des Lebens bestanden haben." In an unpublished letter from December 1, 1925. Archive Pierre Radvanyi. She would still invite the Mannheims to her wedding and many years later during exile, when the Radványis and Mannheims had gone separate ways and the latter were safely in England, Mannheim tried to help the Radványis to flee France.

[15] "Das ganze Seminar war wirklich da. Als äußerste Linke ging eine Korschschülerin / sehr lieb / als Zentrum ein Kaplan (in Kutte) als Rechte Hitlergorpins [?], die erst im Lauf des Essen wahrscheinlich merkten, daß sie bei Juden waren u nun ihr ganzes Leben an der unauslöschlichen Schande leiden, von Juden bewirtet worden zu sein. Es war alles sehr komisch" (July 21, 1925 to L. Radványi, Archive Pierre Radvanyi.)

[16] Anna Seghers, "Wiedersehen mit den Gefährten," in *Kunstwerk und Wirklichkeit*, II, ed. Sigrid Bock (Berlin: Akademie-Verlag 1971), 19.

[17] "Mein Studium interessierte mich so sehr, daß es mich ganz absorbierte. Aber meine Phantasie arbeitete und arbeitete, produzierte jedoch nichts. Als ich dann eines Tages zu schreiben anfing, brach's wie ein Sturzbach aus mir heraus: ich schrieb, studierte, schrieb studierte—wie 'ne Verrückte, das ging bis zur Erschöpfung. Da merkte ich, daß beides nicht lange durchzuhalten war: ich entschied mich fürs Schreiben." Quoted in Achim Roscher, *Positionen I*, 144.

[18] "Ich habe so feste, sogar ganz fest umrissene Gedanken, daß es mir fast zu viel ist. Ich muß mich beschränken u ich weiß nicht, wie man es macht" (I have such firm, even firmly delineated thoughts, that it is almost too much for me. I have to limit myself and do not know how one does it), she confided to Radványi (prob. May 22, 1925, Archive Pierre Radvanyi, Orsay, France). Anna Seghers, *Und ich brauch doch so schrecklich Freude: Tagebuch 1924/1925*, ed. Christiane Zehl Romero (Berlin: Aufbau, 2003); "Die Legende von der Reue des Bischofs Jehan d'Aigremont von St. Anne in Rouen," "Jans muss sterben," and "Die Toten auf der Insel Djal. Eine Sage aus dem Holländischen," in *Erzählungen 1924–1932*, ed. Peter Beicken (Berlin: Aufbau, 2014).

[19] Ludwig Curtius, *Deutsche und antike Welt* (Stuttgart: Deutsche Verlagsanstalt, 1950), 239.

[20] For a more detailed account see Christiane Zehl Romero, *Anna Seghers: Eine Biographie 1900–1947* (Berlin: Aufbau, 2000).

[21] "[Briefe an Georg Lukacs]" (Letters to Georg Lukacs), first published in *Internationale Literatur*, May 1939.

[22] For a more detailed account see Romero, *Anna Seghers: Eine Biographie 1900– 1947*, 133ff.

[23] Unpublished seminar paper: "Anfang und Entwicklung der frühromanischen Grabplastik" (Beginning and Development of Early Romanesque Grave Reliefs), Archive Pierre Radvanyi, Orsay, France.

[24] See Christiane Zehl Romero, "Heldenbuch—Spuren eines verlorenen Manuskripts," *Argonautenschiff* 19 (2010): 155–263.

[25] Philipp Schaeffer (1894–1943) was a fellow student of Reiling's in Sinology and a close friend. He was a resister during the Third Reich and was executed in connection with the Schulze-Boysen/Harnack trials.

[26] György Káldor (1900–1958), a member of the Budapest Sunday Circle and close friend of Laszlo Radványi, also studied in Heidelberg as well as Vienna.

[27] Heinz Pflaum (1900–1962), a fellow student of French literature, perhaps a family friend and most likely a suitor. He was a cousin of Gershom Scholem and

through him Netty Reiling may have met Walter Benjamin already in Heidelberg when the latter visited. In 1925 Pflaum emigrated to Palestine, where he became a Professor of Romance Languages and Medieval Literature.

[28] Carlo Mierendorff (1897–1943) was a friend of Carl Zuckmayer and Netty Reiling may have met him through Zuckmayer. He was a poet and writer and became a Social Democratic politician and member of the Reichstag. A fierce opponent of the Nazis and his former fellow student Josef Goebbels in Heidelberg, he was imprisoned in a series of concentration camps, including Osthofen, a model for the concentration camp Westhofen in Anna Seghers's *The Seventh Cross*. If Netty Reiling did not know him in Heidelberg, it is very likely that she knew about the persecution and death he suffered in the Third Reich.

[29] Anna Seghers, *Und ich brauch doch so schrecklich Freude: Tagebuch 1924/1925*, ed. Christiane Zehl Romero (Berlin: Aufbau-Verlag, 2003), 16 (Entry of Thursday, December 23, 1924).

[30] György Lukács, *Tactics and Ethics: Political Essays 1919–1929*, ed. Rodney Livingstone, trans. Michael McColgan (New York: Harper & Row, 1972), 8.

2: Who Is the Narrator? Anna Seghers's "The Excursion of the Dead Girls": Narrative Mode and Cinematic Depiction

Peter Beicken

THE TITLE OF Anna Seghers's novella "The Excursion of the Dead Girls" sounds uncanny, as adventure and diversion are contrasted with the theme of death. This "masterpiece" is considered the author's only autobiographical work, one closely linked in theme and chronology to her life story.[1] Because in this requiem for her female schoolmates, as well as her own parents, Seghers "reveals facts of her life, her youth, and the time of exile, nevertheless in the form of a narrative creation."[2] Doing "memory work" the author envisions things past, her youth and homeland (*Heimat*), while also mourning the lost promise of an idyll that was crushed by the events of history.[3]

Who is the narrator and how is the story told? In this first-person narration there is generally a distinction between the narrating self and the experiencing self, contrasting the remembering I with the remembered I, Seghers at the time of her exile with the figure of Netty in her childhood. The treatment of the authentic and the autobiographical in Seghers not only recollects the excursion as an episode in her childhood, but also addresses different levels of time and facts of history up to the time of narration in the year 1943. This concerns actual events from Seghers's life story as well as from history, for instance references to Emperor Wilhelm II and the First World War; figures such as Hitler and Goebbels; the crossing of the Rhine by allied troops after the war, and later the re-occupation of the Rhineland by Hitler and the *Wehrmacht*.[4] Additionally, the text refers to the Confessional Church (E 288) or "Bekennende Kirche," which Seghers calls "Bekenntniskirche,"[5] the Nazis' doctrine of "racial defilement" and the concentration camps (E 290); and the People's Court (*Volksgerichtshof*. E 298). In addition, there are topographical references, such as to Petersau(e), an island in the Rhine, Amöneburg (E 300), and to Nonnenwerth, another island (E 301); and although her hometown, Mainz, is not mentioned by name, Seghers lists several streets such as Christhof Street (Christofstrasse), as well as the Christhof church, the late-Gothic church (St. Christoph), a ruin after it was destroyed in a bombing raid in 1942 (E 302). Seghers also mentions Flachsmarktstrasse (E 303–4), where her father's shop was located on the market itself, and the Bauhofstrasse (E 304), from which, in the novella, she fearfully "turns into her own street" to get to her apartment building on Kaiserstrasse (also not named), where her mother is waiting for her.

I. The Authentic and the Grouping of Figures

Seghers fictionalizes the authentic material in the novella, even those characters that depict historically verifiable models. In what Stanzel has called "scenic presentation," Seghers portrays two time frames, the narrative present time of her exile in Mexico contrasted with the look back at her youth in Germany while also referencing events in the period between the excursion and the present day Nazi state.[6] The foregrounding of the visual and the cinematic mode of narration enhances the "illusion of immediacy."[7] "Excursion of the Dead Girls" is not a traditional "novella of remembrance" typical of Theodor Storm; Mayer pointed this out, when he claimed that Seghers "*is* the girl Netty" of her youth, while at the same time she is "well-versed in all the knowledge of the later time periods."[8] Constantly, this later knowledge of history is layered with the look back at the day's excursion before the First World War as "voice-over commentary" to what is being cinematically narrated, whereby commentary is given on different time periods up to the year 1943, most notably on the life stories of the girls who die later together with aspects of Seghers's own biography.[9] In addition, there is the "double optics" or "doubling gaze" resulting in the montage of visual representation that is designed "to make the young girls comprehensively visible" and a knowing narration that brings the girls, in their later life situations, especially those in which death is involved, close to the reader through voice-over narration.[10] Thus, "friendship and harmony of youth in the pre-World War I period" are juxtaposed to "proving oneself or failing to do so in the Third Reich."[11] It is the contrast between an apparently untroubled "childhood idyll" and a Hades realm in which destruction and death extinguish almost all of the thirteen girls and their two teachers except for Seghers, the early witness and later narrator.[12]

Seghers divided up this contingent of female figures into two opposing groups. One group consists of resisters and victims: Leni, Sophie Maier, and the younger teacher, Miss Sichel, all three of whom are killed by the Nazis. The older teacher, Miss Mees, who always wears a big cross instead of a swastika on her chest and belongs to the Confessing Church, is brought before the infamous Volksgerichtshof, but in the end seems to survive. Two additional girls in this group, Lore and Gerda, commit suicide. Admired by the others for her *joie d'vivre*, Lore is exceptional because she is involved in love affairs while still at school. Later on, her lover, an ardent Nazi supporter, accuses her of disgracing the Aryan race because of her involvement with a Jewish paramour. Subsequently she takes an overdose of sleeping powder. Gerda, like Miss Sichel and Seghers herself, is based on a historical figure. In the novella Gerda is a fictionalized portrait of the author's childhood friend, Ria Denk.[13] Denk, however did not gas herself, as Gerda does in a moment of despair when she comes home and finds that her husband has displayed the swastika flag outside the window out of fear of losing his position as a state-employed teacher. Two more girls, Lotte, who joins a religious order, and Liese Möbius, a fearless person who gives hope to her neighbors in the air-raid shelters, are killed in bombing attacks.

As a negative contrast there is a group of girls who eventually succumb to Nazism. Among them are Marianne, Ida, and Nora, and opportunistic followers such as Elli, Else, Katharina, and Marie Braun. They all perish in bombing raids in Mainz or other places. However, Nora's death is not confirmed in the novella. Except for Ida, all of these girls married Nazis, notably Marianne and Elli, or married into families who are loyal to the Nazi regime.[14]

The male figures in the novella are less developed except for Otto Fresenius, Marianne's first love and her soon-to-be fiancé, who was killed early in the First World War. The same fate was suffered by Leni's brother, who was also an early war casualty. Widow-like Marianne was embittered by her loss, as was Ida, who became most resentful after her fiancé was killed in action. Both women join the Nazi movement, as does Else, who together with her carpenter husband Ebi, dies in a bombing raid. Their three children and Ebi's apprentices perish in the raid as well. Marie Braun, her father, and the rest of her family suffer the same devastating fate.

Among the male anti-Nazi resisters is the figure of Fritz, who meets Leni during home leave from the front and marries her. Later, Fritz is reported to the Nazis by Marianne's husband Gustav Liebig, who had made a fast career becoming a major in the SS. Liebig wants Fritz to join the SA or serve under him in the SS, but when he does not, Liebig denounces him. Both Fritz and Leni are active in the underground, printing and distributing illegal leaflets. Tipped off by Liebig, the Gestapo arrests Fritz, who, ironically, is taken away by Walter, the former dance partner of Elli, one of Netty's schoolmates. While Fritz disappears and is never heard of again, Leni is put into a concentration camp where she is starved to death. However, Seghers does not relate the fates of Liebig or Walter, the Nazi henchmen. Like Fritz, Herbert Becker, Sophie Meier's boyfriend at the time of the excursion, is an enemy of the Nazi state whom Seghers meets during her exile in France, where he moved after his fight against the Franco regime in the Spanish Civil War. Seghers does not give any more information or further clues about Becker's fate. Except for Becker, who seems to be modeled after a historical figure, all other male characters in the novella are fictional. This is also true for the male group that arrives on the little steamer *Remagen* that lands near the café where the girls of the excursion are taking a break and shouts ring out: "Mr. Neeb! Mr. Reiss! Otto Helmholtz! Eugen Lütgens! Fritz Müller!" (E 292) Thus the girls identify and welcome the upperclassmen of the boys' Gymnasium. The young Mr. Neeb, who has taken a liking to Gerda, is also among the teachers. Later, the teacher Reiss is mentioned again as having outlived his pupils, who were to die in the first war and then the one to follow. He survived unscathed and also refrained from making any statements that might have landed him in prison or in a concentration camp (E 297). This is clearly a critique of the teacher as an authority figure who escapes harm while so many of his students get killed.

Considering Seghers's portrayal of historical figures, Barbara Prinsen-Eggert has emphasized the author's art of reflecting reality and pointed out that up to now no real-life models for the two prominent girl characters, Leni and Marianne, have been found.[15] Her research also divulged that there was a Professor Reiss at the secondary school for girls in Mainz, but not at the boys' Gymnasium. In addition, she notes that Neeb was a "well-known art historian of repute" (380), not a secondary-school teacher like his fictional namesake, who became complicit in Gerda's death by suicide (E 295). Ria Denk, whose daughter Christel Wolpert corresponded with Seghers after meeting her in Mainz after the Second World War, was unlike the fictional Gerda in that she did not marry a teacher and also did not die the way alleged in the novella.[16] In a letter to Wolpert, Seghers states that in her novella "there are not photographic images of some teachers and girls, rather external and inner characteristics of different human beings are blended and much is invented."[17]

The necessity of art to create a reality contrary to the real does not prevent the artist from aiming at the reality, as is evident in the double optics that Seghers employed. For using this doubling gaze, she engages the method of cinematic vision, while utilizing, on the other hand, the above-mentioned voice-over commentary that grafts historical knowledge onto the true-to-life portrayal of the excursion in a kind of montage. Thus, there is the looking-back of "retrospective narration" and, at the same time, the commenting that also "remembers something that is supposed to happen still," a concept that Wolf also has labeled "remembered future" (500).[18] Several times this not-yet-happened is expressed in sentences in the subjunctive mood or future tense. For example, it is mentioned that the girls all revere their favorite teacher Miss Sichel, but that one of them "would later spit on [her] and deride her as a Jewish sow" (E 290). In

contrast to these anticipatory sentences in the subjunctive, there are passages with comments that assert events that have happened in historical
reality. For example, Seghers mentions her mother Hedwig Reiling's
deportation to a Polish concentration camp in 1942, a painful revelation
by the author to be sure.

An important example of an inevitable happening can be seen in
Seghers's description of her mother's appearance at the ending of the interior stories or *Binnenerzählung*. As the author wonders about the dark and
smooth hair and the still-young look of her mother, she becomes aware of
her own soon-to-be-gray hair. Using the past tense, the tense in which she
tells the story, she adds: "She [her mother] stood there blithe and upright,
destined for an active family life with the ordinary joys and burdens of the
everyday, not for a cruel, agonizing end in a remote village whither she had
been banished by Hitler" (E 305). This is not narrated as something that
has not yet happened or as remembered future, but is relayed with the
painful certainty of the actual death of her mother, which she the daughter
learned about only a year or more after the fact, and after she had tried
several times in 1940 and 1941 to secure a visa for her mother to leave
Nazi Germany, attempts that ultimately failed.[19]

After Paris fell to the Germans in June 1940, Seghers and her husband
and children were in great danger of being arrested, but were able to
escape from France. They left France and went into transatlantic exile in
March 1941, arriving in Mexico in June of that year. Later, in spring 1943,
Seghers learned that her mother had been deported from Mainz in March
1942 to the Polish transit ghetto in Piaski near Lublin. Whether her
mother died of illness or hunger in this ghetto, or was murdered in one of
the extermination camps is still unknown.[20]

Seghers felt immediately compelled to write a story about her childhood and her parents, but at the end of June 1943 she suffered severe
head injuries in a hit-and-run accident that sometimes has been considered a possible assassination attempt. At night on a broad street she was
hit by a truck and ended up badly hurt, lying unconscious in a hospital for
days. She recovered very slowly, and after months of convalescence was
left with residual effects such as impaired vision and memory loss.[21]
However, while she was still in the hospital, Seghers experienced distinct
memories of her childhood and youth. While the full recovery continued,
she began writing her requiem-like novella, which, in addition to the dead
girls, also commemorates her father and mother. In March 1940, Isidor
Reiling passed away two days after he was forced by the Nazis to sell his
business far under price. Subsequently, his wife Hedwig had to leave their
apartment for a Jewish house in Mainz. From there, she was deported
with other Jews from the city and the state to Poland. There were a total
of one thousand deportees.[22] Whereas Seghers has Netty experience her
mother's youthfulness and beauty, while also referring to the future event

of her deportation and death, her father's death is referred to in a peculiar way characterized by denial, as Netty, confirming the double optics of the novella's narration, expresses her childhood fear that her legs would fail her in the attempt to climb the stairs to be received by her mother: "Only as a very small child had I felt a similar uneasiness, fearing a disaster would prevent our reunion. I pictured how she was waiting for me in vain, just a few steps away. Then I was comforted by the thought that, should I collapse here from exhaustion, my father would soon find me. So he wasn't dead after all" (*E* 305). In view of the many deaths that the novella narrates, Netty's assertion that her father isn't dead after all appears to maintain the perspective of the child while suspending the author's view and knowledge that her father had indeed died in 1940. It is a doubling of perspectives indicative of a retrospective wishful utopia that suspends the inevitabilities of real history by having the child's view prevail in the ahistorical.

II. Visual Representation and Cinematic Narration

The terms "daydream" and "dreamlike" were used in early reviews (1946) of the "Excursion ("Tagtraum," "traumhaft," A 135–38), while related terms like "dreamer" and "knowing dreamer" have been used later by others such as Werner Baum, although Mayer has categorically rejected such characterizations: "Anna Seghers does not 'dream' of the excursion in Mexico" (124).[23] Gertraud Gutzmann sees Netty as the sole narrator,[24] as does Birgit Maier-Katkin, who also argues that in the interior stories, after the frame story (*Rahmenerzählung*) has been established, Netty enters a different "state of mind," that is, "the realm of dream," and that she "reawakens" from her "state of dream" in the final narrative frame.[25] However, it is not convincing to conceptualize Netty in this way, namely as a narrator engaging in "mindful travel" who moves between the states of dream and reality.[26] Nevertheless, the idea of mindful travel comes close to the concept of experiencing virtual realities in film. Elements such as "flashbacks and flashforwards" or "looking back and looking forward" that concern cinematic representations of time, as well as elements such as "dissolves" and the "montage principle" are among the inventory of filmic concepts in Seghers's novella.[27]

The way Seghers ties the two periods in her life together in her narration, the time when she was a "Rhenish school girl" on her class excursion some years before the First World War, and the time when she was a "tired emigré in a remote village during her Mexican exile, burdened by an unfamiliar environment," as Mayer observed,[28] shows a dialectic of time. This dialectic informs the layering and interplay of cinematic representation and commenting narration. Netty's experiences of the momentary, the here and now of the excursion, are told with visual directness, while vivid insights are given into her life situation. At the same time, the exiled author splices, montage-like, her up-to-date historical knowledge into the narrative process, so that Netty as a figure of momentary experience is distinguished from the figure of the first-person narrator. For example, the history-conscious first-person narrator applies her knowing view in the following way when gazing at the two girls, Leni and Marianne, on the seesaw:

> Now everything that people had told me and written to me about the two of them seemed impossible. If Marianne held the board so carefully for Leni, plucked grass from her hair so tenderly, and even slung her arm around Leni's neck, then it was impossible that she was later so harsh in refusing to do Leni a good turn. Impossible that she could say she had no concern for a girl who at some time, at some place, happened to have been in her class. (E 287)

The first-person narrator relies on hearsay and letters that make it impossible for her to believe the immediate impressions that Netty as the figure of momentary experience gathers while watching her two classmates: with their good-natured interaction; their loving trust in each other; their soulful togetherness; and their heartfelt friendship. What unfolds visually as enchantingly beautiful is called into question by the narrator, who employs the doubling optics of first-person narration, which contrast the amicable images with the disillusioning knowledge of Marianne's later inhumanity to Leni. Thus, Seghers conveys the shocking fact that human lives can move into diametrically opposed realities, where a wonderful childhood idyll is turned on its head by the ghastly Nazi reality.

Seghers's cinematic mode of narration is inspired by her fervent interest in the movies, and she incorporated filmic elements into even her early stories.[29] The avant-garde style of narration in the "Excursion" is reminiscent of the experimental way Seghers composed her story "On the Way to the American Embassy" ("Auf dem Wege zur amerikanischen Botschaft") in 1930. Maier-Katkin has compared the visual complexities of the "Excursion" to "futuristic pictures," while noting the "dense, disjointed, and fragmented style" as well.[30] The narrative appears divided into sequential sections by separating means that resemble film cuts, notably jump cuts that have an alarming effect. The resulting episodic structure gives the impression of "conflicted mnemonic flashes."[31] As Dorrit Cohn has observed, the back and forth in the first-person narrative presents "moments of remembrance and the remembered moments" (185) resulting in a "mnemonic a-chronology" (185) that breaks up the continuity of the chronology through disjunction, leading to the prismatic, avant-garde nature of the narrative.[32]

III. The Cinematic Elements in the "Excursion"

This section traces the most obvious cinematic elements in the novella.

a. The narrative gaze or gaze of the (female) narrator. For example: the gaze focused on the dog "with outstretched legs, covered with dust and still as a cadaver" (E 284).

b. The use of a camera-eye or narrative camera. For example: while the organ of vision is mentioned, the gaze explores a particular sight: "Although my eyes burned from heat and fatigue, I could see the stretch of path that led from the village into the wild" (E 283).

c. The use of cinematic composition, that is, the use of mise-en-scène that links certain characteristics of the visual field and makes it thoroughly composed. For example: "Through a gap, I could see gray-brown mountain slopes, stark and wild like a moonscape, [. . .]" (E 283).

d. The slow change from the panoramic view of an establishing shot to a visual detail by zooming in. For example, after the mention of the generally "wild" and moonscape-like scene there is a narrowing perspectival signal: "At the edge of the gorge I saw the corner of the white wall that had captured my attention [. . .]" (E 284). Another example of the zooming gaze concerns the narrator's visual investigation of the rancho, which is contrasted with the village. After a general visual impression—"its squat house, windowless along the path, looked uninhabited"—the gaze then focuses on the gateway and a detail: "The grillwork, neglected and crumbling, had fallen from the entry gate. Yet in the arch of the gate were traces of a coat of arms worn away by countless rainy seasons" (E 284–85).

e. The sequencing of scenic episodes by use of filmic cuts and suture montaging that links the individual units into larger sequences. This occurs especially with scenes that are focused on Leni and Marianne, the main pair of friends, who first appear in the seesaw episode and in many scenes on the terrace of the café restaurant, where the addition of Marianne's lover Otto Fresenius creates a remarkable triangulation of love and friendship that occupies a large part of the "Excursion" right up to the end of the novella, when in a final scene Leni and Marianne appear walking arm in arm in the streets of Mainz on their way home.

f. The use of voice-over commentary in the intervening first-person narration. For example: in the seesaw scene, the focus is on the two best school friends and their lovely apparent unison, as Leni "pushed off forcefully with her big feet in boxy, buttoned shoes" (E 285). This focus on a detail is expanded upon by the narrator, who comments: "I recalled that she always wore boots handed down from an older brother" (Ibid). The narrator then interrupts the present scene and offers an insight into an event of the future that she relates as an event of the past that has already happened: "True, this brother was (to be) killed in the autumn of 1914 in the First World War" (Ibid). (The translation here adds the "to be" which makes it future perfect, whereas Seghers's text clearly states: "Der Bruder war freilich schon im Herbst 1914 im ersten Weltkrieg gefallen." [*A* 124]) Observing the two classmates, Netty can't yet know of Leni's brother's unfortunate death, though it is interjected into the seesawing scene. Seghers continues her intervention when she relates her bewildered reaction: "I was amazed that Leni's face showed no trace of the grim events that ruined her life. Her face was as smooth and clear as a fresh apple. It showed not the least bit, not the faintest scar from the blows dealt her by the Gestapo when she refused to provide information against her husband" (E 285–86). Again, immediate visual impressions are contrasted with historical knowledge and probing questions. A particular feature of Leni dating from her schooldays, her "furrowed brow" (E 286), gives her "mirror-smooth apple face" an "energetic expression" "for any demanding occasion," and it is complemented by the "crease in her forehead" in "all kinds of strenuous activities" (Ibid). This crease later becomes a visual signal of both Leni's suffering in the Nazi period and her defiance of the Nazi authorities, and it is emblematic of her steadfast anti-fascist stance. One revealing occasion is when she is beaten by the Gestapo, who want information on her resister husband Fritz. Another instance occurs when she is put into the concentration camp, where she soon dies of starvation. As narrator, Seghers recalls that this crease between Leni's brows had already become a permanent feature by the time of Hitler's rise to power, when she took leave from her friends in her hometown and fled the country. What makes the symbolism of this visual detail remarkable is Seghers's art of linking apparently minute details to momentous events of history, of contrasting the cinematic gaze with shocking historical knowledge delivered by the poignant voice-over commentary.

g. There are copious juxtapositions of thematic aspects and visual depictions of various locations and points in time in the characteristic sequenced episodes that are treated to flashbacks, flash forwards, dissolves, and montages. These are all important film elements that give the "Excursion" a very recognizable cinematic appearance in its visual mode of representation and narrative structure as well.

h. The "Excursion" uses the frame-narrative that is often found in traditional novellas, particularly in the "novella of remembrance" à la Theodor Storm, although Mayer has observed that Seghers differs from this narrative convention.[33] Rather she uses the framing in a remarkably unusual and innovative way. While the traditional frame-narrative is often introduced by an authorial narrative voice before other narrated figures take on the task of remembering and storytelling, Seghers makes a radical departure from these conventions by starting the "Excursion" with a noticeably truncated scene between the first-person narrator and the owner of the pulqueria in Mexico. Namely, this scenic depiction begins specifically with an answer to a question that is not stated, but needs to be surmised by the reader from the response: "No, from much farther away. From Europe" (E 283). The incompletely narrated dialogue is then followed by an exchange of looks that has the Mexican study the forlorn refugee "as if searching for some sign of my bizarre past" (Ibid). Subsequently, Seghers as narrator collects vivid impressions of the moonscape-like wilderness she finds in this part of Mexico. The visual perceptions show her keen interest in capturing the essence of nature; she was a student of art history and studied landscapes, as they often reveal the suffering of human beings.[34] It is into this arid, hostile natural environment that she places herself and the owner of the pulqueria, "now squatting on the ground beneath the enormous shade of his hat" (E 283). The man with the sombrero hat may seem like a Mexican cliché, but Díaz Pérez suggests that the pulqueria owner in the forbidden landscape resembles the "author's unbearable exile situation,"[35] which provides her, the novella tells us, with a rather "questionable refuge" but not yet a "salvation" (E 283). While the exchanges of words and looks are a sign of interpersonal communication, a sense of strangeness prevails as the interaction discontinues. Seghers stresses not the togetherness in place and time, but the dissociation, as she pointedly observes of the former questioner: "He was no longer studying me. Neither the village nor the mountains held his attention. He stared without moving at the only thing that still puzzled him: an absolute void" (E 283). The bizarre foreignness, the wild and the void are turned into absolutes at the conclusion of this otherworldly encounter that turns into an alienating side by side.

As Seghers continues to take in the strangeness of the place that alienates her, she addresses her difficult past, the flight into exile, and says that her "longing for unusual, outlandish adventures that once made me restless had long since been quenched, beyond measure. There was only one adventure that could inspire me now: the journey home" (E 284). While she is reckoning with the wild turns in her life and also gazing in fatigue at the hostile landscape around her, she is filled with homesickness and the stirring desire to travel back home. It does not take much to realize that only mind travel will be available to her.

i. The use of dissolve is the one crucial cinematic element that Seghers uses innovatively and to a stunning effect at this moment in her novella when she is facing dust, haze, and fatigue. Yet, despite the perceptual difficulties, the space behind the white wall she has been looking at "shone green" (E 284) suggesting a contrasting space of lushness and restoration. As Seghers approaches the wall and steps through the gateway, phenomenal changes in her viewing take place. As if the white wall were a screen for the desired mind travel, a film of a past action begins to roll. At first there is the auditory, the "regular creaking" of the seesaw, then a sense of smell of a familiar green landscape. This moment of the memory film as a recollection of a past event is marked by another amazing moment, an auditory instant, as Seghers suddenly hears her name called out: "Netty!" (E 285) While the Mexican wilderness fades out, the dissolve has taken the first-person narrator via mind travel to Netty's childhood. After the scene with Leni and Marianne seesawing and Netty standing by as patient observer and camera's eye, a string of episodes unfolds to make the memory film a vivid reality interlaced with the narrator's voice-over comments covering the gruesome facts of personal and German history and counteracting the apparently idyllic events of the excursion.

j. Having returned to her hometown at the end of the excursion, the girl Netty shares with the narrator the desire for homecoming. As she moves through the streets from the landing where the boat docked towards her own street, a "twinge of fear came over" her, as though she "could sense it had been destroyed" (E 304). The narrator bestows on Netty a premonition of the historical devastation that has become painful knowledge for the adult exile who had learned about the air raids and destruction of Mainz in the years 1942 and 1943. The proximity of her home and the vision of her mother waiting for her on the small veranda inspires Netty to speed up her steps and, as the mother catches sight of her and waves, she tries to rush up the stairs. At that moment the second significant dissolve begins. Like with the first dissolve, there is a haze again, this time in the stairwell where the girl Netty is in a "gray-blue fog of fatigue" (E 305). Ultimately, she is unable to climb the stairs, not even to the first landing, as her legs fail her and the staircase becomes insurmountable and beyond reach. As fear of disabling exhaustion and disaster settles in, Netty sees her father, "not dead after all" (ibid.) as the one who will find and, naturally, help her. But this staircase episode fades out and the second dissolve transitions to something more decisive: "Now the dishes were clattering" while additional auditory perceptions come into focus, namely "the smacking of hands on dough in familiar rhythm" and "turkeys screeching in the courtyard" (ibid.), which turns out to be the Mexican scene of the beginning with the owner of the pulqueria "still at his old spot" (E 306) and with someone else, a friend or relative, squatting there as well. Díaz Pérez has noted that in the way this renewed encounter is told, the narrator seems to be accepting the scene and is also being accepted by the Mexicans as well.[36] By revisiting her homeland in the both exhilarating and painfully disillusioning memory film, Seghers has come to appreciate the people and land of her exile, after having cherished her past in Germany with memories of kinship, beauty, and goodness, which are contrasted with the shocking human failures, war, and the atrocities of the Shoah.

The two dissolves, the one initiating the transition from the beginning frame to the interior stories at the site of the white wall and the other taking us back from Netty's homecoming scene to Mexican exile, make use of cinematic elements that uniquely usher in and bring closure to the memory film that forms the narrative core of the "Excursion." Noteworthy is Seghers's artful way of keeping separate but also fusing the self of exile and the childhood self, as she successfully joins the Mexican scene at the end with her concerns about time and the "assigned task" (E 306) by her teacher to write about the excursion for the next "German lesson" in school (E 299). But as the "Excursion" concludes, the teacher's assignment has been accomplished in a larger sense: in the work of remembrance that fills the memory film in the novella.

IV. Filmic Narration, the Refound Self, and the Recovered Homeland ("Heimat")

Seghers's use of cinematic elements gives her "Excursion" a distinct avant-garde appearance. One particularly impressive achievement is the innovative linkage of storytelling and visual representation that facilitates the memory film. This involves a certain paradox, as the narrator mentions several times that her vision is plagued by fatigue and pain, although there are copious references both in the narrative frame and in the interior stories to intense looking at individuals, scenery, sites, and landscapes that result in varied visual perceptions and unique depictions. While the novella uses autobiographical material, Seghers avoids mentioning her impaired vision as a result of the accident she suffered in exile. Instead she poeticizes the difficulties in seeing by referring to the heat in the desert-like terrain, including the "shimmering haze" and the "cloud of dust" so "that the near faded and the distant cleared like a Fata Morgana" (E 284). This ambiguity in the field of vision suggests the transitions of fading out and fading in of natural vistas in the cinematic dissolves described earlier, which pointedly climax in the visual transformation that is preceded by auditory signals such as the distinct call "Netty!" This creates a special auratic-epiphanic moment of the self that is found again and its identity reaffirmed.

The memory film also visualizes magic moments of childhood and friendship, female awakening to intimacy, and close encounters of people in love. Throughout her novella Seghers enhances the depiction by endowing the scenes with an intensity of sensory perception. Also, the visual recording of the narrative camera eye is often enriched by voice-over comments that assert impressions as truths beyond doubt. While the scenic depiction in such episodes has been compared to vivid "dream images" of Netty's past, there are instances when the here and now of the narrator is portrayed, for example in the surprise moment when she hears her child-hood name being called out.[37] Bringing together her distant past with the recent experience of being hospitalized after the accident, Seghers's reac-tion is very telling: "Startled at the sound of my old name, I grabbed my braids with both hands even though in school I'd always been mocked for doing this. I was amazed that I could grab the two thick braids—so they hadn't been cut off in the hospital after all" (E 285). It is an instant of stunning self-encounter after an almost forgotten past and a most recent brush with possible death. However, photos document that the author's long hair, usually tied in a bun at the back of her head, had been cut off during her hospital stay.[38] The documentary evidence indicates that Seghers often avoids including specific biographical material, instead tak-ing poetic license to fictionalize the autobiographical. The reluctance to use unaltered biographical information fosters Seghers's tendency to depict different periods in her life in the attempt to shape her memory film with visions of the now and then and to fuse or juxtapose the transformed personal and the experienced historical.

The interior stories of the "Excursion" begin with the seesawing scene, and Seghers has the narrator comment on Leni as a loving friend whose life is destroyed by her best friend's cruel disloyalty. It is a horrify-ing event that the narrator contrasts with Marianne's exceptional beauty as it comes into clear view in this episode. The visual focus moves laterally to Marianne, the "prettiest girl in our class, her long, thin legs crossed in front of her on the board. [. . .] Nothing but charm and mirth could be seen in her face, as noble and as perfectly shaped as the faces of the medi-eval stone maidens at the cathedral in Marburg" (E 286). When compar-ing Marianne's appearance to the statues of the ten bridesmaids who in the Gospel of Matthew (25:1–13) represent the five wise and the five foolish virgins, Seghers speaks of a cathedral in Marburg when the cor-rect identification is the Magdeburg cathedral.[39] Being aware of Marianne's later "heartlessness, culpability, or coldness of conscience," the narrator nevertheless forgets all later knowledge about her, as she is "delighted at the sight of her" (E 286). While the memory film presents the action, a jolt moves through Marianne's taut, slender body every time she adds to the bounce of the seesaw without pushing off, and she looks "as if she could just as easily fly away, a carnation between her teeth, her small, firm breasts in an outgrown smock of green linen" (ibid). Clearly, the visual details reveal Marianne's attractive physical appearance but also her laziness, insofar as she lets Leni do all the hard work of pushing the seesaw while she enjoys the carefree abandon and lightheartedness of a girl whose budding beauty stands in contrast to the worn linen of her gown.

Time and again, the narrative camera catches these two girls in an intimate embrace as they move, "each of them with one arm around the other, their heads touching" (E 287). This image of loving togetherness of two girlfriends nevertheless causes the narrator to recall: "Directly I felt a bit sad as seemed to happen to me so often in my schooldays, a bit left out of the shared games and close friendships of the others. Then the two of them paused and took me into the middle" (ibid). While both Leni and Marianne offer a gesture of inclusion, Seghers recollects a sense of being an outsider in her school, sometimes seen as a "loner."[40] The scene might also obliquely address being Jewish in a predominantly Christian environment.

The sweet triangulation between Leni, Marianne, and Netty gets challenged and fluctuates when Otto Fresenius, Marianne's "favorite suitor and dance partner" (E 292), arrives on the *Remagen* and is seen by the narrator as a proverbial fairy-tale prince who "would have swum right over to us to be with his girl" (E 293). His presence transforms Marianne, "always a lovely, healthy girl," into "such a wonder of tenderness and grace that she stood out from all the schoolgirls like a marvel" (E 293). With the approval of his mother, Otto is set on marrying his sweetheart, but is drafted into a student battalion and killed in action in the Argonne forest when a shot from French sharpshooters tears him apart. Seghers attributes to Otto's noble character the exemplary "traits of propriety and a shared respect for human dignity that would have prevented" his beloved Marianne "from disavowing her school friend" Leni, who, "like a sister, a steadfast companion in love's joy and pain," had served as "a conscientious go-between for letters and clandestine meetings" between Otto and Marianne (E 293). The triangulation of mutual love in the here and now is reinforced by Seghers's visualization of touching and intimacy, as Marianne never removes her one hand from Leni's shoulder while she gives Otto her other hand, confirming the sense of love that all those present witness. Regarding the cinematic arrangement of these gestures, Seghers exults with bathos: "They were the first to give us a true idea of what it was to be a loving pair as nature itself intended and joined together, not something dreamt of, not read about in poetry or tales or classical drama, but tangible and real" (E 294). While the body language visually manifests true intimacy, it also reveals in a utopian sense the physiognomy of noble humanity.

When the time comes for the separate departure of the boys and girls, Marianne lets go of Otto's hand and her arm slips off of Leni's shoulder. She remains standing, "alone in her row of girls, lost in thoughts of love. Despite this most earthly of all sentiments, she stood out from the other girls in her near-unearthly beauty" (E 297). Having emphasized Marianne's exceptional beauty, which is contrasted by the major flaws of her character, Seghers then singles out Otto's unfortunate fate by claiming, ironically, that because of his early death "devotion was granted him for all time, and all evil spared—all temptation, all base impulses and disgrace" (E 298).

The fickleness and collapse of close friendship and intense love are exemplified in Marianne's betrayal of Leni. Seghers expounds on this deadly disloyalty almost as a constant theme in her voice-overs when she relates the closeness of the two girls as best friends from the seesawing scene to their very last walk together, which the camera eye follows as both have left the ship and are on their way home through the streets of Mainz. Departing from these two friends, Netty sees them walking "arm in arm to the Rheinstrasse" and their loving intimacy is detailed with charming visual details such as Marianne having "a red carnation between her teeth" after she had "stuck just such a carnation into the ribbon around Leni's Mozart braid" (E 301). But then the narrator turns to a gruesome contrast, asserting a horrible historical truth: "I can still see Marianne with that red carnation between her teeth, even as she is giving vicious replies to Leni's neighbors, even as her half-charred body is lying in smoking shreds of clothing in the embers of her parents' house" (E 301). Up to this point, the elaborate sequencing of scenes featured Leni and Marianne, particularly the latter, as fairy-tale-like figures of beauty and closeness. But from the opening scene of the memory film, the narrator's voice-over comments establish a counter-current that relates Marianne's betrayal. Now it is her terrible death in a bombing raid that puts an end to an ultimately infamous life. However, as the narrator relates this point of closure, one historical fact is mentioned that serves an almost consoling purpose. Enlightening the reader about Marianne's harrowing fate, the narrator also informs the reader that Leni's child "sent by the Gestapo to a remote National Socialist reformatory, survived the bombardment" (E 302). Clearly, Seghers's narrative strategy is to sequence multiple episodes of the idyllic and contrast them with revelations that break the stream of apparently idyllic interactions between beautiful human beings by revealing sobering truths about those same humans' moral and ethical downfall in connection with the horrible events in recent German history.

In striking contrast to the friendship between Leni and Marianne and its sad ending, Seghers depicts the deportation of Netty's classmate Sophie Meier and their Jewish teacher Miss Sichel. By the time the two characters are taken away "in a sealed train car crammed full" with many other deportees on their way to the camps and certain death in Poland, their shiny black hair has turned completely white. The narrator asserts: "Sophie was already withered and wizened like a twin sister when she drew her last breath in Miss Sichel's arms" (E 298). With this sobering image of human intimacy in the face of deadly cruelty, Seghers creates a visual memorial to the victims of the Shoah. While she does not mention it explicitly here, the author also commemorates her mother's deportation on the same train as Miss Sichel, although she probably did not know this fact at the time she was writing the "Excursion" from the fall of 1943 through the first few months of 1944.

V. Conclusion

The novella is a tripartite requiem. The *Rahmenerzählung* of the Mexican exile situation through the visually striking depiction of a remote and barren landscape frames the *Binnenerzählung*. These interior stories contain, in a string of cinematic scenes, the memory film of the excursion in the author's childhood. Seghers's innovative use of voice-over comments serves the purpose of deconstructing an apparently idyllic event by confronting the reader with the tragic fates of the dead girls and others whose deaths symbolize the many human failures and horrors of German history. Notably, the cinematic narrative visualizes these doomed girls on the excursion and focuses on various topographical locations: the café, an oasis-like locale compared to the Mexican wilderness; the boat trip on the Rhine as a visual hymn to the homeland, with the moving camera taking in the iconic, fairy-tale-like landscape; and the way back to an erstwhile home that has been irreconcilably lost in the bombings. Seghers creates a precarious juxtaposition between the desire for a comforting homecoming and the impossibility of returning back home. Whatever magical welcome and existential safety that home seems to guarantee have fallen victim to Nazi brutality and wartime air raids that extinguish the lives of both the innocent and the guilty.

Who narrates this novella? The "Excursion" shows the author's remarkably personal way of narrating, in an avant-garde style and dual vision, the memory film of her childhood as well as her predicament as an exile in a foreign land far away from her home country. Oscillating between the hope for a utopian idyll that fosters close friendship and love and the disillusioning annihilation of such promises of a community of lovely humanity, Seghers focuses on her childhood self Netty as an experiencing self in the now of the past, while giving this figure of innocence the companionship of a history-wise narrator who becomes the teller of devastating truths. These truths are not only about the barbarism of Nazi regime but, as the contrast between Leni and Marianne reveals, about the righteous and their dignity in suffering as well as those who lose themselves to the enemies of humankind. According to Gutzmann, Seghers as an author of exile, also focuses on the future, on a time after the defeat of the fascist regime, in order to envision and facilitate a better postwar Germany.[41]

As a requiem for the dead girls, for her parents who perished under the Nazis, and for the many others victimized by the Nazi regime, the

"Excursion" is not only the fulfillment of an assigned task for school, but a memorial for all those victims whose struggles against fascism need to be remembered and honored for the sake of the decent and righteous in a recovered homeland.

Notes

[1] Sonja Hilzinger, *Anna Seghers* (Stuttgart: Reclam, 2000), 120.

[2] Hans Mayer, "Anmerkung zu einer Erzählung von Anna Seghers," *Sinn und Form* 14.1 (1962): 121.

[3] "Erinnerungsarbeit": Ute Brandes, *Anna Seghers*, Köpfe des 20. Jahrhunderts, vol. 117 (Berlin: Colloquium Verlag, 1992), 58.

[4] Anna Seghers, "The Excursion of the Dead Girls," trans. Helen Fehervary and Amy Kepple Strawser, *American Imago: Psychoanalysis and the Human Sciences* 74.3 (Fall 2017): Wilhelm II and the First World War: 293; Hitler and Goebbels: 302; occupation of the Rheinland: 300. Subsequent references to this translation will be in parentheses in the text using the abbreviation E.

[5] Anna Seghers, "Der Ausflug der toten Mädchen," in *Anna Seghers: Die Erzählungen 1933–1947, Werkausgabe*, vol. 2.2, ed. Silvia Schlenstedt (Berlin: Aufbau, 2011), 131. Subsequent references to the original German novella will be to this edition in parentheses in the text using the abbreviation A.

[6] Franz K. Stanzel, *A Theory of Narrative*, trans. Charlotte Goedsche (Cambridge: Cambridge University Press, 1984), 142.

[7] Ibid., 127.

[8] Hans Mayer, "Anmerkung zu einer Erzählung von Anna Seghers," 124.

[9] Stanzel, *A Theory of Narrative*, 118.

[10] Hans Mayer, "Anmerkung zu einer Erzählung von Anna Seghers," 123; Christiane Zehl Romero, *Anna Seghers: Eine Biographie 1900–1947* (Berlin: Aufbau, 2000), 382; Mayer, "Anmerkung zu einer Erzählung von Anna Seghers," 123.

[11] Mayer, "Anmerkung zu einer Erzählung von Anna Seghers," 123.

[12] Heike A. Doane, "Die wiedergewonnene Identität: Zur Funktion der Erinnerung in Anna Seghers Erzählung 'Der Ausflug der toten Mädchen,'" in *Ästhetiken des Exils*, ed. Helga Schreckenberger (Amsterdam: Rodopi, 2003), 289.

[13] Romero, *Anna Seghers*, 76–77.

[14] Simonetta Sanna, "Die Sehnsucht nach einem friedlichen Deutschland. Das Schicksal deutscher Frauen zwischen kriegerischer Geschichte und stiller Landschaft in Anna Seghers 'Der Ausflug der toten Mädchen,'" *Argonautenschiff: Jahrbuch der Anna Seghers Gesellschaft* 5 (1996): 184–87.

[15] Barbara Prinsen-Eggert, "Mädchenfreundschaften," *Argonautenschiff: Jahrbuch der Anna Seghers Gesellschaft* 8 (1999): 380.

[16] Ibid.

[17] Ibid., 379.

18 Robert Cohen, "Die befohlene Aufgabe machen: Anna Seghers' Erzählung 'Der Ausflug der toten Mädchen,'" *Monatshefte* 79, no. 2 (1987): 186; Christa Wolf, *Die Dimension des Autors: Essays und Aufsätze, Reden und Gespräche 1959–1985*, 2nd ed. (Darmstadt: Luchterhand, 1987), 324.

19 Romero, *Anna Seghers*, 37–39.

20 Ibid., 38.

21 Ibid., 404.

22 Ibid., 38.

23 When the book publication of "Der Ausflug der toten Mädchen" first appeared in New York in 1946, three reviews followed using the terms "traumhaft" etc. The reviews are reprinted in Anna Seghers, *Der Ausflug der toten Mädchen und andere Erzählungen* (Berlin: Aufbau Taschenbuch Verlag: 1995), 135–39; Werner Baum, *"Bedeutung und Gestalt": Über die sozialistische Novelle* (Halle, Mitteldeutscher Verlag: 1968), 95, 97.

24 Gertraud Gutzmann, "Literary Antifascism: Anna Seghers' Exile Writings 1936 to 1949," in *Facing Fascism and Confronting the Past: German Women Writers from Weimar to the Present*, edited by Elke P. Frederiksen and Martha Kaarsberg Wallach (Albany, NY: State University of New York Press, 2000), 89.

25 Birgit Maier-Katkin, "'Kahl und wild wie ein Mondgebirge'—Exile and Mind Travel in Anna Seghers' 'The Excursion of the Dead Girls,'" in *Exiles Traveling: Exploring Displacement, Crossing Boundaries in German Exile Arts and Writings 1933–1945*, ed. Johannes F. Evelein (Amsterdam, New York: Rodopi, 2009), 300.

26 Ibid., 305.

27 Kurt Batt, *Anna Seghers: Versuch über Entwicklung und Werke* (Frankfurt am Main: Röderberg, 1973), 181. See also Heinz Neugebauer, *Anna Seghers: Leben und Werk* (Berlin (West): DEB Verlag das europäische Buch, 1978), 111. See also Sonja Hilzinger, "Im Spannungsfeld zwischen Exil und Heimkehr. Funktionen des Schreibens in der Novelle 'Der Ausflug der toten Mädchen,'" *Weimarer Beiträge* 36.10 (1990): 1578.

28 Mayer, "Anmerkung zu einer Erzählung von Anna Seghers," 120.

29 Peter Beicken, "'Erotische Phantasien' und Bilder im Kopf. Filmisches in Anna Seghers' Erzählungen. Teil II: Erzählfilmisches in 'Jans muß sterben,'" *Argonautenschiff: Jahrbuch der Anna Seghers Gesellschaft* 18 (2009): 103–13.

30 Birgit Maier-Katkin, *Silence and Acts of Memory: A Postwar Discourse on Literature, History, Anna Seghers, and Women in the Third Reich* (Lewisburg, PA: Bucknell University Press, 2007), 143. See also her "'Kahl und wild wie ein Mondgebirge,'" 305.

31 Maier-Katkin, "'Kahl und wild wie ein Mondgebirge,'" 305.

32 Dorrit Cohn, *Transparent Minds: Narrative Modes for Presenting Consciousness in Fiction* (Princeton, NJ: Princeton University Press, 1978), 185.

33 Mayer, "Anna Seghers' 'Ausflug der toten Mädchen,'" 124.

34 Helen Fehervary, *Anna Seghers: The Mythic Dimension* (Ann Arbor: University of Michigan Press, 2001), 35.

35 Olivia C. Díaz Pérez, "Das Bild Mexikos und die Exilerfahrung im Werk von Anna Seghers," *Argonautenschiff: Jahrbuch der Anna Seghers Gesellschaft* 11 (2002): 93–94.

36 Ibid., 93–94.

37 Neugebauer, *Anna Seghers*, 113.

38 Romero, *Anna Seghers*, 33, 34. See also the illustration on those pages.

39 Gertraud Gutzmann, "Anna Seghers' 'Ausflug der toten Mädchen' als ein Beitrag der Literatur zur Neugestaltung Deutschlands," in *Das Exilerlebnis: Verhandlungen des Vierten Symposium über Deutsche und Österreichische Exilliteratur*, ed. Donald G. Daviau and Ludwig M. Fischer (Columbia, SC: Camden House, 1982), 482.

40 Romero, *Anna Seghers*, 70–71.

41 Gutzmann, "Anna Seghers' 'Ausflug der toten Mädchen,'" 482.

3: Anna Seghers's Rubble Literature, 1947–49

Ute Brandes

O N AUGUST 2, 1949, after Anna Seghers had been in postwar Berlin for about two years, she wrote to her American literary agent Maxim Lieber: "I have also noted very many things about both the land in which I live and other countries. Different specific situations and conversations in the last two years. The events of the last years prevent me from sending them to you."[1]

Why exactly was she so hesitant to publish these pieces? During her exile years Anna Seghers had already voiced specific ideas about how writers could help to "denazify" Germans. She wanted to take part in such an education project as early as 1942. In her essay "Volk und Schriftsteller" (The People and the Writer, 1942) she talks about her views that writers should live among their people, feel responsible for their country, and act upon their mandate to reeducate their audience after the fall of National Socialism.[2] In her 1944 essay "Aufgaben der Kunst" (The Functions of Art) she goes a step further, speaking of the desired themes: "The artist of today must think of points of attack by which we can free the mentality of the fascist youth of monstrous delusion, of deceitful conceptions, of bossiness and mechanical obedience controlled by rigor-mortis-like uptightness."[3] Such "Angriffspunkte" (points of attack) would be to write very realistically about the true postwar conditions of the individual, the people, and humanity ("Individuum," "Volk," "Menschheit"). The writer must bring to the conscience of her readers "the humiliation in which Germany fell, in order to make it still more terrible because of the realization of this humiliation, through the ruthless itemization of all that followed, all marks of political impotence, which not only mark the existence of the nation but also stigmatize the existence of every person in the nation, with countless, often only subconscious, effects" (197).

In addition to the depiction of post-fascist German reality in its actual shape, Seghers finds the themes of foreign peoples in their struggles for humanity to be an especially important topic for writers who have been in exile. Throughout the rest of her life she continued to develop her concept of writing about foreigners, their differences, and their struggles for autonomy and independence from colonial rule. Many of these postwar stories, from *Das Argonautenschiff* (The Ship of the Argonauts) and the *Karibische Geschichten* (Caribbean Stories) to *Crisanta* and *Das wirkliche Blau* (The True Blue), *Der Führer* (The Leader), and *Drei Frauen aus Haiti* (Three Women from Haiti) are considered today to be among the best of the works she wrote after her return to Germany.

Seghers's third aesthetic principle was to continue the flexible, open, and modernist forms of writing for which she had argued in her 1938/39 correspondence with Georg Lukács, today best known as part of the "Expressionismus-Debatte"[4] (Expressionism Debate). In times of social and historical change, she wrote there, the best realistic art has the "tendency to make one conscious through reality" by incorporating fantasy, dreams, legends, and fairy tales into realistic texts, using montage, collage, reportage, and sharp film-like cuts. Both the *inner* and *outer* reality of a person should thus receive attention when writing about the individual with all his or her concerns and characteristics.[5] Most of her works, from *Die Gefährten* (The Wayfarers, 1932) to her latest novel to this point, *Die Toten bleiben jung* (The Dead Remain Young; finished in Mexico 1946, published in Germany 1949) had been written with such modernist techniques—without a central narrator, without one unified fable. In a string of parallel chapter plots, small narrative units are cut with intersecting scenes, asking the reader to come up with a synthesis between different perspectives and strands of narrative.

These three concepts for her writing at that time—stark depictions of postwar social reality, non-racist foreign topics, and writing with a range of modernist techniques—are present in the many unpublished or later not republished short stories, reportages, a lengthy drama fragment, and other pieces that Seghers wrote during her first two years after returning to Berlin. They are more complex and nuanced than what was desired by the Soviet zone and East German cultural policy at that time. Most of all, they lack the positive outlook on a socialist future. Many of the sketches, narratives, and tales with postwar Berlin themes are still located in the Anna Seghers Archive at the Academy of Arts in Berlin; they were either not published at all or appeared in East and West German newspapers or journals in the late 1940s. They were not selected by Seghers herself to appear in the several editions of her collected works that were published in East Germany. There are some wonderful texts among them which deserve to be thought of as part of the "Rubble Literature" themes and styles written by contemporary postwar authors, all of them still in exile or living in the Western Zones.

Anna Seghers's first years in Berlin turned out to be even harder than she had imagined during her exile in Mexico. As a German Jew who had lost her mother and many close friends in the Holocaust, and as a Communist, she felt alienated; her private letters about having entered an "Ice Age" in Berlin are well known by now.[6] In those first few months in spring and summer 1947 she was looking for the few Germans who had dared to resist—in jails, in concentration camps, in the underground. To close friends she expressed her feelings of resentment toward most "ordinary" Germans who were preoccupied with their own losses and fears while not reflecting upon their compliance and the terrible cruelties and destruction of the Third Reich.

Immediately after her arrival in Berlin, Seghers began to write down her impressions of the mentality of postwar Germans in letters, sketches, and articles. A mixture of alienation and dismay is already visible in the unpublished essay "Ich bin genau vor drei Wochen in B. angekommen" (I arrived in B. exactly three weeks ago):

> I came to B. exactly three weeks ago . . . I experience again the untouched energy in the old friends who escaped concentration camps and all persecution. . . . I find the folly again in men and women who have learned nothing, but nothing in the meantime. . . . I watch to see whether children sing the ancient song that could have been written yesterday: Cockchafer fly / father is in war / mother is in Pomerania / Pomerania has been burned to pieces / cockchafer fly.[7]

Because of her own Western experience in exile, where much more open discussions were the norm, her expectations for a responsible literature were quite different from the instructions of the Moscow Communist Party officials or the SED (Socialist Unity Party Germany) mandates in her first few years back in Germany.

Many of Seghers's texts of that time, as well as a longer, aesthetically very interesting play *Die Feier* (The Celebration), remained unfinished.[8] But even those anecdotes, scenes, reportages, and short stories published around 1947–50 that were of great literary merit were eventually held back by Seghers herself from further publication in the several editions of her collected works. We need to ask today: In terms of early East German goals for literature, were they possibly too complex? Were they too dark in their attempt to reeducate readers? Not always upbeat in their stark realism? Or is it because they lack the perspective of a coming and better Communist future? Or can we, today, read them as Seghers's contribution to the genre of "Rubble Literature" being written by other postwar authors at the time?

Most texts are set in the Soviet sector of Berlin and in Eastern Germany in the postwar era. There are only three or four fragments among them that are situated in foreign locations and at previous times. They express unease about the future, and some document a lingering Nazi mindset. Among the topics Seghers takes up are disoriented children in displaced persons camps; prostitution as a commodity; the Black Market; and German fear of Russians and the Red Army. Several fragments concern lingering racist attitudes among medical workers. Other topics include a

young woman who discovers that she lives in the former apartment of a
Nazi criminal; an entertainer who condoned Nazi violence out of vanity;
and the ambivalent political messages adults give to children as they
quickly readjust their political views after the war. In the following, I will
look especially at those texts that bear a striking resemblance to the contemporary genre of "Rubble Literature."

The first, *Die Feier*,[9] is an unfinished, lengthy play with innovative
dramatic techniques that make visible the historical situation, the postwar
location, and the mental insecurity of the characters. Seghers wrote this
play to be staged in the renowned *Deutsches Theater* at Schumannstrasse,
the previous theater of Max Reinhardt, where her friend Wolfgang
Langhoff had been the director since 1946. Like her, he had joined the
German Communist Party in 1928, and she most probably knew him in
the last years of the Weimar Republic. She was familiar with his Düsseldorf
agitprop group "Nordwest ran" (Northwest, let's go), with his imprisonment in the concentration camp "Bürgermoor," where he had first staged
the famous song "Die Moorsoldaten" (The Moorsoldiers) in a revue; she
knew about his escape from Germany in 1934 and his exile in Zurich. In
1947 they met up at the "Kulturbund" (Cultural Alliance) in Berlin's
Jägerstrasse (Hunters Street) and then, in spring 1948, they both went to
the Soviet Union with a delegation of writers.[10]

Langhoff seemed very receptive to Seghers's innovative ideas, and in
the first version of the play there are numerous requests addressed to him,
asking for his ideas and staging suggestions. For example, Seghers makes
"Vorschläge zu einer Rahmenhandlung" (suggestions for a frame) or
writes to him "Achtung auf folgende Punkte . . . Langhoff, erinnere dich
an den Film *The Green Pastures!*"[11] This American film was made in 1936,
with music by the exiled Erich Wolfgang Korngold. In the second copy of
the manuscript the notes to Langhoff are missing, although his name
shows up again later in the text—maybe a mistake by Seghers, who was
very busy writing. It is not known why their collaboration did not come
about.

Seghers's play consists of separate scenes, which at times are reminiscent of Brecht's epic theater, but they are even more abstract in montage and stage techniques. Only some of the past scenes are told by
narrators: most historical episodes are played out on stage, with dimmed,
and then slowly increased lighting marking these as historical scenes,
while the original actors sit in the dark on stage. Diverse plot strands and
intermittent frames appear, together with characters that are part of the
frames. The non-chronological time within the scenes—before, during,
and after the war—is intended to make German war guilt clear, together
with its historical origins and current effects. The overall temporal frame
is November 7, 1947, the thirtieth anniversary of the Bolshevik
Revolution.

People with very diverse goals and travel destinations are waiting for their train connections, in the noise and confusion of a bunker that is now used as a waiting area and night shelter. In the chaos of the diverse travelers only a small group speaks about the revolution; most persons in the play do not seem to know or care about the date. An episode in the novel *Die Toten bleiben jung* is similar to the beginning scene of the play: in the last weeks of the war a young bombed-out woman listens to the hard-to-understand conversation of two friends, enemies of Hitler, in an overcrowded train compartment. In the hopeless confusion and noise of the many voices, she listens, and then she puzzles about the sense her own life makes, and the guilt that her country bears. Soon she wants clarity, and after the train's arrival she goes searching for one of the speakers. She finds him and is admitted to his apartment, but the novel leaves open whether she knows how to phrase the right questions to him.

An important element of the unfinished play is Seghers's radical lighting technique which focuses on persons, groups, scenes, or separate dialogues. Pairs or groups of characters speak to each other, wanting to pass the time. When they talk about a past event, a spotlight comes on and the scene is not only narrated but enacted. Some of the scenes have titles: "Die Fahne" (The Flag), "Sein Tod" (His Death), "Psychologie" (Psychology), "Das Viereck" (The Square), "Die Stiefel" (The Boots), "Nachtasyl" (Night Asylum), and "Wartesaal" (Waiting Room). Again and again the action is interrupted by other conversations. All interruptions are motivated by the noise and confusion in the bunker.

A very interesting example of the innovative lighting technique is the scene "Das Viereck," in which the author also includes sounds that arouse certain memories in the characters. At first only the scene in the bunker is illuminated, then the sounds of the travelers are slowly dimmed, and one can make out a room. Two people speak. The lighting slowly focuses on a spot on the wall: the stage directions say "Das Viereck, wo vor dem das Bild hing, wird unmerklich heller und heller" (The square, where formerly the picture hung, becomes imperceptibly brighter and brighter). The psychological effect is heightened by the music: "Solange das Viereck hell ist, hört man diese Lieder von weither" (As long as the square is lit up, the songs are perceived from afar).

Among the uprooted persons in transit are the young bombed-out woman already mentioned, who wants to start a new life in another city, a disabled young soldier, and an old woman, mothers with their children, swindlers, Nazis, and many more. They talk about bombings, dead spouses and sons, und whatever else was lost: houses, jobs, body parts, money. They fear the danger of relying on promises during such uncertain times, they speak of the impossibility of obtaining legal papers, and they talk of their hopes of making a better life in the West or in the East. Most conversations show persons who suffer from loss, doubt, and disappointment.

They do not understand or have not even asked who is to blame for the destruction of their country. Almost entirely, a positive perspective is reserved for the small group of persons who celebrate the Russian Revolution. However, their part in the play is small, compared to the confusion, boredom, and strife which make for the predominant atmosphere in the bunker.

Not clearly taking sides as to its intended political message is the scene "Die Stiefel." Seghers first sent it as a separate one-act drama to her literary agent Bronislaw Buber in Paris in 1948, but it was then aired in 1949 on East German radio. A young German veteran, recently returned from the Eastern front, believes he recognizes a sleeping Soviet soldier by the impossibly patched boots he wears. Some time before, during a house search in Odessa, the German soldier had been commanded to shoot a Russian partisan in hiding. After searching several apartments, he suddenly sees the Russian hiding in a pipe behind a wall. Actually, he only sees his patched boots sticking out of the pipe, and out of fleeting empathy he does not report him to his SS sergeant. Back at home after the war, the veteran, compared to his father, is much more sincere in facing up to the past. However, Seghers also tells about his indifference to the shooting of Russian civilians during the war. She leaves open whether he is ready for a new beginning in postwar Germany.

Another example of Seghers's writings that record the contradictory reality she found in postwar Germany is "Das Dorf S. in Mecklenburg" (The Village S. in Mecklenburg)—published in a Heidelberg newspaper—a few months after her arrival in Berlin.[12] This is another valuable text not to be found in any of her collected works editions. The reportage-like short story was in another version titled "Vorher Während Nachher" (Before During Afterwards).[13] The story begins with the fairytale-like village S. being admired by tourists who look out of their train window and see a quaint little town, made up of pretty thatched-roof houses. But in reality, this village has a terrible secret: two years before, during the last few weeks of the war, a train with about 6,000 women prisoners bound for the concentration camp Bergen-Belsen was held up on the railroad tracks close to the station. Any prisoner trying to flee was immediately shot by the SS guards. For two days, the villagers heard the screaming and moaning women, crying out for food and drink, but they did not come to help. About fifty-three corpses, shot by the SS or starved to death, were found two years later when several mass graves were discovered next to the tracks.

Seghers was especially interested in recording the mentality of a village like this, which had first complied with evil and then had hushed it up, so that its own guilt would not become publicly known. Available to her were three different perspectives about the village and its crime. First, the archival files contain a report written by one of the surviving women prisoners, who vividly describes the terrible conditions in one of the railway cars and the prisoners' increasingly desperate cries for help. Second, Seghers worked from the transcript of a radio interview with an East German official whose testimony about the crime reflects the predominant ideology of "coming-to-terms" with fascism in the Soviet zone. The SS was guilty, the radio speaker says, not the villagers, who were witness to the terrible crimes and learned from this experience firsthand about the true character of fascism. And third, Seghers traveled to the village herself to meet some of the locals and to learn about their peculiar thinking and lifestyle, honed by ages of poverty, conceit, and seclusion. Contrasting the tourists' fairytale myth with real historical and mental conditions in the village, however, her own focus is on depicting the villagers' guilt in the context of the experiences of generations of these farmers, their treacherous defense of the little property they own, and their mistrust and fear of any outsiders. Her explanation of the conditions is a social and historical one, not primarily motivated by ideological interpretations. By presenting all perspectives about the crime, Seghers assumes that her readers will look for their own conclusions.

The literary jewels among these earliest stories after the writer's return to Germany are the three anecdotes that make up the cycle *Die Kinder des zweiten Weltkrieges* (The Children of the Second World War), written in 1947 and 1948, and published only once, in 1953. In their sparse, Kleist-like language they capture the children's trauma in a raw manner. They are not written with the intent to give a positive outlook for the future, as Seghers's later stories tend to do. It is remarkable how intensely the writer edited these texts, how often she rewrote and sharpened them—several versions, each one shorter, exist among her papers. In an objective, matter-of-fact tone, all three texts transmit the mental devastation of children caught up in war. Both the beginning and the end tales, with their parallel plots, frame the middle; the cycle is structured like a triptych. Seghers experiments here with epic foreshortening. In the most concise form she foregoes any narrative embellishment in order to express the children's anguish.

The first of these amazing stories is "Die Puppe" (The Doll) in which a little girl, just liberated from a concentration camp, receives a doll from a relief organization. She cries: "Warum gebt ihr mir ein totes Kind zum Spielen?" (Why do you give me a dead child to play with?). The vignette contains a first longer sentence, which sums up all information as to time, place, and action, and drives it toward the climax in the following short sentence. Her traumatic experiences in the concentration camp are this little girl's reality. The attempts of the adults to appease her amount to an insult of her most inner, personal dignity which enabled her to survive the camp in the first place.

The middle, somewhat longer, anecdote "Kindergarten" seems to signal a beginning normalcy in the dialogue between two little girls who are waiting for a parent to pick them up at the end of their day. In a sharp turnaround, one of the girls, being sure that no father will ever come again, must experience the dad of the other girl showing up. Then her mother comes. She is at a loss to console her daughter—it was she who always told her daughter that her dad would come home after the war.

The third little story, "Schulaufsatz" (School Essay), is probably the most artful one of the cycle. It leads us into the childlike world of fairy tales. A little girl, shopping in the town market with her mother, flees when bombs fall from the sky. She never sees her mother again. In a panic she runs, screaming, into the deep woods to hide. At night, a huge animal comes and threatens to devour her. It looks at her, and then it turns away. She thinks that it did not perceive that she was a child—she was so wild and shaggy—the animal must have thought she was a beast as well. The regression of the little girl into a wild creature is the only means for her to survive in the chaos of war. The story is a reversal of the fairy tale *Rotkäppchen* (Little Red Cap). In this "Anti-Märchen" (anti-fairy tale) the child becomes the wolf's chum. This new existence protects it from being eaten, and it deflects from her mother's death. Only the title, "Schulaufsatz" (School Essay) suggests an attempt by a teacher at dialogue and normalization. Yet no positive development can be made out that would lead the child out of her shock and despair and back into a state of normalcy.

Among these early texts there is also a file that documents Seghers's sharp protest over an unauthorized editing job, which naively aimed to make her text into a more acceptable, simple story. Her "Passagiere der Luftbrücke" (Passengers of the Airlift, 1948) was changed by the editors of the journal *Aufbau* (Building-Up) while the author was traveling, away from Berlin.[14] The Seghers reportage is introduced by a motto, a famous verse from Shakespeare's *Merchant of Venice*, in which a Jewish merchant relates anti-Semitic clichés. Seghers continues with a second remark, which is in italics. This functions just like a reply to Shakespeare: in Heine's "Shakespeare's Girls and Women" a London theater visitor, seeing these clichés acted out on stage, cries: "The poor man is wronged!" (Dem armen Mann geschieht Unrecht!). The 1948 Aufbau version of Seghers's reportage deletes the italic text and changes some words in the essay. The writer's subtle argumentation about Jewish displaced persons who had survived various concentration camps now appeared to support racism and fascist ideology.

Within the reportage, the author continues her earlier narrative technique of indirectly providing meaning just as in the two corresponding mottos at the beginning. She first restates anti-Semitic clichés still circulating in Berlin which suggested that all Jews are black market dealers, gangsters, and profiteers. She then confronts this cliché with the realities of the displaced persons' activities while waiting for their evacuation to different destinations, their various achievements in the camps, on theatrical stages, in schools, and in daily cooperation.

Eagerly taken up by the press of the American sector, the journal *Sie* (She) came up with a grotesque reaction, accusing the "Kleist Preis Trägerin Anna Seghers" (Kleist-Award Holder Anna Seghers) of anti-Semitism, slander, and attempting to attract former Nazis to the newly founded SED Party. In the Soviet sector, the *Berliner Zeitung* (Berlin News) and *Neues Deutschland* (New Germany), possibly encouraged by Seghers's seeming rejection of displaced persons, related episodes of these "asozialen Elemente" (asocial elements) who thankfully would now have to leave Berlin. After Seghers returned from her travels and read this reception of her reportage, she wrote a seething letter to *Aufbau*. By cutting and editing her text, she said, her publisher had provoked such misunderstandings. This letter was not published.[15] One of Seghers's subtle narrative methods which, in this reportage, first takes up clichés and then refutes them without stating an authorial perspective, was only deciphered in a 1998 study that analyzed textual strategies in another Seghers text.[16]

Seghers's political worries overshadowed her life and literary work at this time. A first public reprimand went her way in September 1948, after the Cold War was firmly established. Walter Ulbricht demanded that authors should be concerned with the new developments in society, instead of writing about exile and concentration camps. She had then been accused in October and December 1948 *Neues Deutschland* articles of not paying attention to socialist topics in her writings.[17] After the Anti-Zionist campaign in Moscow in March 1949 and the attacks on Western exiles in the summer of 1950, Seghers became more and more cautious.[18]

In describing Seghers's unpublished sketches, fragments, dramas, and reportages, some critics have attempted to make sense of the reasons for the author's unwillingness to finish or to publish them. Most agree with the Eastern German critic Inge Diersen that, although this literature was written with the clear goal of reeducating readers, Seghers was not yet able to make positive stories out of the new, postwar realities in the Soviet zone of Germany.[19] Yet in the second volume of Christiane Zehl Romero's *Anna Seghers* biography, some of these texts are discussed as documents of Seghers's difficult beginnings in Berlin which, if further pursued, would have led to a very different literary work:

> What can be made out in these fragments and *forgotten* works that deal with the current times are the sober view that was open to contradictions, with which Seghers looked at the conditions after her return, and her strenuous attempts to master the present times by writing in several genres. It is open to speculation how her works would have developed if she had followed these beginnings further and in future had relied more on her skeptical outlook and less on her hopes.[20]

A study of Anna Seghers's essays written in Mexico City, has shown that in 1947 and 1948 Seghers was writing with an amazing continuity. She held on to the literary principles she had developed in exile and was not yet willing to comply with the political and aesthetic cultural policies of the Soviet zone. The required ideological harmonizing that motivated her publisher's editorial changes and censorship incited her anger at first. However, time passed, and by the 1950s she voluntarily gave in.

Instead of further searching for the political and aesthetic implications of her increasing compliance with the demands of East German cultural policies, however, I suggest that we look at her early postwar work in Germany under the rubric of "Rubble Literature" (Trümmerliteratur). Seghers's participation in this postwar genre by Western and exiled authors proved to be true to her literary principles, as defined in Mexico. A comparison with other writers shows that Seghers's aesthetic and literary innovations are striking. Consider Robert Neumann. His *Kinder von Wien* (Children of Vienna), a novel written in 1946 by the Austrian writer and satirist, was written during his London exile. In it, a group of six orphaned children survive in the basement of a bombed-out house, barely surviving by prostitution and thievery. Just as in Seghers's texts, Neumann's theme is the social and psychological displacement of children in the ruins of postwar Europe.

Or consider Wolfgang Borchert's "Das ist unser Manifest" (This Is Our Manifesto) and his drama *The Man Outside* (Draußen vor der Tür), both written in a language of stark reality, which includes allegory and dreams, expressing lost illusions, hopelessness, and human destruction. Further examples include Heinrich Böll's early novels, his *Haus ohne Hüter* (House without Guardian) or the short story "Wanderer kommst du nach Spa . . ." (Wanderer if you come to Spa . . .) with their soldier protagonists having lost their ideals, their homes, and sometimes their entire families. Or the word-sparing lyrical I in Günter Eich's "Inventur" (Inventory). All these authors write in a simple, non-beautified, direct language and attempt to start from scratch. The exile authors Neumann and Seghers are also concerned with the displacement of children in war, with Jewish themes, and with the Holocaust, and they deal with these themes in a stark and often brutal simplicity.

The participation of Anna Seghers in this postwar genre by Western authors proved to be true to her literary principles, as defined in Mexico. Rubble literature was concerned with finding the "Angriffspunkte" (points of attack) Seghers was looking for, it featured non-racist and international themes, and it suggested the internal and external lives of her characters by incorporating their dreams, nightmares, and fantasy into a matter-of-fact language. Seghers's sketches and dramatic scenes, in addition, invented new modernist montage forms; new stage emphases by lighting and sounds; new, complex forms of reportage and narrative. It is to be hoped that these works will be published together soon, as outstanding examples of the distinct genre of German *Trümmerliteratur*.

Notes

Parts of this article were published in German in *DDR-Literatur: Eine Archivexpedition*, ed. Ulrich von Bülow and Sabine Wolf, 172–86 (Berlin: Ch. Links Verlag, 2014). Other parts were published in English as "Anna Seghers's Efforts to Write about German Reality, 1947–1950," forthcoming. All translations in this chapter are mine.

[1] Anna Seghers to Maxim Lieber, August 2, 1949. In Anna Seghers, *Briefe, 1924–1952* (Letters, 1924–52), ed. Christiane Zehl Romero and Almut Giesecke (Berlin: Aufbau, 2008).

[2] Anna Seghers, "Volk und Schriftsteller," in *Über Kunstwerk und Wirklichkeit: Die Tendenz in der reinen Kunst*, vol. 1, ed. Sigrid Bock (Berlin: Akademie-Verlag, 1971), 191–97.

[3] Anna Seghers, "Aufgaben der Kunst," in *Über Kunstwerk und Wirklichkeit: Die Tendenz in der reinen Kunst*, vol. 1, ed. Sigrid Bock (Berlin: Akademie-Verlag, 1971), 197–201; here, 197.

[4] Georg Lukács, "A Correspondence with Anna Seghers," in *Essays on Realism*, ed. Rodney Livingstone, trans. David Fernbach (Cambridge: MIT Press, 1980). See also Hans-Jürgen Schmitt, ed. *Die Expressionismus-Debatte: Materialien zu einer marxistischen Realitätskonzeption* (Frankfurt am Main: Suhrkamp, 1973).

[5] Christiane Zehl Romero, *Anna Seghers: Eine Biographie, 1947–1983* (Berlin, Aufbau, 2003), 61.

[6] Anna Seghers, *Hier im Volk der kalten Herzen: Briefwechsel, 1947*, ed. Christel Berger (Berlin: Aufbau Taschenbuch Verlag, 2000). See also AS to Georg Lukács, June 28, 1948, in Bock, *Über Kunstwerk und Wirklichkeit*, 4:154. See also Monika Melchert, *Heimkehr in ein kaltes Land: Anna Seghers in Berlin, 1947–1952* (Berlin: Verlag für Berlin-Brandenburg, 2011).

[7] Four typed pages, Anna Seghers Archiv (ASA) 362.

[8] Partly published in Ute Brandes, "Anna Seghers, Die Feier: Fragment eines Dramas; Aus dem Archiv der Akademie der Künste," *Sinn und Form* 66 (2014): 785–91.

[9] Anna Seghers Archive (ASA) Signature, Akademie der Künste, Berlin, 147.

[10] Ester Slevogt, *Den Kommunismus mit der Seele suchen: Wolfgang Langhoff—ein deutsches Künstlerleben im 20. Jahrhundert* (Cologne: Kiepenhauer & Witsch, 2011).

[11] "Be aware of the following points . . . Langhoff, remember the film *The Green Pastures*." ASA, Signature 147.

[12] *Rhein-Neckar-Zeitung*, Heidelberg, September 13, 1947.

[13] This longer version was first published in *Argonautenschiff* 7 (1998): 31–38.

[14] The original reportage, plus press articles, Seghers's protest letter to *Aufbau*, and a comment are in Klaus Schulte, "'Ich wollte eine widerwärtige Erscheinung verständlich machen': Editorische Anmerkungen zu Anna Seghers' 'Passagiere der Luftbrücke' und zu ihrem Protest gegen redaktionelle Eingriffe in den Text bei seinem Abdruck in der Zeitschrift 'Aufbau,'" *Argonautenschiff* 8 (1999): 89–102.

[15] ASA Signature, 295.

[16] Elizabeth Bense and Karl Schulte, "Wann ist 'Jetzt'—wo ist 'Hier'—wer sind 'Wir'? Sprach- und literaturwissenschaftliche Bemerkungen zu einigen Details im Textverfahren von Anna Seghers' Erzählung 'Der Ausflug der toten Mädchen,'" *Europe Plurilingue* 7 (March 1998): 47–82.

[17] Martin Böttcher, "Zeitliteratur und Literatur für unsere Zeit" and "Dichter im Niemandsland," in *Neues Deutschland*, October 1, 1948 and December 12, 1948.

[18] Romero, *Anna Seghers: Eine Biographie*, 36, 64, 151.

[19] Inge Diersen, "Jason 1948—problematische Heimkehr," *Argonautenschiff* 1 (1992): 107–28.

[20] Romero, *Anna Seghers: Eine Biographie*, 87. Emphasis in the original.

4: Anna Seghers and the Struggle to Tell Stories about the Nazi Past in the Early German Democratic Republic

Stephen Brockmann

W HEN ANNA SEGHERS returned to Germany in 1947 and settled in the Soviet zone of occupation, the literary world was already eagerly anticipating her arrival. Seghers's great anti-Nazi novel *Das siebte Kreuz* (The Seventh Cross),[1] which had appeared in Mexico in 1943 and in the United States a year later, was considered so important for postwar German literature that the country's leading cultural-political weekly, *Sonntag*, had begun publishing it in serialized form in its first issue, on July 7, 1946. The novel dominated subsequent issues of the newspaper for most of the rest of the year, finally reaching its conclusion—the famous words "All of us felt how ruthlessly and fearfully outward powers could strike to the very core of man, but at the same time we felt that at the very core there was something that was unassailable and inviolable"—on December 15.[2]

Partly as a result of the fame of this novel, Seghers was hailed as a genius when she arrived in Germany less than a year later. In the pages of *Die Weltbühne*, a key literary-cultural biweekly that had been intentionally (re)created to remind its readers of the Weimar-era journal of the same title, the former anti-Nazi resistance fighter and writer Jan Petersen, a long-time comrade of Seghers, called her the "shaper of our era" and proclaimed that the role of a writer with such creative power would be crucial for serving the cause of "truth and bringing it closer to people."[3] Seghers's work, he believed, could, "for hundreds of thousands . . . for millions of readers, make the confusions of our chaotic era clearly visible, thus transforming the seemingly insoluble into a profound, path-breaking understanding, which" would be "the only basis for conscious and intentional action."[4] The editors of *Die Weltbühne* greeted Seghers's arrival in Germany enthusiastically and declared Petersen's article to be not only the first overview of the writer's work ever published but a necessary response to the problem that, at this point, few members of the German reading public had access to Seghers's writing of the previous twelve years, since books by Seghers had been banned during the Nazi period.

Seghers was aware of the expectations being placed on her. She shared the hope that through her work she would be able to shed light on what Petersen had called "the confusions of our chaotic era." Like Petersen, Seghers viewed her task as not just literary or artistic but also pedagogical. As she put it in a letter she wrote to a friend at the time, "I came back because I can do the most for the people I know best. . . . Through books that will come into being here, I want to help prevent the mistakes of the past from ever being repeated."[5]

Several years after her return to Germany, Seghers publicly gave even more powerful expression to her belief in her own and other writers' responsibility for educating Germans, particularly young people. In July of 1950, at the founding congress of the East German Writers Union—an organization for which Seghers was to serve as president from 1952 to 1978—Seghers insisted that writers had a responsibility to eradicate any possibility of a fascist revival among the younger generation. "It is our assignment to make sure that they will never be guilty" again, she proclaimed.[6] And she warned: "It will be my fault, too, if any one of them should become guilty; because this, too, is part of the writer's work."[7] Obviously this was a high bar for any antifascist writer—so high, in fact, that one might wonder whether Seghers was setting herself up for inevitable failure. After all, in a post-Nazi world filled with large numbers of German young people who had served in Hitler's armies and helped to subjugate foreign countries, how was it possible even for a writer with extraordinary powers "to make sure that" German young people would never again "become guilty"?

Seghers knew that reeducation would be difficult, and almost all the works that she dedicated to narrating the development of the young East German state, from the novella "Der Mann und sein Name" (The Man and His Name, 1952) to the full-scale novels *Die Entscheidung* (The Decision, 1959) and *Das Vertrauen* (Trust, 1968) dealt either directly or indirectly with the education of German young people away from Nazism and toward an antifascist, antiracist democratic perspective. It was hardly a coincidence that "Der Mann und sein Name," Seghers's first such work, ended with the words "It won't be easy."[8] Seghers knew that these words applied both to herself and to the young people whom she viewed as a key audience, particularly for this novella. It was precisely the challenges faced by such young people that she frequently sought to describe in her literary works. Both she and they had a difficult task ahead of them: Seghers as an educator and young people as students and learners who would have to rethink their previous existence.

The task of reeducation applied not just to Seghers alone, of course, but to the postwar situation generally in all four occupation zones, where words like "reeducation" and "denazification" were commonplace. As early as September 1944, Seghers's friend and colleague Johannes R.

Becher, the most important cultural-political figure in the German Communist Party and later in the Socialist Unity Party (SED, founded in 1946), had accepted the party's directive that he and his colleagues—many of whom were then still in exile in Moscow—should "draft measures for the ideological reeducation of the German people in an antifascist-democratic spirit and . . . formulate specific tasks that will be assigned to literature, radio, film, and theater" in the furtherance of denazification.[9] In Becher's view, the task of reeducation was nothing less than "*national liberation and reconstruction on the most massive scale in the area of ideology and morals.*"[10]

Seghers's postwar speeches and writings demonstrate that she accepted the task of reeducation as her own, and that she sincerely hoped to carry it out successfully. Her short story "Der Ausflug der toten Mädchen" (The Excursion of the Dead Girls, 1943),[11] one of the greatest works of twentieth-century narrative prose in the German language, had dealt precisely with the experiences, educational and otherwise, of her own generation of Germans born around the turn of the twentieth century. The story revolved around a homework assignment given to the semiautobiographical narrator Netty by her favorite teacher, Miss Sichel, to "write up an account of the school outing for our next German lesson" because, as Netty reports, "I liked to travel and . . . write essays."[12] The story presents itself as the completion of this assignment decades later, after the horrific death of Miss Sichel—whose only "crime" was that she was Jewish—in a Nazi concentration camp. The narrative thus constitutes a commemoration of the inspirational impact that Miss Sichel once had on her adoring pupil, who has managed—virtually alone among her classmates—to survive the cataclysmic course of twentieth-century German history. "All at once I was mindful of my teacher's charge to describe the school outing in great detail. Tomorrow or yet this evening, once my fatigue had passed, I would carry out the assigned task."[13] The act of writing and telling stories is, for Netty, a way of giving order and meaning to human life. "I wondered how I should spend my time, today and tomorrow, here and there, for I now sensed an immeasurable stream of time, untethered like the air. As children we were ever reminded, rather than humbly surrendering to time, to take command of it in some measure."[14]

The act of writing is connected—also for Anna Seghers—to this overcoming of time. If one conceives of the "outing" that Netty describes as not just a particular school trip on a fine spring day a year or two before the outbreak of the First World War but the entire panorama of twentieth-century German history up through and even beyond the end of the Second World War, as well as the disastrous impact of that history on actual individuals—Netty and the girls and boys with whom she once went to school—then not just this one story but also much of Seghers's subsequent writing can be viewed as an attempt to carry out precisely the assignment given to Netty by Miss Sichel: specifically, to overcome time, and the destructive history associated with it, through storytelling and the sense- and meaning-making inherent to it. As Robert Cohen has argued, what underlies Seghers's attempt to carry out her task is not cheap or easy opti- mism but rather "comprehension of historical necessity."[15]

The ultimate goal of storytelling, for Seghers in the postwar period, is to prevent a repetition of what the German historian Friedrich Meinecke, in 1946, called "the German catastrophe" by making it clear to young people that they have a unique role to play in the unfolding of history: "No one, when there was still time to do so, ever recalled to us this our shared journey. No matter how many school essays were yet to be written about this country and about its history, and about our love for this shared land, never was it mentioned that our bevy of girls nestled together, glid- ing upstream in the oblique afternoon light, rightfully belonged here."[16] Seghers believed that her primary postwar task was to remind German young people that they "were especially a part of this homeland" and its history, and that their actions, therefore, mattered—not in spite of Germany's problems but precisely because of them. This self-assigned task corresponded to Seghers's long-standing conception of the writer's role more generally. As Helen Fehervary has shown, even in her earliest work Seghers had indicated a "readiness to take her place among the legions of chroniclers and storytellers who passed on to subsequent generations the knowledge, fancy, and wisdom inherent" in the stories people tell each other in order to make sense of the world.[17] In the postwar period this readiness became, for Seghers, a political and moral duty.

The figure of the adolescent Fritz Hellwig in *Das siebte Kreuz*, who lies to Gestapo agents when asked to identify his own stolen jacket—thus giv- ing the novel's protagonist Georg Heisler, who has escaped from the fic- tional Westhofen concentration camp, a decisive head start against the Nazis who are trying to recapture him—represents Seghers's hope that German youth might not be irredeemably corrupted. However the fear that German youth might instead already be beyond all hope of redemp- tion also haunts the novel:

> These were our thoughts on that terrible morning; then for the first time we voiced our conviction that if we were to be destroyed on that scale, all would perish because there would be none to come after us. The almost unprecedented in history, the most terrible thing that could happen to a people, was now to be our fate: a no-man's-land was to be established between the generations, which old experiences would not be able to traverse. If we fight and fall, and another takes up the flag and fights and falls too, and the next one grabs it and he too falls—that is natural, for nothing can be gained without sacrifice. But what if there is no longer anyone to take up the flag, simply because he does not know its meaning? . . . The best that grew in the

land was being torn out by the roots because the children had been taught to regard it as weeds. All those lads and girls out there, once they had gone through the Hitler Youth, the Work Service, and the Army, would be like the fabled children nurtured by animals who finally tore their own mothers to pieces. (146–47)

Although Fritz Hellwig is a Hitler Youth boy initially caught up in the Nazi worldview, he gradually learns to distance himself from it, both because of his own innate goodness and as a response to discreet but carefully targeted comments, gestures, and suggestions from a well-meaning, non-Nazi adult, the gardener Köhler, who serves as Fritz's unobtrusive but effective antifascist educator:

> He thought of his own sons. They belonged partly to him, and partly to the new State. At home they were his, they sided with him when he said that tops were still tops in the State, and bottoms were still bottoms. Away from home, though, they wore the regulation shirts and shouted "Heil!" at the proper moment. Had he done all in his power to strengthen their resistance? By no means! (229)

Here—as frequently happens in Seghers's works—a character is faced with a fundamental decision about whether or not to support a just cause—in this case whether to give the young Fritz Hellwig advice on how to thwart the Gestapo. "What a decision! What a world!" Köhler thinks (229). Partly on behalf of his own sons and their future, and partly because of his concern for Fritz, Köhler decides to help the youth, and this seemingly minor choice ultimately makes a decisive difference: "All the hundreds of coats made by that factory were undoubtedly alike. The Gestapo need only telephone. The zippers are all alike to the sixteenth of an inch. The pockets are all alike. But if for instance a key or a pencil had worn a hole in the lining, the Gestapo could never prove that it hadn't. That's the difference that you must obstinately hold to" (229). This is only one example in Seghers's work of an older character helping a younger one to thwart Nazis, and to escape their worldview. There were to be many others in the postwar period.

The most prominent story that Seghers told about the (re)education of a young man away from Nazism was her novella "Der Mann und sein Name," which appeared toward the end of 1952 and was widely discussed in subsequent months as a crucial contribution to early GDR literature, since critics viewed it as the first major work in which Seghers tried to describe social development in the nascent East German state.[18] The story revolves around a young Nazi man who served in the Nazis' most notorious organization, the SS, in a concentration camp, and who subsequently returns to civilian life in Germany, managing to evade Soviet authorities, to take on a false name, and to pass himself off illegitimately as a hero of the anti-Nazi resistance. The protagonist Walter Retzlow—who calls himself Heinz Brenner because that was the name of the antifascist whose identity he has appropriated—even joins and becomes a respected member of the SED. The party does not manage to uncover this deception on its own; rather, in a moment of crisis—when, quite by chance, he runs across a former Nazi associate of his—the young protagonist breaks down and reveals the truth to authorities. His reward for his honesty is a severe reprimand and expulsion from the party, in spite of the fact that he truthfully claims to support the SED and its goals. The party, however, is not interested in Walter's inner life, or in the drama of his psychological transformation from a Nazi into a socialist. "And don't say you belonged to us on the inside. What does 'inside' mean?" one of his older comrades snarls at him after his confession (179). Walter Retzlow admits, "confessions don't help anyone, only work helps" (150).

Unlike Seghers, SED leaders—in this story and in the reality that Seghers was both depicting and critiquing—do not want to hear about the psychological development of young people. Their lack of interest in an honest account of Nazism in Germany, which is thematized in the story, became a topic in official and semi-official reactions to Seghers's work as early as 1949–50, with the publication of the novel *Die Toten bleiben jung* (The Dead Stay Young), which dealt directly with the history of Nazism.[19] Seghers had defended her approach to exploring the problem of fascist mentalities in her work in a speech she gave at the 1950 Writers Union congress. She warned that fascism had attacked not just German cities and the German language but also the national psyche, and she asserted that the destruction left behind continued to threaten society even in the postwar period: "This confusion of language, which continues to exist today . . . is merely a reflection of the confusion found on the inside of people for many years, a devastation that is far greater even than the devastation of our cities."[20] It was precisely this confusion that Seghers hoped to address, and clear up, in literary works such as "Der Mann und sein Name."

Why was Seghers's first major story about the early GDR the account of a young Nazi who falsified his name and passed himself off as a heroic socialist resistance fighter? The answer is that Seghers knew that East German society was above all else a post-Nazi society, and that it was therefore, inevitably, full of former members and supporters of Hitler's party. As she put it in 1950, a few years before she wrote "Der Mann und sein Name," "the new human being doesn't fall out of a blue sky into democracy. He has all the imperfections and stains of capitalism as he begins to build the new society, and thereby himself, after so many years of Hitler's fascism."[21] Indeed, the changes that were happening in the early GDR—above all the changes in human beings themselves—were fascinating not in spite of the country's Nazi past but precisely because of it: because "this change has happened here, in this country, which has brought so much disaster and terror to other nations and to itself."[22]

Seghers suggested at the 1950 Writers Union congress that the progress being made in the GDR was astonishing because it was "happening on the same soil that was once the proving grounds for Hitler's fascism. It is a magnificent buildup that is occurring, unique in world history."[23] Seghers believed that the GDR was full of promise for the future, but she also knew that former Nazis would not find it easy to transform themselves into peace-loving democrats and socialists. The reality was that most Germans had not been heroic anti-Nazi resistance fighters, and that a great many of them had been conformists, opportunists, or even criminals. Seghers also knew that the Nazis had subjected German youth to intensive ideological brainwashing in schools and organizations such as the Hitler Youth, the Wehrmacht, and the SS. She knew that large numbers of young people living in the GDR had gone through precisely such conditioning prior to the end of the Second World War, and that the effects of this conditioning would not immediately disappear simply because the Nazis had lost the war and the Soviets had triumphed. Rather, Seghers believed, it would take a long period of careful reeducation to effect a change of attitude on the part of German young people. Hence the story of a young Nazi and his slow, painful conversion to socialism was more typical for the situation of a post-fascist Germany than the story of an unblemished resistance fighter, however noble. The story of such a man, Seghers believed, was "especially characteristic."[24]

Many readers and critics agreed with Seghers that her novella "Der Mann und sein Name" had put its finger on the core of the transformation then occurring in the GDR. As one representative report in *Sonntag* noted, "We know of no [other] example of postwar prose that deals in such a short space, in a lean form reduced to the essentials, with a theme so important and typical as the characteristic human path of a German in five postwar years from fear and despair through boredom, indifference, and apathy, to the threshold of reflection and cleansing."[25] A lecturer in Dresden who helped to didacticize the novella for students at the technical university there proclaimed enthusiastically:

Anna Seghers did not let herself be seduced into depicting Walter Retzlow's transformation as an uncomplicated, purely pleasant affair. Because Anna Seghers succeeds in depicting the essentials of this reality, this process of transformation in a concrete artistic image, she touches the hearts of many people who remember having experienced "the same" thing. What guarantees the hero of the story our most profound sympathy is the parallelism between his fate and our own experience. Countless Germans did not get their right names until after 1945, did not become what they could be until then. In the figure of Walter Retzlow, Anna Seghers has created a symbol of this powerful process of transformation and has shown countless people the process of their ideological transformation and brought to consciousness what would otherwise, for a great many, have remained hidden.[26]

The same lecturer admitted in a 1956 letter to Seghers that one of the reasons for the story's power over him was its resemblance to his own ideological transformation: "'Der Mann und sein Name' has . . . pulled me into its orbit a number of times and has done me a great service. I have learned to see my own life, my own ideological development, in an entirely new light. Through this story the developmental process of my own consciousness has become clear."[27]

In spite of the wide attention that her story received, Seghers also came in for criticism for what some readers saw as her pessimism with respect to Germany's difficult postwar transformation. Such readers generally wanted the novella's protagonist to enjoy a more upbeat, triumphant fate, because they believed that a happy ending would engender greater optimism about the future of the GDR. As a concerned reader from Halle wrote in a ten-page letter to Seghers in August of 1953, "the reader should be inspired to imitation, or at least to encouragement. But even with the best of will, such inspiration or merely encouragement can hardly develop in view of the life of the protagonist and his [girlfriend] Katharina, which has not got happier at all. It is as if he were still bearing his burden or some other weight. 'Their farewell was quiet,' 'He was standing stark and stiff. . . .' and the last sentence: 'It won't be easy': is an ending like that the appropriate result of a liberating deed?"[28]

Seghers wrote back to her interlocutor from Halle in September of 1953 with a patient defense of literary realism, as opposed to idealism or propaganda: "A reader often believes that a figure in a book should behave as he himself would recommend. But the figures in a book don't behave according to the suggestions of readers and also not according to the suggestions of the author, they behave the way they behave in reality." Although this answer did not initially satisfy its recipient, he subsequently responded with a grateful letter to the author acknowledging that she had been right all along:

> Your explanations have made a lot clear to me, actually even a lot more than what you said in the letter itself. At first almost everything you wrote . . . annoyed me. It wasn't until a few weeks later that I began to come around, then gradually to understand this and that, and now it appears to me that you were right pretty much all across the line. And that's why I'm only now answering your letter.

According to this reader, learning to appreciate the subdued optimism of Seghers's novella—an optimism that for him had seemed more like pessimism—was like learning to appreciate particularly challenging classical music. One had to listen to such music again and again in order to appreciate its nuances. "Yes, and that's the way it seems to be with your letter (and probably also with your writings): one has to read it many times, and by doing so one learns to read correctly and does not miss what's in it and behind it." The pedagogy in which Seghers was interested was a difficult process, not a matter of cheap victories.

The figure of Robert Lohse in Seghers's two East German novels, *Die Entscheidung* (1959) and *Das Vertrauen* (1968) was also a former youth led astray by Nazism who has—thanks at least in part to the help of conscientious educators—transformed himself into an anti-Nazi and begun to devote himself to the education of German young people.[29] At the beginning of *Die Entscheidung*, Robert understands, as he tells a former friend and comrade who is now a high party official, that relatively few Germans truly understand what is happening in postwar Germany, with the transformation of the Soviet zone: "'You can count the people,' he finally said, 'who really understand what's happening here, that something new is beginning, something completely different, and who really believe it.'"[30] The process of conversion and transformation to a new way of life, in other words, is painfully slow. As another character in the novel explains to his wife, who lives in the West, "Where we live, things still look shabby. Where you live, what's needed is what makes people greedy and crazy for money. Where we live, people are changing. It's happening on the inside. You can't see it in the shop windows." But this character, a talented engineer who is trying to convince his wife to move east, then asks himself silently, "have many people truly changed? I shouldn't pull the wool over her eyes" (314). At the end of *Die Entscheidung*, after an encounter with one of his own inspirational former teachers, a committed antifascist, Robert Lohse decides to devote himself to the education of the young: "Suddenly he felt clearly that nothing was finished; something new had begun" (625).

Seghers's second GDR novel, *Das Vertrauen*, recounts the events leading up to the uprising of 17 June 1953, including mistakes made by both the party and individual workers. Many of these mistakes revolve around failures of trust, and of democratic process. This novel, too, deals centrally with the education of young people and the importance of genuine human connections between teachers and their students in order for real growth and change to occur. As one of Robert Lohse's colleagues warns him, too many socialists view society as changeable but the individuals in it as fixed:

> You're strange people. You have ideas like no one else, about change and why and how. Yes, you swear by it, if it's the world you're talking about, for instance here, where everything inside and out was a pile of rubble, and you want to change it, and you're succeeding. But if it's an individual human being you're talking about, then you look at him as if he were a block that's the way it is, fixed, immovable, unchangeable.[31]

As one character in the novel points out, genuine human change cannot happen simply by administrative fiat. Rather, it constitutes a long and difficult internal process: "You can't change anyone through orders" (202).

One of the central functions of literature, as depicted in *Das Vertrauen*, is that, precisely because of its fictional nature, it is able to address reality, and thus the possibility of human change, in a way that other forms of discourse—which tend to assume a static human being—cannot. In the book written by Robert Lohse's former friend and comrade Herbert Melzer, for instance, reality seems, at least to Robert, to "crackle." "However weak we may be, it crackles and hisses like a forest fire. Far stronger than real reality" (272). Literature can burn like a fire, because it conceives of reality, and human beings, as changeable, as combustible material. Through the power of the imagination, literature provides access to the thought processes of other human beings, and, in Robert's case, it helps him to understand himself better.

Literature thus gives readers insight into the ways that human beings can, over time, gradually transform themselves. As Robert Lohse's lover Lene acknowledges, the book that he is reading is capable of achieving something that nothing else can: "In this book . . . something must be happening that he can find nowhere else" (280). Herbert Melzer's friend Helen Wilcox, who reads the book Herbert has written after its author's death, muses on the paradox that she knows her deceased acquaintance and his former comrades better through the book than she knows any actual human beings in reality: "She thought as she fell asleep: the most important people in this book are dead. And even if they're still alive. I would never meet a single one. But through the book I'm closer to them than to the people I know or may yet get to know" (284). Literature, in essence, becomes a kind of school that never closes, as Lohse's beloved former teacher Karl Waldstein muses at the end of the book: "He had the feeling that, through Melzer's book, his schoolhouse door would always remain open, and through that door thousands of young people would go in and out. Even after there was no trace left of him, Waldstein, and no trace of Robert or Richard or even Thomas, who was the youngest of them" (311). Literature thus has the potential to make educational processes permanent and self-perpetuating. Or at least this was Seghers's hope.

In addition to providing her own accounts of young people and their ideological transformations, Seghers, throughout her life in the GDR, also encouraged younger writers to address their own personal and political development in their writing. She believed that an honest depiction of such ideological transformations on the part of younger writers who had previously been implicated in Nazism constituted a crucial element in the development of postwar German literature. One of the most prominent interventions by Seghers with respect to a younger East German writer in the mid-1950s—precisely the moment when the younger generation was beginning to emerge on the postwar literary scene—concerned Franz Fühmann, a talented writer and poet who was himself a veteran of Hitler's Wehrmacht and who made no bones about his previous support for Nazism. In 1953 Fühmann published a poetic, semiautobiographical account of his own ideological transformation from Nazism to socialism, the long-form poem *Die Fahrt nach Stalingrad* (The Journey to Stalingrad), which, although purely socialist in its ideological focus, echoed the complex diction and vocabulary of Friedrich Hölderlin. In Fühmann's depiction the emergent world of the antifascist GDR was not a hesitant and difficult new beginning, as Seghers usually depicted it, but rather a triumphant certainty expressed in deliberately old-fashioned language and syntax:

> O world, which arose, victorious and against
> the old that was in us, that we placed
> in its path! Irresistible as light it came
> into the night of our soul, probing the traces and scars
> of all events, destroying the nesting
> shadows, solving the riddles of the inmost heart. O future:
> It exists! It is real. It is here. We can walk the path toward it,
> the path to the human world. And in the arduous, painful movement
> > toward it
> we understood it and we understood Germany. And our
> life lay, backward and forward, open to our eyes,
> and it led: from the end to the beginning,
> it led to the free fatherland.[32]

Seghers publicly welcomed Fühmann's attempt to tell the story of his own ideological transformation, declaring that the young poet "had thereby, for us, begun to express one of the most important topics in a poetic way."[33] Nevertheless, Seghers charged Fühmann with using an obscurantist language and form that rendered any concrete depiction of his own personal transformation impossible. "The desire that one often senses among our young people to express exciting, important things in the form of great pathos, which seems appropriate to them, carries a danger," she warned. "Our life and our language are in need of concreteness. We want to create a concrete effect. With hymn-like, unbounded language the danger arises . . . that something important may be hidden."[34] Seghers, in other words, wanted not grand pathos and highfalutin diction but rather a concrete account of how and why a young man gradually learned to acknowledge his own mistakes. "What has transpired in a soldier of Hitler's Wehrmacht that he is now a fighter for peace?" she asked.[35]

Several months later, in a speech delivered at the January 1956 congress of the East German Writers Union, Seghers again returned to the subject of Fühmann specifically and the younger generation's literary accounts of its own ideological transformations more generally. She proclaimed that "every piece of incompletely understood life demands structuring so that one can comprehend the present completely."[36] Younger writers' relative silence about their own concrete experience of the Second World War, and the problems associated with it, created, Seghers believed, "a gap not just in our literature but in the consciousness of the people." What postwar German literature needed, she suggested, was an inside view from the perspective of the very younger generation that had been seduced by Hitler and the Nazis. "The writer," Seghers proclaimed, "must, with the means of his profession, make clear to the people why, how, and for what our youth, seduced and subdued, went to war for fascism; he must make us understand how the bewilderment happened; step by step, as precisely as a factory or a fortress is obscured via a smoke machine in war."[37]

In "Der Mann und sein Name" Seghers had attempted to provide a sober account of how such a young person painfully extricates himself from Nazism; now, however, she was urging younger writers like Fühmann, who had themselves been seduced by Nazism, to make use of their experiences and show, from their own unique perspective, how young people had gradually gone astray. "We need . . . books that show what young people who went to war, seduced by fascism, are experiencing: their doubts, their despair, and their transformation as a result of painful experiences."[38]

Seghers singled out Fühmann as one of the few members of the younger generation who was honestly attempting to address this topic, but she demanded more. Truthful war literature, she insisted, was a necessary precondition for ideological change in Germany, because it would help readers to become truthful as well: "Only if he [the author] is up to the topic, only if he unsparingly shows what such a person was and what he has become, and how, only then will the reader believe him and change, even if he is still caught in old lies."[39] It was not enough simply to proclaim, as Fühmann had, "O future: It exists! It is real. It is here." Seghers admitted that it was "no easy task to describe how young people, confused and bewitched by Nazi lies, took part in Hitler's barbaric war of aggression." Nor would it be easy to show how young people "at first voluntarily or in shock took part in cruelties against nations that were defending their freedom," or how these same young German Nazis "abruptly or gradually understood to what end they had been misused and began to hate war and fascism."[40] Nevertheless she believed that such accounts of difficult ideological transformation were essential for the future of Germany, and of German literature.

One can view much of Fühmann's subsequent writing, from his war stories of the 1950s to his semiautobiographical work *Das Judenauto* (1962), as a response to Seghers's interventions. Indeed, it is also possible to examine the development of other East German authors of the younger generation, such as Christa Wolf, as a similar response to such interventions on the part of Seghers. Much of Wolf's work was autobiographical or semiautobiographical, and much of it dealt, like the work of Fühmann, with the problem of ideological transformation. Via the younger generation in whom Seghers showed so much interest, her approach to storytelling, and to the truth of fiction, was to have a profound impact on the subsequent history of East German literature.

Notes

[1] Anna Seghers, *The Seventh Cross*, trans. James A. Galston (New York: Monthly Review Press, 1987).

[2] Ibid., 344; Verena Blaum, *Kunst und Politik im SONNTAG, 1946–1958: Eine historische Inhaltsanalyse zum deutschen Journalismus der Nachkriegsjahre* (Cologne: Wissenschaft & Politik, 1992), 125.

[3] Jan Petersen, "Anna Seghers: Gestalterin unserer Zeit," *Die Weltbühne* 2, no. 4 (February 15, 1947): 159–63, 160. All translations from German-language sources, here and elsewhere, are my own; however, citations from published English-language translations of Seghers's works are by the relevant translator.

[4] Petersen, "Anna Seghers: Gestalterin unserer Zeit," 160.

[5] Christiane Zehl Romero, *Anna Seghers: Eine Biographie, 1947–1983* (Berlin: Aufbau, 2003), 22.

[6] Anna Seghers, "[Rede auf dem II. Deutschen Schriftstellerkongreß 1950]," in Seghers, *Über Kunstwerk und Wirklichkeit I: Die Tendenz in der reinen Kunst*, ed. Sigrid Bock (Berlin: Akademie, 1970–71), 76–84; here, 80.

[7] Seghers, "Rede," 80.

[8] Anna Seghers, "Der Mann und sein Name," in Seghers, *Erzählungen, 1950–1957*, ed. Ute Brandes (Berlin: Aufbau, 2009), 101–99; here, 199.

[9] Jens Wehner, *Kulturpolitik und Volksfront: Ein Beitrag zur Geschichte der Sowjetischen Besatzungszone Deutschlands, 1945–1949*, 2 vols. (Frankfurt am Main: Peter Lang, 1992), 1:64.

[10] Magdalena Heider, *Politik-Kultur-Kulturbund: Zur Gründungs- und Frühgeschichte des Kulturbundes zur demokratischen Erneuerung Deutschlands, 1945–1954 in der SBZ/DDR* (Cologne: Wissenschaft & Politik, 1993), 17. Emphasis in the original.

[11] The most recent translation of Seghers's *Ausflug der toten Mädchen*, by Helen Fehervary and Amy Kepple Strawser, appears in a piece called "Three Tales from Dark Times," *American Imago: Psychoanalysis and the Human Sciences* 75, no. 3 (Fall 2017): 283–306.

[12] Seghers, "Three Tales from Dark Times," 299.

[13] Ibid., 306.

[14] Ibid.

[15] Robert Cohen, "Die befohlene Aufgabe machen: Anna Seghers' Erzählung 'Der Ausflug der toten Mädchen,'" *Monatshefte* 79, no. 2 (Summer 1987): 186–98; here, 196.

[16] Seghers, "Three Tales from Dark Times," 300.

[17] Helen Fehervary, *Anna Seghers: The Mythic Dimension* (Ann Arbor: University of Michigan Press, 2001), 28.

[18] Stephen Brockmann, "From Nazism to Socialism in Anna Seghers' 'Der Mann und sein Name,'" *German Studies Review* 37, no. 2 (May 2014): 297–316; here, 297.

[19] Stephen Brockmann, *The Writers' State: Constructing East German Literature, 1945–1959* (Rochester, NY: Camden House, 2015), 149–53.

[20] Seghers, "Rede," 80.

[21] Anna Seghers, "Über die Entstehung des neuen Menschen," in Seghers, *Über Kunstwerk und Wirklichkeit III: Für den Frieden der Welt*, ed. Sigrid Bock (Berlin: Akademie-Verlag, 1971), 242–50; here, 248.

[22] Seghers, "Über die Entstehung," 242.

[23] Seghers, "Rede," 81.

[24] Seghers, "Über die Entstehung," 248.

[25] "'Der Mann und sein Name': Eine notwendige Diskussion," *Sonntag*, May 31, 1953, 4.

[26] Unpublished manuscript, Anna Seghers Archive, Academy of the Arts, Berlin, #645, 32–33. I want to give my thanks to Helga Neumann at the Academy of the Arts for allowing me to examine this and other unpublished material. I also owe a debt of gratitude to Pierre Radványi for allowing me to quote from unpublished material connected to his mother, Anna Seghers. Here and elsewhere, at the request of the Anna Seghers Archive, I am withholding the relevant names associated with such unpublished material. These names, at any rate, are not necessary for my argument.

[27] Anna Seghers Archive, Academy of the Arts, Berlin, #1799.

[28] Ibid., #1188. The citations in the following paragraph, including Seghers's response, are also from this source.

[29] For a useful overview of Seghers's writings about East Germany, particularly the novels *Die Entscheidung* and *Das Vertrauen*, see Loreto Vilar, *Die Kritik des realen DDR-Sozialismus im Werk Anna Seghers: "Die Entscheidung" und "Das Vertrauen"* (Würzburg: Königshausen & Neumann, 2004); and Sylvia Fischer, *Dass Hämmer und Herzen synchron erschallen: Erkundungen zu Heimat in Literatur und Film der DDR der 50er und 60er Jahre* (Bern: Peter Lang, 2015), 101–42.

[30] Anna Seghers, *Die Entscheidung* (Berlin: Aufbau, 1985), 77.

[31] Anna Seghers, *Das Vertrauen* (Darmstadt: Luchterhand, 1977), 37.

[32] Franz Fühmann, *Die Fahrt nach Stalingrad* (Berlin: Aufbau, 1953), 41–42.

[33] Anna Seghers, "Fahrt nach Stalingrad," in *Über Kunstwerk und Wirklichkeit II: Erlebnis und Gestaltung*, ed. Sigrid Bock (Berlin: Akademie-Verlag, 1971), 120–25; here, 125.

[34] Seghers, "Fahrt nach Stalingrad," 122.

35 Ibid., 124.

36 Anna Seghers, "Der Anteil der Literatur an der Bewußtseinsbildung des Volkes [Rede auf dem IV. Deutschen Schriftstellerkongreß 1956]," in *Über Kunstwerk und Wirklichkeit I*, 90–115; here, 110.

37 Ibid.

38 Ibid.

39 Ibid.

40 Ibid., 111.

5: *Aufbauzeit* or *flaue Zeit?*
Anna Seghers's GDR Novels

Hunter Bivens

IN THIS CHAPTER I explore socialism as a problem of narrative and emplotment in Anna Seghers's late novels, *Die Entscheidung* (The Decision, 1959) and *Das Vertrauen* (Trust, 1968), which together are formal experiments in an open epic form that grasps East German socialism in its essentially worldly character and nonsynchronous temporal dimensions, while at the same time providing a model for a the novel genre as a form of cognitive mapping in a moment of far-reaching social crisis and transformation.[1] Without drawing a blanket homology between economic plan and literary plot, or making any claim that there is something political or socialist about the process of literary emplotment *per se*, I argue that plot is a problem for epic narratives that seek to depict socialism as an emergent life world, raising questions about both narrative causality and historical agency. Seghers's work is unique within the corpus of German socialist realism in explicitly thematizing this problem, but less in the form of political didacticism than through the representation of necessity and contingency in the text as an explicit exploration of the organizing capacity of emplotment. The historical adequacy of narrative in Seghers's work consists in successfully bringing the collective dimension of being and acting into visibility. This collective capacity in Seghers's narratives should not be understood in terms of the effacement of individual experiences into some sort of totalitarian unity, but rather as a mode of third-person mediation that allows for the preservation, transmission, and coordination of experience and agency between subjects across space and time; it is, in short, a plan. Seghers reminds us in her 1973 address to the Eighth Writers' Congress of the GDR, "socialism does not mean a narrowing, but always an expansion of the field of vision, because I have chosen a standpoint from which I can see the furthest in any direction."[2]

In this essay I take *Die Entscheidung* and *Das Vertrauen* as test cases for this socialist narrative perspective, and I will attend to both what Seghers's late novel structure makes possible and where it finds its limits; as though Seghers had formally solved a problem that history itself had yet to resolve. Although they share some characters and scenarios from Seghers's 1949 *Epochenroman* of the Weimar Republic and Third Reich,

The Dead Stay Young, the later novels share more formally and thematically with one another than they do with this earlier novel. Both focus on the fictional East German steel town of Kossin in the GDR's formative years of 1947 to 1953.[3] Furthermore, they situate Kossin in a worldly representation of socialist construction, Germany's national division, and the Cold War, moving across the axes of postwar geopolitics, from West Germany to New York, from Paris to Mexico, all under the shadow of the Soviet Union.[4] Instead of focusing on one central protagonist, the novels portray an ensemble of characters connected to each other in direct and indirect ways throughout the two books.

Die Entscheidung chronicles the workers' struggles to build up Kossin as a People's Owned Enterprise, and the machinations of the Benthiem family, the steel mill's former owners (along with their West German and US backers) to subvert the rebuilding of the mill, and by proxy the larger socialist project in the young GDR. *Das Vertrauen* continues this narrative, but focuses on the crisis year of 1953, beginning with the fallout of Stalin's death and culminating in the events of June 17. The central problem of both novels is the *novum* of socialism, of representing what is new in this new social formation. In the GDR, "they are doing something completely new," a character in *Das Vertrauen* remarks, "and they need every single one of us. What they're doing's never been done before. It's hard to do. Hard to understand even."[5] Seghers takes this difficulty seriously in both novels. The disappointments of the *Aufbauzeit*, which she describes in her notes for *Das Vertrauen* as "spiritless time," or *flaue Zeit*, resonate in a curious dissonance between the form of Seghers's GDR novels and their content.[6] In what follows I will elucidate the ways in which both novels thematize the tension between their formal aspirations and their historical context through the tropes of *Vertrauen* on the one hand and *Zufall* on the other, between *Aufbauzeit* and *flaue Zeit*.

This aporia of freedom and necessity also is the essential contradiction of something like the plan at a philosophical level. In the wake of Khrushchev's Secret Speech at the twentieth Congress of the Communist Party of the Soviet Union, Ernst Bloch, in a 1954 essay, "Über Freiheit und objektive Gesetzlichkeit, politisch gefasst" (On Freedom and Objective Lawfulness, Grasped Politically), argued that to take the well-known maxim according to which "freedom is insight into necessity" seriously in a Marxist fashion is to insist on the actuality of Spinoza's thesis that "freedom involved making one's affects and ideas adequate to the world." Peter Caldwell, in his analysis of the discussions opened up by Khruschev's speech, notes that the speculations of GDR economists such as Fritz Behrens shared an affinity with Bloch's work.[7]

For Bloch this means thinking through the dynamic and dialectical aspects of each of these poles, the "not-yet become" and the "not-yet conscious," that is, the poles of what is possible in the world and what it is possible to envision as a potential or concrete utopia, as they are brought together in what Bloch calls "anticipatory consciousness": a "planning, future-oriented activity." This activity, for Bloch, "was essentially labor, conceived of as human sensuous activity, practice that mediated human and world" in the sense described by Marx in his "Theses on Feuerbach" (124). Adequacy would then denote forms of thought and practice wherein freedom and necessity are neither contradictory nor related to each other in a closed and determinate manner. Rather, both terms are open, but in a specific and historically grounded way, so that "'freedom' as 'insight into necessity' becomes 'the will to realize' a new world based on the real potential of the existing world" (126).

This notion of adequacy resonates with a history of left avant-garde techniques of representation that Alberto Toscano and Jeff Kinkle call "an aesthetics of the plan" or "socialist cognitive mapping" in their recent work *Cartographies of the Absolute*.[8] At the same time, Toscano and Kinkle point to "the antinomies of communist aesthetics," deriving from a tendency toward the fetishization of political and industrial infrastructures—that is, the party and the factory as expressions of a reified historical necessity (87). *Die Entscheidung* and *Das Vertrauen* do not solve these contradictions, but in these novels Seghers develops an epic style that is *adequate* to the complexities of socialist transformation in the German context.

The explicit negotiation of the problem of contingency and emplotment is thematized for the characters of Seghers's postwar duology as the problem of random chance on the one hand and trusting familiarity, or *Vertrauen*, on the other. As Kurt Batt reminds us, *Vertrauen* is Seghers's privileged figure for terrestrial providence: not otherworldly transcendence but a "unity of insight and emotion that saturates every life impulse." In Seghers's poetics *Vertrauen* stands for the "comportment of solidarity, wealth of relationships, reciprocal attentiveness, and capacity for bonding" that are the human substance of the socialist plan.[9] Furthermore, conceiving contingency, or *Zufall*, in terms of the opacity or breakdown of *Vertrauen* changes our understanding of both terms. If, following Reinhard Koselleck, "wherever chance is made use of historiographically, it indicates an inadequate consistency of given conditions, and an incommensurability in their results,"[10] then a historically and aesthetically adequate narrative form for the *Aufbauzeit* must account precisely for the "inadequate preconditions" of German socialism, as Seghers was well aware.[11]

In a 1959 interview with Christa Wolf, Seghers explains her intention with *Die Entscheidung*: "For me the main thing was to show how in our times the break that splits the world into two camps affects every part of our life, even the most private, even the most intimate."[12] How does one relate a notion of social crisis and transformation as a massive recalibration of the very intimate relations between all of the dispersed affects, passions, and projects within and between individual subjects on the one hand, and the impersonal mediations of social objectivity on the other, in terms of a literary or narrative mode? Perhaps this is nothing but the problem of the novel as genre, which Lukács already described as "the epic of an age in which the extensive totality of life is no longer directly given," and where the contradiction between the protagonist and the world becomes the central problem of the work.[13] In fact, as Christa Wolf noticed, there is something profoundly "non-novelistic" about Seghers's GDR novels.[14] "The outward form of the novel," as Lukács argued, "is essentially biographical";[15] whereas in Seghers's late epic works the world has become "smaller and sharper," as Wolf puts it.[16] Seghers's novels do not offer "the history of a subject or subjects removed from their limited context," but rather narrate the emergence of "new societies" and "new forms of human living together." "These great processes," Wolf writes, "are only to be registered in their complex epic multiplicity" (54). Seghers's GDR novels formally refuse the narrative closure that the fate of the bourgeois novel's protagonist guarantees. This interweaving, but open structure is reflected in the closing lines of *Die Entscheidung*, as Robert Lohse muses: "The most important threads were knit together. At once he felt clearly that nothing had come to a close; something new had begun" (*E*, 619).[17]

Inge Diersen has suggested that the unifying element in *Die Entscheidung* is the experience of the Spanish Civil War shared by the three main protagonists, a figure for "a compositional interweaving of active characters that personally have nothing to do with one another and know little to nothing of each other's mutual existence, but stand directly before one another on the class front in the struggle for one and the same cause."[18] In other words, Seghers's novels take for their protagonist a network of indirect relationships that constitute a historical situation of emergence. The social, epic character of this narrative form is encompassed in Wolf's observation that *Die Entscheidung* has no minor or secondary characters but rather "the kernels of dozens of novels," a "host of plots" that Seghers patiently weaves into a "network of relationships."[19] At the same time, this form of narrative is historically concrete; it depends on socialist construction itself, not as an aspiration but as a fact, as its condition of possibility.[20] Andreas Schrade has pointed out that "the people then can only be represented in its entirety if it becomes visible as a historical power in its unity."[21] The wager of these novels is that the *Aufbauzeit* is such a moment, one where the objectivity of the historical situation cuts through the multiplicity of everyday life and forms a contradiction through which something like the people might emerge into the field of the visible.

The far-flung narratives of *Die Entscheidung* and *Das Vertrauen* can perhaps best be read less as symptomatic of the author's difficulty in portraying the construction of socialism as a unified process as than a representation of the actual confusion and uncertainty of the 1950s themselves. "There's only over here and over there," as one of *Die Entscheidung*'s characters puts it. "There's only this terrible border, these fragments of life" (*E*, 326). The novels will then be tasked with a vocation of gathering these fragments, not through an act of will, but by making visible the social interdependency of the characters across time and space. The opening scene of *Die Entscheidung* is the key moment of transmission, in this sense linking the Spanish Civil War to socialist construction in postwar Germany, evoking the antifascist solidarity of the past in the face of the post-fascist desperation of the present. In this scene, SED (Socialist Unity Party) functionary and Spanish Civil War veteran Richard Hagen arrives in the ruined steel town of Kossin to deliver a speech to the mill workers, who have been turning out cooking pots and such just to scrape by, on "the new relationship to work."[22] The link to the antifascist struggles of the Popular Front is established through the reminiscences of Robert Lohse, who is in the audience and recognizes his childhood friend and fellow Spanish Civil War veteran Richard. This is October 1947, when "doubt and bitterness clung to the rubble like scabies" and "it looked as though" the ruins of Kossin "could draw everything back into themselves in the night that had been dug out of them during the day" (*E*, 13). Richard has come to announce SMAD (Sowjetische Militäradministration in Deutschland) Order 234, providing for the resumption of industrial production in the Soviet zone.[23] This opening sequence places the aporias of the plan at the heart of Seghers's duology, since Order 234 was an important tool for suppressing the workers' councils that had sprung up in the SBZ (Soviet occupation zone) since 1945 and in introducing an East German variant of the Soviet Stakhanovite movement. Seghers depicts Order 234 as a historical turning point for the German people. The weary and excitable Kossin workers, Seghers writes, "were stirred up now, because they were always getting stirred up about something special, and they sensed that this could be something special" (*E*, 9). The double valence of "something special" (*etwas Besonderes*) in this sentence opens up the structuring question of the novel: is the construction of socialism just old wine in a new bottle? Is this "something special" really "the new," a world historical event, "by chance now and here" (*E*, 18)? "What's new here," the old worker Janausch challenges Richard. "When they want something from the workers they promise us the moon . . . it was like that in the days of Kaiser Wilhelm II and in the Weimar Republic and under Adolf Hitler more than ever. Why should it be different now all of the sudden" (*E*, 15–16)? Seghers describes the restlessness of the workers shuffling out of the hall after Hagen's speech: "Even if you didn't believe in it or didn't care one way or the other—for an instant something new had flashed into their muddled lives" (*E*, 18). The task of the narrative will then be to bring the *Aufbauzeit* into continuity with the antifascist struggle in Spain, and Seghers accomplishes this through the plot line that follows Herbert Melzer, Richard and Robert's comrade from Spain, as he writes his own novel, which will then appear as a sort of feedback loop at the conclusion of *Das Vertrauen*.

In other words, can "the new relationship to work" heralded by Order 234 stand as a historical sign, in the sense that the enthusiasm of German onlookers for the French Revolution stood as an index of human progress for Kant in the eighteenth century?[24] The historical sign for Kant is not the event of the revolution itself but the reaction to the event, and for Seghers the question is not the fact of Order 234 but rather that of the structure of feeling of the East German workers. Thus the SED functionary Martin speculates after his speech on the occasion of the inaugural tapping of the Kossin Works' first open-hearth furnace: "He had wanted to grab what was in their faces and hold firm to it with what he said . . . if I had pulled it off, to maintain that feeling of triumph, they would all have been transformed, everything would be different. They would have been prepared for events that outdid this event. For the power that belongs to them" (*E*, 167). Seghers shares with the mass of East German *Aufbauliteratur* a view of work as socially constitutive, but for Seghers the production of material goods, infrastructure, and dead labor is of only secondary importance. In her response to the infamous *Nachterstedter Brief*, Seghers wrote that a literary depiction of work should not depict labor itself but rather the "processes happening inside people." Literature should "not only represent the construction of a factory or a city; it should represent what happens with the inner lives of the people involved in this construction. What spurs them on and what holds them back."[25] This is precisely the significance of work in *Die Entscheidung* and *Das Vertrauen*, where labor often seems closer to affect than to activity. *Vertrauen* is the shorthand for the structure of feeling that corresponds to this "new attitude to work" proper to socialism, and it is also what socialist work should produce in Seghers's GDR novels: the ability to feel "what kind of work our work is," that the Kossin works, and by extension, the GDR "is us" (*E*, 167, 152).

Vertrauen and socialist labor are also where Seghers's novels encounter the key aporias of aesthetics of the plan, as Toscano and Kinkle put it, for it is around the thematics of work and trust that her work collides with the weight of the dead labor of industrial infrastructure and bureaucratic *dirigisme*. This aporia is already evident in the opening scene of *Die Entscheidung*, as the historical sign is set by Soviet command. Janausch angrily reminds Richard Hagen that the workers at Kossin scraped together what could still be used and improvised methods of bringing production back underway, "without order number whatever, without bonuses, without piece wages" (*E*, 15–16). This question of *Vertrauen* and command is also at the center, appropriately, of *Das Vertrauen*, with its depiction of the controversies about the production norm increases that led to the strikes of June 17, 1953. As tensions mount in Kossin, Richard, now Party Secretary, argues with the plant's director, Ulsperger, who points out that the very workers complaining about the norms were the same soldiers "who left so much burned earth behind them in the Soviet Union that you could stuff three undivided Germanys in there," concluding, "now they'll have to struggle a little bit" (*V*, 294). Richard responds to Ulsperger: "You can't change anybody with orders . . . it can't be commanded, it has to be understood and advocated for" (*V*, 295).

Yet, this is precisely what Richard is unable to do throughout the novel. This problem introduces *Zufall* into the duology as an index of the social opacity of East German socialism. The inability to communicate "the most important thing" (*E*, 293), which is "to transform everything from the ground up" (*V*, 26), plagues the protagonists of both books. Richard becomes increasingly unable to act as a relay for *Vertrauen* throughout *Das Vertrauen*, lamenting: "There's something about these people . . . that maybe I don't really understand . . . I can't explain it to them. I don't think it's really these people, I think the problem's with me" (*V*, 67). Similarly, when, in a pivotal early scene in *Die Entscheidung*, Robert Lohse is confronted by the arguments of his fellow worker Gerhardt Bechtler (who will later flee to the FRG) that the relationship between work and the wage norms is arbitrary, he experiences a lack of rhetorical capacity, "he felt very strongly that he was not able to properly explain what he held important, in his work and in his life" (*E*, 450). Life and work under socialism are not coincidental in Seghers's postwar work, yet neither is the product of the laws of history or the insight of the party into such putative laws. This is where the language of Seghers's characters fails.

Das Vertrauen contextualizes this inability to articulate the socialist project in the peculiarly post-fascist *and* post-Stalinist history of the GDR itself. Stalin serves the character ensemble in *Das Vertrauen* both as the source of certainty and confidence and as an almost absolute lacuna. The ubiquitous image of Stalin provides, it seems, a literalization of a socialist big Other, interpellating socialist subjects while also closing off the fascist past in the self-evidence of the present.[26] Thus Thomas Helger, the young worker whose story moves into the foreground in this later novel, muses: "Many portraits of Stalin were familiar (*vertraut*) to him from school and from the factory, from meetings and demonstrations; they belonged to the reality that his eyes knew" (*V*, 37). This phantasmatic supplement to the severity of everyday life in East Germany increasingly breaks down as a means of interpellation in the course of *Das Vertrauen*. Richard Hagen, caught up in the pathos of Stalin's death, is shocked to realize that the workers at Kossin are largely indifferent to the event; they are more curious about the details of the news cycle of Stalin's death watch than despairing over the passing of the genial leader of the working class. "There was nothing special [*Besonderes*] to be read in most of the faces." Stalin's death is simply not a historical sign for these workers. "Between Richard's feelings and the feelings of the group of people around him," Seghers writes, "lay an abyss" (*V*, 131).

Richard reveals later: "It's not just Stalin's death that's burdens me, but rather everything that comes to light through his death" (*V*, 134). What exactly might come to light, though, Seghers leaves unclear: is it the indifference of the people that Richard perceives, or is it the revelation of the complex phenomena of repression that we call, inadequately, "Stalinism"? In this context, it is precisely the novel's vagueness that renders it a proper historical novel for the early 1950s for the East German present of 1968, which still lacked a public language to work through the history of socialism. If there is a historical sign of the efficacy of socialism, Seghers does not see it in Stalin. Stalin serves rather as a kind of dead labor of socialism, an immense machinery or infrastructure that imposes itself on the characters of the novels, eliciting their complicity or resistance, as the case may be. Thus Richard is shocked to learn that Soviet authorities had unjustly arrested Ulsperger, whose easy familiarity with the Soviet had previously, in the 1930s, provoked Richard's jealousy. Ulsperger dismisses the whole affair, asking what it matters in the context of today's struggles. Richard's admiration for Ulsperger is only increased by this willingness to dismiss his own experiences of the Purges, but, ironically, this admiration only interjects the problem of chance into the very heart of socialist commitment: "He can shake off what was unjustly done to him, as though it were unimportant, a mistake that met him by chance" (*V*, 440).

It is not Stalin but the capillary processes of socialist life and labor themselves that produce *Vertrauen*, and Seghers communicates this through the form of her novels. As Konrad Woede has pointed out, the fugue-like structure of these books, with its techniques of repetition, "through which the main motif appears in varying contexts and in manifold variations," is itself a modeling of the kind of "arduous learning processes" that would be necessary to realize the promise of socialism, "the categorical devotion to fellow humans through the utilization of social and professional competencies that must first be acquired."[27] Indeed, *Vertrauen*, as Ute Frevert points out, is a force of production in its own right, but is not initially given: "it is volatile and sensitive; it demands effort and investment. It has to be nurtured and actively produced."[28] How, then does Seghers's duology allow for the reentry of this formal imperative at the level of content and diegesis? This is where Seghers's central themes of narrative and pedagogy step into the breach, in the form of Herbert Melzer's Spanish Civil War novel and the school house of Richard, Robert, and Thomas's teacher, Waldstein. Melzer's book, completed shortly before his death in a West German metal workers' strike and published in the GDR, follows fictionalized versions of himself, Robert, and Richard in the last days of the Spanish Republic and reaches Kossin immediately after

June 17. Seghers describes Melzer's novel precisely in terms of a trans-human concatenation of historical experiences. "He did not feel as though he had invented anything," she writes of Melzer, "but as though little by little he could remember everything that had slipped from his memory. This recollection, though, did not concern only things that he had witnessed, but also what happened without him and much later" (*V*, 338–39).

Richard and Robert both read the novel as a confirmation of their political commitment and solidarity, as a historical sign. "Yes . . . that is us," Robert proclaims, "we never let each other down" (*V*, 402). The "we" that Robert evokes is in some sense the collective, epic protagonist of the duology itself, the "un-novelistic" "network of relationships" evoked by Christa Wolf, now gathered and illuminated by the face of the Spanish nurse and antifascist martyr Celia. Seghers, though, does not end on this note of ecstatic reconciliation of history and symbol, but points to its incompleteness, its failure to gather past and present. Herbert's novel, closing with the defeat of the Spanish Republic and the death of Robert, is incomplete without the horizon of socialist construction in the GDR, the "concrete anticipation" that will put everything in its place. Melzer lets the sullen and awkward former Nazi Robert die, rather than sensing the stubborn endurance and empathy that would see Robert through the war as a member of the French Resistance and make him a beloved mentor in Kossin (*V*, 406–8). In failing to image a social order where Robert could be who he wanted to be (*V*, 431), Melzer's novel falls behind the historical reality of the struggle in Spain as the moral basis for a new social formation.

Rather, it is Waldstein, the antifascist teacher, who is able, in his reading of Melzer's novel, to perform this gathering role. In the last pages of the duology, Robert and Richard visit their former teacher at his school, now housing and educating refugee children from the Democratic People's Republic of Korea, and Waldstein grasps the reality and the lacuna of Melzer's Spain novel: "Waldstein supposed that if Melzer was still alive, he would certainly have sought one of them out. Then he would also have noticed that he had omitted something important, essential in their life, a life that he had fully placed himself within, even if only up to a certain instant" (*V*, 454). Seghers herself would make good on Melzer's incomplete narrative. Indeed, before Melzer's death, he envisions a follow-up to the Spain book that very much resembles Seghers's duologue, and *Das Vertrauen*'s closing is a complicated *mis en abyme* with Waldstein, a central figure in Melzer's novel, praising and criticizing that very novel. In Melzer's unwritten book, "he wanted to show these people, who had survived the war," that is Richard, Robert, and Herbert himself, how they insist on "a simple, bright life," and how "they were placed before new, unexpected decisions that would blow them apart again like a cold blast of air" (*E*, 544). What, however, will keep them, these protagonists of the book within the book, from being blown apart by the winds of the Cold War is precisely this mutual feedback of pedagogy and narrative. Waldstein "felt that his school house would always stand open in Melzer's novel" (*V*, 455).

Vertrauen now is lifted from individual characters to the "network of relationships" portrayed, and this is perhaps a bridge to our current situation, in the light of a general emergent consensus that wage-labor can no longer function as a basis of social integration.[29] As capital increasingly frees itself from the need for direct labor in order to produce surplus value, while at the same time clinging to the wage form in order to forestall the emergence of social forms outside the law of value, what emerges, following Fredric Jameson, as the truth of capital is unemployment and the "extinguishing" of non-commodified social practices.[30] In this situation, we are increasingly amputated from labor in the sense that Bloch evokes above, as "concrete anticipation." If socialism will no longer be imaginable in terms of the emancipation of labor, perhaps the forms of sociality and collectivity historically implicit in labor might migrate to other social realms, so that with the amputation of labor as a form of social integration, a notion of socialism comes into view that is no longer about the production of goods per se, but about the production of the forms of social intercourse themselves, a re-igniting of the vitality of social togetherness. Seghers, I would argue, offers us a model for the kind of post-novelistic epic forms adequate for that post-capitalist horizon.

Notes

[1] I am using "worlded" here in the sense developed by the World Literature Group at the University of California, Santa Cruz, as a way of thinking about culture that recognizes the necessarily global perspective of the local, among other things. See Christopher Leigh Connery, "Worlded Pedagogy in Santa Cruz," in *The Worlding Project: Doing Cultural Studies in the Era of Globalization*, ed. Rob Wilson and Christopher Leigh Connery (Santa Cruz: New Pacific, 2007), 1–13; here, 3. On cognitive mapping, see Fredric Jameson, "Cognitive Mapping," in *Marxism and the Interpretation of Culture*, ed. Cary Nelson and Lawrence Grossman (Chicago: University of Illinois Press, 1988), 347–57.

[2] Anna Seghers, "Der sozialistische Standpunkt läßt am weitesten blicken," in *Aufsätze, Ansprachen, Essays, 1954–1979: Gesammelte Werke in Einzelausgaben* XIV (Berlin: Aufbau, 1984), 361–69; here, 364.

[3] For a detailed account of Seghers's negotiation of the 1950s, see the fourth through the sixth chapters of Christiane Zehl Romero, *Anna Seghers: Eine Biographie, 1947–1983* (Berlin: Aufbau, 2003).

[4] See Sigrid Bock, "Erzählen in unfasslicher Zeit: Einige Bemerkungen zur Roman-Dilogie *Die Entscheidung* und *Das Vertrauen*," *Argonautenschiff* 22 (2013): 115; and Helen Fehervary, "*Die Entscheidung* und *Das Vertrauen* im Rahmen der Weltliteratur," *Argonautenschiff* 22 (2013): 125–38.

[5] Anna Seghers, *Das Vertrauen* (Berlin: Aufbau, 1968), 407. Unless otherwise noted, all translations are my own. Further references to this work are given in the text using the abbreviation *V*.

[6] This note is quoted by Alexander Stephan in "Kommentar," in Anna Seghers, *Die Entscheidung* (Berlin: Aufbau, 2003), 657. Further references to this work are given in the text using the abbreviation *E*.

[7] Peter Caldwell, *Dictatorship, State Planning, and Social Theory in the German Democratic Republic* (Cambridge: Cambridge University Press, 2003), 121.

[8] Alberto Toscano and Jeff Kinkel, *Cartographies of the Absolute* (Winchester, UK: Zero Books, 2015), 87, 85.

[9] Kurt Batt, *Anna Seghers: Versuch über Entwicklung und Werk* (Leipzig: Reclam, 1980), 235.

[10] Reinhart Koselleck, *Futures Past: On the Semantics of Historical Time*, trans. Keith Tribe (New York: Columbia University Press, 1985), 116.

[11] See Inge Diersen, "Jason 1948—problematische Heimkehr," in *Unerwünschte Erfahrung: Kriegsliteratur und Zensur in der DDR*, ed. Ursula Heukenkamp (Berlin: Aufbau, 1990), 72–99.

[12] Anna Seghers, "Gespräche und Interviews, I," in *Aufsätze*, 399–406; here, 401.

[13] Georg Lukács, *The Historical Novel*, trans. Hannah Mitchell and Stanley Mitchell (Lincoln: University of Nebraska Press, 1983), 56.

[14] Christa Wolf, "Das Land, in dem wir Leben," *Neue Deutsche Literatur* 9, no. 5 (1961): 49–65; here, 54.

[15] Lukács, *The Historical Novel*, 77.

[16] Wolf, "Das Land in dem wir leben," 54.

[17] On Seghers's chronicle-like narrative structure, see Walter Benjamin, "A Chronicle of Germany's Unemployed," in *Selected Writings, Volume 4, 1938–1940*, ed. Howard Eiland and Michael W. Jennings (Cambridge, MA: Belknap, 2003), 126–34.

[18] Inge Diersen, "Kompositionsfragen zu Anna Seghers Romanen 'Die Toten bleiben jung' und 'Die Entscheidung,'" in *Kritik in der Zeit: Der Sozialismus— seine Literatur—ihre Entwicklung*, ed. Klaus Jarmatz (Halle (Saale): Mitteldeutscher Verlag, 1970), 464–75; here, 465, 472.

[19] Wolf, "Das Land in dem wir leben," 57–58.

[20] Ibid., 56; Diersen, "Kompositionsfragen zu Anna Seghers Romanen," 474.

[21] Andreas Schrade, *Entwurf einer ungeteilten Gesellschaft: Anna Seghers' Weg zum Roman nach 1945* (Bielefeld: Aisthesis, 1994), 54.

[22] On Seghers's first visit to "Kossin," see Seghers, "Was geschah und was bleibt," in *Aufsätze*, 294–98.

[23] Eric Weitz, *Creating German Communism, 1890–1990: From Popular Protests to Socialist State* (Princeton, NJ: Princeton University Press, 1997), 349–53.

[24] Immanuel Kant, "A Renewed Attempt to Answer the Question 'Is the Human Race Improving?'" in *Political Writings*, ed. Hans Reis (Cambridge: Cambridge University Press, 1970), 176–90; here, 181.

[25] Seghers, "Zum Nachterstedter Brief," in *Aufsätze*, 58–64; here, 61.

[26] For a psychoanalytic reading of East German literature, see Julia Hell, *Post-Fascist Fantasies: Psychoanalysis, History, and East German Literature* (Durham, NC: Duke University Press, 1997).

[27] Konrad Woede, "Verlauf und Folgen der Podiumdiskussion zu der Rezeption der Romane *Die Entscheidung* und *das Vertrauen*," in *Argonautenschiff* 22 (2013): 157–67; here, 158.

[28] Ute Frevert, "Trust as Work," in *Work in a Modern Society: The German Historical Experience in Comparative Perspective*, ed. Jürgen Kocka (New York: Berghahn Books, 2010), 93–108; here, 98.

[29] See Wolfgang Engler, *Bürger, ohne Arbeit: Für eine radikale Neugestaltung der Gesellschaft* (Berlin: Aufbau, 2005).

[30] Fredric Jameson, *Representing Capital: A Reading of Part One* (London: Verso, 2011), 20–21, 93, 125.

6: The Time of Decision in Anna Seghers

Benjamin Robinson

I.

ANNA SEGHERS'S 1959 novel of socialist construction *Die Entscheidung* (The Decision) marks a turning point in the reputation of an author whose literary career, had the Cold War taken a different course, would surely have been one of the most celebrated in modern German letters.[1] Although this essay will not directly justify my assessment, I am far from alone in considering Seghers one of the great writers of the past century in terms of the imaginative range of her material, the discipline of her formal and affective registers, and the power of her social vision. The effect *The Decision* had on her reputation is only partly related to the strengths and weaknesses of the novel, which remains an affecting work even as its narrative particularities differ from those that lent her pre-Cold War work its well-deserved fame. It is not a novel of elemental revolt against the degradation of life, as her early works were, but in a more indirect way it depicts a revolt against the vulgar temporality of the judgments of her time—it is, in this sense, a novel about acting on principle. Here, then, elementary values of dignity, care, and bodily communion do not rise up against the weight of indifference and persecution. Those values, although invoked, are held in check by a proposition about the direction of the present that is much harder to portray as experiential grounds for revolt. Panning the novel for what they took as its naïve adherence to the official doctrine of the Socialist Bloc, West German critics vigorously provincialized Seghers's cosmopolitan reputation.[2] Even as her imagination in this period took her stories to settings spanning centuries in countries in Africa, China, and the Caribbean, her work was tied to the ideological discourse of an unprincipled present. It was not viewed as pursuing aesthetic strategies capable of transforming readers' taste in lasting ways; rather, the work was characterized as trying to influence readers to make a decision for East Bloc socialism that flew in the face of casual common sense—as, arguably, her characters' decisions seem to do.[3] Socialism in these critics' eyes was so tainted by dictatorship that such a perverse aim could only indicate the bad faith of an ideologue, not the sensuous convictions of an artist. While

Seghers doubtless "paid a substantial price for her politics of affirmation," in terms of the compromises with power that weigh down her biography, I want to emphasize what remains aesthetically searching about the ways in which *The Decision* still affirms what we cannot help but read as a bleak depiction of a socialist state.[4] In a telling irony of twentieth-century aesthetics, the stylistic techniques Seghers had developed to express revulsion at daily working life in the Weimar Republic and fascism—her portrayal of the crushing force of habit in juxtaposition to the ecstatic beat of danger— serve here to affirm daily life in socialism by means of a surprising inversion of the narrative counterpoint.

Before turning to *The Decision*, indeed, to the counterintuitive example of one of its unpromising, stock characters, I want to convey my sense of Seghers's talent in order to clarify how the special problems of the novel—which as the editor of *neue deutsche literatur*, Wolfgang Joho, put it, depicts "not the struggle *against* something, but *for* something"[5]— relate to Seghers's persistent themes and styles. Her talent, to be sure, does not reside in the psychological charm of her writing or in the effervescence of her prose. Her characters are not the hyper-individualized figures that we associate with the high modernism whose contemporary she was. Love in the romantic sense, that great driver of the bourgeois novel, is virtually absent from her plots, and she was not attracted to the comedic genres underlying postmodernism such as satire, parody, picaresque, or burlesque. On the contrary, such comedic forms resist what Helen Fehervary calls the "chiliastic thematic that is at the core of Anna Seghers's prose."[6] This chiliasm, with its resonant call *de profundis*, ties her style to the agonized spirituality of Expressionism, even as she moves toward the critical topicality found in the countervailing modernist movement of the New Objectivity. If not distinguished by subjective realism, playfulness, or intimacy, Seghers's writing is, from the very first, marked by its serious engagement with the social milieus it chronicles. As her novels become increasingly referential—demanding a high degree of historical competence from readers—their style continues to foster a sense of engagement deeper than their systematic panorama of current events. Christa Wolf, in her essay on Seghers's celebrated resistance novel *Das siebte Kreuz* (The Seventh Cross), aptly formulated its sensibility as resting on a "feeling for the 'now' of the epoch," a temporal attunement more interior than the literary reportage prominent in the era. Wolf, however, ties the sensibility to the "author's consciousness of her present," reflecting her own interest in bringing authorial autobiography to bear on the construction of literary fiction.[7] Whereas Wolf's fiction draws primarily from the non-fictional genres of biography and autobiography, Seghers's writing draws from different genres. Seghers writes above all in fictional analogue to chronicle forms, from mythical legends to newspaper reports, using her "consciousness of the present" to animate not first-person memories but third-person histories. Although Wolf overstates the role of the first person (whether fictive or real), she does highlight the characteristic layering of time (*Zeitschichten*) in Seghers's work.[8] Such temporal layering takes on different characteristics when it is read with respect not to biographical but to historiographic time. Emphasizing different modalities of time in historical writing, Reinhard Koselleck distinguishes a *longue durée* of institutional time from the repeating time of people occupying institutional roles in a medium term. Together these temporalities comprise a ground against which a layer of singular events emerges in different compositional patterns. It is these rhythmic patterns of time that I want to focus on in Seghers's prose. My interest is less different *tenses* of historical time (that is, the relationship of a narrative utterance to a sequence of plot events), and more what linguists call the different *aspects* of historical time. Grammatical aspect refers to the way language captures the quality of time's internal flow—whether a phrase captures, for example, a state, an action, a habit, an iteration, a process of becoming, an inception, a conclusion, or a singularity.[9]

As Fehervary has argued, the emphasis in the secondary literature on Seghers's politics—though an inseparable part of her identity as a writer—has led to a reduced sense of her aesthetics, in which it is seen as more or less mimetic of events and discourses of her day (*AS*, 1). Responding to this reduction, Fehervary has demonstrated how Seghers is "the quintessential pictorial writer. Everything she wrote revolves around pictures and derives its significance from them" (*AS*, 13). At the same time, these pictures insert readers into an omnitemporal "mythic world" (*AS*, 4)—where, according to John Lyons, the semantics of omnitemporality "says that something has been, is and always will be so."[10] This omnitemporal dimension serves as a "bass line," in Jean Starobinski's words, against which the variable temporality of modern time can be gauged.[11] Thus Seghers's aesthetics, even when her novels are set in a more or less urgently represented historical present, represents less a fictionalized image of contemporary political historiography than a distinctive chronotope (Bakhtin's term for a literary time-space) that relates her present to a legendary omnitemporality, or—and this will be my argument about the distinctive quality of *The Decision*—to the timelessness of a gnomic proposition.[12] Timelessness differs from omnitemporality in that the question of time does not arise, not even in the sense of a legendary "always." "Obvious examples of timeless propositions are the so-called eternal truths of mathematics and theology."[13] Although propositions familiar from the antifascist resistance appear in *The Decision*, such as "there is a time of the persecutor and a time of the persecuted,"[14] the truths of resistance are no guide to constructing socialism, where the identity of the revolutionary agent is not that of the persecuted, but the "new wo/man" building the new order. The propositions do not echo Ecclesiastes' "there is a time," but concern instead the unconditional goals of "what's at stake in our efforts" (175). Seghers's challenge in *The Decision* was to find a literary analogue to a proposition about the truth of the new order—the literary equivalent, as it were, of the gnomic revolutionary slogans over factory gates. Given the difficult constraints, but urgent presence, of the socialist state, she sought to personify socialist truth in the functionary figure whose representation did not depend on internal focalization in the narrative discourse but on equating the functionary's social role with a transcendent goal. The functionary is not an archaic or legendary character (represented in the omnitemporality of mythic diction) but precisely a character serving the timeless function of an equation, embodying the truth of a new order; indeed, a new order that on the face of it had little truth to recommend it as it was constantly falling prey to the vulgar, chaotic events of the Cold War. From the alternation between habitual present and legendary past characteristic of her early works, the chronotope of *The Decision* shifts to a busy present filled with characters who alternately fall prey to their time and bear a timeless truth.

In the following I want to pursue the idea of Seghers's chronotopes in order to foreground a basic contrast that clarifies the logic of the switch between the earlier and later novels. To put it concisely, the common denominator of all Seghers's novels, whether early or late, can be seen in each one's effort to escape, by means of both theme and style (or story and discourse), the habitual temporality of everyday plot events. The difference resides in the divergent temporal quality of the liberation or escape. In the early works the escape is mostly into legendary time, where the insight into the revolution is grasped by the reader, not the characters. In the late works, the escape is into the timelessness of a true proposition. Here the insight into truth is presented as an event in the plot. Thus, although the truth is grasped by a character with reference to the story's time, it concerns a state of affairs that is timeless. As an aside, the narrative problems Seghers is grappling with—conveying a sense of suprapersonal truth to characters caught in finite, human-scale historical time—closely parallel those raised in contemporary narratives that grapple with anthropocentric agency in the face of the geologically scaled environmental challenges of the Anthropocene era.[15]

II.

The distinction of *The Decision* can be brought out with reference to an unpromising figure, Martin, a genre-typical figure of socialist realism—a Communist of the first hour, a fighter in Spain and the underground, a concentration-camp survivor. He plays only a small role in the novel, connecting its protagonists to a dangerous and heroic past, as well as connecting the novel itself to Seghers's previous novel, *Die Toten bleiben jung* (The Dead Stay Young), the first of Seghers's final three novels, a realist trilogy focused on contemporary German political and social struggles from the 1918 revolution to the June 1953 uprising against the East German state. When we meet Martin in *The Decision*, he is attending a ceremony celebrating the first tapping of molten steel from an open-hearth furnace refurbished out of the expropriated wreckage of a giant steel combine. He drops in to speak at the official event, but does not hang around to socialize with his mates after their success. He is more activist than comrade, which means that he always has more work to do—which busyness seems to be the long and short of Martin's story. Nonetheless, as a means of personifying the revolution—the primary, enduring theme of Seghers's oeuvre—Martin presents a remarkable contrast to the way Seghers personified the revolution in her prewar works.

I want to compare the passage introducing Martin with the opening lines of an early work of Seghers's, her 1928 novel *Aufstand der Fischer von St. Barbara* (Revolt of the Fisherman of Santa Barbara), in order to establish the contrasting paradigms for personifying the revolution. Let me begin with Martin's first appearance in the plot of *The Decision*, which comes about a quarter of the way into the novel. We have, to be sure, already learned about Martin in the backstory of Richard Hagen, another impossibly busy Communist functionary figure who belongs, however, to the generational cohort of the novel's other protagonists. In that episode, which takes place outside the plot, we learn how Martin, who had collapsed from hunger in a concentration camp, was commended to Richard's care by the Communist underground, with the simple instruction, "we are obligated to make sure Martin gets through" (46).

> Martin—the same Martin safeguarded [behütet] by Richard in the concentration camp—had come from Berlin for the celebration. He'd wanted to use his speech to grasp and hold onto the expressions people wore on their faces. But the excitement fled from his words. For many it had ebbed as soon as the air was no longer crackling with sparks, passing away with the steel as it flowed into the ingots. For some the excitement lasted only minutes, for others into the night, for a few it lasted forever. . . . Everyone in Kossin understood [that Martin had to go to his next appointment]. Everyone, everywhere, for years. (165)

Before turning to the earlier passage, I want to remark on a few features of our introduction to Martin. First of all, Martin, like the revolution, has been transmitted to the future by an act of safeguarding. This safeguarding—programmatically announced by the title of Seghers's preceding novel, *The Dead Stay Young*—is characterized as transmitting the revolutionaries themselves, who are the characters of Seghers's plots, as well as transmitting the excitement or spirit of the revolution. It is in other words a matter of passing along the agents of the revolution in the cause and effect of the plot as well as passing along the spirit of the revolution in the narrative discourse. The two elements, the agents in the plots, and the insight in the discourse, are crucial variables in Seghers's work. One more remark concerns my claim that Martin allegorically represents the revolution as an agent in the plot rather than a metaphor in its telling. Martin, as I have pointed out, is a minor figure not involved in any of the complications of the story. Moreover, the diction of the passages in which he appears is unremarkable. There is little focalization on any interior awareness of time and space, although the temporal clauses are prominent. We read, for example, that the excitement ebbed at the same time as the sparks faded. The temporal synchrony mediates the metaphorical equivalency of revolutionary excitement and poured steel. This vivid sense of duration then becomes explicitly thematic, with the mention of lengths of time increasing from a few minutes into timelessness. Nonetheless, the lyricism of the passage is minimal and what is emphasized is that Martin is ceaselessly busy—where busyness has a disjointed temporal flow unlike the directed flow of becoming or achieving an end. Martin's busyness, and the more or less perfunctory expository prose in which it is represented, is the counterpoint to the description of his longing for timelessness, for the permanent ecstasy of the revolution.

The iconic first lines of *Revolt of the Fishermen* open by foreshadowing the end of the plot. The novel's time thus has from the first an unusual temporality. The story flows forward from a beginning that already harbors the end—its primary development will not be in the causal series of plot events but in the metaphorical intensity of Seghers's prose. The plot will end in defeat, but the revolution will outlive the plot, just as, for the chiliastic thinkers of the German revolutionary movement of the nineteen teens and twenties, the political action survives each of its historical defeats to become an event that disrupts and transcends the historical sequence (*AS*, 73–74).

> The revolt of the fishermen of Santa Barbara ended with their putting out to sea belatedly on the same terms as the preceding four years. One can say that the revolt was already over before Hull was extradited to Port Sebastian and Andreas died on the lam among the cliffs. The prefect shipped out after he reported to the capital that peace had been restored on the bay. Santa Barbara actually now looked just like it looked every summer. But long after the soldiers had withdrawn, and the fishermen were at sea, the revolt was still sitting on the empty market square, white and barren in the summer, and thinking calmly about its own, those whom it had borne, raised, nurtured and safeguarded [behütet], for the sake of what was best for them.[16]

Although *Revolt* begins *in medias res*, the simplicity of its diction points beyond the busy series of events. Its laconic solemnity expresses what is arguably Seghers's most characteristic juxtaposition—the habitual with the violent, the static with the dynamic. On the one hand, her oeuvre persistently depicts wearied, laboring bodies whose boredom and pain so focalizes her narrative account that time and space shrink to a vanishing point of dull repetitiveness. On the other hand, in counterpoint to the rhythm of pain-dulled figures, we find singular bodies, physically and spiritually ready to extend themselves, to make contact, either brutal or tender, but open and exposed to another quality of experienced time— time that might either flow into itself, gathering, waiting, or suddenly burst open, dispersing into a wider, transcendental realm.[17] In the case of *Revolt*, the gathering body, simultaneously protecting and coiled, does not belong to a character situated in the cause and effect of the narrative diegesis, but is a metaphorical personification of the revolution. Even in the deixis of these first sentences, adverbs such as "belatedly," "the pre-ceding four years," "before," and "after" point to a past sequence of time that resolves itself into a paradoxical *nunc stans*, a "now" that remains as an inconclusive "every summer." This omnitemporal site is where we find the revolt sitting calmly apart from the busyness of daily life, taking care of its own.

The revolt, we read, "was still sitting on the empty market square." "Comparable," as Fehervary puts it, "to the mythical-maternal, at repose in itself, encompassing both the quiet grief of a pieta and the hope of a young Madonna."[18] The revolution is the maternal body resisting the physical degradation of the fishermen and the emaciated bodies of their families who subsist under the crushing circumstances of hard labor and insufficient wages. The image is one of powerful simplicity, expressing a faith that is difficult to render authentically. Writing in her diaries as the German revolution was being liquidated in January 1919, the graphic art-ist Käthe Kollwitz, to whose lithographs Seghers's novel has been com-pared,[19] wistfully cited a literary image from Maxim Gorki—an ingathering God caring for his revolutionary martyrs: "As God takes the souls up to himself after death: 'now, my pure, my beloved, have you erred and suf-fered enough?'"[20] Kollwitz, as a "compatriot of Kant rather than Dostoyevsky," felt Gorki's "great, simple faith" to be beyond her reach. We see in this passage that Seghers's ability to represent such faith shares something with Gorki's or Dostoyevsky's sublime simplicity. It is not, however, a faith that her fiction was able to maintain in such a nobly simple form after 1945. As the historical reference point for the Communist revo-lution switched from the spontaneous rebellions of impoverished commu-nities to European states under Soviet military occupation, the quality of the revolutionary faith that Seghers represents proves to be a delicate act of changing aesthetic balance.

III.

Comparing these two passages, from *Aufstand* of 1928 and from *Die Entscheidung* of 1959, we see that they both exhibit how Seghers shifts the representation of experienced time from the busyness of the present into some other temporal experience. From this common point, where her fictional chronotope complicates any simple reflection of the historiography of the present, the texts go in different directions. I want to highlight two fundamental distinctions. First, whereas the enduring revolt in the 1928 passage is represented metaphorically in the novel's discourse, in the 1959 passage the revolution has become personified as a character in the plot. There are, to be sure, agents of the revolution in the early novel, such as the two characters named in the quoted passage, Hull (the agitator) and Andreas (the young fisherman inspired by Hull). Ultimately, however, they do not transmit the spirit of the revolution within the plot. Hull's extradition and Andreas's death are narrated in a mixture of naturalistic terms and mythopoeic diction. For example, we read of Andreas in realistic external time that he "had already tumbled over, was caught in the stones, his face smashed beyond recognition."[21] Then, separated by a dash, a new clause switches from a punctual, perfected grammatical aspect into the durative, non-telic becoming of the mythic discourse. "—but something inside of him ran on and on, ran and ran and finally dispersed into the air in every direction with an indescribable joy and lightness." I want to suggest that Seghers is distinguishing between the naturalistic bearers of the revolution (in the plot) and the archaic spirit of the revolution (in the discourse).

When we turn to *The Decision*, however, we see that this distinction has qualitatively changed. Martin is a busy, but not quite naturalistically described figure—while he always has more to do, his life lacks the eventual temporality of a personalized character. As an allegorical figure of the revolution, he has become polished into a schematic ideal—but an ideal whose trace remains firmly inscribed within the plot: "His trace, carefully covered over in fascist countries, firmly pressed into the earth in socialist ones, was far plainer than the man himself. Since he no longer had his own family . . . he seemed to possess no everyday [gewöhnliches] life of his own with its many trivial details, with petty secrets, tender, sad, frustrating, meaningful only to him but without trace and consequence for others" (167). Instead of the distinction between the bearer of the revolution and the spirit of the revolution running between plot and discourse, the bearer and the spirit are both within the plot of the later novel. At the same time, although Martin is a character and not a metaphorical personification, he clearly isn't written in a way to become a figure of identification in the text. Seghers is quite literal about presenting him as a trace (*Spur*) of moral authority furrowed into the landscape of socialist Germany—his power emanates from a timeless, generic space in which we'd search in vain for the portrait of a flesh-and-blood man. In this sense, Martin personifies a literary "image" of the didactic and propositional language of the Communist Party doctrine. In the *Dialogic Imagination*, Bakhtin writes of novels as presenting an "image of language" that describes how some non-fictional idiom, whether visual, aural, linguistic, or haptic, is incorporated into the fiction of a novel.[22] Seghers presents two distinct images of revolutionary insight in the cases of Martin and Andreas. Andreas's insight is expressed through literary access to his consciousness at the moment of his death, which reveals how he "dispersed into the air in every direction with an indescribable joy and lightness." He feels joy in revolutionary sacrifice, but shares it only by becoming transfigured through death into literary discourse. Martin's insight, by contrast, is expressed without direct experience of his consciousness. He is attributed a backstory and memories, but their experiential dimension is limited to what is necessary in order to convey the allegorical significance of the functionary for the revolutionary proposition. Though he is a figure within the plot, his challenge is not itself within the plot time; it is to make the temporal setting stand out as such, to communicate, within the story, what kind of story the story of the real socialist present is. Martin's importance consists in a didacticism that Seghers, in a letter to Lukács at the height of the leftist realism debates of the 1930s, defined as the substance of aesthetic realism, "namely a tendency to render reality conscious" (eine Tendenz zur Bewußtmachung von Wirklichkeit).[23] It is important to note that the genitive preposition "von" in the German is both subjective and objective—that is, it can mean either that realism makes reality conscious of itself (subject) or makes us conscious of reality (object). What we see in Seghers's aesthetic development is that whereas before real socialism, this consciousness was *for us*, disseminated in the novel's discourse, once socialism arrived as reality the insight shifted from discourse to plot, to the represented reality becoming conscious of itself within the narrated events: "[Martin] thought: if I don't accomplish that much, don't make it clear to at least some part of the people in the Elbe factory what kind of time our time is, what kind of work our work is, if I don't succeed in that, then it was in vain that Richard stole a potato for me every day to keep me alive in the concentration camp" (167).

IV.

Of course, Martin occupies only a small part of the story of *The Decision*. Understanding realism as a frankly didactic aesthetic category, Seghers was well aware that she would fail to reach her literary goals were she only to depict fictional characters coming to an insight, rather than to enlighten actual readers. In her presidential address to the 1956 Congress of the East

German Writers Union, she cites a young reader who bemoans novels that presume a positive socialist attitude, beseeching her, "Why don't you write about how individual people, going through difficult inner and outer struggles, come to the correct perspective?"[24] In fact, there are several pivotal characters in *The Decision* who, like Andreas in *Revolt*, die so that we readers might, through the affecting portrait of their inner struggles, understand the decision we need to make. As much as Martin allegorically depicts a proposition along the lines of Marx's dictum "Communism is the riddle of history solved, and it knows itself to be this solution," his opaque subjectivity does not commend him as a figure for the reader's identification. It is the highly individualized characters who attract our identification. And yet far from undermining my claim about the distinct aesthetic quality of the late novels, I think these characters are the best evidence on its behalf. For if in the earlier novels the characters into whose dying minds we are allowed to enter transmit the aesthetic epistemology of the text to the reader, here those same characters transmit a lesson that conflicts with Martin's proposition. Martin, represents, in a sense, the reprimand of the timeless against the omnitemporal, the true against the mythical. At the same time, *The Decision* sends a mixed signal: the individuals whose subjectivity is depicted do not arrive, through their difficult inner and outer struggles, at the same perspective conveyed by the plot.

I will conclude by considering the death of Katharina, the gentle Rhineland Catholic wife of the socialist engineer, Riedl, who resists following her husband's example and committing her faith to the secular socialist state in the East. In one of the most memorable plot sequences of the novel, Katharina dies in childbirth crossing over the inner German border to meet her husband at the steel plant where he works in the GDR. The scene of her death, like that of Kedenneck or Andreas in *Revolt*, is written so as to retard the action to the very edge of transcendental deliverance. Having finally crossed the unmarked border, Katharina bursts into tears, unaware she has arrived in the new land. When the peasant midwife reassures her that she is in the "German Democratic Republic," all Katharina can muster in response is "I? Here?" before she closes her eyes. "In the midst of her joy the labor pains began anew. Her thoughts stopped. Astonishment and fear were stronger than anything" (605). Rather than ending with something like Andreas's revelatory lightness, Katharina's thoughts turn from joy to fear—to something more like the doubt of Christ in the face of a merely natural death on the cross. The insight is, perversely enough, reminiscent of the insight we glean from another young mother in *The Dead Stay Young*, Elizabeth, who dies, not in labor, but cradling her young child, "curled up like a hedgehog" in her arms.[25] I call this a perverse association, because Elizabeth is the Baltic aristocratic wife and cousin of a cruelly decadent SS officer. But like the death of Katharina in *The Decision*, the scene of Elizabeth's death in *The*

Dead Stay Young is the novel's most haunting, the affecting mood fostered by a similar ritardando in which time flows from the natural sequence of cause and effect into the messianic rhythm, just to the verge of the *nunc stans*, the eternal now, then back to nature. As her will fades, there is a rare instance of free indirect style: "How benevolent was the snow!" Her mind then settles into the cadence of the Lord's Prayer, repudiating the Führer's hateful Reich for the healing seasons of God, and the winter's final benediction. "At home it is always quiet, even now. The snow is quiet; for yours is the kingdom, the power and the glory, amen!" (579).

What we behold in their minds at death is just the creatureliness of human being. In *The Decision* Katharina's priest, Father Traub, articulates the suffering principle *creatus sum* against the pathos of her husband's rationalistic faith in the new man. It is the counterpoint to the Promethean thesis of earthly redemption represented by Martin. The reader's experiential insight, the one we take from the novel's mythic discourse in scenes such as that of Katharina's death, contradicts the timeless insight into Communism's resolution of history that we gather from the outer struggles to get the steel plant up and running that are depicted in the plot. That is not to say that the novel is incoherent, or that the position of affective identification trumps the position of rational understanding. Rather, it is to emphasize the importance of the particular chronotope in understanding Seghers's work and its relationship to real socialism in the GDR. The rhythmic counterpoint in the late, real socialist novels is a fugal inversion of that in the earlier novels. Rather than escaping debased, ordinary time into the legendary time of suffering and revelation, the reader of *The Decision* discovers that the mythic revelation is withheld, interrupted by the allegory of real socialist principles, with its busy efforts tending toward the riddle of history's final resolution. Katharina dies miserably, the peasant midwife's mattress soaked in her blood; a beautiful girl, "like an apparition from another world" (605), hands the surviving child to Katharina's socialist husband. Lest we mistake her for truly an otherworldly angel, we immediately read that the girl "later became a crane operator" (606). The timeless truth of *The Decision* does not refer to the gentle mythical seasons of death and rebirth, but demands to be grasped without delay in the eternal present of socialist construction.

Notes

[1] Anna Seghers, *Die Entscheidung* (Berlin: Aufbau, 2003); Colin Smith, "All Quiet on the Eastern Front?" and Cettina Rapisarda, "Women and Peace in Literature and Politics: The Example of Anna Seghers," both in *German Writers and the Cold War: 1945–61*, ed. Rhys W. Williams, Stephen Parker, and Colin Riordan

(Manchester: Manchester University Press, 1992), 7–26; here, 22; and 159–80; here, 159, respectively.

[2] Valentin Merkelbach, "Fehlstart Seghers-Rezeption: Vom Kalten Krieg gegen die Autorin in der Bundesrepublik," in *Anna Seghers Materialienbuch*, ed. Peter Roos and Friederike J. Hassauer-Roos (Darmstadt: Luchterhand, 1977), 9–24.

[3] Marcel Reich-Ranicki, "Die geistige Kapitulation der Anna Seghers," *Die Welt*, September 3, 1959; Martin Kane, "Existentialism or Ideology? The Early Works of Anna Seghers," in *Anna Seghers in Perspective*, ed. Ian Wallace (Amsterdam: Rodopi, 1998), 7–28; here, 9.

[4] Ute Brandes, "Anna Seghers's Politics of Affirmation," in Wallace, *Anna Seghers in Perspective*, 175–98; here, 182.

[5] Gerd Labroisse, "Bild und Funktion Westdeutschlands in Anna Seghers' Romanen *Die Entscheidung* und *Das Vertrauen*," in *Anna Seghers Materialienbuch*, ed. Peter Roos and Friederike J. Hassauer-Roos (Darmstadt: Luchterhand, 1977), 133–51; here, 133.

[6] Helen Fehervary, *Anna Seghers: The Mythic Dimension* (Ann Arbor: University of Michigan Press, 2001), 66. Further references to this work are given in the text using the abbreviation *AS*.

[7] Christa Wolf, "Das siebte Kreuz," in *Christa Wolf/Anna Seghers: Das dicht besetzte Leben; Briefe, Gespräche und Essays*, ed. Angela Drescher (Berlin: Aufbau, 2003), 69–84; here, 78.

[8] Christa Wolf, "Zeitschichten," in *Die Dimension des Autors: Essays, Reden, Gespräche, 1959–1985* (Darmstadt: Luchterhand, 1987), 353–63; Hans Jochen Vogt, "What Became of the Girl: A Minor Archaeology of an Occasional Text by Anna Seghers," *New German Critique* 82 (Winter 2001): 145–65.

[9] Bernard Comrie, *Aspect: An Introduction to the Study of Verbal Aspect and Related Problems* (Cambridge: Cambridge University Press, 1976), 5.

[10] John Lyons, *Semantics*, vol. 2. (Cambridge: Cambridge University Press, 1977), 680.

[11] Marc Augé, *Non-Places: Introduction to an Anthropology of Supermodernity* (London: Verso, 1995), 77.

[12] Ibid., 681.

[13] Ibid., 680.

[14] Seghers, *Die Entscheidung*, 521. Further references to this work are given in the text using the page number alone. All translations from German in this chapter are by Benjamin Robinson.

[15] Bernhard Malkmus, "'Man in the Anthropocene': Max Frisch's Environmental History," *PMLA* 132, no. 1 (2017): 71–85.

[16] Anna Seghers, *Aufstand der Fischer von St. Barbara* (Berlin: Aufbau, 2002), 5.

[17] Christine Zehl Romero, *Anna Seghers: Eine Biographie*, vol. 2 (Berlin: Aufbau, 2000), 328; Bernd Leistner, "Warten und Wartenkönnen: Beobachtungen zu einem Leitmotiv im Werk von Anna Seghers," *Zeitschrift für Germanistik* 1, no. 4 (1980): 389–97.

[18] Helen Fehervary, "Commentary," in Seghers, *Aufstand der Fischer*, 100–163; here, 114.

[19] Ibid., 140.

[20] Käthe Kollwitz, *Ich sah die Welt mit liebvollen Blicken*, ed. Hans Kollwitz (Wiesbaden: Fourier, 2001), 193.

[21] Seghers, *Aufstand der Fischer*, 92.

[22] Mikhail Bakhtin, *The Dialogic Imagination: Four Essays*, ed. Michael Holquist, trans. Caryl Emerson and Michael Holquist (Austin: University of Texas Press, 1981), 300, 354.

[23] Anna Seghers, letter to Georg Lukács, 28 June, 1938, in *Über Kunst und Wirkichkeit: I. Die Tendenz in der reinen Kunst*, ed. Sigrid Bock (Berlin: Akademie, 1970), 173–81; here, 179.

[24] Stephen Brockmann, *The Writers' State: Constructing East German Literature, 1945–1959* (Rochester, NY: Camden House, 2015), 286.

[25] Seghers, *The Dead Stay Young* (London: Eyre & Spottiswoode, 1950), 579.

7: Filling the Void with Stories: Anna Seghers's Conceptual Metaphors

Jennifer Marston William

I. Seghers's Prose of Stasis and Motion

THE WORKS OF ANNA SEGHERS are so richly varied, and so numerous, that sweeping generalizations about them prove futile. At the same time, a number of thematic, stylistic, and linguistic patterns emerge quite clearly across her oeuvre. For instance, much of her prose is characterized by a rhythmic quality that parallels the motions of the wind, the sea, the rolling fog, and other natural elements that not only serve as her physical backdrops but also contribute to her "mythic topographies."[1] Seghers's language often reflects the stasis and motion that her characters experience as they find themselves dealing with frustrating, challenging, and sometimes seemingly hopeless situations. Examples of this contrast of stasis and motion are abundant in Seghers's work, with the degree of movement often changing noticeably from one sentence to the next, as in the opening chapter of *Aufstand der Fischer von St. Barbara* (Revolt of the Fisherman of Santa Barbara, 1928), with its juxtaposition of verbs that indicate motion or momentary inactivity: *gehen / zögern; rennen / gähnen* (to go / to hesitate; to run / to yawn).[2] Seghers creates a powerful sense of rhythm and an often lyrical style through a combination of techniques, such as repetition, onomatopoeia, alliteration, assonance, and evocative lexical choices (particularly verbs). Her style is one of simplicity, not overdone or forced. Yet Seghers's writing is by no means apolitical. Her stories often feature humans coping with natural forces such as the wind and the sea but are also very much about humans coping with other humans, struggling to coexist amidst stark ideological difference.

On the whole, despite taking a critical stance toward depicted political events and their ramifications, Seghers's writing conveys a certain—while neither blatant nor naïve—optimism. Although this optimism is grounded partly in a socialist belief in progress, it also marks Seghers's unrelenting belief in humanity. She demonstrated time and again through her stories how seemingly small actions can make a large positive impact. Taking a cognitive-literary approach, in my essay I elaborate how her use of conceptual-metaphorical language skillfully highlights humankind's potential to fill the inherent emptiness of human existence with meaning.

II. Conceptual Metaphor, Personification and Animation

Two terms that are integral to this essay, namely conceptual metaphor and personification, require some clarification in the context of cognitive-literary studies. First, the term *conceptual metaphor* can be misleading, as the phenomenon that this term represents is often conflated with the figurative, predominantly literary language that analogizes two things or ideas; for instance, in the reference work *Key Concepts in Cultural Studies*, the expression "to step in the right direction" is listed among others in the entry on metaphor without it being differentiated from the other examples as a conceptual, orientational metaphor.[3] "Love is a rose" is a metaphor of the figurative literary sort, while LOVE IS A JOURNEY is a conceptual metaphor (and the standard typographical representation for this is with all capital letters and a slightly smaller font). The metaphor "Love is a rose"—to be differentiated from the simile in Scottish poet Robert Burns's well-known verse "My love is like a red, red rose"—"assumes an imaginary identity" between the two terms.[4] In standard metaphor theory, the tenor (a rose, in this case) and the vehicle (love, in this case) allow for a comparison to be drawn between something concrete and something more abstract. In the case of the conceptual metaphor LOVE IS A JOURNEY, both concepts are quite abstract, and the metaphor manifests itself through further expressions that often involve verbs or adjectives, such as "we have come so far in this relationship" or "the unfaithful spouse strayed."

Conceptual metaphor underlies human cognition and relates to embodied experience. Orientational metaphors such as HAPPY IS UP; SAD IS DOWN; HIGH STATUS IS UP; LOW STATUS IS DOWN[5] are reflections of our thought processes and result in figurative expressions such as "to feel down / up," or "to look down on / up to" another person. It is important to note that such conceptual metaphors are, as cognitive linguist George Lakoff and philosopher Mark Johnson emphasize, based on physical orientations that are also culturally determined and reinforced. While some conceptual metaphors are pervasive across cultures and even seem universal, others—such as those depicting temporality—are highly culturally dependent. There is not a simple, straightforward correspondence between conceptual metaphors and perceptions of temporality in a given culture. As Perry Link notes in his study of conceptual metaphors in Chinese, there is often inconsistency across temporal expressions within a language. For instance, in English, we can say that something lies "before us" when we are actually talking about the future, while at the same time referring to our past "*fore*bears," those who came before us.[6] Despite considerable differences between Western and Chinese cultures, Link reports in his study that the conceptual metaphors in Chinese and English are more similar than they are different.[7]

A more precise term for conceptual metaphors would be something like "cognitive underpinnings." These conceptual utterances reflect our perceptions of reality and are apparent not only in literary texts but in everyday speech as well. These are, as Lakoff and Johnson have famously termed them, the metaphors we live by. Conceptual metaphors are a type of figurative language that is not always recognizable as such, because these expressions reflect ingrained conceptualizations. Before conceptual metaphors became an object of study, metaphors were easier to define. In his 1972 book on metaphor, well-known literary critic Terence Hawkes described figurative language—of which metaphor was understood to be "the most fundamental form"—as that "which doesn't mean what it says," and as "usually descriptive."[8] However, these characterizations are too reductionist to apply to all conceptual metaphors. If we take, for instance, Lakoff and Johnson's conceptual metaphor IDEAS ARE RESOURCES, it does not make sense to say that this metaphor does not mean what it says, nor is the metaphor particularly descriptive. Rather, the function of this conceptual metaphor is best seen in its manifestations in everyday speech— "He *ran out of* ideas. Don't *waste* your thoughts on small projects."[9] This language is figurative, since thoughts are not commodities that can be literally wasted or run out of as if there were a finite number of them. But this is how the human mind tends to conceive of things, as the infinite is not within its grasp. At the same time, literary writers such as Seghers often work creatively with these cognitive underpinnings, manipulating them and adding linguistic flourish to them such that readers become more aware of their inherently metaphorical nature than they would be when using them in their everyday communication. An analysis of these kinds of expressions and the concepts behind them offers some insights into a writer's mindset and, at times, into mentalities or worldviews that were prevalent during a particular historical era.

A second essential term to be clarified is personification, the definition of which is debated within various fields of study. As Dorst notes, the understanding of what should be "counted" as personification "will depend greatly on the analysts' field of research (psychology, literature, linguistics, visual arts) and on whether personification is studied at the linguistic, conceptual, communicative or cognitive level."[10] For my purposes, Lakoff and Johnson's definition is the most applicable: personification is an ontological conceptual metaphor by which "the physical object is further specified as being a person. This allows us to comprehend a wide variety of experiences with nonhuman entities in terms of human motivations, characteristics, and activities."[11] In literature as well as in everyday speech, something non-animate may be given metaphorical agency and presented as having some level of control over the animate beings around it. Personifications may be conventionalized such that we hardly notice them as metaphorical—for example, the idea that lamps "give" us light[12]— or, their metaphoricity can be clearer, and consciously employed. In the case of literary language, we can often assume at least some level of deliberateness in their usage. Here I am less concerned with degrees or categories of personification than with the overall effects that this type of conceptual metaphor elicits in Seghers's texts, and their implications for the worldviews of the characters during the historical periods in which the author situates them.

Seghers was a master at uniting the stylistic and thematic aspects of her works. Alexander Stephan points to an excellent example of such from *Das siebte Kreuz* (The Seventh Cross, 1942):

> Atemlos wie die Verfolgungsjagd selbst wechselt innerhalb einer knappen halben Textseite die Perspektive nach der Aussage von Füllgrabe vor der Gestapo von Westhofen über die Verbreitung von Heislers Steckbrief und die Beobachtungen von Röders Hauswartsfrau bis zu Röder selbst. Unruhig pendelt der Bericht zwischen Wurz und Aldinger, als dieser sich seinem Heimatdorf nähert. Nervös wie die Beteiligten springt die Erzählung zwischen den Gedanken von Paul Röder und Fiedler hin und her, als es darum geht, die Vertrauenswürdigkeit des Gegenüber einzuschätzen.[13]

> [Breathless as the pursuit itself, the perspective changes within a half a page, after Füllgrabe's statement before the Westhofen Gestapo about the distribution of Heisler's wanted poster and the observations from Röder's housekeeper as well as from Röder himself. The report oscillates anxiously between Wurz and Aldinger, as the latter approaches his home village. As nervously as the participants, the narration jumps back and forth between the thoughts of Paul Röder and Fiedler as they attempt to gauge each other's trustworthiness.]

In his description of how the author changes perspectives in the novel, Stephan bestows personification on the narrative here—it is breathless, anxious, and nervous; alternating, oscillating, and jumping. This personification reflects the agency that non-living entities also often enjoy within Seghers's texts. On the one hand, this anthropomorphism often lends her work a fantastical, even magical, fable-like quality. On the other hand, it is a constant reminder of circumstances that seem completely out of human control. Such contrasting portrayals have a strong effect on the reader, who also alternates between being swept into a realm of apparent fantasy and then back out into a cold, harsh reality.

While Seghers included a number of explicitly paranormal and mystical scenes in her early works particularly,[14] she more commonly portrayed realistic scenarios in which the lack of human control is evident. Frequently she accomplished this effect via personification, as the non-animate comes alive through her carefully considered verb choices. In the story "Grubetsch" (1927), for example, the conceptual metaphor consists of a remarkable combination of the natural and the supernatural in the depiction of the fog: "Der Nebel hatte die ganze Stadt, in der [Martin] sich ohnedies schwer auskannte, völlig verhext" (The fog had completely jinxed the entire city, which [Martin] hardly knew well in any case).[15] There are many straightforward, non-personified mentions of fog in Seghers's works as well—it is a regular presence in the gripping tale of *Das siebte Kreuz*, to name but one—contributing to a leitmotif of uncertainty that is fitting for many of her characters and their often unclear circumstances. It is not a mere coincidence that the first-person exiled narrator of *Transit* (1944) describes his future as "nebelhaft" (nebulous).[16] At the same time, an exploration of fog as a conceptual metaphor reveals an ambivalence typical of Seghers's works, in which symbols with a single and definitive meaning are rare. In the story "Bauern von Hruschowo" (Woodcutters of Hrushovo, 1929), it is not the fog that is personified but the forest, which lays the fog around like a comforting blanket to the men within its reach: "In der Mulde stieg der Nebel wie Rauch. Die Männer fühlten sich vollkommen geborgen. Der Wald legte den Nebel um sie herum wie eine Mutter die Röcke um ihre Kinder" (In the hollow, the fog rose like smoke. The men felt completely secure. The forest laid the fog around them like a mother puts coats around her children).[17] With its folktale-like quality,[18] this story expresses a largely cooperative rather than adversarial relationship between nature and humans, reminding us that broad generalizations about symbols in Seghers's work—for example, a statement like "fog always indicates an obstacle for her characters"—are not possible.

The wind is another natural element that Seghers often makes explicitly animate, for instance in *Grubetsch*: "Ein böser Zugwind kam durch die Torfahrt, schlug [Anna] ins Gesicht" (A wicked draft came through the gateway, hitting [Anna's] face).[19] In German as in English, it is common to say that the wind hits us in the face; that is, it is a metaphor we live by. While this may not be identified as figurative language (the wind can, after all, be physically felt on our face), it is nonetheless conceptually metaphorical and a personification that is a direct result of the verb choice. As linguist Morton W. Bloomfield argues, "the verb not the noun is crucial to personification because it frequently enables us to determine whether the noun, which appears to be a personification, is to be regarded as animate or not."[20] The accumulation of such verb-based conceptualizations in Seghers's works enhances the storytelling on multiple levels: it can make the depicted environment seem dangerous; it contributes to suspense; and it adds a layer of alluring detail. In this scene from *Aufstand der Fischer*, the wind wields its power against throngs of people:

> Die Leute von St. Barbara standen in dichten Haufen auf dem Marktplatz. Es war nach Sonnenaufgang, scharfer Wind, steigende Flut. So viel sie waren, man konnte das Wasser rauschen hören. Je schärfer der Wind wehte, je lustiger die Lichtchen hupften, die er über den Hafen und die Dächer versprenkelte, desto verzweifelter wurde die Stille.[21]

> [The people of St. Barbara stood in dense crowds in the marketplace. It was after sunset, biting wind, rising tide. As many as they were, one could still hear the water rushing. The more bitingly the wind blew, the more playfully the little lights hopped around that [the wind] sprinkled over the harbor and the roofs, the more distraught the silence became.]

The imagery here is at once beautiful, powerful, and ominous. Adding to this atmosphere are the "little lights" (die Lichtchen) that are likewise personified, frolicsomely hopping around at the wind's behest. The stormy wind at the harbor becomes even stronger and is described a couple of pages later as "zügellos" (unrestrained; literally, without reins).[22] The wind is not only given agency through Seghers's language; it is also depicted as ungovernable, untamable, and unstoppable. Any humans in its way are at its mercy. Seghers relies on conceptual metaphor, in this case that of personification, to convey the sheer magnitude and strength of natural forces in relation to the people enduring them.

While many of the instances of personification in Seghers's works contribute to a foreboding atmosphere, this is not always the case. Sometimes the personifications are humorous or whimsically appealing because of their novelty, as in this passage from "Grubetsch": "Martin kam zurück, stellte die Lampe vom Schrank auf den Tisch. Er zündete an, Marie holte den Topf und setze sich. Die Lampe legte ihren Arm rund um alle drei" (Martin came back, set the lamp from the closet onto the table. He lit a cigarette, Marie fetched the pot and sat down. The lamp laid its arm around all three of them);[23] or in the description of the demonstration procession in "Auf dem Wege zur amerikanischen Botschaft" (On the Way to The American Embassy, 1930) that "zog sich auseinander wie eine Harmonika" (stretched out like an accordion).[24] This latter story, with its stream-of-consciousness style, also exemplifies how Seghers builds rhythm into her texts. The alternating movement and stasis of the procession (*der Zug*) mimics the narrative movement, its ebb and flow being reflected in the repetition of entire sentences. Seghers's playful, lively language is that of a natural storyteller and creates appeal for a wide audience, which was always one of her goals as a writer.

III. Ontological Container Metaphor
Die Leere (emptiness)

A perusal of her collected works confirms that the descriptor *leer* (empty) and the noun *die Leere* (emptiness) were clearly among Seghers's favorites, in addition to the noun *Öde* (barrenness, desolateness) and the adjective *öde* (barren, desolate, bleak, dreary). See for instance the novel *Transit*, in which the protagonist comes to be comforted by the sea that he used to hate—"diese unmenschliche Leere und Öde" (this inhumane emptiness and desolateness).[25] Sometimes these words are used in an apparently simple manner to describe physical conditions and to paint a picture of a scene's deserted or even desolate atmosphere.[26] Seghers also uses *leer* in her depictions of temporality, such as the empty time her protagonist in *Transit* spends waiting for his exit visa to escape Nazi-occupied Europe: "Mein Besuch erschien mir damals verfehlt, der weitere Abend leer" (My visit seemed to me at the time to be a failure, the rest of the evening empty).[27] But beyond this function of *leer*, I argue that its recurrence in both literal and figurative contexts points to an existential emptiness motif that spans across Seghers's works and that she underscores by her frequent use of the container metaphor.

Lakoff and Johnson explain our tendency to conceptualize borders, even when there are none, by the fact that "each of us is a container, with a bounding surface and an in-out orientation."[28] It is thus in our nature to view the world in terms of bounded entities, and to conceive of abstract ideas in a similarly contained way. In English, for example, one can get "into" and "out of" trouble; similar conceptualizations are found in German: *in Schwierigkeiten geraten* (to get into difficulties), and *aus den Schwierigkeiten herauskommen* (to get out of difficulties). A close look at how Seghers uses the conceptual container metaphor, particularly in respect to the notion of emptiness, provides some clues as to what the writer might have had in mind with her depictions of characters who often find themselves in fateful circumstances, and who also tend to be relentless in their searches for greater meaning. By way of illustration, in what follows I briefly examine the novella "Der Mann und sein Name" (The Man and His Name, 1952) in relation to the container metaphor of emptiness, a sustained conceptual metaphor that highlights Seghers's talent for implicitly inviting the reader to more carefully consider the moral ambiguity of the postwar period as well as the intensive individual struggles of rebuilding a life during such times.

With its theme of German soldiers and SS officers returning home from the war, "Der Mann und sein Name" can be placed loosely in the tradition of *Heimkehrerliteratur* (returnee literature), although many such works were written by young male authors who had themselves returned from the war. Protagonist Walter Retzlow is a former SS officer trying to find his footing in the Soviet zone of occupation in 1948. He is at first described only as "der Junge" (the boy), giving the reader a sense of his youthfulness as well as hinting at the identity games that soon ensue. His mental state parallels the world around him in its desolation, as Seghers expresses through her characteristically compact syntax and vivid imagery:

> Der junge Mensch hatte keine Hoffnung mehr. Er hatte Angst, und er fror. . . . Es war ihm nicht nur kalt, weil er keinen Mantel trug. Die Welt war geborsten, und er war allein in einem Erdspalt, und außen war es so öde wie innen." (91)

> [The young man didn't have any more hope. He was scared, and he was freezing. He wasn't only cold because he wasn't wearing a jacket. The world had shattered, and he was alone in a gap in the earth, and outside it was as desolate as it was inside.]

Eventually the reader learns that the main character's name is Walter Retzlow, but after being mistaken for the devoted antifascist Heinz Brenner, he takes on that identity instead. When asked to fill out a registration form with his name and other details, he is momentarily unable to do this:

> Der Junge dachte: Nur schnell was schreiben.—Sein Kopf war hohl. Er las die Fragen, die vorgedruckt waren: Name—Geburtsort—Alter—Familienstand—Beruf—Parteizugehörigkeit—Truppenteil. Es fiel ihm aber nichts ein. Er starrte in die leeren Rubriken, die er ausfüllen sollte. (93)

> [The boy thought: just write something quickly.—His head was hollow. He read the preprinted questions: Name—Place of Birth—Age—Marital Status—Occupation—Party Membership—Military Unit. But nothing occurred to him. He stared into the empty boxes that he was supposed to fill.]

This description of the protagonist's lack of action can be read on two levels: literally, there are blanks on the form that he needs to fill in with his personal information; figuratively, there are "blanks" in his memory that also need to be filled in. Ultimately, he chooses to take this opportunity to start fresh by providing someone else's identifying information in these empty spaces. Under this guise, Retzlow-Brenner becomes an exemplary Socialist and comes to see his past mistakes. The ruse does not last forever, however, and he is expelled from the SED after finally confessing his deception. Still, all is not lost, as he starts a new life with Katharina, and the novella's closing lines reflect the reality of his new situation: "Sie werden sich liebhaben. Es wird nicht leicht sein" (189; They will love each other. It won't be easy).

Given the emptiness that Retzlow feels earlier in the narrative, when his heart is "leicht" (light), the work's final words are more hopeful than they might seem otherwise. The earlier passage depicting his state of mind shortly after his return is as follows:

Es war ihm auf einmal leicht ums Herz. Er war aber dadurch nicht froher. Im Gegenteil. Das Gefühl von sinnloser Leere wuchs, als sei er mit seiner Angst auch das letzte Gewicht losgeworden und wirbele federleicht wie ein welkes Blatt in der leeren Luft. Er dachte: Wie unwichtig ist das alles. Warum habe ich mich gerettet? Der Führer ist tot. Das Reich ist zugrunde gegangen. Ich geh auch zugrunde. So oder so. (97)

[Suddenly he was light-hearted. However, he wasn't happier. On the contrary. The feeling of pointless emptiness grew, as if he had, along with his fear, shed the last weight and was whirling like a withered leaf in the empty air. He thought: how unimportant this all is. Why did I save myself? The Führer is dead. The Reich has perished. I am also perishing. One way or another.]

The emptiness and light-heartedness he is experiencing at this point is actually a combination of hopelessness and apathy. Readers may not easily sympathize with an SS officer who (by his own admission later in the text) chose to follow orders so blindly, but Seghers's portrayal ensures that we understand him as flawed but young, with the potential (and probably the time) to change, and as despondent but with a chance to turn things around.

The path to a brighter future is not an easy one, psychologically, for the protagonist. His surroundings frequently mirror his inner emptiness in such descriptions as "Der Platz sah kahl und menschenleer aus" (95; The square looked bare and free of people). The term *menschenleer* evokes not only the physical absence of people on the square, but also the lapse in humanity that had characterized the years of Nazi Germany, the repercussions of which were still strongly apparent. Seghers had used *menschenleer* in her earlier work *Das siebte Kreuz* as well,[29] surely with similar connotations in mind for the novel's setting of Nazi Germany.

When Retzlow runs into his best friend, Helmut, the latter reminds him about the influential nationalist book *Das Dritte Reich* (The Third Reich, 1923) by Arthur Moeller van den Bruck, who claimed that if Germany was defeated, "dann sei sein Untergang so gewaltig, so toll sei der Abgrund, daß alle Menschen und alle Völker mit ihm in den Abgrund gezogen würden" (99; then its downfall would be so massive, the abyss would be so tremendous that all humans and all peoples would be pulled with it into the abyss). Retzlow's immediate reaction is one of silence and pain: "Er spürte für einen Augenblick einen scharfen Schmerz. Als könnte er in der unsäglichen Leere noch einmal fassen, was er verloren hatte" (99;

He felt for a moment a sharp pain. As if in the unspeakable emptiness he could once again grasp what he had lost). The abyss appears previously in the text as a striking metaphor characterizing the minor character Hermann Müller's postwar state of mind, on the brink of the "Abgrund des Irrsinns" (89; abyss of insanity). The abyssal imagery describing Germany's downfall complements that of the individual, existential "unsäglichen Leere" (unspeakable emptiness) and profound loss experienced by this young man who has returned from war. Yet there is hope for him. Among the more than a dozen appearances of *leer* (or related forms) in the novella are two instances of the phrase "die Leere der Welt" (the emptiness of the world). The first time, Retzlow's frustration is clear: "Womit hätte auch das Menschenherz auf die völlige Leere der Welt antworten sollen, als mit Verzweiflung oder mit Langeweile" (110; With what else should the human heart have responded to the complete emptiness of the world, other than with despair or with boredom)? The next time, though, the phrase appears in a positive context, when Retzlow has this realization after a conversation with a friend: "Die Leere der Welt war doch ausgefüllt. Der Abgrund hat sich doch geschlossen" (129; The emptiness of the world was in fact filled up. The abyss closed itself up after all). Since emptiness always implies a contained space—whether the boundaries enclosing it are physical or imagined—there is always the potential for filling that space, for existential fulfillment. In this way, Seghers employs the conceptual metaphor to show how her character's understanding of his situation has changed—how all is by no means perfect, but all is by no means lost.

The German noun *die Leere*, comparable to its English equivalent "emptiness," is not a typical concrete noun, since it is something that cannot be perceived with the senses. But it is also not a strictly abstract noun such as "love." Emptiness is a state created and recognized by the perceived absence of either something physical or something abstract. An empty feeling can be depressing, when the lack of something essential is emphasized, or it can be promising, when the possibilities for filling that void are highlighted. The character Retzlow exemplifies both of these poles with his despondence, particularly at the story's beginning, and his various opportunities for fulfillment as time goes on. This polarity corresponds with the ambivalence that characterizes so many of Seghers's stories, whose endings often leave readers wondering if the author wrote them with a sense of optimism and hope in mind, or one of pessimism and despair. Such endings are perfectly fitting for the kinds of extreme historical situations about which she often writes, in which it could not be uncommon for people to feel hopeful one moment and despondent the next. Retzlow's plight reflects this ambivalence, both on an individual and a collective level. As Hunter Bivens notes about the protagonist's fall from grace, "For the workers, Retzlow loses his status as an object of identification and imitation, as a role model, but at the same time his story becomes an event that opens onto a discourse about history, politics, and experience."[30] Something similar could be said about Seghers's readers, who also are not likely to identify with Retzlow in the end, but who gain a greater understanding of the complexities of the postwar era through the author's nuanced portrayal of an individual's attempts to fill an existential void when it seemed all had been lost.

IV. Conclusion: A Hopeful Ambivalence

Helen Fehervary eloquently articulates the multivalence of Seghers's writing in terms of the reader's role: "At once hopeful and tragic, the world of Seghers's prose offers neither individual nor collective resolution. As readers, we are not so much invited to identify with a narrative subject as we are called upon to engage ourselves in the larger flow of the narrative."[31] Although Seghers wrote of revolution and class struggle, her boldly unique way of writing was not always favored by fellow party members. Hers is a style that, "um wirken zu können, weniger die kämpferische 'richtige Linie,' sondern vor allem den Mut zum Träumen, die Öffnung zum Phantastischen braucht" (in order to be effective, needs less of the combative "correct line" but rather, above all, the courage to dream, the port to the fantastical).[32] At the same time, her characters tend to be down-to-earth and grounded—certainly not airily empty— and they display a psychological realism that often makes it easy for the reader to empathize (if not exactly identify) with them as they grapple inexorably with complex dilemmas. Rather than presenting socialism as an unequivocal and immediate solution to these problems, Seghers wrote about it more as the light at the end of the tunnel for many of her characters, who first need to muster the inner strength to make their way toward it.

The final statement of *Das siebte Kreuz* displays the kind of optimistic, hopeful ambivalence that characterizes much of Seghers's work:

> Wir fühlten alle, wie tief und furchtbar die äusseren Mächte in den Menschen hineingreifen können bis in sein Innerstes, aber wir fühlten auch, dass es im Innersten etwas gab, was unangreifbar war und unverletzbar.[33]

> [We all felt how deeply and formidably external forces can reach into the innermost core of a person, but we also felt that there was something in that innermost core that was unassailable and invulnerable.]

While Seghers's texts often focus on the utterly dreadful, both in nature and in civilization, they also remind readers that feelings of existential emptiness are both natural and impermanent. Seghers regularly relied on conceptual metaphor to express a persistent belief in the ability of the human spirit to prevail even in the darkest times. Ultimately, that spirit is neither carried away by the wind, nor swept out to sea by the current, nor obscured completely by the fog.

Notes

[1] Helen Fehervary, *Anna Seghers: The Mythic Dimension* (Ann Arbor: University of Michigan Press, 2001), 13.

[2] Anna Seghers, *Aufstand der Fischer von St. Barbara* (Berlin: Aufbau, 2002), 11. All translations from German in this chapter are my own.

[3] Maja Mikula, *Key Concepts in Cultural Studies* (New York: Palgrave Macmillan, 2008), 127.

[4] Mikula, *Key Concepts*, 127.

[5] George Lakoff and Mark Johnson, *Metaphors We Live By* (Chicago: University of Chicago Press, 1980), 15–16.

[6] Perry Link, *An Anatomy of Chinese: Rhythm, Metaphor, Politics* (Cambridge, MA: Harvard University Press, 2013), 8.

[7] Link, *An Anatomy of Chinese*, 11.

[8] Terence Hawkes, *Metaphor* (London: Methuen, 1972), 1–2.

[9] Lakoff and Johnson, *Metaphors We Live By*, 48.

[10] Aletta G. Dorst, "Personification in Discourse: Linguistic Forms, Conceptual Structures and Communicative Functions," *Language and Literature* 20, no. 2 (2011): 113–35; here, 117.

[11] Lakoff and Johnson, *Metaphors We Live By*, 33.

[12] Dorst, "Personification in Discourse," 121.

[13] Alexander Stephan, *Anna Seghers: Das siebte Kreuz; Welt und Wirkung eines Romans* (Berlin: Aufbau, 1997), 86.

[14] Sonja Hilzinger, *Anna Seghers* (Stuttgart: Philipp Reclam, 2000), 88.

[15] Anna Seghers, "Grubetsch," in *Erzählungen, 1924–1932* (Berlin: Aufbau, 2014), 11–71; here, 26.

[16] Anna Seghers, *Transit*, ed. Silvia Schlenstedt (Berlin: Aufbau-Verlag, 2001), 19.

[17] Anna Seghers, "Bauern von Hruschowo," in *Erzählungen, 1924–1932*, 150–64; here, 160.

[18] See Fehervary, *Anna Seghers: The Mythic Dimension*, 132.

[19] Seghers, "Grubetsch," 33.

[20] Morton W. Bloomfield, "Personification-Metaphors," *Chaucer Review* 14, no. 4 (Spring 1980): 287–97; 287–97; here, 288.

[21] Anna Seghers, *Aufstand der Fischer* (Berlin: Aufbau, 2002), 66.

[22] Seghers, *Aufstand der Fischer*, 68.

[23] Seghers, "Grubetsch," 21.

[24] Anna Seghers, "Auf dem Wege zur amerikanischen Botschaft," in *Erzählungen, 1924–1932*, 165–88; here, 165.

[25] Seghers, *Transit*, 43.

[26] Seghers, *Aufstand der Fischer*, 85, 87; Anna Seghers, "Der Mann und sein Name," in *Erzählungen, 1950–1957* (Berlin: Aufbau, 2009), 101–99; here, 120. Further references to this latter work are given in the text using page numbers alone.

[27] Seghers, *Transit*, 44.

[28] Lakoff and Johnson, *Metaphors We Live By*, 29.

[29] Anna Seghers, *Das siebte Kreuz: Roman aus Hitlerdeutschland*, ed. Bernhard Spies (Berlin: Aufbau, 2000), 139, 291.

[30] Hunter Bivens, "Anna Seghers' 'The Man and His Name': *Heimat* and the Labor of Interpellation in Postwar East Germany," *German Studies Review* 30, no. 2 (2007): 311–30; here, 325.

[31] Fehervary, *Anna Seghers: The Mythic Dimension*, 2.

[32] Sonja Hilzinger, *Anna Seghers* (Stuttgart: Philipp Reclam, 2000), 112.

[33] Seghers, *Das siebte Kreuz*, 421.

Part II.

Expressions of Modernity: Using Storytelling Unconventionally

8: Storytelling and Telling Stories in Heine's Prose Fiction

Robert C. Holub

NOT ALL GREAT WRITERS are great storytellers, especially not in the traditional sense of storytelling. In order to construct a story, a writer has to possess specific talents and a certain temperament. A good story must have a beginning, a middle, and an end. It must cohere to the extent that characters are consistent psychologically throughout the various phases of the story. The actions and activities of the characters must be motivated by a credible psychology, and the events must develop in a logical pattern. Elements of the story must be carefully arranged to elicit reader responses. Often suspense is a reaction storytellers seek to evoke, and for each reaction the author is trying to provoke in the audience, he or she must apply appropriate techniques. Narration must demonstrate the same type of relationship to characters throughout, and the narrator has to remain consistent in tone and level of diction. If the writer is composing a short story or a novella, we will often find a focus on one event or a series of related events, but even in cases of shorter prose fiction we count on consistency in characters and character development, logical plots, and psychological credibility. With longer prose fiction, such as novels, there are additional demands for attention to detail and development. The reader expects an exposition when new characters are introduced, or when the scene shifts from one place to another. Descriptions must be consistent from one part of the novel to another. Obviously some modernist tendencies in prose fiction play with these conventions, intentionally disappointing readers' expectations and the norms that have become established for fiction. But even in the case of the deviation from narrative norms, the writer must display a command that allows the reader to appreciate the deviation as part of the compositional strategy. If the deviation from norms and consistency appears to result from a mistake or deficient capacity, then the writer fails to accomplish his purpose and will be considered lacking in talent.

It is quite possible to imagine a writer who is constitutionally unable to accomplish storytelling in this traditional sense, yet who is an outstanding prose stylist and insightful author. Heinrich Heine is a case in point. In his early years he experimented with many genres and forms. As a young man he began writing lyric poetry, composing sonnets, ballads, and other types of verse with a number of different metrical patterns and rhyme schemes. He soon discovered that he was well suited to these shorter forms, and throughout his life, even in the years when political journalism was foremost in his creative activities; he continued to compose poetry and to experiment with both formal and substantive elements. But Heine was obviously not content to be considered solely a poet, and we therefore find him, especially in his formative years during the 1820s, turning to other genres to test his own limits as a writer. In the first half of the decade he composed two tragedies: *Almansor* (1823) and *William Ratcliff* (1823). Neither met with success in Heine's or subsequent eras, and he likely drew the logical conclusion from his theatrical efforts rather early in his career, never attempting another stage production.

Heine did experiment with prose fiction, however, and we have evidence from both the 1820s and the 1830s of his desire to establish himself in this genre. In the early 1820s, as a result of his involvement with the Association for the Culture and Scholarship of Jewry (Verein für Cultur und Wissenschaft der Juden), he embarked on an ambitious project to compose a novel dealing with the plight of Jewry during the fifteenth century. The *Rabbi of Bacherach* (*Rabbi von Bacherach*) was based on research Heine conducted as a member of the Verein and deals thematically with a period in European history that recalls the drama *Almansor*. The exact date of the occurrences in the novel is not mentioned, but the narrator recounts the history of Jewish persecution, mentioning specifically the construction of four churches to honor Saint Werner, whose death in 1287 had led to a fierce pogrom against the Jewish population in the Rhine region. The narrator sets the story of the *Rabbi* two centuries after these events, and we can conclude that we are dealing with the life of Jews during the late fifteenth century, at the time, therefore, when both Muslims and Jews were subject to European persecution. The origins of the *Rabbi* lie undoubtedly in the first half of the 1820s, but there is evidence that Heine ceased work on the manuscript in 1825, taking it up again only a decade and a half later when he was already residing in France. The reason for his abandonment of the project and his decision to turn to it again may well have been connected, respectively, with his conversion to Protestantism in 1825 and the Damascus crisis in 1840, but we should not exclude the possibility that he recognized in 1825 that he was encountering structural difficulties in writing in an epic form. Although the composition of Heine's two other attempts at longer works of prose fiction may not entail the same bifurcated origins, it is possible that he conceived *From the Memoirs of Herr von Schnabelewopski* (*Aus den Memoiren des Herren von Schnabelewopski*) and *Florentine Nights* (*Florentinische Nächte*) in the 1820s and resumed work on them in the 1830s. Although Manfred

Windfuhr, the editor of these two texts in the Düsseldorf edition of Heine's writings, argues that they are works solely composed in the 1830s, Klaus Briegleb, who edited the Hanser edition, detects two or even more periods of composition. If we assume composition in the 1820s and in the 1830s, with a significant hiatus between them, they we may be dealing again with Heine's recognition of difficulties in planning and writing a longer piece of prose fiction. All three works were eventually published in different volumes of the *Salon* series and rounded out their respective volumes, which contained longer, complete pieces. Even if Windfuhr is correct, however, the fact that Heine aborted each of his three novels indicates something about his abilities as a storyteller, as we defined them above. He was unable to sustain a piece of prose fiction, and his novels remained fragments, never appearing as self-sufficient books.

If we examine the novels we can understand better the problems Heine was encountering. His most traditional novelistic attempt was undoubtedly the *Rabbi*, which Heine appears to have conceived as something like a Jewish alternative to the writings of Walter Scott; as Jeffrey Sammons points out, it is a conscious attempt to produce a "Romantic novel with Jewish materials."[1] One problem that Heine faced was simply that he did not have sufficient command of the history and traditions he was attempting to capture. His personal acquaintance with Judaism was spotty, and although in connection with the Association he had conducted research to bolster his knowledge of Jewish communities in the medieval period, he was certainly no expert in this area. The main difficulties he encountered, however, were related to compositional flaws rather than matters of substance. Like Scott, he had achieved his initial success with poetry, but unlike the Scottish novelist, his transition to historically based fiction was fraught with irresolvable structural problems. These problems stem from Heine's inability at this point in his writing career and, indeed, at any point during his lifetime, to construct a story that coheres, pursues a meaningful plot line, and manages to successfully resolve an important conflict or conflicts developed in the initial stages of the book. Sammons has identified four "tensions" that would be worthy of novelistic treatment in the *Rabbi*: the conflict between the threatened Jews and the Christian communities that surround them; the guilt incurred by the Rabbi upon abandoning his fellow Jews when he escapes to Frankfurt; the discrepancy between the ideals of Judaism and the reality of Jewish life in the ghetto; and the contrast that appears in the third chapter between the rather traditional Rabbi Abraham and the dashing, emancipated Don Isaak Abarbanel. He carefully pursues each of these tensions and points to plausible barriers Heine would have encountered in trying to resolve each.[2] To a certain extent Heine had bitten off more than he could chew: there are too many themes and they are too disparate, even if he did have the constitution to resolve them. He was unable to compose in the first three chapters an exposition with the potential for development, one that would be able to drive the plot for a sustained piece of prose. His deficiency does not necessarily lie in the stories he tells and the characters he invents—there are moments of brilliance, both tragic and comic, in this fragmentary work, as well as some beautiful prose—but in his inability to construct a larger framework that will lead to a successful historical novel.

It is quite possible that Heine became aware of his limitations, since the forms he selected for his other two novels departed from the historical novel of Romantic origins. He wrote to Moser on June 25, 1824 with regard to the *Rabbi*: "On this occasion I noticed that I am utterly lacking in the talent of storytelling."[3] *From the Memoirs of Herr von Schnabelewopski* announces itself to be something quite different in its title. As a memoir it will be written in the first person and deal with experiences, a narrative perspective perhaps better suited to a noted lyric poet. And in adopting the persona with the comic sounding Polish surname, it promises to contain humor, a mode at which Heine was adept, as we witness in many of his poems and his early reportages. But the title also informs the reader that it does not strive for a complete and rounded narrative, since we will have something "out of" the memoirs: selections, presumably of the most pertinent and highly crafted passages. This structure provides Heine with more flexibility to do what he does best, enabling a potpourri of thoughts and topics as the eponymous protagonist proceeds on his journey from Poland to Amsterdam. The chapters include, among other things, satirical accounts of institutions in Hamburg, a city with which Heine was obviously very familiar; an abbreviated version of an old Danish ballad adopted from a collection by the Grimms (Herr Vonved); the tale of the Flying Dutchman; and various reflections on religion. The structure of his novel, which resembles prose drawn from the picaresque tradition,[4] plays to Heine's strengths, since Schnabelewopski encounters new persons and situations at successive stations of his travels and can include, since it is a feigned memoir, reflections on experiences as well as legends and poetry that occur to him. Heine is more comfortable with this sort of variety and the opportunity to employ free association. The looser overall narrative does not interfere with Heine's ability to inject witty remarks, make humorous observations, and tell stories on a more reduced level.

The structure Heine utilizes for his third attempt at a novel is similarly constructed with shorter narratives and maximum flexibility in mind. The framework for *Florentine Nights* involves a Heine persona, Maximilian, who consults with a physician about the deteriorating health of his patient, Signora Maria. Maximilian's appointed task is to entertain Maria with fantastic and foolish stories, so that she does not have to converse and needs only to listen passively and preserve her strength. Maria is destined to die, and so the framework has a natural trajectory, and since we are dealing with evening visits, the novel is conveniently divided into the tales

Maximilian relates on separate nights. This compositional arrangement recalls Boccaccio's *Decameron*, where the framework similarly serves as the occasion for the telling of separate tales, connected only by the homogeneity of the group.[5] As Sammons observes, we are dealing here less with a novel than with "a series of *Novellen* related within a frame."[6] Despite choosing a structure conducive to telling stories and allowing the kind of associative material at which Heine excelled, he managed to compose only two "nights," and the "novel" breaks off abruptly with Maximilian grabbing his hat and quickly exiting Maria's bedroom. The two most noted sections of the work feature the description of a performance by the violinist Niccolò Paganini in the first night, and in the second, Maximilian's recollection of a strange group of London street performers and the fate of Mademoiselle Laurence, the exotic dancer in this ensemble, whom the narrator later encounters in Paris in rather different circumstances. There are some perversely erotic passages in the first night, and the story from the second night breaks off abruptly with no discernible resolution to the many odd threads in its exposition.

Heine obviously did not fare better in trying to complete a novel comprising a more serialized structure, whether picaresque or a collection of novellas in a loose frame: like the *Rabbi*, *Schnabelewopski* and *Florentine Nights* remained fragments, and Heine evidences no desire to return to them in the last decade and a half of his life. With regard to *Schnabelewopski* we could say that the material was going nowhere. The protagonist completes his journey to Amsterdam, but this city appears to be an endpoint for his wanderings. Thus the continuation of writing would have to have entailed further stories and encounters in the Dutch city. But there was no real trajectory, no conflict that was built up through the initial fourteen short chapters and that needed resolution. The loose structure enabled successful individual "stories," but these stories do not add up to a success in overall storytelling. *Florentine Nights* poses similar compositional problems. The framework adopted by Heine certainly enabled him to continue with additional "nights," if he had so desired, but in the first two he did not take advantage of the structure with convincing material. Most commentators agree that this fragment is one of Heine's most contrived and unsuccessful works. The framework story is marred by various types of ambiguity, but there is no attempt to drive them toward resolution. And the two initial "nights" are unconvincing as independent tales, seemingly unrelated to each other, and disconnected from the frame. Undoubtedly this lack of promise contributed to Heine's decision to proceed no further.

Heine was thus unsuccessful in writing three types of novels: the historical, Romantic novel; a variety of the picaresque novel that follows a central figure on various adventures; and a novel structured as a framework for relating individual and perhaps even quite different novellas in sequence. These failures at the craft of storytelling in larger formats, however, do not mean that he lacked talent to tell stories on a more modest scale. Indeed, in each of the "failed" novels there are moments of successful storytelling, from the opening tableau of Bacherach in the *Rabbi* to the depiction of the odd London street artists in *Florentine Nights*. Heine's forte was obviously not storytelling writ large, but telling stories within a more confined space and with an energy and wit that exhausts itself before leading to more epic conflicts. Azade Seyhan notes that Heine's "manner of interactive, performative storytelling and the dream narratives that frequently wander into Heine's stories require a realignment of reading habits based on expectations of a linear, undisrupted narrative."[7] He had developed this storytelling talent in his earliest prose works, the correspondence articles from Berlin and about Poland, and it is in evidence in the series of mostly prose writings that was grouped under the *Travel Pictures* (*Reisebilder*). In these latter pieces the combination of a peripatetic, first-person narrator and a definite geographical location that supplies a beginning and end point provides an ideal structure for shorter observations and critical remarks, but also succinct forays into storytelling. Stories could be used to reinforce the overall thematic grid and become part of an interweaving of elements that contributed to a larger, coherent pattern.

Heine's mastery of storytelling occurs in the only "travelogue" that departs from an actual journey, *Ideas: The Book of Le Grand* (*Ideen: Das Buch Le Grand*). Heine's critics have recognized that it is among the most successful works he wrote, and quite possibly his most accomplished piece of prose. Heine himself was obviously pleased with what he had produced, although most of his comments relate to the political content rather than the structural perfection he had achieved. In a letter to Karl Varnhagen von Ense in October 1826, he describes the piece as an autobiographical account "written in the most daring humor,"[8] and three months later he cites the furor it will cause in the public: "The book will create quite a stir, not because of private scandal, but because of the great world interests that it treats; Napoleon and the French Revolution are depicted as large as life."[9] And in June, Heine compares his recently published first edition of the *Book of Songs* (*Buch der Lieder*) with *Book of Le Grand* in terms of political impact. The poetry is a "harmless merchant ship," which "will sail under the protection of the second volume of travel pictures into the sea of oblivion." This second volume, which featured *Book of Le Grand*, by contrast, is compared to a "warship" that has "all too many canons on board."[10] Anticipating that these canons, once fired, would create a dangerous situation for him as author, Heine sailed to England on the day the book was released in order to witness from a distance what its fate, and his fate, would entail.

The impact Heine anticipated from *Book of Le Grand* was achieved not merely because it contained controversial attitudes toward Napoleon and the French Revolution, as well as critical attitudes toward Germany, but because the author invented a framework in which he could effectively unite the various autobiographical and historical topics with wit and irony. The principle that organizes the dispersed remarks and narratives that make up this text is, as critics already recognized at the time, one of subjectivity. The various elements of the work all relate to the first-person narrative persona who is supposedly speaking to an otherwise unidentified "Madame," a married and sympathetic listener. Subjectivity as an organizing principle for telling stories appears initially to be the very antithesis of what authors customarily employ in longer works of prose fiction. The Western tradition has hailed objective narration as a standard, and in the *Rabbi* Heine was no doubt making a bow toward this tradition. But objectivity places different organizational demands on the author, and, as we have seen, Heine was unable to fulfill them. Both memoirs containing a series of encounters and serialized novellas with first-person narrators at center stage were halfway measures that proved to be dead ends as well. Only in the *Travel Pictures* from the 1820s and in *Book of Le Grand* in particular does Heine come up with a solution to his compositional dilemma. We might even conclude that it is the lack of objectivity, the free movement and associations of a subject reflecting on conventions and events, that allows for the telling of relevant stories and for the political associations and innuendos that were so important to the author.

The subjective nature of the narrative does not mean that it lacks structure; indeed, it is perhaps more rigid in its organization than any of the other *Travel Pictures*. In the first and last quarter of the work the narrator associates himself with a poetic persona who very much resembles Heine, but who assumes various guises. At different points he imagines himself and presents himself to "Madame" as an Italian knight, an Indian Count, and a broken-hearted lover. In these sections the dominant themes are familiar from the Romantic literary canon: love, death, and suicide. It is hardly coincidental that these are the themes taken up by Heine in much of the early poetry collected in 1827 in the *Book of Songs*. At the close of the fifth chapter and throughout the next quarter of the book, however, the loosely structured narration, which had moved from one persona to another, shifts focus: here the narrator takes on the identity of the author, reflecting autobiographically about his youth. We are transported in the prose to Heine's birthplace and to the haunts of his youth. The major event he discusses in this section is the invasion of the French army into the German Rhineland at the beginning of the nineteenth century. Napoleon and his drum-major Le Grand become symbols of emancipation for a backward, anesthetized Germany unwilling to follow in the footsteps of the French Revolution. In the third quarter of the work, after the demise of Napoleon and the death of Le Grand, the narrator reflects on a variety of themes from the ensuing Restoration Period, including academic scholarship, the writing profession, and the political absurdities following the Congress of Vienna in 1815. The work closes with the return to the diverse Romantic masks and motifs we first encountered in the initial five chapters.

Within this framework the narrator is able to tell stories. In the first and last quarter of the text the stories can be reduced to the kernel contained in the motto of the first, second, and twentieth chapter: "She was lovable, and he loved her. He, however, was not lovable, and she did not love him" (248, 250, 308).[11] That this motto is reportedly drawn from an "old play" refers both to the ubiquity of this theme in the history of drama and literature, and to Heine's own endeavors in the first part of the 1820s to write about this theme in his lyric poetry. The narrator makes several allusions to Goethe, especially to *Werther*, as well as to the actual suicide of Heinrich von Kleist, and cites the early play *Almansor* in the course of these chapters. Biographically oriented Heine scholars have identified Heine's thematic treatment of unrequited love with his disappointment in wooing his cousin Amalie, but the more salient point is that Heine in his early writings and in the chapters of *Book of Le Grand* finds different ways to relate this commonplace narrative, and to relate it without the tragedy that terminates the life of a Werther or Kleist. Thus the mysterious woman whom the narrator encounters by chance on the corner of the "Strada San Giovanni" saves him from death, and he is able to continue his reflections on the pleasures of life in the following chapter. Similarly the narrator, breaking off suddenly from the Romantic parody concerning "little Veronica," "pious Ursula," the old soldier, and the brown dachshund— "But I don't want to tell this story today"—has a sudden urge to tell "another story," "the real story that was supposed to be told in this book" (304). In the following chapter he relates the tale of the knight and Signora Laura, his love for her, and her failure to return his affections. This is, indeed, the tale, repeated in many guises in the text and encountered in myriad forms in the tradition, which must be related. Again, in chapter 20 the avoidance of suicide from unrequited love becomes the initial topic in the one-sided discussion with "Madame." In the first and last quarter of *Book of Le Grand* Heine has not only told stories and variants of stories about fraught love relationships—he has made the telling of stories a central theme for reflection.

Throughout the text, but in particular in its middle sections, Heine treats the reader to further humorous reflections on telling stories. As we have seen above, the traditional art of creating prose fiction usually entails a narrative trajectory that proceeds from a conflict or tension that is developed sufficiently to make it worthy of a resolution that is the telos of the narrative. Digressions from the main task of narrative are therefore hindrances to conventional storytelling and should be excluded. But if your task is foregrounding the telling of stories, that is, relating variants on a central theme, and adding reflections on political questions of the times, then the manner in which the narrative proceeds will be different, and the recognition of this difference may even become part of the narrative structure. We should not be surprised, therefore, to find Heine referencing his own apparently chaotic compositional method. In the thirteenth chapter the narrator brings up the topic of composition, insisting against all the evidence in his text that his seemingly digressive style is really to the point: "In all previous chapters there is not a line that does not belong to the topic. I write concisely, I avoid all superfluity, often I even neglect the necessary" (284). We might want to note that in this passage the fiction of speaking—as we have seen, Heine continuously interjects "Madame" as a form of direct address—is here abandoned for writing, but it is a writing informed by the spoken word. We are obviously supposed to understand this self-reflection on the writing process as ironic—in the classical sense of not saying what one means. But like so much of Heine's irony, it is also meant seriously. Since Heine's project in *Buch Le Grand* has no mimetic pretensions to objectivity, since it is not intended to recount for us a single story with one trajectory, but to tell subjectively a variety of interrelated stories with overlapping themes, there is no external constraint on the direction of the text. Where writing follows the associations of a mind rather than an ordered pattern imposed on it by the conventions of traditional storytelling, nothing can be out of place and everything has a place. The stories Heine tells add up to a novel that can be captured, not by traditional storytelling, but only by an overriding agenda that favors the multiplicity of stories and reflections over a falsely conceived narrative coherence.

If Heine had found a solution to his compositional dilemma as early as the mid-1820s, why did he continue to search for alternatives that were both more traditional and less suited to his unique talents? It is quite possible that he originally conceived the structures for his three fragmentary novels at about the same time he was developing the "Ideas" that culminated in *Book of Le Grand*. There are indications of a concern with autobiography, for example, in *Schnabelewopski*, and we can be certain that the conception of the *Rabbi* as a historical novel predated his writing of the *Travel Pictures*. It is not out of the question, therefore, that Heine was experimenting with various forms in the 1820s, that he put away the least promising of his attempts at prose fiction when he recognized that they presented him with compositional aporias in storytelling, and that he took them up again only in the politically repressive atmosphere of the late 1830s as fillers for various volumes of the *Salon* series. (Only *Schnabelewopski* appears prior to the repressive measures taken against the Young Germans in 1835.) He worked on them at that point, but may have regarded them already as failures that would remain fragmentary. It is also possible that he simply harbored greater ambition for his prose fiction during the first two decades of his writing career. He may have wanted to emulate other greater writers of the previous generation or have had in mind a rivalry with Goethe, whose accomplishments in all genres was widely recognized. In this case Heine's early preoccupation with drama while writing lyric poetry was supplemented by a turn to various prose forms in the 1820s and 1830s. Alternatively he may have believed that prose fiction opened up greater markets for him, since he had to be concerned with his writing providing part of his livelihood. No matter what the reason was for his novelistic experiments, he was ultimately perspicacious enough to understand that his future as a writer did not lie with traditional prose forms. But unfortunately, focusing on journalism in the 1830s as his main exercise in prose, he never returned to the compositional solution that had fostered his greatest success in telling stories.

Notes

[1] Jeffrey L. Sammons, *Heinrich Heine: The Elusive Poet* (New Haven, CT: Yale University Press, 1969), 310.

[2] Ibid., 306–9.

[3] Heinrich Heine, *Säkularausgabe: Werke, Briefwechsel, Lebenszeugnisse* (Berlin: Akademie Verlag, 1970), 20:168 (25.6.1824).

[4] The relationship to the picaresque tradition is disputed. It was first mentioned by Wolfgang Menzel in his review of the work in 1834 and promoted by Manfred Windfuhr in "Heines Fragment eines Schelmenromans: Zu den Memoiren des Herren von Schnabelewopski," in *Heinrich Heine*, ed. Helmut Koopmann (Darmstadt: Wissenschaftliche Buchgesellschaft, 1975), 232–56. Windfuhr's contention was disputed in Gerhard Kluge, "Heinrich Heines Fragment *Aus den Memoiren des Herren von Schabelewopski* und das Problem des Schelmischen," in *Der moderne deutsche Schelmenroman: Interpretationen*, ed. Gerhart Hoffmeister (Amsterdam: Rodopi, 1986), 41–53. Dieter Arndt reaffirms the picaresque nature of the work in an examination of the scenes about Hamburg: "Heinrich Heine: Aus den Memoiren des Herren von Schnabelewopski oder Ein Pikaro am Jungfernstieg," *Heine-Jahrbuch* 36 (1997): 40–69. Andreas Schirmeisen, on the other hand, argues that the text is a parody of a *Bildungsroman*: "Heines 'Aus den Memoiren des Herren von Schnabelewopski': Eine parodistische Negation des Bildungsromans?" *Heine-Jahrbuch* 35 (1966): 66–80.

[5] Bettina Knauer, "Heinrich Heines 'Florentinische Nächte': Form und Funktion novellistischen Erzählens und esoterischer Allegorik," in *Aufklärung und Skepsis*, ed. Joseph A. Kruse, Bernd Witte, and Karin Füllner (Stuttgart: Metzler, 1999), 433–45, cites several other similarities between Boccaccio and Heine, among them that both were writing in troubled times; for Boccaccio the time of the plague, for Heine the time of political repression. Christine Mielke, "Der Tod und das novel-

listische Erzählen: Heinrich Heines 'Florentinische Nächte,'" *Heine-Jahrbuch* 41 (2002): 54–82, emphasizes the novella cycle as a way to keep death at bay.

[6] Sammons, *Heinrich Heine*, 326.

[7] Azade Seyhan,"Veiled Gestures: Aesthetic Performance contra Censorship in Heinrich Heine's 'Florentinische Nächte,'" in *"Es ist seit Rahel uns erlaubt, Gedanken zu haben": Essays in Honor of Heidi Thoman Tewarson*, ed. Steven R. Huff and Dorothea Kaufmann (Würzburg: Königshausen & Neumann, 2012), 139–50; here, 142.

[8] Heinrich Heine, *Säkularausgabe*, 20:271 (28.7.1826).

[9] Heine, *Säkularausgabe*, 20:281 (10.1.1827).

[10] Heine, *Säkularausgabe*, 20:303 (30.10.1827).

[11] Page numbers refer to volume 3 of Heinrich Heine, *Sämtliche Schriften*, ed. Klaus Briegleb (Munich: Hanser, 1976). Translations from Heinrich Heine, *Poetry and Prose*, ed. Jost Hermand and Robert Holub (New York: Continuum, 1982).

9:   Modernist Haze: Topographical Textures in Paul Klee and Franz Kafka

Kristy R. Boney

IN MODERNISM the silhouette of a great city usually takes center stage and looms over the individual. Early-twentieth-century social philosophers such as Georg Simmel explored the city as a subject and attempted to explain urbanity through a conceptual system. In his essay "Metropolis and Mental Life" (1903) Simmel claimed that the most difficult challenge of modern life stems from individuals' attempts to preserve their autonomy in the face of the "intensification of nervous stimulation," which is the result of the increased tempo of city life.[1] The city becomes a unique place that offers untold potential for the individual; it is *the* active topography, and it is part and parcel of the modern individual's experience. For example, Mann's account of the decline of Achenbach in a plague-infested Venice conveys an erosion of a stagnated European culture; Joyce's Dublin provides a "photograph" of a city at the turn of the century, and Musil's Vienna offers a quiet urbanity next to Döblin's hectic Berlin. Place names in literature give an immediate entry to the writing. Topography becomes a metonymy of meaning, since it is not pre-existing in itself—it gives solidarity, continuity, and durability to the life that is lived within it. Yet for quintessential modernists Franz Kafka and Paul Klee the topography is less than an urban bustling place for untold potential. Rather, Klee's and Kafka's topographies offer a topographical texture to modernism that visualizes and showcases intricate oscillating processes of emancipation and isolation, as well as connection and estrangement, ultimately marking modernist space.

Kafka's detached visual descriptions help to create the anonymity of the modern experience and allow the reader an illusion of freedom.[2] Indeed, Kafka's stories are incessantly explained as first and foremost fantastic, but other descriptions include prohibitive, tangled, and downright disorderly. The individuals often become barred from or mired in their topography while trying to resolve their conflict. Yet the visual descriptions of topography are as integral to the story as are the characters and plot twists. Without the visual element, one would become as slow and stuck as Kafka's country doctor, who, in trying to escape the sick patient becomes as lethargic as the old man in a snow desert.

Similarly, Paul Klee, a Swiss contemporary of Kafka, an early teacher of the visionary Bauhaus art movement, and an expressionist painter, often captures in his visual art a topography that mirrors Kafka's. Klee had a deep attachment to German Romanticism that sets him apart from other modernist painters, who either disregarded or manipulated German Romanticism for irony.[3] For Klee, a picture concerned the ego and the world in the sense of the Romantic sublime. A picture was in the highest sense a "comparison to the totality of the All."[4] Although not nostalgic, Klee searched for a unity in his art that reached beyond fragmentation. He sought to create images that would serve as symbols, an all-embracing unity that corresponds with man and the world. According to his "Creative Credo," one of Klee's essays on artistic creation, the artist should take his own life experiences and transform them into a journey to the invisible parts of the world. He is often re-quoted when he writes: "Art does not reproduce the visible; rather it makes visible."[5] Their works hazy and dream-like, both Kafka and Klee visualize modern topographies as certainly disrupting tangibility and continuity, but ultimately they reorganize (or in Klee's words, make visible) how one understands modernist experiential space and time.

In his *Zimmerperspektive mit Einwohnern* (fig. 9.1), Klee creates a topography that traps and misleads the eye. The piece appears to be a room with a table that is drawn within lines. In the 1920s Klee painted a series of rooms with lines of perspectives. The effect is one of playful transparency.[6] The eye follows a line, or a path, but the path is not obvious: It becomes turned around, or is blocked, and retracing it does not necessarily help in finding a clear way around the room. Similarly, the painting *Architektur* (fig. 9.2) consists primarily of squares and uses only four colors: blue and yellow, and then green and purple. The painting was part of a series on Magic Squares, in which Klee uses colors and chiaroscuro—the treatment of using light and shading—and the result is a study of a rhythmic repetition of similar elements. Andrew Kagen explains Klee's technique as "polyphonic." It is a musical reference that involves two or more lines of melodies, instead of one melody that is accompanied by harmony.[7] In Klee's "Pedagogical Sketchbook" he writes that blocks should be placed in a way to establish equilibrium. If they were to be placed symmetrically on top of each other, then the perception is incorrect psychologically, since a person views ones further away (or higher vertically) as smaller, than those closer to the ground.[8] While the painting appears to be a simple organization of blocks, there is, as in *Zimmer*, no clear pattern. We cannot follow along the same path without obstacles, but there is still a sense of rhythm and order. For Klee, this type of frustration is not necessarily a direct result of the anonymous self in the city, but rather it depicts a more realistic description of the world as a whole. He writes that when graphic imagery confines itself to outlines, it "has a fairylike quality and at the same time can achieve great precision. The purer the graphic work—

Figure 9.1. Paul Klee, Zimmerperspektive mit Einwohnern (Room Perspective with Inhabitants), 1921, 24. Oil transfer drawing and watercolor on paper on cardboard, 48.5 x 31.7 cm. Zentrum Paul Klee, Bern.

Figure 9.2. Paul Klee, Architektur (Architecture), 1923. Oil on Pavatex (cardboard), 58 x 39 cm. Inv. NG 7/69. Bpk Bildagentur/ Staatliche Museen, Berlin, Germany. Photo: Jörg P. Anders. Art Resource, NY.

that is, the more the formal elements underlying linear expression are emphasized—the less adequate it is for the realistic representation of things" (*CC*, 5). Thus he is not aiming for a slice of life. On the contrary, his "Credo" insists that art is a journey, and it follows a topographic plan in which several elements—lines, planes, space—produce forms that create an energy charge or movement. Ultimately, the charge allows incredible possibilities for expressing ideas—an emancipation from isolation or limitation, a texture to allow for new perspectives. In other words "to make visible" is not about changing perspective but about making the movement visible as it is being created.

Klee's ideas of visual movement are useful in reading Kafka's works. In the story fragment *Das Schloss* (The Castle, 1926), K., who is employed as a school janitor, is the main focus. K's path is seemingly open, but as is typical for Kafka, he is consistently blocked. Most of the novel recounts his strange encounters as an outsider with the townspeople as he tries not to be overwhelmed by the village's bureaucracy in his quest to contact Klamm, a castle official. Ironically, K.'s occupation is that of a land surveyor—one who should be able to envision and draw lines of topography with precision. Yet, K. (who never measures or surveys land) is unable to see the castle in distinct exactness or even approach it, despite its being outlined "distinctly in the clear air" (16):[9]

> It was neither an old knightly castle, nor a showy new structure, but rather an extensive complex of buildings, a few of them that were two stories, but most of them were low and crowded close together . . . K. saw only a single tower, and could not make out whether it was a residence or belonged to a church. Flocks of crows were circling around it; . . . It was a round building, partly covered with ivy. There were small windows, with the sun streaming in—there was something ludicrous about the sight, as it was built into the shape of a balcony at the top, with insecure, irregular battlements, crumbling as if drawn by an anxious or careless child as they stood out, zigzag fashion, against the blue sky. (16–17)

The topography here is comparable to Klee's visuals—not word for word, but in patterns, energy, and texture. Kafka's description of the castle is a hazy, imprecise, though detailed topography, and its function reaches across several planes. As in Klee's "Credo," the description provides a medium for the plot, the mood, and the movement of the story: this topographical center could be argued as the city or arena that Simmel refers to as the topography for the modernist individual, albeit very provincial considering the mass of ivy and the flock of crows. Kafka even refers to the castle as that which one could take for a "small city" (16). The topography is foreboding, not only evoking how the castle reaches into each of the characters' lives, decisions, and actions but also setting the mood for K.'s stay and the events that are to come. This includes examples such as K's inability to reach the castle, to have a meeting with the high castle official Klamm, to have more than a dysfunctional relationship with Frieda the barmaid, and to control his laughable assistants. But while the picture is not exact, there is still a coherent structure. The topography becomes evocative, and there is a vague resonance, or an acrobatic, dancing movement caused by the colors (Klee) or words (Kafka), creating an intuitive experience.

This movement is essential to Klee and Kafka. Paths for both artists are always ambiguous and the direction is never clear, but at the same time there is a struggle against paralysis. For example, in Klee's most famous painting, *Hauptwege und Nebenwege* (fig. 9.3), depicting a series of strata that form into large paths, one can only deliberate on the network of paths as a set of possibilities. Different viewpoints are possible, but none can be absolute. Incidentally, Klee completed his most iconic work after a trip to Egypt. Most interpretations read the painting as obviously representing Egyptian grain fields, interspersed with the Nile. It is a bright, radiant, and timeless landscape that reaches toward the river, as indicated by the wide swaths of blue at the top. In Kafka's *Der Verschollene* (The Man Who Disappeared, 1927) Karl Rossmann's direction—like the painting—is always ambiguous, and the fragment's inconsistencies lend itself to a network of topographies and possibilities as if the paths were visualized by Klee. This fragment is not set in a remote country with a castle, but rather in the newly formed America. Karl Rossmann comes to New York as an immigrant teenager following a scandal with a housemaid in Germany. His first encounter is with a stoker for a ship who has also come into difficulties, but the story jumps from episode to episode, detailing various encounters Karl has in America. In terms of topography, in Kafka's narrative the places are already changed from what the reader has instant access to via the place name to what Kafka writes. For example: In *Der Verschollene*, San Francisco is in the East and not the West, and a bridge links New York with Boston instead of Brooklyn. By confusing the place names, Kafka distorts any type of metonymic meaning connected to the topography, even if, to quote Klee, "the main action can be in the landscape or the main action can be in the artist. Conflict between the subjective and the objective yields perfect unity."[10] Wolfgang Iser's theory of narrative comes close to explaining Kafka's playful frustration of the topography. He explains narrative tension as a triad of the real, the fictive, and the imaginary. In this triad, the referential reality and fictional features "do not constitute an end or an entity unto themselves. Rather, they provide the medium through which a third element emerges"—the imaginary.[11] In this third element of fictional replacements of real place names, Kafka highlights that in this America there is no exclusive path. The narrative is open, full of space, energy, and forward movement. Similar to Klee,

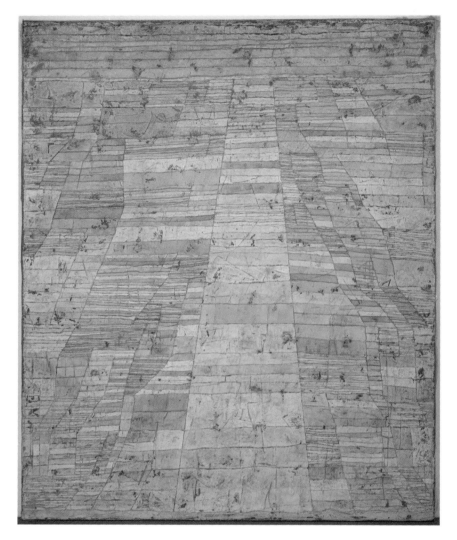

Figure 9.3. Paul Klee, Hauptwege und Nebenwege (Highways and Byways),
1929. Oil on canvas, 83.7 x 67.5 cm. Museum Ludwig, Cologne, Germany.
Photo: Sabrina Walz © Rheinisches Bildarchiv, rba_d039386_01.

through the topography, the writing and story resist confinement and
inertia. When Rossmann enters New York harbor, the first thing he sees is
a *German* Statue of Liberty, but he presents it with an aura of movement:
"Her arm with the sword loomed newly aloft and around her form wafted
the free and fresh air."[12] And a short time later, in the "stoker" episode,
Rossmann looks out of the boat's window and sees a busy harbor full of

Figure 9.4. Paul Klee, Hafenscene (Harbor Scene), 1923, 163. Watercolor on primed paper on cardboard, 23 x 31 cm. Sara Hildén Art Museum, Tampere, Finland.

barges, zooming motorboats and swimmers: "A movement without end, and much restlessness, transmitted by the impatient element of the helpless people and their work!" (18). As a topographical metaphor, the harbor scenes are a precursor, a foreshadowing of Rossmann's travels, and a concrete visual to Rossmann's path and story. The "stoker" episode takes place in the city and the tempo is fast, strange, and somewhat alienating, from the commotion surrounding his lost baggage to the drama of befriending the stoker. But Karl does not try to preserve his identity; he moves from station to station, characters surface and disappear, and his journey becomes a strange, turbulent, and restless ride.

While it is tempting to understand Kafka's topography solely as a reproduction of a hierarchical world that structures itself with status, bureaucracy, guilt, victimization, and absurd systems, to do so would suggest that Kafka's world is ordered with great precision, instead of using forms (to use Klee's language) that offer a "formal symphony" of the "possibilities of variation. . . . The work of art, too, is above all a process of creation; it is never experienced as a mere product" (*CC*, 6–7). For example, Klee's *Hafenszene* (fig. 9.4) and Kafka's *Der Verschollene* are the product of dynamic activities. Both should be viewed not as static, or as frozen in the moment, but as movement. In one of his Bauhaus lectures and in his *Pedagogical Sketchbook*, Klee discusses a type of multidimensionality that is found in overlapping forms and techniques and perspectives.[13] He is offering not only a spatial overwriting of events but also a temporal one. His images present a simultaneous set of events: the ships in his harbor slides overlap, but the viewer should consider all the possible dynamic relations between the lines, shapes, and colors. This kind of overwriting is also the essence of *Der Verschollene* and Karl's constant movement. The topography creates a nexus of connection and estrangement and simultaneously of isolation and emancipation. For Karl, no one station stands alone, and each one adds to his composition. He describes his impression of America shortly after he leaves his uncle's house:

> The bridge that connected New York with Boston hung delicately over the Hudson and trembled, when one squinted. It appeared to be completely empty, and under it stretched the inanimate and smooth band of water. Everything in the big cites appeared to be empty and uselessly constructed. One could hardly tell any difference between the big and small houses. In the invisible depths of the streets life went on and about in its own way, but above ground there was nothing to see but a light haze, which didn't really move but appeared to be chaseable without much effort. Even in the ports, the biggest in the world, peace had settled in for a bit, and one might have believed, undoubtedly influenced by a memory of an earlier view from a distance, that one could see a ship, pushing forward slowly. But one could not follow it for long; it disappeared from view and could not be seen again. (90)[14]

The spatial topography here collapses into itself—the city, streets, and harbor merge in the haze, and the haze connects the entire topography into one temporal moment. There is no bustling tempo of city life in which we see individual struggles, but rather a genesis of something larger—a simultaneous picture of the past, present, and future. In this, Kafka is channeling Klee's idea of the artist as philosopher and shows the world as one possibility of many.

Furthermore, one can read the same dynamic structure in *Das Schloß*, or even Kafka's *Der Prozess* (The Trial, 1925). In *Das Schloß*, the fragmented topography goes beyond the castle, and the texture of it becomes more vibrant—it is not alienating in its description but suggests something less mutable, albeit ungraspable. As a result, the precision throws the metonymy of meaning off balance. The topography of flux is comparable to a game. Klee plays games with tones and shapes the way a child might play with building blocks. In Klee's *Burg und Sonne* (fig. 9.5), it is easy to discern the recognizable landscape motif that is reminiscent of Kafka's castle—realistic and recognizable influences, and yet simultaneously abstract and subjective. Klee's picture is composed of bright and colorful

Figure 9.5. Paul Klee, Burg und Sonne (Castle and Sun), 1928. Canvas.
Erich Lessing / Art Resource, NY.

triangles and rectangles with a sun shining apart from the structure, but still created by the lines. The variety of geometric shapes adds depth to an otherwise abstract painting. Klee draws parallels with the child's ability to bring together—without self-consciousness, but rather with intuition—representation, decoration, and imagination. Consider again his quote from his diary that "the main action can be in the landscape, or the main action can be in the artist. Conflict between the subjective and the objective yields perfect unity" (236). Equally, Kafka plays games with the various scenes in his storytelling, and he even suggests that it was a "child's hand" that designed the castle's structure: Do we smile or squirm when K. and Frieda awkwardly roll on the taproom floor? Are we horrified and indignant, or do we chuckle at the schoolhouse incident when the school cat frightens K. and Frieda during the night, and K. punches an assistant, hurts the cat, and ultimately irritates the teachers? And do we guffaw or become irritated (like K.) with the assistants clamoring to get back into the schoolhouse?

And similarly, the storytelling style is simultaneously humorous and perplexing in *Der Prozess*. Also a fragment, the narrative centers on the protagonist Josef K, who wakes up one morning to police in his room. The police inform him that he is on trial, but Josef K cannot find out what he is accused of. The narrative follows K's quest to understand the accusation, protest his innocence, and delve into the judicial system. In one such scene K. converses with the painter Titorelli. He notes that Titorelli should paint a realistic portrait, but Titorelli dismisses his comment and asserts that even though he paints their portraits, he has never seen the court figures— it's all just an invention. From this lens, "the totally of the whole" (to use Klee's words) is less the singular picture of K. trying to get into the castle, or Joseph K's wrangling with the courts, but more about the (playful) variety of meanings that is implied in each of the conversations and experiences.

This same playfulness is coupled with movement. When Josef K. (ironically mistaken as a house painter) notes one of Titorelli's portrait paintings, "made with pastel colors and pale and unclear. . . . [Titorelli took] a pastel crayon from a small table and he added a few strokes to the edges of the figure but without making it any clearer . . . 'That's the figure of justice,' said the painter, finally. 'Now I see,' said K., 'here's the blindfold and here are the scales. But aren't those wings on her heels, and isn't she moving?'"[15] The ensuing discussion concerns justice and victory and the figure is cloaked in shadow. The fact that Titorelli himself usually paints moorland landscapes and gloomy themes that no one takes seriously hearkens to the inability to grasp something concrete—a good metaphor of Josef K's journey. For Klee—and in many of Kafka's stories—it is the most exact observation and subsequent contemplation of something's realistic nature that allows for the portrayal of the object to be simultaneously abstract and objective. Consider also the description of Gregor in *Die Verwandlung* (The Metamorphosis) to understand how a human turned vermin would look: from the image of his legs wiggling in the air to trying to roll over. Yet that image (or ability to name it exactly) is abstract, if not absurd. Walter Benjamin, in a letter to Gerhard Scholem, wrote: "Kafka lives in a *complementary* world. (In this he is closely related to Klee, whose work in painting is just as essentially *solitary* as Kafka's work in literature)."[16] Examples of Klee's work dating from 1892 to 1930, document his persistent interest in cartography, but he also learned from maps how to break away from three-dimensional illusionism. Just as historical places such as Prague and Bohemian castles, and also travel reports of America, grounded Kafka's literary world, the maps provided Klee with models of visual images that give specific information about visible reality. Both could then construct a vision with recognizable topographical motifs and symbolic content. In doing so, both generated a dynamic tension between symbolic and iconic representations of space.

But a better example of where recognizable landscape motifs are encoded with thematic and symbolic content is better exemplified in Kafka's *Der Verschollene*. Carl Steiner has already pointed out that historically America has been depicted in German literary studies as that big symbol "full of countless and diverse possibilities, a sanctuary for the oppressed and demoralized Europeans, an asylum for the persecuted."[17] Steiner places *Der Verschollene* as part of a general development of a literary topos, from Goethe's *Wilhelm Meister*, Auerbach's Keller, and even later Karl May, the popular writer who wrote stories about the American West. He does argue, however, that Kafka doesn't use America as an asylum, but rather as a place where Karl becomes a victim of circumstances, as a place where he fights for existence. Certainly one can read the descriptions about the exceedingly loud and active hotel dormitory (that incidentally was constantly swathed in a Klee-like haze of workers' cigarette smoke) as one in which one's individuality is oppressed: workers were playing at all hours, getting ready, washing, and wrestling. For the sleep-deprived, the scene is stress-inducing, but also playful:

> The sleeping hall was not a quiet bedroom. While everyone had different times of free time during twelve hours that consisted of eating, sleeping, leisurely enjoyments and other jobs, the dorm was always busy. . . . Consequently, every bed stood in its own cloud of smoke and everything was covered in a general haze . . . it was impossible to enforce, although the majority agreed in principle that the lights in the dorm should be turned off at night. (118–19)

There is no sense of loneliness, anxiety, or horror, but liveliness. This isn't Gregor's boxed-in and isolated room from *Die Verwandlung*, or the suffocating streets of Joseph K.'s Prague, nor is it the inapproachable bleary castle. Karl is lamenting his lack of sleep, but the inability to sleep keeps him moving to the next station. Because of the haze, we can use the techniques from Klee to create polyvalent connections, taking different perspectives and creating a variety of meanings. Moreover, this is not the first instance of haze: when Karl first takes up with his uncle, he lives in a high building and his view is hazy. In the distance "out of a heavy haze" looms a cathedral, and the street always has "ever crowded traffic . . . as if a glass ceiling hung over the street and could at any minute break with great force" (35). Karl's travels with his friends Delamarche and Robinson are often swathed in fog (while on the road), or smoke (while in a room with Brunhelda). The haze suggests that it is the process and not the station or the endpoint that is more important. In other words, one cannot deny isolation, but neither can one forget about emancipation. In his *Creative Credo*, Klee writes: "A formal cosmos is ultimately created from abstract elements, independent of their groups as concrete objects or abstract things such as numbers and letters" (10). For example, in all of Klee's works up until this point, or, to use an example, his *Komposition mit Fenstern* (Composition of Windows, 1919), there are a variety of shapes of different colors—dark and light, and when they are placed next to each other, these abstract elements show a tension between architecture and image, between the abstract and the objective, and between the decorative and the illustrative. But in the process of analyzing, there is, despite the abstract individual elements, a single poetic wholeness.

And in all Kafka's works we are still able to piece together wholeness. In *Das Schloss* we read through fragments and strange scenes and yet are still able to garner the oppressing and absurd nature of a higher authority that the topography reflects, or at least we are able to peer through various windows and reconcile a cosmos. For example, in "Amalia's story," Olga explains the whole alleged affair of their family's downfall when the castle official Sortini spies the lovely Amalia and she rebuffs his advances, or when K. becomes a janitor for the school. Yet through these two equally unrelated events, K. not only discovers the lives of various villagers but also finds connections between Olga and Barnabas, between Frieda and Olga, between Amalia and the landlady, and between Barnabas and the castle. Individually they are abstract compositions, but together they ultimately tie K. closer to the village. Paradoxically, the series of unrelated events frees him from Frieda—she mistakes his visit to Olga and Amalia as a romantic betrayal and leaves him. Frieda and not K., it turns out, wants to leave the village: "If you want to keep me, we have to immigrate, anywhere, to the south of France, to Spain." K. responds, "What could have trapped me in this terrible country, except for the longing to stay here?" (180). The oscillating process of K.'s isolation and emancipation is not a simplistic voyeur's view, but rather an obstructive view that can be viewed as a poetic whole. Another example is in *Die Verwandlung*, when Gregor peers out of the window. He sees the hospital across the street, and he says if he did not know on what street he lived, "he would have believed he was looking out from his window into the solitude, in which the gray sky and the gray earth unite indistinguishably" (76–77). Again, it is a fragmented and hazy topography, but the whole scene is metonymical in meaning. Gregor is losing sight of his former self as a part of the system in the city. His transformation is a process that leads to the real metamorphosis of the story—his sister's blooming sexuality. But like the hazy view of the hospital, we gain lucidity or understanding in stages and in blocks, and while the journey is something foreign and intangible—waking up as an unwanted vermin—we certainly recognize it. Thus it becomes more than a singular quest or a fundamental principle, but rather a journey that links the accidental (like alienation) to something essential (like puberty). Ultimately, there is not a collage in Klee's work—it does not remind us of Dadaism, which celebrates chaos and, by default, alienation. At the same time, though it is fragmented, there is a sense of the whole (albeit ungraspable) in Kafka. Like Klee's blocks that ultimately create a rhythm or order, Kafka's characters, too, search for belonging in un-orderly topographies. Even though they are constantly frustrated, all characters still persist in putting their topography of experiences together, creating a precarious balancing act.

Haze does not cloak the two artists completely, however. In the Oklahoma Theater episode of *Der Verschollene*, Karl Rossmann joins a welcoming crowd, and he gets on a train to see the "carefree nature" of America. When he arrives, he sees a landscape of angels: a hundred women dressed as angels in white cloths and wearing wings on their backs are blowing golden trumpets. They are standing on different sized pedestals, although one cannot see the pedestals, because they are covered by the angel costumes" (203). The women are balancing precariously in the wind, and by the end of the fragment Rossmann has found a place to fit in. In fact, Kafka confessed to Max Brod that this was to be where Rossmann ended his journey. This episode is similar to Klee's *Seiltänzer* (fig. 9.6) or even one of his many angel representations. Klee started drawing such figures as acrobats or jugglers around 1912. Constance Naubert-Riser writes that it was his "means of suggesting the modern artist's vulnerability and marginality in an unsettled art market. Given the precariousness of the times, the act put on for an audience by a circus performer symbolized perfectly the situation of the artist who was obliged to 'take risks' in order to attract attention and carve out a niche for himself in a market that placed a premium on innovation."[18] The face of the tightrope walker is open and unsketched. Through the face, however, Klee draws two straight horizontal lines connecting the eyes visually to the ladder. The lines of the ladder and the other spots are thematically connected as eyes, suggesting a composition of a cross and references to Christianity that connects with the eye of imagination.[19] The theme of balance was paramount to Klee and in a lecture to his Bauhaus students, he said that the "tightrope walker with his pole [is a] 'symbol of the balance of forces.' He holds the forces of gravity in balance (weight and counterweight). He is a pair of scales."[20] The tightrope walker in this print is balanced on a structure of horizontal, vertical, and diagonal lines that looks precarious but perfectly balanced. And in terms of angels—he drew more than 130 of them—Klee viewed them as winged hybrids—half man and half heavenly beings that serve as mediators between the world here and the other world. While *Angelus Novus* is most famously connected to Walter Benjamin's notion of history as an ongoing process of catastrophe, many of the angels reflect his situation at the present time.

This lack of haze in Kafka too represents balance. Kafka notoriously wanted to belong, while also wanting to be free. In wanting to leave Prague, he wrote Max Brod in 1922 (the same year he wrote *Das Schloss*): "I am away from home and must always write home, even if any home of

Figure 9.6. Paul Klee, Seiltänzer (Tightrope Walker), 1923. Lithograph, 44 x 26.8 cm. AM81-65-872. © CNAC/MNAM/Dist. RMN-Grand Palais / Art Resource, NY.

Figure 9.7. Paul Klee, Wandbild aus dem Tempel der Sehnsucht (Mural from the Temple of Longing), 1922. Watercolor and transferred printing ink on gesso on fabric mounted on cardboard, 30.2 x 39.4 cm. Metropolitan Museum of Art, The Berggruen Klee Collection, 1984.

mine has long since floated away into eternity."[21] Scholars regularly remember that Kafka, unlike his contemporaries, stayed in Prague until September 1923, when he finally left Prague for Berlin with Dora Dymant. The topographies in both of the artists' works are in essence mythic, in that they express a timelessness that is not stuck in stasis. It is not the type of modernism in which the self is cut off from the past and present and hurtles forward at a dizzying pace so it cannot take root. Rather, these visual journeys find root beyond the city and exhibit themselves best in concretizing an epic totality outside the city and in a larger and grander visual topography, thus finding permanence.

In conclusion, from the perspective of Klee, his *Wandbild aus dem Tempel der Sehnsucht* (fig. 9.7)—which incidentally was also completed the same year as Kafka's *Das Schloss*—depicts the paradox of paralysis and movement, and of modernist energy. There are the semblances of walls, or houses, but they are still fragments with an energy in the form of arrows shooting out to somewhere other than home. For Klee, approaching an external landscape was not a matter for interpretation but a matrix of experience—there is in his painting scale, color, atmosphere, memories, and continuity. And topography is nothing more that the writing of experience. Thus the forward and eternal energy that is implied in Klee's arrows is similar to that of the characters in Kafka's narratives. They are always moving, changing, and acting contrary to the norms. Their existence gives depth and complexity to Kafka's narrative topography. Kafka plants subtle clues in the narrative that suggest that the castle is not the monolithic enemy that K. imagines it to be, even though the haze that envelops the castle in the opening lines of the book never quite lifts. In fact, Kafka told Brod that K. was supposed to die, worn out and exhausted. On his deathbed, "the community was to assemble, and from the castle itself the word was to come that though K.'s legal claim to live in the village was not valid, . . . he was nonetheless to be permitted to live and work there."[22] That ending is certainly compatible with the underlying paradoxical spirit of the novel—he may be doomed, but he will traverse this topography in order, according to Brod "to get clear about ultimate things" (ix). Or, in *Der Verschollene*, when Rossmann is kicked out of his uncle's house, he finds himself on the open road, amazed, and no longer in a city. "He could not determine with certainty in which direction New York lay . . . Finally he said to himself that he didn't necessarily have to go to New York, where no particular person expected him. So he chose a direction and went on his way" (64–65)—modernist impulses full of paradoxical movements.

Notes

[1] Georg Simmel, "The Metropolis and Mental Life," in *Simmel on Culture*, ed. David Frisby and Mike Featherstone (London: Sage, 1997), 184.

[2] Leena Eilittä, "Kafka and Visuality," *Kulturpoetik* 6, no. 2 (2006): 233.

[3] Rezae Riese Hubert, "Paul Klee: Modernism in Art and Literature," in *Modernism: Challenge and Perspectives* (Urbana: University of Illinois Press, 1986), 213.

[4] Paul Klee, *The Diaries of Paul Klee: 1898–1919* (Berkeley: University of California Press, 1964), 208.

[5] Paul Klee, "Creative Credo," in *Paul Klee: Watercolors, Drawings, and Writings*, 5 (New York: Abrams, 1969). Further references to this work are given in the text using the abbreviation *CC*.

[6] Paul Klee, *Paul Klee: The Thinking Eye; The Notebooks of Paul Klee*, ed. Jürg Spiller (London: G. Wittenborn, 1961).

[7] Andrew Kagen, *Paul Klee: Art and Music* (Ithaca, NY: Cornell University Press, 1983), 119.

[8] Paul Klee, *Pedagogical Sketchbook*, trans. Sibyl Moholy-Nagy (New York: Präger, 1956).

9 Franz Kafka, *Das Schloß* (Frankfurt am Main: Fischer, 1997), 16. All translations of excerpts from this work are mine. Further references are given in the text using the page numbers alone.

10 Klee, *The Thinking Eye*, 195.

11 Wolfgang Iser, *The Fictive and Imaginary: Charting Literary Anthropology* (Baltimore: Johns Hopkins University Press, 1993), 1.

12 Franz Kafka, *The Complete Stories* (New York: Schocken, 1972), 7. Further references are given in the text using page numbers alone.

13 Klee, *Pedagogical Sketchbook*.

14 Franz Kafka, *Der Verschollene* (Frankfurt am Main: Fischer, 1983), 90. All translations of excerpts from this work are mine. Further references are given in the text using page numbers alone.

15 Franz Kafka, *Der Prozess* (Frankfurt am Main: Fischer, 1979), 186.

16 Walter Benjamin, "Letter to Gerhard Scholem," June 12, 1938, in *The World of Franz Kafka*, ed. J. P. Stern (New York: Holt, 1980), 176–77.

17 Carl Steiner, "How American is *Amerika?*" *Journal of Modern Literature* 6, no. 3 (1977): 455–65; here, 455.

18 Constance Naubert-Riser, *The Great Parade: Portrait of the Artist as Clown*, ed. Jean Clair (New Haven, CT: Yale University Press, 2004), 150.

19 David Ferrell Krell, "The Way Back Down: Paul Klee's Heights and Depths," *Research in Phenomenology* 43, no. 3 (2013): 336.

20 Paul Klee, *Paul Klee* (New York: Parkstone International, 2013), 200.

21 Franz Kafka, *Letters to Friends, Family, and Editors*, trans. Richard Winston and Clara Winston (New York: Schocken, 1990), 340.

22 Kafka, *Das Schloß*, ix.

10: Synthesis and Transtextuality: The Jewish Reinvention of Chinese Mythical Stories in "Shanghai Ghetto"

Weijia Li

FROM 1938 to 1941, between 17,000 and 20,000 European Jewish refugees fled the Nazi terror to the Chinese harbor city Shanghai, the only place that did not enforce requirements for travel or immigration documents, because of the so-called "International Settlement" that was established by the British and French colonial powers. In 1943 the Japanese occupation authority forced the Jewish refugees in Shanghai to move to a restricted area in the city, known as the "Designated Area for Stateless Refugees," and often referred as the "Shanghai Ghetto." Thus the refugees' hope to use Shanghai as a temporary waiting room for their transfer to North America or elsewhere was shattered. They ended up spending a decade in China, during which time their quest for a culturally enriching life brought to fruition numerous Jewish writings on China.

One notable example is Willy Tonn, a German-Jewish émigré who during his exile in China from 1939 to 1949 contributed numerous articles to German-Jewish newspapers and English periodicals published in Shanghai. His experiment with a literary hybrid of various intercultural and interreligious elements resulted in several mythical narratives—legends, parables or tales—published in Shanghai's major English newspapers.

In this essay I investigate the aesthetic apparatus in Tonn's reinvention of "Chinese" tales that incorporate diverse European and Asian cultural elements. My aim is threefold. First, from a hermeneutic perspective, I will illustrate how Tonn's storytelling strives for an aesthetic synthesis of Western and Eastern mythological narratives, which was in line with the search for interreligious, cultural *Synthese* (synthesis) in the spirit of Jewish renewal, a cultural movement during the Weimar Republic. Second, my intertextual analysis will reveal that Tonn's narrative can be seen as a playful experiment of transtextuality that transcends the discourse of originality concerning fictions dealing with transnational mythological themes. Finally, adopting a transcultural angle, I will argue that Tonn's writing encompasses Martin Buber's notion of the oriental spirit of Judaism.

Willy Tonn and China

Willy Tonn was born on January 28, 1902 in a German-Jewish family in Berlin.[1] In 1920 he became a student at the Friedrich Wilhelm University Berlin. From the summer semester 1921–22 to the winter semester 1924, Tonn completed a total of seventeen Chinese courses taught by renowned Sinology scholars such as Erich Schmitt (1893–1955), Erich Haenisch (1880–1966), and Otto Franke (1863–1946). These courses focused on reading Chinese authentic texts, mostly classics on Confucianism, Taoism, and Buddhism, along with other selected works in Chinese literature.[2]

It is highly plausible that Martin Buber sparked Tonn's interest in China. Tonn exchanged correspondence with Buber from the 1920s to the 1950s, a long-lasting intellectual interaction spanning Germany, China, and finally Israel, where they both settled for the rest of their lives. Buber's view of China and his encounter with Chinese mysticism played a significant role in the discourse of cultural Zionism and the idea of Jewish renewal. Buber's essay "The Teaching of the Tao." published as an afterword for his *Reden und Gleichnisse des Tschuang Tse* (Sayings and Parables of Chuang-tzu, 1911) had "a great impact on the German Youth Movement."[3] His notion of the oriental spirit of Judaism is anchored in his encounter with Chinese Taoism, a potential inspiration for Tonn's decision to pursue Chinese Studies. Reciprocally, Tonn's training in Chinese language and culture also enabled him to contribute to Buber's intensive encounter with Chinese Taoism in the 1920s. For example, Buber discussed with Tonn in a letter dated March 2, 1927 the translation of Chinese Taoist poems.[4] Tonn and Buber were both included in a "Chinese" circle around Richard Wilhelm, the renowned German translator of *Tao Te Ching* and other Chinese classics. In 1928, Buber delivered a speech entitled "China und Wir" (China and Us) dealing with Chinese Taoism, at Richard Wilhelm's China Institute at the University of Frankfurt.[5] Tonn contributed articles to the *Ostasiatische Rundschau*, founded and edited by Richard Wilhelm.[6] As such, Tonn's study of Chinese language and culture enabled him to play a unique and essential role as a culture mediator during his exile in China.

During his exile years in China, writing and publishing served as Tonn's intellectual fulfillment, something that was essential for émigré scholars. On June 1, 1939, merely a month after his arrival in Shanghai, he published a translation of several Chinese humorous pieces from the Ming Dynasty (1368–1644 CE) in the *Gelbe Post*, Shanghai's only German periodical focusing on East Asian cultures, founded in 1939 by A. J. Storfer, a Jewish refugee from Vienna. In 1939 alone, Tonn contributed nine articles to the *Gelbe Post* including book reviews, essays on Chinese customs, and translations of Chinese folklore. In addition, he soon began to contribute articles written in English, as it was not only the lingua franca in the foreign-controlled international settlement in Shanghai, but also the most commonly used language besides Chinese in the publishing sectors and business world of the metropolitan city. In the following years, Tonn published essays on Chinese culture and art, and free adaptations of Chinese literary works, in *The China Journal*, one of the most influential English magazines published in Shanghai, whose editor-in-chief Bruno Kroker was a German refugee as well. At the same time he earned his own column "Der ferne Osten" (The Far East) in the largest German-Jewish daily at that time, the *Shanghai Jewish Chronicle*. The years of 1941 and 1942 marked the most fruitful period for Tonn's writing. He became a regular contributor to major English newspapers published in Shanghai, such as *The Shanghai Sunday Times* and the *Shanghai Evening Post & Mercury*.

Thus Tonn emerged as Shanghai's most productive émigré writer with unparalleled China-expertise among the Central European Jewish refugees in the city. Besides his essays introducing Chinese culture, philosophy, art, music, and classic literature to Western readers, Tonn wrote several fictional works, mostly anecdotes or stories with adaptations of Chinese literary motifs or themes. A close examination of his reinvention of these "Chinese" stories represents a unique case for understanding the trajectory of the Jewish search for interreligious, aesthetic *Synthese* (synthesis).

Reinvention of "Chinese" Tales

Tonn's literary experiment with a hybrid of various intercultural and interreligious elements reached its high in August and September 1942 when he published a series of "Chinese" tales in the English newspaper the *Shanghai Evening Post & Mercury*. One of those tales, "The Lucky Fisherman's Dream"[7] is a story that adopts elements of Chinese folklore.

In "The Lucky Fisherman's Dream" the protagonist Ling Mei-ho was a poor fisherman from Ningbo, a Chinese coastal city. One day, he sailed out on the ocean and landed on a "magic island," where he discovered a marvelous palace belonging to the "Dragon-King Hai Long Wang." He then prayed for the mighty power of the Dragon-King and lamented his harsh life as a fisherman. He wished that the Dragon-King, the sovereign ruler of the sea, could "render the sea favorable" to him. Yet while he was praying, the island started to tremble, and he soon realized that the alleged magic island was in fact the back of a "gigantic sea serpent." He was thrown into the ocean and fought for his life in the waves. Eventually he reached an unknown seashore covered with stiff rocks. Guided by a mystical "thin voice" in the air, he then entered a cave, where he encountered a kingdom of ants and was welcomed by the "King of the Mighty Purple Ants." Those "magnanimous and invincible" ants were the rival of the sea serpents and thus decided to protect the fisherman. To make up for the loss of his boat, the king of ants guided him to a sacred place called "Kin-hu-men," meaning "Gate to the Gold Lake." The ants then dove into the lake many times and each brought back a half-gram of gold each time until sunrise. The king of ants then handed over to the fisherman the pile of gold dug out by the ants from the Gold Lake. After saying goodbye to the kingdom of ants, the fisherman left for home, yet he fell asleep on the way. At the end of the story, the fisherman woke up from his mysterious dream and found himself lying in his boat and "blinking upon the infinite picture of sky and sea."

At least at the semantic level, "The Lucky Fisherman's Dream" stays true to its Chinese "authenticity" by faithfully adopting Chinese mythical themes and elements such as the Dragon-King and actual names of the geographical locations in the story. At the hermeneutic level, Tonn's story invites a Taoist interpretation of the fisherman's dream. The fact that the fisherman woke up from his dream of a mysterious adventure suggests a Taoist observation of human beings' fate in their interaction with infinite nature. Neither his worshiping the mighty power of the Dragon-King nor the generosity of the gold-digging ants would change the fisherman's life, a life deeply embedded in the enormity of nature. Despite this "Chinese-ness" suggested in the narrative, however, Tonn's story is not just an imitation of a Taoist tale: it aims to create a synthetic mythical facet in the narrative by weaving together mythical traditions from different cultures.

Synthesis of Mythical Elements in Storytelling

"The Lucky Fisherman's Dream" can be seen as Tonn's transnational literary experiment that blends elements from European and Asian mythologies and cultural traditions in this "Chinese" tale. The mythical figure of the sea serpent in the story warrants a closer look if we wish to appreciate Tonn's apparatus for achieving such a synthesis of Western and Eastern mythological narratives. In the story, the fisherman was dismayed when he found out that the island was "in fact the back of a gigantic sea serpent. The alleged "dragon" dove into the sea, and a loud voice exclaimed: 'Fool! Your death is pronounced! You dare come hither and pray, indeed!'" In the following passage, the "Mighty Purple Ants" who provided refuge for the fisherman detest the sea serpents. The king of the ants denounces his rival in the sea: "Those absurd fluttering and colorless sea serpents, ridiculously calling themselves 'white dragons.'" Whereas in Chinese folklore dragons or "Long" enjoy a largely sacred status and thus serve as a supreme, iconographic subject for worship,[8] a sea serpent is a rare if not completely absent motif in the Chinese cultural tradition. Likely due to the predominantly inner-continental characteristics of Chinese culture, it is hardly possible to find references to sea serpents in any major works of

Chinese literature and folklore. On the other hand, sea serpents or sea monsters represent a recurrent motif in many European and Eurasian maritime cultures, such as the sea serpents in *Laocoön* and the sea monster (kētos) of Ethiopia in Greek mythology.[9] Indeed, the sea serpent as a mythological theme is mostly depicted in oceanic cultures of the Western hemisphere, from Old Norse mythology to Mediterranean folklores. Along with sea serpents, sea monsters are a common motif in Judaic and biblical literary traditions, such as the Leviathan that is often referenced in both the Tanakh and the Old Testament.

Like the sea-serpent depiction, the mysterious gold-fetching ants are foreign to Chinese folklore. Although ants are featured in Chinese fable tradition, no reference to gold-fetching ants can be found in any known Chinese tales and stories. Yet interestingly, one can easily find literal references to "gold-digging ants" in the works by the ancient Greek historian Herodotus (484–425 BCE) who, as a matter of fact, provided an account of gold-digging ants in his monumental work *The Histories* (also referred to as *The History*). In his depiction of the Indians living in the desert in the Bactria region of north India, Herodotus writes:

> In this desert, and sand, there are ants that are in bigness lesser than dogs but larger than foxes. Some of them have been hunted and captured and kept at the palace of the Persian king. These ants make their dwelling underground, digging out the sand in much the same fashion as ants do in Greece, and they are also very like them in form. The sand that they dig out has gold in it.[10]

Thus Tonn's "Chinese" tale may also have roots in ancient Greek mythology. Obviously, it is hardly possible to identify the single origin of those mythical elements or to assign them to any distinct national cultural tradition. In this sense, Tonn's storytelling penetrates various mythical dimensions across national and ethnic "borders," thus essentially serving as a synthesis of different cultural and religious elements.[11] In the story about the Chinese fisherman's dream, Tonn employs the motif of dreaming, a common motif in both Judaic-biblical and Asian literary traditions, as a vehicle and the agent for achieving literary synthesis. As in the fisherman story, it is easy to identify as a central theme in Tonn's many other writings on China the coalescence of Western and Eastern cultural references and the resemblance between European and Chinese traditions.

Tonn's interblending of Western and Eastern mythical elements speaks to Martin Buber's notion of synthesis between Orient and Occident. The search for such "synthesis" is one of the most prevailing themes in the works of German-Jewish scholars and intellectuals during the Weimar Republic.[12] Synthesis is indeed a central theme in what Martin Buber referred to as the "Jewish Renaissance." In his writings, synthesis is a concept that "denotes above all the reciprocally creative meeting of the Orient and Occident."[13] Buber's encounter with Hinduism, Buddhism, and later Chinese Taoism, along with his engagement with German mystics, evidently set the stage for his revival of Jewish mysticism.[14] In 1909 he published *Ekstatische Konfessionen* (Ecstatic Confessions), an anthology on mystical traditions from various cultures, in which he collected Indian and Chinese mythical stories, along with Christian and Jewish legends. In the following years, Buber published two major collections of Chinese Taoist tales and ghost stories: *Reden und Gleichnisse des Tschuang Tse* (Sayings and Parables of Chuang-tsu, 1910) and *Chinesische Geister- und Liebesgeschichten* (Chinese Ghost and Love Stories, 1928). Yet, it appeared that Tonn aspired to extend what Buber had achieved in pursuit of synthesis. He clearly moved beyond simply collecting Eastern mythical themes or ghost stories. He sought ways of interblending European and Asian narrative traditions, which is reflected in his reinvention of some other "Chinese tales" that were published along with the fisherman story in the *Shanghai Evening Post & Mercury*: "The Beggar of Soochow" was a story depicting a penniless Chinese beggar's rise to successful businessman by defeating a Chinese gang, a re-creation of the Western urban legend in Chinese settings.[15] "Tang, The Wily General" is a playful parody of Carlo Gozzi's *Turandot* (1762).[16] "Pa-Pao's Golden Peach" is an invented story modeling Chinese fairy tales.[17] "Darwin Was Wrong: The Apes Found an Ancestor in Old Ah-Pei" was an imitation of traditional satirical fiction of the Ming Dynasty (1368–1644 CE), yet blended with European evolution theory.[18] Beyond his search for East-West synthesis, Tonn's storytelling also reveals the complexity of his intertextual engagement with transnational and transcultural referentiality, a discussion of which follows.

A Playful Experiment of Intertextuality

"The Lucky Fisherman" is not confined within a single Chinese mythical dimension; rather, it engages in traditions of Japanese ghost stories inspired by Chinese folklore. To illustrate the apparatus of intertextuality in the story, a close reading and examination of the text is in order. The arguably most intriguing passages in this "Chinese" tale are the first three paragraphs, which serve as a scenic description of the sea and provide the settings for the story:

> Azure eternity of depth lost in height, sea and sky interblending through luminous haze. The day is of spring, and the hour morning.
> Only sky and sea—one wide enormity. In the fore, ripples are catching a silvery light and threads of foam are swirling. A little farther off and motion is no more visible, nor anything else but color—dim warm blue of water widening away to melt into blue of air. Horizon there is none; only distance soaring into space, infinite

concavity hollowing before you and hugely arching above you, the color deepening with the height.

But far in the midway-azure there appears to hang a faint, faint, vision of an island. While palace towers and curved roofs glimmer, illumined by a soft sunshine—the Palace of the Dragon-King Hai Long Wang.[19]

The mythical quality of the opening scene illustrated in the first three paragraphs determines the fable-like settings of the story about the fisherman's adventure. Despite its clear reference to the Chinese mythological figure of the Dragon-King, some readers of Tonn's story published in Japanese-occupied Shanghai could probably have recognized the Japanese roots of the opening scene.

Indeed, the initial depiction of the seascape in "The Lucky Fisherman's Dream" is almost identical with the opening passage of "Hōrai," a Japanese story collected in the book *Kwaidan: Stories and Studies of Strange Things*, first published in 1904 by Lafcadio Hearn (1850–1904), a Greek-born American who lived in Japan from 1889 to 1904, best known for his writings on Japan and notably his collection of Japanese tales and ghost stories. Hearn's "Hōrai" starts as follows:

> Blue vision of depth lost in height,—sea and sky interblending through luminous haze. The day is of spring, and the hour morning.
>
> Only sky and sea,—one azure enormity . . . In the fore, ripples are catching a silver light, and threads of foam are swirling. But a little further off no motion is visible, nor anything save color: dim warm blue of water widening away to melt into blue of air. Horizon there is none: only distance soaring into space,—infinite concavity hollowing before you, and hugely arching above you,—the color deepening with the height. But far in the midway-blue there hangs a faint, faint version of the palace towers, with high roofs horned and curved like moons,—some shadowing of splendor strange and old, illumined by a sunshine soft as memory.[20]

Clearly, the vast majority of the text in the opening paragraphs in Tonn's story is largely identical with the first two paragraphs in Hearn's retelling of the Japanese tale "Hōrai." Does Tonn's excessive adoption of the text in "Hōrai" suggest an inconceivable act of "plagiarizing intertextuality"?[21] A keener examination of the interrelation between the two texts—both Western adaptations of Eastern mythical elements—will support interpretations that neither elicit an accusation of plagiarism nor support an argument for the restoration of originality. As such, the suggested interpretation will "move away and beyond the reductive and accusative discourse erected under the label of plagiarism."[22]

In Hearn's "Hōrai," the text passage immediately following the mysterious scenic description of the "azure enormity" may provide an insight into Tonn's motivation for his "plagiarizing borrowing." It reveals that the actual subject of the scenery description in "Hōrai" was a Japanese painting inspired by Chinese folklore: "What I have been trying to describe is . . . a Japanese painting on silk, . . . and the name of it is SHINKIRŌ, which signifies 'mirage.' But the shapes of the mirage are unmistakable. Those are the glimmering portals of Hōrai the blest; and those are the moony roofs of the Palace of the Dragon-King" (174). Hearn's reason for depicting the classical painting is to emphasize the mirage and its mysterious quality of an ancient vision. Thereafter, Hearn's narrative turns around to reject the conventional imagination of *Hōrai* as an Elysian place: "It is not true that sorrow and death never enter *Hōrai*—neither is it true that there is not any winter. The winter in *Hōrai* is cold;—and winds then bite to the bone."[23] At the end of "Hōrai," Hearn's narrative returns to the theme of mirage: "Remember that Hōrai is also called Shinkirō, which signifies mirage,—the Vision of the Intangible. And the vision is fading,— never again to appear save in pictures and poems and dreams."[24]

On the surface, Tonn's literal "borrowing" from Hearn's "Hōrai" could be seen as a "secret" intertextual reference, hence an act of plagiarism. The modern definition of plagiarism was established in the era of Romanticism, which valued the creativity and originality of artistic works, including literature.[25] Evidently, Tonn's story failed to use quotation marks for the "borrowed" text passage and it neglects to credit its source by indicating the reference to Hearn's "Hōrai." Yet I argue that Tonn's "plagiarism" was a playful experiment with intertextuality, a type of transtextual relationship between texts.[26] Specifically, for the readers of Tonn's story, mainly subscribers of the English newspaper *Shanghai Evening Post & Mercury* in the 1930s, the "Lucky Fisherman's Dream" not only revealed its transtextual interrelation with Hearn's "Hōrai," but also probably made the invisible quotation marks perceptible.

Lafcadio Hearn's writings about Japanese culture, including the collection *Kwaidan*, gained their popularity in the 1930s in China. Ironically, when Japan's aggression toward China heightened and the military attack on Shanghai took place in the early 1930s, Hearn's works were the "most widely read in China."[27] From 1930 to 1941, seven editions of *Kwaidan* were published. For many Chinese and Westerners, Hearn's writings about Japan became a means of making sense of the connection between Japanese Shintoism and its military aggression.[28] Hearn was known for his stylistic peculiarity, such as clustering of words of color, for example "azure eternity," "silver light," and "dim warm blue," as well as one of his most favorite themes, the "interblending" of sky and sea.

Alongside readers' familiarity with Hearn's works, the stylistic "break" between the scenic description of the "azure eternity" and the narrative of the fisherman's dream discloses an unsubtle transition from the settings of the story to its plot line—from texts borrowed from Hearn's "Hōrai" to

Tonn's own narrative of synthesis. Moreover, when "The Lucky Fisherman's Dream" was published in the *Shanghai Evening Post & Mercury*, its first two paragraphs on the seascape were printed in boldface, whereas the third paragraph depicting the Palace of the Dragon-King and the rest of the narrative were printed in regular typeface. Thus both stylistically and visually the scenic description of the seascape is largely a stand-alone segment in the story. To make the invisible quotation marks even more perceptible, echoing the first three paragraphs, Tonn ends his narrative in the final paragraph with the exact same scenic description of the sea, as he relates how the fisherman awoke from his dream:

> It was noon when the dazzling sunbeams awakened him. He found himself lying in his junk and blinking upon the infinite picture of sky and sea—one wide enormity—azure eternity of depth lost in height.
> . . .
>   Azure eternity of depth lost in height, sea and sky interblending through luminous haze. The day is of spring, and the hour noon.[29]

This final paragraph even has its own title, "Azure Eternity," a theme that is not directly involved in any aspect of the plot. Thus Tonn both starts and ends his narrative by borrowing from Hearn's text. In between, he continues to blend various mythical elements from different cultures. Consequently, we can interpret his plagiarizing transtextuality as a playful experiment with interliterary synthesis. His storytelling represents an attempt to reconcile cultural encounters and intersections between West and East, Europe and Asia, and China and Japan. From this perspective, the paradigm of his plagiarizing intertextuality shares the characteristics of what would be considered today the writings of postmodernity.

Moreover, Tonn's story is not merely a transtextually and transnationally blended tale. The story also serves as a reflection of his Shanghai exile. For the fisherman, the evil of the Dragon-King and the promise of the gold-digging ants only exist in dream. He has to wake up and face the azure eternity, endlessness both in time and space. For the Central European Jewish refugees in China, Shanghai provided a sanctuary, far away from war and mass murder in Europe. Yet its terrible economic conditions, unbearable climate and unhygienic environment, and its isolation from the rest of the world because of the breakout of the Pacific War, nonetheless imposed a hollow dream for the Jewish refugees who once hoped to use it as merely a waiting room for their further immigration to other parts of the world. The "lucky" fisherman's dream is an allusion to the Shanghai exile. Its quasi-secret reference to many Jewish refugees' lament about Shanghai is revealed when one reads Hearn's "Hōrai." The paradigm of demystification of the Hōrai-Elysium, "It is not true that sorrow and death never enter Hōrai;—neither is it true that there is not any winter," can find its parallels in many biographical accounts of refugee experiences in Shanghai.[30] By excessively borrowing from the description of the seascape in "Hōrai," Tonn extends his Shanghai parable into an "alien" text. Thus his storytelling fulfills Martin Buber's imagination of the "fully achieved parable as one that begins with the image and ends with a tale."[31]

In 1949, Tonn, like many other Zionism-minded Central European refugees, left Shanghai for Israel after ten years of oriental exodus in East Asia. In the newly founded Jewish state Tonn continued his project of bridging Western and Eastern cultures by organizing Israel's first East Asian art exhibition and editing a commented German edition of *Tao Te King*. He exemplified Buber's notion of the oriental spirit of Judaism, namely that the Jews' destiny is "to link Orient and Occident in fruitful reciprocity" and "to fuse the spirit of the East and the West in a new teaching."[32]

To conclude, inspired by Buber's notion of the oriental spirit of Judaism, Tonn's reinvention of Chinese tales employed a transnational, transtextual apparatus. Within the narrative scope, he created a synthesis of different mythical elements from various cultural and religious traditions. Beyond the textual level, his storytelling promotes intertextual and inter-literary dialogues and challenges the conventional mode of reading. Furthermore, from a cultural-historical point of view, Tonn's invention of Chinese tales resonates with Buber's idea of Jewish renewal and thus provides a unique case of German-Jewish writings on China, a paradigm of the German-Jewish-Chinese discourse reflected in literature, which deserves further exploration and close examination in the scholarship of German Studies, Jewish Studies, and Chinese Studies alike.

Notes

[1] Franz Steiner & Co., Material Part 1, Willy Tonn Collection 1920–88, Leo Baeck Institute, AR 7259, MF 862, Reels 1–4, Box 3, Addenda 4.

[2] Personal Papers, ibid., Box 1, Folder 1.

[3] Maurice Friedman, "Martin Buber and Asia," *Philosophy East and West* 26, no. 4 (1976): 411–26; here, 415.

[4] Letter from Buber dated March 2, 1927, Correspondence with Martin Buber, Willy Tonn Collection 1920–88, Leo Baeck Institute, AR 7259, MF 862, Reels 1–4, Box 1, Folder 6.

[5] Jonathan R. Herman, *I and Tao: Martin Buber's Encounter with Chuang Tzu* (*Albany: University of New York Press, 1996*), 242.

[6] Willy Tonn, Letter to Dr. M. Wiener, Shanghai, 8 July 1941, Willy Tonn Collection 1920–88, Leo Baeck Institute, AR 7259, MF 862, Reels 1–4, Box 1, Folder 10. Also see a letter from Richard Wilhelm to Willy Tonn dated 5 March 1929, Willy Tonn Collection 1920–88, Leo Baeck Institute, AR 7259, MF 862, Reels 1–4, Box 1, Folder 6.

[7] Willy Tonn, "The Lucky Fisherman," *Shanghai Evening Post & Mercury*, September 22, 1942, 5.

[8] Chengming Ji, *Zhong guo chong long xi su* (Tianjin: Tianjin gu ji chu ban she, 2002), 53.

[9] Daniel Ogden, *Dragons, Serpents, and Slayers in the Classical and Early Christian Worlds: A Source Book* (New York: Oxford University Press, 2013), 4.

[10] Herodotus, *The History*, trans. David Grene (Chicago: University of Chicago Press, 1987), 256.

[11] I owe many thanks to Helen Fehervary, whose extraordinary book *Anna Seghers: The Mythic Dimension* (Ann Arbor: University of Michigan Press, 2001) has been a great source of inspiration for this essay.

[12] Michael Brenner, *The Renaissance of Jewish Culture in Weimar Germany* (New Haven, CT: Yale University Press, 1996), 120–21.

[13] Martina Urban, *Aesthetics of Renewal: Martin Buber's Early Representation of Hasidism as Kulturkritik* (Chicago: University of Chicago Press, 2008), 100.

[14] Maurice Friedman, *Martin Buber: The Life of Dialogue* (London: Routledge, 2002), 29.

[15] Willy Tonn, "The Beggar of Soochow," *Shanghai Evening Post & Mercury*, August 13, 1942, 5.

[16] Willy Tonn, "Tang, The Wily General," *Shanghai Evening Post & Mercury*, August 25, 1942, 5.

[17] Willy Tonn, "Pa-Pao's Golden Peach," *Shanghai Evening Post & Mercury*, August 29, 1942, 5.

[18] Willy Tonn, "Darwin was Wrong: The Apes Found an Ancestor in Old Ah-Pei," *Shanghai Evening Post & Mercury*, September 2, 1942, 5. A longer version of the story was first published with the title "The Lord of the Apes" in *The China Journal* (March 1941): 111–16.

[19] Willy Tonn, "The Lucky Fisherman," 5.

[20] Lafcadio Hearn, *Kwaidan: Stories and Studies of Strange Things* (Tokyo: Tuttle, 1971), 173.

[21] Christopher L. Miller, *Blank Darkness: African Discourse in French* (Chicago: University of Chicago Press, 1985), 7.

[22] Dominic Richard David Thomas, "Intertextuality, Plagiarism, and Recycling in Ousmane Sembene's Le docker noir (Black Docker)," *Research in African Literature* 37, no. 1 (Spring 2006): 77.

[23] Hearn, *Kwaidan*, 175.

[24] Ibid., 178.

[25] Umberto Eco, *The Limits of Interpretation* (Bloomington: Indiana University Press, 1994), 95.

[26] Gérard Genette, *Palimpsests: Literature in the Second Degree*, trans. Channa Newman and Claude Doubinsky (Lincoln: University of Nebraska Press, 1997), 1.

[27] Rie Askew, "The Critical Reception of Lafcadio Hearn outside of Japan," *New Zealand Journal of Asian Studies* 11, no. 2 (December 2009): 41–71; here, 53–54.

[28] Ibid., 53.

[29] Tonn, "The Lucky Fisherman," 5.

[30] For a description of the challenge of the harsh living conditions and the Jewish refugees' surprise about the coldness of the winter in Shanghai (which was partly due to the European imagination of Shanghai's alleged tropical weather), see Ernest G. Heppner, *Shanghai Refuge: A Memoir of the World War II Jewish Ghetto* (Lincoln: University of Nebraska Press, 1993), and David Kranzler, *Japanese, Nazis & Jews: The Jewish Refugee Community of Shanghai, 1938–1945* (New York: Yeshiva University Press, 1976).

[31] Martin Buber, "Afterword," *Chinese Tales: Zhuangzi, Sayings and Parables and Chinese Ghost and Love Stories*, trans. Alex Page (Atlantic Highlands, NJ: Humanities Press International, 1991), 90.

[32] Marin Buber, *On Judaism*, trans. Nahum N. Glatzer (New York: Schocken Books, 1967), 78.

11: American Children Writing Yiddish: The Published Anthologies of the Chicago Sholem Aleichem Schools

Elizabeth Loentz

Between 1912 and 1977 Chicago was home to six Yiddish secular school organizations: the National-Radical schools (1912–18), the Poalei Zionist and Jewish National Workers' Alliance (*Farband*) schools (1913–60), the Workmen's Circle schools (1919–65), the Nonpartisan Labor Children's Schools, later called the Children's Schools of the International Workers' Organization (1929–70), the Borokhow School (founded in 1920), and the Sholem Aleichem schools (1925–77).[1] In theory, they had much in common. Their leaders were members of "progressive," left-oriented political movements who sought to counterbalance the "capitalist" ideology transmitted by American public schools; and they believed that maintaining the Yiddish language and culture (as opposed to the Hebrew language or religion) both in the Diaspora and Eretz Israel was the key to uniting the Jewish people worldwide.[2]

The Sholem Aleichem (ShA) Schools were the last Chicago secular Yiddish schools to close their doors, offering classes until at least 1977. Unlike the other secular Yiddish schools in Chicago, which were affiliated with political organizations, the ShA Folk Schools were by principle nonpartisan, as outlined in their 1927 mission statement:

> The Sholem Aleichem School is a nonpartisan educational institution which aims to spread the thought of a modern, progressive secular and national education in Yiddish; to teach the Yiddish language, Jewish history, Jewish literature, the Bible, Jewish songs, folklore; and to acquaint the Jewish child with the Jewish holidays and Jewish traditions. The Yiddish schools are an end to themselves and are not built to serve any political party or group. . . . The cultural needs of the Jewish community demand that cultural and educational work be truly nonpartisan (not anti-partisan). . . . The Sholem Aleichem school group is outspokenly Yiddishist because the Yiddish language binds together the dispersed communities of the Jewish people and gives them a unifying element as a national-cultural unit. The Yiddish language is also an important instrument for continued national-cultural creativity.[3]

With a deliberate focus on the fine arts and commitment to involving students in "living" Yiddish culture, the schools produced a Yiddish radio show and taught folk music, recitation, acting, and dance. From the mid-1930s the school group also operated the Children's Art Studio, led by prominent figures in the Chicago Jewish arts community, such as Todros Geller.[4] One year after the ShA schools were founded, school leaders organized a Chicago branch of the New York-based Sholem Aleichem Folk Institute (ShAFI), which sought to bring parents and the larger Jewish community into their fold through women's clubs, PTAs, reading circles, drama and music clubs, holiday celebrations, and cultural events. The organization was responsible for many of the more auspicious Yiddish cultural events that took place in Chicago during its existence, including readings and lectures by David Pinski, H. Leivick, Moyshe Leib Halpern, Mani Leib, and Shmuel Niger; a Zhitlowsky week, organized in conjunction with the first ShA school graduation in 1930 (Zhitlowsky himself handed out diplomas to the sixteen graduates); and the immensely popular Friday night dinner discussions, which included such diverse topics as "What is religious socialism?," "What is Abnormal Psychology?," "The possibility of agrarian-industrial Jewish colonies in America," and lectures on Yiddish literature.[5]

The ShAFI also published yearbooks and commemorative volumes, including the six collections of students' original Yiddish-language writing, published between 1928 and 1950, that are the subject of this essay. These collections range in scope and sophistication from self-published, mimeographed pamphlets to an impressive book-length bound volume printed by L. M. Stein's Chicago art press, with cover page art and illustrations by Todros Geller. The collections feature writings by students of all ages and abilities (from the early elementary school grades to alumni in their early twenties) and from a variety of genres (autobiographical compositions, position papers, historical essays, biographies of notable Jews, literary critique, social reportage, stories, songs, short plays, and poems). The student writings provide insight into the composition of the student body (especially the linguistic, political, religious, educational, professional, and economic background of students' parents and families); the curriculum (authors and titles read, textbooks used, the exact nature of classroom and homework assignments, how visits by authors or theater productions were integrated into the curriculum); and students' achievements in terms of language acquisition.

Most importantly, the volumes provided the children with a public venue for telling in their own words, in the Yiddish language, either directly (in autobiographical reflections) or indirectly (in other genres), their stories of being educated in progressive secular Yiddishism while growing up in an American context that was increasingly inhospitable both to the maintenance of heritage languages and to the leftist politics espoused by the schools. My readings focus therefore on how the texts' topics, themes, and content reflect the interplay of the students' own personal and political concerns with the evolving pedagogical agenda of the ShA schools in Chicago. Of especial interest are those texts in which students reflect on the purpose of the schools and on the schools' influence on their lives. Although the schools' leaders publicly espoused radical or progressive Yiddishist ideals until at least 1952, the published students' writings reveal that the gradually widening rift between the schools' leaders and their students (and students' parents) that led to curricular concessions in the 1950s and 1960s and the eventual demise of the schools in the 1970s actually began much earlier.

The first of these collections, the 33-page mimeographed *Ven mir viln* (If we want/will it) was printed by L. M. Steyn in an edition of 150 copies in 1928. Adorned with a cover by Todros Geller, *Ven mir viln* is comprised of stories, poems, songs, autobiographical remembrances, and short essays written and compiled by seven- to twelve-year-old students. In their foreword, the student editors ponder the question "Why do we have a Yiddish school?" They write: "The ShA schools were founded by people who thought that the Talmud Torahs were not educating children in the right spirit. The Talmud Torah teaches children in a fanatical manner, and that keeps them from thinking independently. But in the ShA schools . . . children are taught in the progressive, radical spirit."[6] The students write that they learned to read and write Yiddish; learned about Jewish history, literature, and holidays; and read stories, poems, and plays from Yiddish writers. Several texts in the collection suggest an internalization of the political and cultural agenda of the schools. Sore Hendler and Rivke Vayner's play *"Ven der tate krigt arbet"* (When Father Gets Work), expresses empathy with the children of an unemployed worker (3–4). In her poem "Friling" (Spring) Sore Veksler alludes to the life of Jewish children who live in tenements, and her story "Rokhl" describes the plight of an orphan girl left to take care of younger siblings whom she cannot feed (22, 30–31). Menuha Benamy's essay on the "legend" of Prophet Elijah portrays him "as a heavenly emissary sent to earth to combat social injustice, helping the poor and punishing rich people who showed no compassion for the poor" (21–22). Other texts demonstrate the teachers' efforts to immerse their students in contemporary Yiddish literature. Mendel Zilberman's essay on the poet and dramatist H. Leyvik's visit to their school, Menuha Benamy and Sore Veksler's (age 11 and 12) "reviews" of Leyvik's 1928 drama "Shop," and Yitzkhok Rozenfeld's report on Isaac Raboy's novel *Der yidishe farmer* (The Jewish Cowboy) illustrate both the children's familiarity with contemporary Yiddish cultural production and their class consciousness (16–18, 29).

The 50-page anthology *Zekhtsn* (Sixteen), professionally printed and bound in Warsaw, collects the commencement essays of sixteen 1930 graduates of the ShA elementary schools, who had completed the equivalent of four years of instruction.[7] Teachers Pomerants and Meyzlish write in their foreword:

> We sent the compositions to the printers with all of their virtues and flaws, just as the children submitted them to us . . ., because we wanted to: 1) put a finger on the Yiddish linguistic pulse of our children (all but one of whom were born in America and raised in the average Americanized milieu) . . ., and 2) to use the compositions to inform our continuing pedagogical-methodological work. (n.p.)

The importance of the volume in the world of Yiddish culture is demonstrated by a review by literary critic Shmuel Niger ("What the children themselves are writing") that appeared in the New York daily *Der Tog* (The Day).[8] It is notable, however, that only two of the sixteen students make any reference to the progressive political orientation of the schools.[9] While most essays do not demonstrate the students' *active* reception of progressive ideology, they do demonstrate the schools' remarkable successes in developing students' Yiddishist cultural consciousness. By making them active and fully contributing members of the community at a young age, the teachers instilled in the children the sense of belonging to a living, thriving Yiddish culture. The feeling of being equals with their teachers, who unlike the "dictators" of English public school were their friends and comrades, strengthened this. Rather than merely reading literature, the children met with visiting writers, such as Dovid Bergelson and Perets Hirshbeyn, who let them choose the topics of their discussions. Rather than producing Yiddish texts as mere classroom language exercises, the children's writing and other cultural activities were integrated into the cultural life of the community. Bashe Slobodkin recounts that students' stories, recitations, songs, and tableaus were the centerpiece of poet Avrom Reyzn's fiftieth birthday celebration, which was held before an audience of a thousand people (3–8). The students also dramatized Sholem Asch's *Keyn Amerike* (To America) for the ShAFI Passover celebration. Most importantly, the budding Yiddishists of 1930 took the initiative to found their own student-run youth group, which hosted visits by Yiddish writers and political leaders. At least two graduates even aspired to careers in Yiddish culture (24–26, 33–35).

Yung-Yidish (Young Yiddish), a 134-page hardbound volume produced in 1936 and printed by L. M. Steyn, with illustrations by Etl Steyn, is the most ambitious of the anthologies.[10] Dedicated to the teachers and school activists (*shultuer*) on the occasion of the schools' tenth anniversary, it contains writings by elementary and *mitlshul* (high-school) students as well as from alumni. The volume was edited by the *mitlshul* students, who—as in previous volumes—resolved not to clean up all grammatical errors and Americanisms, so that the language itself would mirror "the

milieus in which the children live." The essays also show students' awareness of events in Germany. Elementary school student Avrom Kohn (age
14) writes: "When we were talking about the horrible situation of Jews in
Germany, I thought that Haman was still alive, that he is alive right now
in 1936. His wife, a witch, took his body when he died and made a spell
that he would return in 1932. He changed his name so that Jews wouldn't
recognize him, but his new name also started with an H, Hitler" (49).

The majority of the middle school students' essays focus on the influence of the Yiddish schools in their lives and profess a strong personal
allegiance to the ideals of "national-radical" or "secular" Yiddishism. One
student, in particular, Elye Shvarts (age 17), writes an account of the origins and development of progressive secular Yiddishism, starting with the
French Revolution and Berlin Haskalah. Shvarts explains that prior to the
French Revolution Jews were separated from Christians by two sets of
"armor," the physical armor of the ghetto and the spiritual "armor" of
their religious beliefs. After the French Revolution had torn down the
physical wall, the Berlin Haskalah began to dent the spiritual armor.
Eventually, Jews embraced Marx's "Third Testament of the Bible," which
taught principles of secularism, equality, and fraternity; while the Torah
remained important as a "masterpiece of world literature" from which
Jews derived their "national traditions," which they adapted to modern
life. He concludes that—despite the acculturist program of the Berlin
Haskalah, which advocated abandoning Yiddish in favor of using the
dominant coterritorial language together with Hebrew for religious purposes—Yiddish, as an egalitarian language to which the masses had access,
had retained its importance as Jewish national language (77–81).

Although personally committed to progressive secular Yiddishism, the
students of 1936 recognized that they were members of a small minority
movement that was rapidly losing ground. Yankl Steynberg (age 17), for
example, writes about giving a speech on "Yiddishkayt" in his high-school
public-speaking class, which had a sizable number of Yiddish speakers and
a Jewish teacher. In his speech he argued that, while his teachers' efforts
to help the students learn proper English and to develop their interest in
modern American literature were laudable, it was even more important for
young Jews to acquaint themselves with Jewish culture:

> We were born Jews and will stay Jews, and we cannot run away from
> this. . . . No one could foresee what is now happening in Germany,
> and no one knows what will happen to us in the future. It is our duty
> to learn as much as possible to prepare for the unknown future, to
> prepare to solve the problems we may encounter. Learning Yiddish
> language and literature and Jewish history should be part of this. (88)

The teacher's and fellow students' reactions to his speech confirmed his
suspicions that progressive secular Yiddishism was already a voice in the

wilderness. When his teacher noted that his statements echoed those of Reform rabbis, he had to explain that he was "talking the talk" of secular Yiddishists whose "rabbi" was Zhitlovsky; but his Jewish teacher had never heard of Zhitlovsky. Steynberg's fellow students countered that his ideas were counterproductive to building a unified American people. When they criticized his "religious" separatism, he had to explain to them that he understood Jewishness not as a religious but as a national category, and that the United States was not a "nation" by his definition. The discussion convinced him that he was speaking a different language than his contemporaries, not only linguistically but ideologically (87–93).

Several essays by recent alumni rejected outright the schools' raison d'être. Mendl Silverman (age 19) cautioned that the *nonpartisan* Yiddishism of the ShAFI was losing its hold on young people, because it could not compete with Jewish political parties, such as the Communists and Zionists and their concrete goals and achievements, such as Birobidjan and Palestine (121). Another alumnus, Yitzkhokh Rozenfeld, accused the ShA schools of cultural chauvinism and producing fanatical ethnocentrists: Not only were the schools not saving Yiddish culture, but Yiddish culture was not worth saving. The demise of Yiddish was not a catastrophe but part of a natural process. Only when such ethnocentricism was overcome would mankind reach a "high stage of development where trivialities such as land and nation disappear and the spirit remains free to expend all its energies on the eternal mystery of the fate of mankind" (131–34).

Afn sheyd-veg (At the Crossroads), a 40-page collection of essays written by ten *mitlshul* graduates on the title theme, with greetings from critic Shmuel Niger and author H. Leyvik, was printed by L. M. Steyn in 1937.[11] The graduates are almost unanimous in their expression of allegiance to the ideals of progressive secular Yiddishist nationalism. National Socialism and the betrayal of assimilated German Jews had served to strengthen their belief in the failure of the assimilationist strategy. Yosl Bronsteyn, for example, writes:

> I must think about German-Jewish youth, who suddenly lost their entire physical and spiritual grounding, because they had no inkling of their Jewish identity and were entirely assimilated. Now they stand there hopelessly, with nowhere to turn. We youths who have enjoyed a Yiddish education are ready to face the world and fight persecution and discrimination, because we are part of a conscious and confident ring of Yidishkayt. (11)

In their congratulatory greeting the teachers proudly note that they were not the "last Mohicans of Yiddish culture" but were sending forth a "new generation, . . . ten Bar-Mitzvahs of modern Jewish culture," who would carry on their work (5). Their students, however, were not quite as optimistic. Hinde Rozenfeld laments how few American Jews remained dedicated to the "great ideals" of Yiddish cultural work. Leyvik Horeker speaks of the difficulty of harmonizing the two completely separate cultural and linguistic milieus between which he commutes (17–18). Elye Svarts blames the schools' programmatic non-partisanship for isolating the students from Jewish political parties, and thus stunting their growth as active participants in real political life (25–27). Bine Zalts, while grateful for what she learned at the schools, concedes that a Jewish state where Jews can live peacefully and securely was a higher priority (19–20).

Oyfn shvel (On the Threshold), a 60-page mimeographed pamphlet with graphics from Todros Geller, was published just two years later in 1939.[12] It includes writings of various genres from both elementary and *mitlshul* students. On the back cover, a message from the the the executive board of ShAFI states: "In these difficult times the schools must become a strong vehicle of resistance against the dark forces that threaten our existence. Our future lies on the path of Yiddish language and culture that connects and unites us around the globe. Wherever we are living, we must lead the next generation on this path" (n.p.).

The intensifying persecution of Jews in Germany prompted students to reexamine their status as Jews in the United States and to reflect on American anti-Semitism. Sixteen-year-old Rokhl Imerman's essay "Jewish Problems" notes that democracy had not shielded American Jews from anti-Semitism. Even in America, anti-Semites distributed pamphlets urging Christians to boycott Jewish businesses; Jews sometimes had to lie about their origins, names, and addresses to get employment; and private universities had quotas. American Jews should not view assimilation as the solution—German Jews, after all, had become so assimilated that they had nearly forgotten their Jewish identity until Hitler reminded them of it (40). In "Save Yourselves, Learn Yiddish!" Musie Gingold (age 18) argues that because Jews have always been stronger in spirit and intellect than in munitions, it is dangerous to neglect Jewish culture and a positive Jewish identity when Hitler was sending thousands of Jews to concentration camps and Chamberlain was closing the gates to Israel (56). An increased interest in Zionism is discernible in this volume, as well. Leybl Pravatiner's "The Blood Libel against Us," for example, is a Zionist-hued anti-defamation essay that acknowledges the "partial truth" of the stereotype of Diaspora Jews as "parasitic and economically exploitative" but blames the presumed Jewish affinity for certain occupations on centuries-long discrimination. Pravatiner concludes that the only way to eradicate anti-Semitism was to found a Jewish state, where Jews, freed from discrimination, could prove that they are a "useful and productive" race (1–5). Etl Fratkin (age 16) advocates for the Poalei Zionist movement in particular, citing its interest in fighting for peace between Arabs and Jews and for the rights of the Yiddish language (39–39a).

Several students address issues of social and economic justice that are not specifically Jewish, such as sixteen-year-old Yosel Oderberg's pro-Union essay on the Chicago stockyards, which also advocates vegetarianism (8–10). Seventeen-year-old Gershon Heller's "The Life of Negroes" is a highly empathetic but nevertheless chauvinistic text informed by his experiences working on Chicago's South Side. Noting the high rate of alcoholism and violent crime there, he patronizingly suggests that many emancipated slaves had been "unprepared for freedom," and that "civilized people" continued to exploit Blacks, forcing them into the worst neighborhoods, charging exorbitant rents, and limiting access to educational and professional opportunities (17–18).

The 200-page volume *Undzer Yugnt* (Our Youth) commemorates the twenty-fifth anniversary of the Workmen's Circle schools in Chicago in 1944, devoting only twenty pages to the writings of ShA school students.[13] This small sampling of essays shows widening rifts between students and activists and between the students themselves, especially in their assessment of the situation of Jews in America. Sheyndl Hoyrst, whose essay highlights Jewish involvement in the war effort, insists: "Jewish children who live in America are happy because they live here. They live in a free country and enjoy the same rights as all US citizens. All Jewish children who don't live here hope that they will some day" (188–89). Khaym Silverman, on the other hand, cautions that American anti-Semitism remains a serious threat. He writes that he has heard claims that Roosevelt and Churchhill were connected with the Jews, that the war was a Jewish war, that America was a Golden Land until the Jews came and ruined it; and that Jews were trying to bring Bolshevism to America (189–90). Skeptical of America's commitment to Jews, a third student, Judith Brodski, insists that the foundation of a Jewish state is the only way to ensure Jewish survival: "As long as the structure of American economic and social life is based on the present system of maximizing profit, the emigration quotas will not be revoked and Jews will not be let into this country" (198).

The final anthology *Afn Shvel* (On the Threshold) is a slim 20-page mimeographed pamphlet edited by Feygl and Yitzkhok Melamdovitsh and self-published in 1950.[14] It comprises writings by eleven elementary school graduates, who began their education there after the Second World War had ended. The congratulatory note from the teachers and activists of the school (who included Chicago sporting-goods manufacturer Jack A. Dubow), is a very tempered version of the schools' earlier professions of radical national secular Yiddishism. It reads, rather innocuously: "You should learn our language, know our history, and become familiar with our holidays. . . . We taught you to love our People and remain loyal to her always. We are confident . . . that you will grow up to be proud good Jews and free citizens of America" (1). Not a single student essay is overtly

Yiddishist; and only one living Yiddish writer is the subject of a student essay, while two students write about Emma Lazarus, a Sephardic-Jewish American writer, who wrote in English (4–5, 14). Shloyme Oberman's essay "Bar Mitzvah" documents the gradually increasing inclusion of religious instruction into the previously programmatically secular schools. Oberman tells us that he learned to sing the haphtarah and say his brokhes, that he wrote a Midrash on Noah, and learned "how to bind tefillin." Oberman's Bar Mitzvah tutor was none other than Muni Mark, his teacher from the ShA school (16–17). The only overt expression of socially progressive politics can be found in Moyshe Klaynsteyn's essay "Israel." The young author's idealized vision of pioneer life in Palestine clearly illustrates his stake in his teachers' progressive orientations: "The pioneer life was a life of justice and equality. The pioneers lived and worked together, believing that it would someday be this way everywhere, that Jewish life would be a model for the whole world." However, he does not suggest that the cultivation of Yiddish language and culture was an integral part of the national project (18).

With the exception of this final collection, the children's writings were all written during the years in which the ShA schools were at their strongest—the decades prior to the Second World War and the Holocaust. From 1945 to the 1970s the schools fought an uphill, ultimately losing, battle for survival. While the schools suffered from perennial financial difficulties, which were exacerbated by demographic shifts within the schools' neighborhoods, these merely accelerated the schools' inevitable decline due to major historical and political events and the resultant reconfiguration of secular Jewish identity in America. With the destruction of centers of Yiddish-speaking Jewish culture in Eastern Europe and the murder of millions of Yiddish speakers in the Holocaust, Yiddish language and culture were left without a geographic point of orientation, without a homeland. Even before the Holocaust, rapidly assimilating American Jews in pursuit of the American dream were abandoning Yiddish. An annual report reveals that as early as 1938, 50 percent of students' parents had no Yiddish books or newspapers in the home, and only 40 percent of students heard Yiddish in the home. The victory of Hebrew over Yiddish first within the Zionist movement and then in the newly founded state of Israel stigmatized Yiddish further—it was not only an immigrant, greenhorn language but also one associated with forced ghettoization, persecution, victimization, and Diaspora.[15]

By 1960 all invitations and publications were either bilingual or in English, and in 1970 school leaders complained that the entire PTA was English-speaking.[16] In the post-Holocaust era the school system that had once celebrated a positive Diaspora identity defined by language, culture, history, and universal ideals—not by a geographic location—collected donations for aid to Israel, participated in city-wide celebrations of the founding of the State of Israel, and featured Israeli songs in their concerts and pageants.[17]

Since the 1950s the shift of orientation away from Eastern Europe and Yiddish to Israel and Hebrew was accompanied by a de-emphasizing of the leftist politics that were central to the mission of the ShAFI in its early decades. This can be attributed in part to fear of the Red witchhunts of the McCarthy era, as well as pro-Soviet Yiddishists' disillusionment following the Stalinist purges and execution of Soviet Yiddishists in 1952. While the 1952 Yearbook still states (in Yiddish) the goal of educating children in the "radical, progressive, Jewish-nationalist spirit," it prints just one year later (in English) that the ShAFI "seeks the best and right way to educate our Jewish children not only as productive Jews but also as intelligent American citizens." The 1958 Yearbook offers the rather innocuous aim, "To preserve and perpetuate those elements of Jewish tradition which are in harmony with Jewish life in America," and "to implant in the children an awareness of the universal principles of Jewishness, which are especially relevant today, such as peace and democracy."[18] Never again do the words progressive, let alone radical, grace an advertisement. The extent of the Americanization of the ShAFI is perhaps best demonstrated by the 1961 PTA social event, "The Homentash Hoe-Down," celebrating Purim with a square dance with caller Hardy Freeman.[19] While the PTA still sponsored Yiddish-language cultural events for its adult members into the early 1960s (especially screenings of sub-titled Yiddish films) and had great success with a fund-raising production of "Dos groyse gevins," starring Yiddish theater star Dina Halpern, they deferred to the American tastes of their children. The budding Yiddishists watched Shirley Temple's *The Littlest Rebel*, Abbott and Costello, and cartoons.[20] The rift between the schools' strictly secular, progressive, Jewish-nationalist, Yiddishist roots and its postwar public identity (ethno-religiously Jewish but nationally patriotic American) is further demonstrated by a 1959 PTA recruiting letter: "Your children are your most precious possessions, and we know that you do everything in your power to protect and shelter them. Your child's religious education should be as important to you as the food you feed them."[21]

By 1965 the school advertised study of the "Torah, Prophets, and Scriptures" and Bar/Bat-Mitzvah preparation on its recruitment flyer.[22] With the downplaying of progressive political thought and activism and the introduction of religion into the core curriculum, the only thing that distinguished the ShA schools from religious schools (with whom they were financially ill equipped to compete) was Yiddish. Whereas the school activists of the 1920s had recognized the importance of involving children in the creation of contemporary living Yiddish culture in projects such as the Children's Art Studio and through publication of their essays and stories, the Yiddish students of the 1970s learned that Yiddish language and culture lived in a nostalgic past. The 1972 Hanukkah concert no longer included poems and stories written by students, recitations of the poems of contemporary modernist Yiddish writers, Yiddish workers' anthems, and the Yiddish version of "America, The Beautiful" but was a program called "Dos shtetl," featuring nostalgic Yiddish songs of ghetto life in Eastern Europe, interspersed with an English-language narration about Zeyde and Bobe's life in the shtetl.[23]

The six anthologies examined here offer unusual and invaluable insights into one community's attempt to maintain and develop what we would now refer to as a "heritage language" via a community-based heritage language program, by documenting—in their own voices—students' stories of their learning experiences and their understanding of the meaning of the Yiddish language and their secular Yiddish education within their individual and collective negotiation of their identities as Americans and American Jews, at a time when the maintenance of heritage languages was not encouraged as it is today but—especially in the case of a low-status, non-territorial or stateless language that possessed little cultural capital—even actively discouraged. The writings, although written during the schools' best years, reveal students' awareness of the difficulties of this endeavor, which was due to negative attitudes toward the use of heritage languages in the United States but also to the disappearance of a Yiddish-speaking homeland in Eastern Europe to look back to, due both to the gradual "natural" process of Jewish acculturation since the eighteenth century and to the destruction of Jewish communities in Eastern Europe by the Holocaust and resultant dominance of Hebrew and Israel over Yiddish and forms of Diaspora Nationalism.

Notes

1 Leonard C. Mishkin, "Out of the Past: Secular Yiddish Schools," in *The Sentinel's History of Chicago Jewry, 1911–1986* (Chicago: Sentinel, 1986), 258–61; Mark M. Krug, "The Yiddish Schools in Chicago," *YIVO Annual of Jewish Social Science* 9 (1954): 283–94.

2 Joshua A. Fishman, *Yiddish in America: Sociolinguistic Description and Analysis* (Bloomington: Indiana University Press, 1965), 21–25; Krug, "Yiddish Schools," 283.

3 Unless otherwise noted, all translations are my own. M. Bronsteyn (M. Brownstone), "20 yor shul-un-kultur-arbet funem Sholem Aleykem folks institut," in *Shul-Pinkes*, ed. Shloime Bercovich et al. (Chicago: Sholem Aleichem Folk Institute, 1948), 607–73; here, 608; translated in Mark M. Krug, "Yiddish Schools," 297.

4 Brownstone, "20 yor shul-un-kultur-arbet," 614, 646, 654.

5 Ibid., 614, 617, 622, 636, 638, 669.

[6] Sholem Aleichem School Number One, *Ven mir viln: Kindershrift fun der Sholem Aleykhem shul eyns* (Chicago: Sholem Aleykhem shul eyns, 1928), 1.

[7] Sholem Aleichem Folk Institute Chicago, *Zekhtsn: A zamlung siem-kompozitsyes fun zekhtsn talmidim-graduirer fun di elementare Sholem-Aleykhem folk-shuln, Shikago* (Warsaw: B. Kletskin, 1930).

[8] Brownstone, "20 yor shul-un-kultur-arbet," 638.

[9] Sholem Aleichem Folk Institute Chicago, *Zekhtsn*, 24–26, 36–37.

[10] I. Kh. Pomerants, ed., *Yung-Yidish: Zamlbukh, Shafungen fun talmidim fun di Sholem Aleichem folkshuln, mitlshul un abituryenten* (Chicago: L. M. Steyn, 1936).

[11] I. Kh. Pomerants and A. Pravatiner, eds., *Afn shayd-veg: Zamlshrift fun der Sholem Aleykhem mitlshul* (Chicago: L. M. Steyn, 1937).

[12] I. Kh. Pomerants, and A. Pravatiner, eds., *Oyfn Shvel: Zamlbukh, Shafungen fun talmidim fun di Sholem Aleykhem folkshuln un mitlshul* (Chicago: Sholem Aleichem Folk Institute, 1939). In box 5, file 55 of the Sholem Aleichem Folk Institute (ShAFI) Papers, Collection 124, Chicago Jewish Archives, Spertus Institute, Chicago.

[13] B. Grobard, ed., *Undzer yugnṭ: Gezamelṭe arbeṭn fun Shikager Arbeṭer Ring miṭl shul un elemenṭar shul talmidim un talmidim fun Sholem Aleykhem folk shuln* (Chicago: Farayniḳṭer miṭl shul fun Arbeṭer Ring un Sholem Aleykhem folḳs insṭiṭuṭ, 1946).

[14] Sholem Aleichem Folk Institute Chicago, *Oyfn shvel: Zamlbukh fun di graduantn fun di Sholem Aleykhem folkshuln* (Chicago: 1950). In ShAFI Papers, box 5, file 55.

[15] Brownstone, "20 yor shul-un-kultur-arbet," 654–56.

[16] ShAFI Papers, box 2, file 21; box 3, file 32.

[17] Ibid., box 1, file 4; box 3, file 34.

[18] Ibid., box 5, file 56.

[19] Ibid., box 2, file 22.

[20] Ibid., file 24.

[21] Ibid., file 20.

[22] Ibid., file 26.

[23] ShAFI Papers, box 7, file 74.

12: A Literary Depiction of the Homeland of Jews in Czechoslovakia and East Germany after 1945

Michaela Peroutková

ACCORDING TO THE PREVAILING HISTORICAL NARRATIVE, around 40,000 to 56,000 Czechoslovak Jews returned from concentration camps and exile to their former homeland in order to start a new life after the Second World War.[1] At the same time, some 3,500 Holocaust survivors came to the Soviet occupation zone in Germany hoping to find a new home there. This statistic corresponds to 3 percent of the Jewish population that had lived in that territory before the war.[2] These figures directly convey the disaster of the Shoah on a factual scale, one that most historians corroborate.[3]

However, such a narrative is just one way of looking at the past. This point of view lacks the phenomenological dimension of the atrocity and does not depict the distressed human condition of the returning Jews and the post-traumatic anxiety they had from being in concentration camps. These experiences, whether in an individual or collective form, are the core of literary narratives dealing with these past events and memories of these events. Paul Ricoeur states that literary narrative offers a view into the human condition, since it conveys human life in its complexity and different modalities. Literary narrative opens a new horizon for understanding the world that surrounds us in the context of the past, present, and future.[4]

Drawing from Ricoeur's perception of narrative, in the following text I pursue the literary narratives about Holocaust survivors returning from concentration camps or exile immediately after the Second World War. The study concentrates on the Czech literary text, *All the Colors of the Sun and the Night (Alle Farben der Sonne und der Nacht)* by Lenka Reinerová and the (East) German novel, *Der Boxer* by Jurek Becker. Both works consist of stories of Jewish survivors in Czechoslovakia and East Germany (the GDR). My analysis explores the differences and similarities between Czech and German literary narratives about Jewish survivors. It encompasses how Czechs and Germans perceived them, the survivors' struggle with anti-Semitism in the pertinent societies, and their quest for self-identity and a homeland.

Despite the small number of returning Jews, they played an important role in the cultural and political life in both countries. In Czechoslovakia, both Czech-speaking and German-speaking Jews, such as Egon Erwin Kisch, Luis Fürnberg, and Lenka Reinerová, were active in cultural life until they were struck by a new anti-Semitic wave that took the form of political trials during the 1950s. The cultural involvement of Jewish artists and writers such as Anna Seghers, Stephan Hermlin, Günter Kunert, Stefan Heym, Peter Edel, Barbara Honigmann, and Jurek Becker in the German Democratic Republic lasted until 1976, when the singer Wolf Biermann was expatriated by the Communist government and consequently expelled from the GDR. In spite of the East German proclamation about the assimilation of Jews, some Jewish intellectuals proclaimed their Jewishness and identified themselves as such. One of them was Jurek Becker, the author of the famous novel and film *Jacob the Liar*.

Jurek Becker (1937–97) was born in the Polish city of Lodz. When he was two years old, he was placed in the local newly built Jewish ghetto, and later spent five years in the concentration camps Ravensbrück and Sachsenhausen. At the age of eight, he went with his father to Berlin because "he had hoped that the discrimination of Jews would be thoroughly eliminated precisely at the place where it occurred in the most horrendous way."[5] Becker did not know any German when he arrived there. He had to learn the language and acclimate to his new home. Jewishness did not play a big role in his life; it was more connected to his father, who represented "the only bridge to Jewishness" and also to the past, which was taboo for his father. The silence about the past troubled Becker his entire life. It was a part of his identity that he knew very little about, and yet it was constantly present in his life. According to him, his memories could be traced only to the end of the war. In order to fill the vacuum before that time, he occupied himself with thoughts about the past, which resulted in his first work about the ghetto of Lodz, the novel *Jakob the Liar*. Although the tale was rejected as a screenplay in 1968, it was published as a novel one year later. A film by the same name, based on the book, was released in 1974 and was a success. The material for the story about a hero from the ghetto of Lodz came from Becker's father, although Becker changed it and wrote a story about a man who pretends to own a radio in the ghetto. The protagonist regularly reports to the other prisoners in the ghetto about the allegedly approaching Red Army that would free them from the Nazis.

Becker's next novel, titled *The Boxer* (1976), also was inspired by his father. The story features strong autobiographical characteristics and depicts a quest for self-identity in the postwar society of the GDR. Insecurity and doubt about self-identity are reflected in the structure of the story. Becker uses a narrator in his novel to relate the story that is being told by the main protagonist, Aron Blank. The narrator listens to Blank and writes down his story, which means that readers learn the narrator's story about Blank rather than Blank's story itself.

Because of this arrangement a conflict arises. On the one hand, the narrator stands for objectivity. On the other hand, it is questionable whether we can rely on his storytelling. In order to solve this dilemma, the narrator appears regularly throughout the whole story in the first person and talks to Blank to make sure that he understands Blank's story. One example of this feature occurs when the narrator introduces Blank, who has created a new identity for himself. The narrator repeats his question: "Why did you make yourself six years younger?"[6] Blank does not answer immediately, just as Becker's father did not answer. Blank mulls over the question and then gives an explanation, which the narrator relates to the reader as follows: "The war lasted six years. Aron was arrested for six years in concentration camps. He could have tried to erase the bad times and with all possible means for him regain the lost piece of his life back" (19).

Aron Blank, like Becker a Holocaust survivor, comes to Berlin after the war and wants to start a new life and rid himself of his troublesome past. He changes his name from Aron to Arno in an attempt to blend in with other Germans. He wants to erase his Jewish identity, which he believes is apparent from the shape of his nose. His wife and two sons died in a concentration camp. His third son is missing, and Blank does not have any information about him. After Blank's arrival in Berlin, he obtains a new apartment that had been confiscated from a former Nazi. He cannot get used to his new life and cannot escape his past in spite of his new identity. "Aron was lying awake and could not protect himself from the last years. His thoughts searched around in there, in death and torture. His two starved children were lying next to him. His wife was constantly dragged from one room to another. She was screaming, and he could not get rid of the repulsive smell" (23). Blank cannot fall asleep in his new home. It is only when he takes refuge in the closet that he finally falls asleep. During the day, Aron looks for his son Mark, whom he left with his neighbor before being deported to a concentration camp.

The "American Jewish Joint Distribution Committee," which helped Holocaust survivors after the war, finds a boy named Mark Berger. His name is different, but the description matches that of Blank's son Mark. The initial meeting between Blank and Mark is very awkward. The boy lacks social skills and knows nothing about his family. Mark, who has been very neglected, does not understand the word "son" and does not know the meaning of the word "fatherland."

After this meeting, a shocked Blank realizes the extent of his son's physical and mental mistreatment. First, he tries to ask Mark about his past, but when he sees his son's negative reaction, he decides not to mention it again. He wants to protect Mark from his own confrontation with the atrocities of the Shoah and from reliving the trauma. However, the opposite occurs. Before the father and the son can form a close relationship, the alienation process that culminates with Mark's emigration to Israel has already started. Not talking about Mark´s origins causes a deep identity crisis. Mark does not know where he belongs; he does not have any friends, and he is beaten up at school. He feels alienated among Germans. This could be, but is not necessarily, due to Blank's attempts at assimilation. He suppresses the past and believes that this way he can build a new life for himself and his son. Nevertheless, he is marginalized by both Germans and Jews and cannot identify with them. He does not trust Germans. He perceives every ordinary German as a perpetrator and avoids Jews because they remind him of his traumatic past. Blank decides to move to the Soviet occupied zone, because he believes that "the Russians dealt with the past more thoroughly than the Western allies did" (151). The Western allies' way of dealing with the past—avoiding confronting it directly—corresponds to Aron's personal strategy to remain silent about the past, even though it haunts him. "The camp is running after you. The concentration-camp barracks haunt you, the stench haunts you, the hunger haunts you, the punches haunt you, and the fear haunts you" (102). Blank believes that by staying silent he can deal with the traumatic events and extreme burden of the past.

The same strategy of silencing the difficult past was implemented in Communist Germany, even though there are different reasons. As Germany also was divided ideologically, it was necessary to emphasize the Communist antifascist resistance and suppress East Germany´s involvement in Nazism. According to the rhetoric of the new GDR government, all the Nazis and their supporters were allegedly in West Germany, which meant that people in East Germany were relieved of responsibility for their past participation in the Nazi regime as well as of critical introspection and self-reflection. Such distancing from perpetrators and the emphasis on Communist victims resulted in the equalization of perpetrators and victims. Becker´s protagonist Aron does not trust Germans, no matter where they live. He is very worried and hesitates when Mark has to go to school because "he did not want Mark to attend a school where people whom he suspected of being fascists and even possible murderers were teachers" (203). These thoughts disturb Aron, but he does not share them with Mark. Therefore his son does not know what his father is afraid of or why he is so afraid. Mark is living among the Germans without any conflicts until he is beaten up at school. He does not understand why this happened; however, his father perceives this attack as a "pogrom on a small scale" (218). Again, Blank does not say this to Mark and instead insists only on finding out the name of the attacker. Mark refuses to tell him unless his father promises not to tell anyone or do anything about it. Blank perceives the attack as a manifestation of anti-Semitism and decides to have Mark learn to box so that he will be able to protect himself. As the title of the novel implies, Mark becomes a boxer. However, he does not understand how to use his skills in a positive way. He beats up a classmate who tells on Mark when Mark draws pictures of male and female bodies on the blackboard. At first Mark lies to his father, although Blank discovers the truth. He is shocked and realizes that he gave his son a two-edged weapon that can be misused. Mark does not show any comprehension of justice or truth, and his behavior resembles the actions of the perpetrators from whom his father wants to escape. In Blank's opinion, boxing should be used only for defensive purposes and not to cause violence. Mark should box to defend himself and to protect people weaker than himself. At the same time, Blank rejects the perpetrators, the Germans, and even victims like himself. Despite all attempts to create a new life, he ends up leading a passive existence, uninterested in the world around him. He finds consolation in alcohol. "Schnapps helps. Alcohol makes things easier. It helps get over the crap" (103–4). Aron adapts the stereotypical Jewish role of victim that is imposed upon him. He takes a passive stance, letting things happen and accepting the external events surrounding him.

He even approves of the East German government's totalitarian methods when they send tanks against protestors in June of 1956. "Tanks are good. Peace will be restored" (255). Indeed, peace was restored after the riots, but at what cost? People had to live anonymously; there was no room for ethnic, cultural, or political plurality. Every East German citizen had to conform to Communist ideology and to the government that implemented that ideology in society. Blank had to assimilate into the German population, but he was still treated differently. As a victim of Hitler's persecution of the Jews, he is eligible for monthly financial support from the state which paradoxically drives him into seclusion. He is not motivated to work and feels marginalized. At a certain point he wonders about his situation: "Is it in the long term an endurable condition to be the victim of fascism and nothing else?" (249). His inability to solve his dilemma is further underscored by East Germans' perception of Jews. They were seen as passive victims of Hitler as opposed to active (Communist) victims who fought for the Jews. From the viewpoint of the GDR, Jews should be grateful to the Communists, since they defeated Hitler and established a new and better Germany that would also be a new home for the Jews. The only caveat was that Jews had to assimilate with the German population. This acculturation process caused two reactions: first, a stronger Jewish awareness, and second, certain apathy. The first-mentioned tendency is exemplified by Blank's friend Kenik and Blank's son Mark, when they both leave the GDR for Israel in order to find a new homeland. Surprisingly, Mark decides to embrace his Jewishness, even though he had not been raised Jewish. Mark felt neither Jewish nor German and found himself in a vacuum. He chooses to become a Jew because his own Jewish background is mysterious to him. Blank cannot change his own attitude anymore. He is stuck halfway between being Jewish because of his past and being an assimilated German non-Jew because of the then current GDR situation. A big paradox in Becker's story is that Aron, the Holocaust survivor, stays alive while his son, who chooses to be Jewish, dies in Israel's six-day war. Blank gives up his identity and his real life; he drowns his life in alcohol. Both protagonists were condemned to an existence without an unconditional homeland; they were accepted under certain circumstances or for a deferred time only.

The second literary work I shall discuss, *All Colors of the Sun and the Night* by the Czech-German-Jewish author Lenka Reinerová, was written during 1956 and 1957. Originally the book was published with the title *The Color of the Sun and the Night (Die Farbe der Sonne und der Nacht)* in 1969. However, all copies were immediately destroyed because of the Soviet occupation of Czechoslovakia. A new version of the manuscript with the title *All the Colors of the Sun and the Night (Alle Farben der Sonne und der Nacht)* did not appear until 2002. Like most of Reinerová's books, this one is autobiographical. Originally written in Czech, the book is an exception; she wrote all her other works in German. The decision to write this particular book in Czech is connected to the circumstances in which the manuscript was written, particularly concerning Czechs. As Reinerová described it, the plot was a quite intimate family issue that had to be treated "at home" in the language of the family.[7] The story explicitly concerns Czechoslovakia and Czech matters and, according to the author, it describes one of the worst periods in her life. With her German-Czech-Jewish background, Lenka Reinerová (1916–2008) was the last representative of the Prague circle in its broader meaning. As a young journalist she worked with Franz Carl Weiskopf, met Max Brod several times, and later established a close friendship with Egon Erwin Kisch. Her mother tongue, in which she wrote all her stories, was German. Nevertheless, she spoke Czech—the language of her father—immaculately. Even in her youth, Reinerová was interested in social and political issues. For this reason she joined the Czech Communist Party and worked with the German Communist newspaper *Arbeiter Illustrierte Zeitung*, whose publisher moved from Berlin to Prague after Hitler's takeover of Germany. Like most of the Jewish intellectuals in the 1920s and 1930s, Reinerová also was influenced by Communist ideology, in which she saw the assurance of peace, justice, and a society in which all people are treated equally. In 1939, as an active Jewish Communist, Reinerová went into exile, and after imprisonment in Paris and West Africa she managed to escape to Mexico, where she stayed until the end of the war. There she met the Prague journalist Egon Erwin Kisch and a number of leftist writers from Germany, including Anna Seghers, Bodo Uhse, and Ludwig Renn.[8] During her stay in Mexico, Reinerová married the Yugoslavian doctor and journalist Theodor Balk, with whom she participated in antifascist activities. After the war ended, the couple first moved to Belgrade in Yugoslavia, where they spent three years. In 1948 Reinerová returned to Prague. Like many Holocaust survivors, she lost her family in the camps and came back to her homeland alone.

Unfortunately, the newly gained freedom in Czechoslovakia did not last long for Lenka Reinerová. Four years after returning to her homeland, she was arrested, this time by the Czechoslovak State Secret Police. This event later served as the basis for her book *All the Colors of the Sun and the Night*. The title already implies that the story focuses on the confrontation of a duality that forms an entity. The two phenomena, the sun and the night, belong together. They create a unity. However, they cannot be seen together at the same time because one part is always missing. The sun represents the hope for a better society, a concept of Communist ideology. And the night represents her bitter disillusionment during her imprisonment, as she faced the reality of a totalitarian regime that had just come to power.

The narrator, a genuine prewar Communist of Jewish origin, is arrested without any explanation in 1952 and remains imprisoned for a year until Stalin's death. She does not know the reason she was jailed. The investigators treat her as if her crime was so obvious that there is no need to explain it. Her Jewish origin is the most crucial issue in the accusation, even though for the narrator herself her Jewishness does not play an important role. While it is not said directly that she is being punished for being Jewish, it is an understated allegation in all of the interrogations. After several pointless interrogations, this issue is finally raised: "'You are Jewish, aren't you?' 'Yes, I am.' 'But why did he say it as another accusation?'"[9] Does it mean that being Jewish is a crime? The absurdity of this suspicion becomes even worse when the investigators blame the narrator for surviving the Holocaust while her whole family perished in concentration camps. "It's interesting. You claim that the Nazis killed your whole family. And you of all people were so lucky. Nothing happened to you. You have to admit that it is at least peculiar" (62). With such manipulative rhetoric the investigators evoke the feelings of guilt from which many Holocaust survivors suffered after the war, since they felt guilty that they had the "privilege" of surviving. In this case, the investigators expediently attack the narrator with this argument in order to devastate her psychologically as well as physically and to coerce her to confess. For many Holocaust survivors, feelings of guilt caused a trauma that was connected with psychological disorders and proved difficult to cure.[10] During the political trials in Czechoslovakia in the 1950s, investigators used this trauma in order to blackmail the defendants and enforce the alleged confessions. Under such psychological pressure, eleven out of fourteen people accused of crimes confessed to having committed acts they had never done and had never intended to do.

In Reinerová's story, the narrator's intimidation does not have the desired effect. Therefore the investigators increase the intensity of the interrogation. She is accused of Zionism. "'Since when have you been a Zionist?' . . . 'I have never been a Zionist.' 'All Jews are Zionists,' he [the investigator] commented in an almost friendly tone, as if he were informing me about the newest scientific finding" (66). The narrator defends herself against the accusation, drawing a parallel between the Nazi regime and the Communist regime. "'You are Jewish even if you conceal it.' 'I never conceal it,' I replied, still quietly but much more firmly. 'I didn't even conceal it from the Nazis'" (65).

The comparison to German National Socialism is an underlying main thread in the whole story, and the memories of the Gestapo are constantly present: "Female Jews to the left, all others to the right. This command was given years ago in the French detention camp for women in Rieucros, . . ." (66). However, back then Communists of different nationalities supported Jews: ". . . a bulwark created by the arrested comrades arose around the group of Jews" (66). The narrator painfully realizes that the political system in which she hoped for a better future is very similar to the Nazi regime that she lived through before and during the war. This is the unknown, dark part of Communism, the night, which so far has been hidden from her and which she is experiencing now with shock and fear. She is deeply shocked by this confrontation with the criminal feature of idealized Communism. She cannot grasp it: "Instinctively, I run both my hands through my hair, maybe to find out whether this is not a bad dream, but rather a bitter truth, like the green uniforms in front of me and the bars in front of the window" (66).

The imprisonment and brutal interrogation evoke memories of Nazi persecution in different camps during the war. However, as Reinerová says, during the war life was not normal, but there was hope that the abnormal situation would end, and a certain degree of normality would be established. Nevertheless, the postwar normality she had desired shows repressive qualities similar to the previous Nazi regime. The anti-Semitism feared and fought by Jews is emerging again, this time in a hidden and sneaky form, because one never knows where and how it attacks you. "The Jew is guilty in many languages and different times, always and everywhere. But here under the excuse of socialism?" (67). It is absurd that the Czech Secret State Security Police interrogate the narrator about the same people and activities as the Gestapo did. It concerns the German left and Communist exile writers who fled from Germany first to Czechoslovakia and later to other, mostly Western, countries. According to the Communist Security Police, these people are highly suspicious because of their German and Jewish origin. "Many emigrants came to Prague . . . certainly, certainly, nothing but immaculate refugees. And it naturally never occurred to you that some of them who graced us with their presence were informers of the Gestapo" (38). This argument sounds completely absurd to the narrator; however, for the new Communist Party transformed under Stalin's influence, these people represented the most dangerous enemy of the state. The Jewish-German origin was the worst combination, since it represented the ultimate unpredictable "other." It contained the detested Jewish element and the hated German component, which unleashed anti-Semitic and nationalistic tendencies in Czechs. Jews in general were perceived with distrust; they were associated with cosmopolitanism, which, according to Stalin, endangered the state because of their lack of loyalty to the national government. Also, they had too many contacts with Western countries, including Israel. The additional German part made it even worse. During the political trials and the persecution of the Jews in the 1950s, the term cosmopolitanism comprised both anti-Semitism and nationalism. The narrator in Reinerová's story refuses to accept this argument. She insists on the prewar Communist ideology and questions the then contemporary party at the same time. "The party? Which party? Not the one that I had been a member of since my Sturm-and-Drang Years, the one that promised all oppressed people the right to live" (22). It gets to the point where the investigators blame the arrested woman for refusing to help the party. "You don't want to help the party as we expected you to. You even cover for the enemy" (75). The narrator does not comprehend the rhetoric of the investigators at all. She feels as if she is in a bizarre panopticon of evil ghosts. And yet they are real. The whole process could have followed a simple procedure, if only the narrator had confessed her crimes. "High treason and espionage for the class enemy, contacts in the West, activities in Yugoslavia, all this. Pack up your things properly. I will record it, you'll sign it, and we will send you home. Is it clear?" (20). It is not so easy for the narrator because she cannot confess to something she did not do, something she finds totally absurd. She is the one who belongs to the class of conscious people who fought against capitalism and was committed to the abolition of classes. She helped ideologically to build up the existence of the workers' movement and supported the Communist party in its antifascist activities. So what is her real offense? The interrogation and the accusation suggest that the biggest crime has to do with her Jewish origin. ". . . maybe the worst accusation from my 'socialist' prosecutor that I could have guessed and that should have never existed: my Jewish descent. It was suspicious to belong to people whose whole families had been barbarically exterminated" (161). From the perspective of the Czech interrogators, the imprisoned narrator was not a victim but rather a perpetrator who had to be removed. This way many Jews in Czechoslovakia were directly or covertly persecuted with the aim of expelling them from the country or of intimidating them to the point that they would conform totally to the Communist regime.

A comparison of the two literary works I have discussed here reveals that both stories show the marginalization of Jewish protagonists from society. The main protagonist, Blank, in Becker's novel gives up his Jewish identity voluntarily. His son, though, tries to adopt a Jewish identity but fails to do so and dies in the six-day war in Israel. Similarly, other Jewish characters in Becker's novel leave East Germany or commit suicide there. They could not identify with the German Democratic Republic as their homeland, since they never felt accepted by society.

The first-person narrator in Reinerová's story does not have any special ties to her Jewish roots. She has assimilated completely and identifies with the prewar Communist ideology. This prewar type of Communism was antireligious and had left behind its initial ideas on nationality and ethnicity. Her Jewish identity is being constructed and imposed on her by the Czech interrogators during her imprisonment. She is labeled as a Zionist, although she had never been engaged in Zionist activities. On the contrary, she belonged to the assimilated, politically left-oriented group of intellectuals. The interrogators ignore this fact completely; they use her Jewishness as the basis for their accusations.

Although in Becker's novel Blank is not openly persecuted in the GDR, he is also not accepted in society. He ends up as an unemployed alcoholic on the margins of society. His traumatic past haunts him, and he has no chance to share it with the Germans. It seems inappropriate to talk about the past, and therefore Blank stands alone with his disturbing memories. Similarly, in the book *All the Colors of the Sun and the Night*, the narrator stays alone with her memories, her painful past even being held against her. Moreover, she, too, is persecuted because she is Jewish. In addition to open anti-Semitism, the narrator is confronted with Czech nationalism. As a German-speaking Jew, she is suspected of not being loyal to Czechoslovakia and, moreover, of having contacts with other German-speaking people endangering the state. This suspicion originates from the claim that the Germans were responsible for the breakdown of Czechoslovakia in 1938. In Reinerová's story, nationalism and anti-Semitism are equally represented, something that, however, cannot be said about Becker's novel. Even though Blank feels alienated in German society and does not trust Germans, he is not confronted with any nationalistic remarks. This can be explained through the different postwar situations in the two countries. Germany defined itself as a homogeneous nationalistic state from the thirties, and nationalism became identical with Hitler's National Socialism. Therefore, after the war, neither part of Germany found it acceptable in any form. On the contrary, before the war Czechoslovakia was a multinational state with 3.5 million Germans, who accounted for the largest minority. They were perceived as the cause of both the disintegration of Czechoslovakia in 1938 and the occupation by Hitler in 1939. For the existence of the reestablished Czechoslovakia, the coexistence of Czechs and Slovaks seemed to be the only possibility. Hence, nationalism was a legitimate ideology that penetrated all social spheres.

In both literary works, Jewish identity is depicted as an unwanted and awkward element that causes problems personally and socially. It is associated with guilt and shame, which determine the life of the protagonists and push them to the margins of society. The father in Becker's novel tries to dispose of his Jewish identity, hoping that he could eliminate the shameful suspicion about his origin, something that is noticeable in his face. The narrator in Reinerová's story suffers from the feeling of guilt because she was the only person in her family to survive the Holocaust. This is artfully used by the investigators to intimidate her and mentally torture her. Blank's decision to change his identity comes from his own motives and inner conviction, whereas the narrator in Reinerová´s story is forced from outside to confess to being Jewish. In both cases, Jewish identity is a stigma that makes it extremely difficult to feel at home in their native countries and to live in East Germany and Czechoslovakia. Both protagonists remain pariahs in society, and both are accepted only conditionally by their homelands.

Notes

[1] The numbers slightly differ based on the source. See Tomáš Staněk, "Němečtí židé v Československu, 1945–1948." *Dějiny a současnost* 13, no. 5 (1991): 42–46. Peter Hallama, *Nationale Helden und jüdische Opfer: Tschechische Repräsentation des Holocaust* (Göttingen: Vandenhoeck & Ruprecht, 2014), 33–63.

[2] Angelika Timm, "Ein ambivalentes Verhältnis—Juden in der DDR und der Staat Israel," in *Zwischen Politik und Kultur—Juden in der DDR*, ed. Moshe Zuckermann (Göttingen: Wallstein Verlag, 2002), 17–34.

[3] The topic of the Shoah in Germany and Czechoslovakia had been extensively researched and discussed by historians, and this was the focal point of the famous *Historikerstreit* in the late 1980s in West Germany. On the extermination of Czech Jews see Hallama, *Nationale Helden und jüdische Opfer*, Petr Brod, *Židé v Československu* (Praha: Česká křesťanská akademie, 2000), and Blanka Soukupová, *Židé v českých zemích po šoa* (Bratislava: Marenčin PT, 2016).

[4] Paul Ricoeur. *The Reality of the Historical Past* (Milwaukee: Marquette University Press, 1984), 1–9. Paul Ricoeur, *Zeit und Erzählung III* (Munich: Fink, 1991), 222–30.

[5] Jurek Becker, "Mein Judentum," in *Jurek Becker*, ed. Irene Heidelberger-Leonard (Frankfurt am Main: Suhrkamp, 1992), 15–25.

[6] Jurek Becker, *Der Boxer* (Rostock: VEB Hinstorff Verlag, 1976), 19. Further references to this work are given in the text using page numbers alone. Translations are my own.

[7] Gitta Honegger, "Prague writer Lenka Reinerová: Kafka's Last Living Heir," *Modernism/Modernity* 12, no. 4 (2005): 659–77.

[8] Most communists who returned to East Germany after the war were of Jewish origin. For more details about the postwar situation concerning Jews in East Germany see Karin Hartewig, *Zurückgekehrt: Die Geschichte der jüdischen Kommunisten in der DDR* (Cologne: Böhlau, 2000), Jeffrey Herf, *Divided Memory: The Nazi Past in the Two Germanys* (Cambridge, MA: Harvard University Press, 1997).

[9] Lenka Reinerová, *Alle Farben der Sonne und der Nacht* (Berlin: Aufbau Verlag, 2003), 63. Further references are given in the text using page numbers alone. Translations are my own.

[10] On the trauma of Czech Holocaust survivors see Alena Heitlingerová, *In the Shadows of the Holocaust & Communism: Czech and Slovak Jews since 1945* (London: Transaction, 2006).

13: Changed for the Better? Alternative Uses of the Transformative Cancer Trope in Thomas Mann's *Die Betrogene* and Nadine Gordimer's *Get a Life*

Kristen Hetrick

Cancer has been a theme in fictional literary works for centuries, but particularly from the twentieth century on. The prevailing representation has been of cancer serving as an impetus for transformative change in either the cancer patient, a person close to the patient, or both. Cancer patients in works of fiction generally experience their illness, and, where applicable, their recovery, over a longer period of time in comparison to more acute illnesses. This allows the sick characters and those around them to think about their lives, and perhaps to change the way they have been living because of having encountered a potentially terminal illness. Such a storyline is what Arthur Frank refers to in *The Wounded Storyteller: Body, Illness and Ethics* (1997) as "The Quest Narrative," in which illness is depicted as a journey that ultimately turns into a pursuit of something such as knowledge or experience.[1] Although not always the dominant depiction of the cancer experience, this portrayal is integral to early fictional cancer works such as Maria Edgeworth's 1801 novel *Belinda*, and Theodor Storm's 1887 novella *Ein Bekenntnis* (*An Avowal*), as well as to more recent texts, such as Margaret Atwood's 1981 novel *Bodily Harm* and Margaret Edson's 1995 play *Wit*. The prevailing depiction in early fictional accounts had been of static, familiar character representations of the cancer patient, often consisting of a virtuous dying woman inspiring those around her, and frequently involving cancer of the reproductive tract or breast cancer. In contrast, the emphasis since the mid-twentieth century has largely been to depict a single unique patient as he or she learns from and changes through the cancer experience. In this essay, however, I will examine two texts that present alternative views of the transformative nature of a cancer experience: Thomas Mann's 1953 novella *Die Betrogene*, and Nadine Gordimer's 2005 novel *Get a Life*. While Mann's work is essentially an indictment of the very concept through his portrayal of the afflicted protagonist, Gordimer's offers a more nuanced depiction of transformative change than the traditionally dramatic one. Each could be viewed as a reflection of the time in which it was written. Mann's text offers no hint of sympathy or understanding for his protagonist, but rather solely his apparent contempt. *Die Betrogene* was published long before the widespread proliferation of first-person cancer memoirs that began in the early 1980s, the vast majority of which conform to a transformative storyline, further popularizing it. Many also concern cancers primarily associated with women, such as breast cancer, and helped to catalyze the de-stigmatization of them. *Die Betrogene* is a response to the trope itself, rather than to this later development. Gordimer's novel, written more than half a century after Mann's, seems to be in dialogue with this explosion of transformative memoirs by offering a storyline that reinforces aspects of the trope but softens the extent of transformation.

In Thomas Mann's oeuvre of works about illness, his final completed work was his single text involving cancer, *Die Betrogene*.[2] Based on an account of an aristocratic woman who suffered a similar fate, this novella tells the story of a Rhenish widow, Rosalie von Tümmler, and her pursuit of the much younger American Ken Keaton in Germany of the 1920s. Rosalie has just turned fifty and lives in Düsseldorf with her unmarried twenty-nine year-old daughter and her teenaged son. When her son requests an English tutor, Rosalie employs the twenty-four-year-old Keaton. She quickly becomes besotted with the attractive young American, and the story then follows her attempts to garner his attention. Eventually, believing the apparent return of her menstruation following years of menopause to be a sign of nature's approval of this relationship, Rosalie becomes emboldened to declare her feelings to Keaton. The two arrange to meet to commence their love affair, but she is not able to follow through on their plans because she begins to hemorrhage. After doctors examine her, they declare that her bleeding has been a result of extensive cancer of the reproductive tract, and Rosalie soon dies.

Mann's choice of cancer type and the infected areas are integral to this text. As Mann describes it: "The bimanual examination . . . revealed a uterus far too large for the patient's age, abnormally thickened tissue in the tube, and, instead of an ovary already greatly reduced in size, a huge tumor. The curettage showed carcinoma cells. Some of them were characteristically ovarian, but others left no doubt that cancer cells were entering into full development in the uterus itself."[3] Her cancer reflects the disease's long-held general association with what Susan Sontag terms a "demonic pregnancy."[4] Mann alters this slightly, though, in that the cancer has spread to the fallopian tubes and ovaries. As the organs responsible for producing and carrying mature, unfertilized eggs to the uterus, they are essential in allowing reproductive potential to become a reality. In parallel, the bleeding that Rosalie mistakes for menstruation is vital to the hope and sense of rejuvenation that had initially been sparked by her interest in Keaton. Had Mann located the cancer solely in her uterus, it would have connoted sexual completion, which does not occur in this story. The association of fallopian tubes and ovaries with mere potential rather than success mirrors the ultimately unrealized potential of this relationship.

Without the initial bleeding, the relationship would have remained completely unrequited; although Rosalie's feelings for Keaton were strong, her perceived lack of youthful potency kept her from making them known. When nature then seems to have granted her a renewed youth, she explains to her daughter that this is the sign nature has given her to indicate its approval of her desire to pursue Keaton (*DB*, 83). As Marguerite De Huszar has argued, Rosalie is able to successfully deny that her bleeding is anything but a reawakening of her fertility because she refuses to accept the image of herself as a reproductively worthless old woman.[5] This transformation due to her cancer is certainly not portrayed as a moment of profound reflection or realization, although Rosalie herself might consider it to be so. Mann instead constructs Rosalie's self-delusion such that the reader will view her as foolish; her bleeding of course makes her no younger than she was before it, but her willingness to believe it leads her to be viewed as a naïve figure. This is then intensified when it is later revealed that the bleeding has been a result of her cancer, making her own interpretation of the bleeding seem even more irrational.

The hemorrhage that precludes Rosalie and Keaton's meeting enriches and complicates the story, as it is the lack of fulfillment in her relationship with Keaton that Rosalie must face in being told that what she took to be signs of rejuvenation are signs of terminal illness. Instead of having to come to terms with the loss of a consummated relationship, Rosalie must face the loss of the hope of that ever happening in the first place. These organs that enable but do not guarantee reproductive success have deceived Rosalie by denying her hope of a true return of her youthfulness and of a relationship with Keaton.

Rather than curse the body that has betrayed her and allowed her to pursue Keaton in vain, she finds a way to reconcile herself with her diagnosis, further emphasizing Mann's depiction of her as a flighty woman. Throughout the novella, Rosalie has identified herself as a "Maienkind" (May child) who finds solace in nature while going through menopause (*DB*, 23–24). Despite the recognition that nature did not grant her rejuvenation, Rosalie remains true to her beliefs. She incorporates her loyalty by explaining to her daughter: "'Indeed, death is a great instrument of life, and if for me it borrowed the guise of resurrection, of the joy of love, that was not a lie, but goodness and mercy.'" Her final words are then: "'Nature—I have always loved her, and she—has been loving to her child'" (*TBS*, 140–41). Rosalie does not hold any malice toward nature for afflicting her with cancer and its associated false promise of rejuvenation, but instead praises it for the resurrection of her ability to desire a man, seeing it as an act of kindness that accompanies the destruction of her physical life. She does not consider herself "die Betrogene," with its negative implication of deceit, but as one blessed to have had this brief reawakening. It was Mann who layered his own interpretation on Rosalie's by assigning this title, underscoring his illustration of Rosalie's naïveté. The human interpretation of nature's processes casts them in a particular light, and as Paul Felder has argued, it is only by accepting death as a part of life that Rosalie can be reunited with nature.[6] This holds true: in order for Rosalie to come to terms with her death and her misinterpretation of her bleeding, she must look at nature differently. Nature becomes inherently indifferent instead of magnanimous, and her cancer becomes a positive occurrence, instead of a cruel irony. Her simplistic devotion to nature is not a positive attribute; rather, it highlights the naïveté that allows for her self-delusion.

Mann's description of the cancer's progression implies that the origins of Rosalie's cancer are partially psychosomatic, further adding to his criticism of Rosalie's persona and beliefs. In the text, the chief surgeon explains to his assistant that "the whole story started from the ovary—that is, from immature ovarian cells which often remain there from birth and which, after the menopause, through heaven knows what process of stimulation, begin to develop malignantly" (TBS, 138). The stimulating factor is Rosalie's longing to be young again, catalyzed by her attraction to Keaton. Before her diagnosis, Rosalie attributes her bleeding to her own yearning to be fertile again, telling her daughter that it was her soul's triumph over her body (DB, 81). This depiction of the cancer's cause is in keeping with the limited knowledge of the biological origins of cancer during the 1950s. The blame for the disease was often placed on something the sufferer had or had not done. Mann does not place the blame fully on Rosalie's desire for Keaton and for her youth, rather also bringing in a vague biological explanation. Although the cells' mutation was initiated by Rosalie's attraction to Keaton, the actual tumors were produced by biological processes, thus freeing Rosalie from being completely at fault. She may have provided the impetus, but nature itself produced the disease from there. Mann's softening of Rosalie's blame in her disease adds weight to the depiction of nature as an indifferent participant in her cancer, instead of either a malevolent or benevolent one; nature proceeded with the disease when the opportunity arose, but it did not seek to destroy Rosalie on its own.

In discussing Mann's portrayal of Rosalie's cancer, James McWilliams has remarked that "Thomas Mann is utterly ruthless in describing the course of the fatal disease. He seems to take delight in the clinical precision with which he destroys his leading figure."[7] Indeed, the detailed descriptions highlight the grave state of her case and emphasize the destruction of her reproductive tract in a manner that seems to be beyond what is necessary in order to convey her terminal condition. One such passage reads: "Not only were all of the pelvic organs already involved; the perito-neum too showed—to the naked eye alone—the murderous cell groups, all the glands of the lymphatic system were carcinomatously thickened, and there was no doubt that there were also foci of cancer cells in the liver" (*TBS*, 138). The graphic details of the disease's progress stand in stark contrast to his protagonist's insistence on the goodness of nature, further contributing to his indictment of her as naïve and unrealistic in her staunch refusal to change her view of nature as benevolent.

Unlike most fictional cancer texts, this work does not focus extensively on the experience of being a patient or enduring treatment. Rather, Rosalie and her family's interactions with the medical professionals are brief. They do attempt surgery, the most effective treatment available at the time, but the disease has spread too extensively to be excised, and so they close the incision and allow the cancer to take its course (*DB*, 125–26). Rosalie's comparatively swift death focuses the reader on her steadfast beliefs instead of on the physical process of dying. Her resolute support of nature is the true focus of the final pages of this work, not her ever-declining physical condition. In providing this relatively abrupt cancer experi-ence, Mann subverts the typical trajectory of a transformative cancer text. The aggressive nature of this case has not given her time to truly examine any aspect of her life and to then potentially change accordingly. The same holds true for those around her, such as her children. In the end, Rosalie has the same views as she had in the beginning; she has simply and quickly crafted a narrative of her disease experience that reaffirms her belief in the goodness of nature. Mann therefore does not imbue this cancer story with the sense of a sincere value inherent in this cancer experience, but rather he repeatedly undermines this concept throughout the novella.

A more recent fictional text, Nadine Gordimer's 2005 novel *Get a Life*, offers another alternative to the traditional transformative narrative. In this work, it is thirty-five-year-old South African ecologist Paul Bannermann who is the cancer patient. When the story opens, Paul is returning to his parents' home for two weeks of quarantine, in order to protect his particularly vulnerable three-year-old son Nickie from any radioactive contamination resulting from the treatment Paul received for thyroid cancer. The complex narrative style of this work interweaves the words and thoughts of the novel's characters, focusing primarily on Paul, his mother Lyndsay, and his wife Benni, as they reflect on Paul's initial diagnosis and quarantine, and then live their lives for the subsequent year. Gordimer here presents a cancer experience that *is* transformative for the central characters, but ultimately in a much more subtle way than one typi-cally finds. As Atul Gawande discusses in his 2014 monograph *Being Mortal: Medicine and What Matters in the End*, research has shown that as the fragility of one's life becomes apparent, one's perspective does indeed shift on how and with whom one wishes to spend the remaining time.

However, in cases where conditions change and uncertainty about survival is lifted, people often largely return to their previously held perspectives and priorities.[8] This is not to say that absolutely no change occurs, but rather that it is less drastic and permanent than the depictions in film, on television, or in fictional texts. Gordimer's portrayal of the cancer experience is more in keeping with this frequent reality of an illness experience, wherein one can, and often does, experience lasting alterations to one's life, but they are not always the substantial changes predominantly depicted.

Consistent with this, Gordimer's choice of thyroid cancer is significant for several reasons. For one, thyroid cancer has one of the most swiftly increasing incidence rates worldwide, in part because with newer technologies it has become easier to identify. Paul's diagnosis, while a surprise to him as a seemingly healthy man, is not as shocking as it once might have been. The five-year survival rates are also exceptionally high at over 98 percent.[9] Therefore Paul's is a best-case scenario where treatment will more than likely end with a positive result. Gordimer focuses only briefly on the surgery and radiation, and in relatively vague descriptions at that. Interactions with the medical professionals are also largely absent, underscoring that the emphasis in this text is not on what occurs while living through active treatment. Instead, it is on the quarantine at the home of Paul's parents, an experience that Gordimer stated in a 2006 interview "alters your whole relationship to the world [. . . and] you begin to face those things that surface, things you probably would have suppressed for the rest of your life."[10] In order to protect his parents and their housekeeper from the radiation, Paul is left alone for the most part, and so he can simply sit and think about various aspects of his life and work while waiting for his quarantine to end. In his parents' garden in particular, Paul finds a retreat from the sick room, and as he reports, it is "the place to be yourself, against orders."[11] Considering his life before and after his radiation, Paul's thoughts focus on several issues: his marriage to Benni, his relationship with his parents, and his work as an ecologist fighting for the conservation of several South African ecosystems.

From the moment of diagnosis a separation develops between Paul and Benni; Paul, in digesting the news of the diagnosis, attempts to "smile in some attempt at recognition of her presence" (*GAL*, 7). This distancing continues as Paul researches the disease without telling her he has done so, and it is particularly evident as their conversations during quarantine become stilted and awkward. On the phone Benni tries to connect to Paul by speaking of her everyday life as they would were they together in person at home. He, however, in his state of quarantine, finds it difficult to connect to her report of the day's activities (*GAL*, 29). These moments alternate with their in-person encounters, where they are able to interact more naturally, albeit without touching. For Paul, this seems to add a new layer of anticipation to their relationship, as the inability to physically even hug adds an element of longing that had long been absent from their married lives. For Benni, however, these moments are uncomfortable, as she believes she can see the strain in him at not being able to touch (*GAL*, 29–32). Thus even in these more intimate interactions, they are not in concert with one another.

As Ileana Dimitriu has asserted, it is in the garden that Paul first begins to truly consider the divide between himself and his wife.[12] Indeed, it is during one of Paul's moments of reflection that he realizes that his professional life and Benni's are ruled by two very different principles, furthering the divide between them. The advertising agency for which Benni works seeks clients who build wild game nature resorts that destroy the natural terrain and replace it with tourist traps. Paul's work seeks in part to protect those very lands, and he sees himself as a man of strong convictions because of it. Benni, in contrast, is a woman with no need for such beliefs, and Paul thinks to himself that he has therefore truly been living in isolation from her all along (*GAL*, 57–58). He considers divorce, but the thought is accompanied by the consideration of whether that would be the right thing to do, given all she has done in the wake of his diagnosis (*GAL*, 58). When Paul resumes his time back at home, divorce or even separation are never mentioned again.

This is not to say that life is immediately as it was before; Paul and Benni must learn how to move forward now, and this new life is accompanied by a continued, if undiscussed, lack of ease with each other. Benni's fears about having sex with Paul after radiation, and his concerns about conceiving the second child Benni proposes they have, are major issues that are not verbally expressed by either. Further, Benni takes it upon herself to establish a new social circle, because she has independently decided that Paul needs new friendships (*GAL*, 102–3, 116–19). By the novel's end, however, their second child has been born healthy. In what Paul describes as a reversal of the "demonic light" that had entered into and then radiated from his body, the child is a positive eminence from Benni (*GAL*, 184). Their lives together seem to be moving forward in general in what Dimitriu referred to as "unexceptional rhythms . . . in a suburban tone."[13] Paul has apparently become reconciled to the differences between him and Benni that had so concerned him earlier in the garden, and while Benni and Paul do not seem to have an enriched, deepened relationship as the result of his illness, they are continuing to live life together happily rather than letting the complication of Paul's illness and treatment cause an irreparable rift. Gordimer's depiction suggests that their lives will continue in this unexceptional manner, in spite of how confronting and surviving Paul's cancer could have drastically changed them.

Paul's parents, Adrian and Lyndsay, are the other significant adults in Paul's illness experience. Paul had had a cordial relationship with them prior to this, but Adrian and Lyndsay's offer to house Paul brings a literal closeness that they had not experienced in years, which then leads to an attendant renewed emotional intimacy. This is evident in moments such as Paul and Lyndsay's spontaneous discussion one night of his environmental research and activism. They explore the importance of Lyndsay's field, law, in finding ways for Paul to fight for the preservation of ecosystems in the face of corporate enterprises (*GAL*, 25–26). However, the disease causes some distance to remain between them. At one point Paul wants to urge his parents to continue on their weekend routine of long walks, which they had given up to care for him, but he does not do so, because it would require them to discuss the reasons he is at their house in the first place (*GAL*, 33). Here again, Gordimer indicates a change in their relationship, but not a sudden reversal of how it had earlier been.

Once Paul leaves their home, his parents initially resume their lives. However, when Adrian stays behind on an archeological trip because of his attraction to their tour guide, Lyndsay's relationship with Paul deepens further. This resulting emotional closeness between mother and son was catalyzed by Paul's quarantine, since "the only one [Lyndsay] can approach is the one who came back in awful radiance to shelter in the childhood home" (*GAL*, 128). This intimacy is intensified by Adrian's eventual death abroad, and it is a positive force in Lyndsay's ability to move past it. In fact, Lyndsay has been promoted to judge by the narrative's end and she has decided to adopt a young girl who is HIV-positive; the bed vacated by Paul will now be occupied by another facing an uncertain illness, cared for by Lyndsay and her housekeeper, as he was (*GAL*, 147–50, 156). Lyndsay's life, like Paul's and Benni's, is moving forward, enhanced by her relationship to Paul and his family. Perhaps this would have happened even in the absence of the quarantine, or perhaps it would have happened without Adrian's departure from the marriage, but the text suggests that it was the combination of the two rather than either alone that enabled it.

Thyroid cancer is commonly associated with radiation accidents, such as Chernobyl; ironically, irradiation of the thyroid gland is also the treatment for thyroid cancer.[14] This connection is not lost on Paul, who, as an ecologist, is seeking to prevent such modern disasters by fighting the construction of a nuclear reactor. As an aside during a discussion with a colleague, Paul even remarks: "I'm my own experimental pebble-bed nuclear reactor," but this link remains unexplored as Paul continues his work; it does not seem to inspire him to be any more interested in stopping the project than he was pre-diagnosis, and it remains only one of several proposed projects he and his two colleagues are working to stop (*GAL*, 59). Rather, it is once again the sojourn in the garden that is significant. In spending extended time in the very place where his awareness of nature was first developed, Paul begins to wonder if his ecological efforts are truly as effective and vital as he had always believed. He ponders the idea that we may simply not live long enough to see what he refers to as the "survival solution" that results from an ecological disasters because "perhaps whatever civilization does to destroy nature, nature will find its solution in a measure of time we don't have" (*GAL*, 93, 168). This is not to say that he consequently finds his ecological work to be futile or unimportant, but it means that he does begin to consider the grey areas of ecological protection rather than taking a hard-line stance on it. There have also been some clear-cut victories from their work, however. The nuclear reactor project is at least temporarily halted, along with a proposal to build ten dams in another region (*GAL*, 185). As Byron Caminero-Santangelo has pointed out, this indicates that there will be no finite, absolute victory in Paul's efforts and in those of his colleagues, but that a more nuanced understanding will still yield positive results through their work.[15] This shift in Paul's perspective may be the greatest alteration that he undergoes because of his quarantine, but it is still an incremental shift rather than a dramatic epiphany; he now considers his work's goals with a greater understanding of what progress might mean, but he has not abandoned his prior efforts entirely.

Gordimer has said that this work is about survival, and that Paul's ultimate decision in surviving is to move forward, living essentially as he had been pre-diagnosis.[16] Karina Magdalena Szczurek has argued that Paul's cancer, like the nuclear reactor project, may only have been temporarily arrested, and the future is uncertain.[17] However, by the final page there is hope in the form of the family's new children and Paul's current cancer-free status that the central characters have all found a way to move past the illness experience in a relatively undramatic, understated manner.

Despite the maxim stating that there is "no pain, no gain," one does not always gain something from illness. With cancer, there is a wide spectrum of personal experience that ranges from truly life-changing and transformational in a positive way to the exact opposite. The fictional accounts most often written are those of the former, doubtless in part because that is what makes for the type of story audiences frequently want to read: someone facing this frequently debilitating illness and making the most of it by significantly changing for the better. For Rosalie in *Die Betrogene*, though, her cancer experience is ultimately not transformational, allowing Mann's critique of her and her beliefs to be writ large. For Gordimer's Paul in *Get a Life*, the change is more modest in nature, integrating his cancer experience into his life in a way that effects positive change but also allows him to carry on with a comfortable existence in favor of dismantling and rebuilding his life entirely. In each case the author presents an alternative to the traditional transformation trope, and one that is in part a product of its time. Mann, writing decades before transformative cancer memoirs became common and popular, offers a harsh rebuttal to the inherent value of the illness that is generally depicted in fictional works, while Gordimer, writing in the wake of the transformative cancer memoir's popularity and prevalence, does not reject it entirely but instead offers a more subtle positive trajectory for her cancer patient's post-diagnosis life. While these two stories of illness were crafted decades apart on separate continents, their authors' portrayals of cancer narratives that diverge from the traditional, expected story progression bridge those divides, allowing them to stand together as compelling counterpoints to the trope of the transformative cancer experience.

Notes

1 Arthur Frank, *The Wounded Storyteller: Body, Illness and Ethics* (Chicago: University of Chicago Press, 1995), 115–36.

2 Andreas P. Naef, "William E. Adams: Thomas Mann and *The Magic Mountain*," *Annals of Thoracic Surgery* 65 (1998): 285–87. Mann himself had a lung cancer successfully resected in 1946, but his diary entries bear no evidence that he knew it was a cancer: he had been told it was an abscess requiring surgical intervention (285).

3 Thomas Mann, *Die Betrogene* (Frankfurt am Main: Fischer, 1953), 83. Further references are given in the text using the abbreviation *DB*. In English, *The Black Swan*, trans. Willard R. Trask (Berkeley: University of California Press, 1990), 137. Further references to this work are given in the text using the abbreviation *TBS*.

4 Susan Sontag, *Illness as Metaphor* (New York: Farrer, Straus & Giroux, 1978), 13–14.

5 Marguerite Allen De Huszar, "Denial and Acceptance: Narrative Patterns in Thomas Mann's *Die Betrogene* and Kleist's *Die Marquise von O*," *Germanic Review* 64 (1989): 121–28; here, 121–22.

6 Paul Felder, "*Die Betrogene*, 'Unverkennbar von mir,'" *Thomas Mann Jahrbuch* 3 (1990): 118–38; here, 133.

7 Ibid.

8 Atul Gawande, *Being Mortal: Medicine and What Matters in the End* (New York: Metropolitan Books, 2014), 99–100.

9 National Cancer Institute Surveillance, Epidemiology and End Results Program, "Cancer Stat Facts: Thyroid Cancer," accessed 6 November 2017, https://seer. cancer.gov/statfacts/ html/thyro.html.

10 Nadine Gordimer, "Radiation, Race, and Molly Bloom: Nadine Gordimer Talks with *Bookforum*," interview by Kera Bolonik, *Bookforum* Feb./March 2006, http://www.bookforum. com/archive/feb_06/gordimer_interview.html.

11 Nadine Gordimer, *Get a Life: A Novel* (New York: Farrar, Straus & Giroux, 2005), 49. Further references to this work are given in the text using the abbreviation *GAL*.

12 Ileana Dimitriu, "Nadine Gordimer: Getting a Life after Apartheid," *Current Writing* 21 (2009): 117–37; *The Free Library by Farlex*, accessed 6 November

2017, https://www.thefree library.com/Nadine+Gordimer%3a+getting+a+life+after+apartheid.-a0221205451.

[13] Dimitriu, "Nadine Godimer," n.p.

[14] M. Hatch et al., "The Chernobyl Disaster: Cancer Following the Accident at the Chernobyl Nuclear Power Plant," *Epidemiological Reviews* 27, no. 1 (2005): 56–66. Hatch et al. found in their 2005 study that thyroid cancer in children was the most common cancer to have occurred in the vicinity of Chernobyl after the meltdown (63).

[15] Byron Caminero-Santangelo, "Never a Final Solution: Nadine Gordimer and the Environmental Unconscious," in *Environment at the Margins: Literary and Environmental Studies in Africa*, ed. Byron Caminero-Santangelo and Garth Myers, 224–26 (Athens: Ohio University Press, 2011).

[16] Maureen Isaacson, "Love, Radiation and Other States of Being," *Sunday Independent*, December 4, 2005.

[17] Karina Magdelena Szczurek, "'Come Rap for the Planet': Matters of Life and Death in Nadine Gordimer's *Get a Life* (2005)," *Werkwinkel* 4, no. 1 (2009): 35–69; here, 56.

Part III.

The Personal Narrative: Storytelling in Acute Historical Moments

14: Problems and Effects of Autobiographical Storytelling: *Als Pimpf in Polen: Erweiterte Kinderlandverschickung 1940–1945* (1993) and *A Hitler Youth in Poland: The Nazis' Program for Evacuating Children during World War II* (1998)

Jost Hermand

I.

STORYTELLING IS ONE OF THE OLDEST, if not the oldest, form of literary discourse. People always wanted to tell others about interesting historical events, legendary adventures, or their own life stories—no matter whether these were really true or only imaginary. In fiction this aspect of the purely interesting was from the outset accepted as "poetical." In historical or autobiographical retelling of facts, on the other hand, everything was expected to be "true." But what is truth? This is one of the oldest questions in this regard, as we know. Isn't every story, even those that pretend to expose only the bare facts, at the same time the product of specific individuals who arrange their stories according to their own convictions based on conscious or subconscious ideological aims, or on their supposed capability to remember the facts exactly? So many questions, so few answers, as the saying goes.

II.

As a case in point, I would like to problematize my own autobiographical report, *Als Pimpf in Polen*, which I wrote in the early 1990s, describing my dreadful experiences in the Nazi program for evacuating children during the Second World War.[1] Although German fascism had always been one of the central interests of my literary and political investigations, I had never written anything up to that point about my traumatic experiences of those years. My sudden interest in this phenomenon resulted mainly from the following occurrence. When I was in Berlin after German reunification in 1989, I heard from several schoolteachers there that some of their pupils in the eastern section of that city were joining neo-fascist organizations that attributed the rising unemployment of their parents to the evils of capitalism. Their exposure to these right-wing groups led them to see the new socioeconomic situation as a cold, competitive struggle for life where even the concepts of solidarity propagated during the forced socialism they had experienced under the Honecker regime were disappearing. Fed up with the restrictions of this system, they were suddenly told by their neo-fascist group leaders that during the Nazi period there had been a real national people's community (Volksgemeinschaft) based on solidarity and even camaraderie and friendship, and this was increasingly attractive to them. Therefore, I decided to unmask this myth by writing a short book about my own experiences in the Hitler Youth organization and my camp experiences during the Second World War, which were based only on competition and brutality without any traces of solidarity.

III.

Instead of relying only on my well-developed, long-range memory of experiences that took place fifty years earlier, I went about this project in the following way. As a scholar I first, of course, searched for other autobiographical writings as well as historical accounts of this topic. The most difficult task was to find any of my former comrades in suffering (Leidensgenossen) from these camps, but I could find only one, since the others had either left Berlin after 1945 or were killed as fifteen- or sixteen-year-old members of the so-called Volkssturm in the last battle of the war at Halbe, south of Berlin, where they were ordered to fight against the advancing Red Army until the bitter end. My former Paul von Hindenburg school in Berlin-Wilmersdorf refused to give me any information on possible survivors, and a trip to Poland, where I wanted to see my former camps again, also did not bring back any memories. The most helpful trip in this respect was a visit to the Bundesarchiv in Koblenz, where I found out that the only two books about this topic that came out in the postwar period were by the two leading male and female overseers of these camps, namely Gerhard Dabel and Jutta Rüdiger.[2] Both authors describe the camps in a rather post-fascist way as romanticized experiences for all those approximately three million teenagers who were sent to these camps in the years 1940 to 1945 for so-called "humanitarian reasons," that is, to rescue them from the attacks of the "evil British and American bombers." Neither pointed out, however, that Adolf Hitler and Baldur von Schirach, the

NS-Youth Leader (Reichsjugendführer) and later on the administrator of the entire children's evacuation program, had planned these camps as early as the early 1930s in order to take away all children from their parents and teachers and to transform the entire educational system into a camp system. Dabel and Rüdiger praised it, as I said, either as a romantic, youthful adventure or as a way of breaking down the older class barriers and thereby paving the way to a more "democratic" society. In reality, Hitler as well as Goebbels and Schirach had not dared to implement this plan in the middle of the 1930s, because they feared negative reactions from the overwhelming majority of parents, but starting in 1940 the bombardment of German cities finally gave them the chance to declare the evacuation of children to camps to be a "humanitarian act."

IV.

In my case, it all started in the fall of 1940, when British planes dropped their first bombs on Berlin. Two weeks later the schools were closed, and all children between eight and fifteen years old were sent to camps, mostly to older schoolhouses in the so-called Reichsland Warthegau, which had been incorporated into the Greater German Reich after the invasion of Poland in September 1939. According to the Social Darwinist principle that the strongest should always be in command, the Nazis left it open whether the teachers or the Hitler Youth leaders would be in command of these camps. In camps where the teachers took over the power, the conditions were almost bearable, as I later heard from others of my generation. In camps where the Hitler Youth leaders were in charge, the general conditions became almost intolerable. I was exposed to both of these forms of leadership. In the first camp, in Kirchenpopowo, near Posen (1940–41), where the teachers were in control, the conditions were almost humanitarian. The second one, in Groß-Ottingen, near Alexandrowo (1942–44), was hell. Here we had almost no school education but were constantly subjugated to a paramilitary drill of the worst kind. The orders of the day were marching, singing military songs, beating each other up, incarceration of the worst kind in stinking outhouses, sexual brutality, killing of animals, exercises in so-called courage by stabbing oneself in the leg or eating ten live frogs at once, working in the fields, and sports, always sports. According to Nazi concepts of the aims of such camps, Groß-Ottingen was not an aberration but the supposedly ideal camp to train the master race for the future Europe. There was no feeling of solidarity, no camaraderie, but only the principle of the survival of the fittest in the struggle for life, according to Hitler's maxim: "I envision my youth as a pack of young wolves, and the leader should always be on top."

V.

So much for the legendary myth of the national people's community, of solidarity among comrades. The opposite prevailed. All of us, forty-five boys of the same age, came to accept the Social Darwinist pecking order. The Hitler Youth leader with his club in hand was always in full command, and we were so afraid of him that we went along with all forms of brutality. I was fully aware that I was number 18 in my room of twenty-two boys, and I accepted this rank and was brutalized accordingly by the stronger ones. There was no chance to change it. The three teachers did not get involved in the daily routine, which always started out with us dressed in Hitler Youth uniforms, daggers hanging from our belts, raising the flag, and singing the song "Morning light, morning light, shines me to my early death" (Morgenrot, Morgenrot, / Leuchtest mir zum frühen Tod). The irony of all this was that such over-brutalization did not lead to the result the Nazis had hoped for. Instead of turning us into strong, proud members of the Aryan super race, we started to rebel in the fall of 1944 against the constant paramilitary drills. Granted, this was solely an adolescent rebellion caused by puberty and not by ideological motivations. Politically, we had been left totally in the dark, not knowing anything about Aryanism, the Nazi leadership, or the war events. In the Groß-Ottingen camp there was no electricity, no running water, no newspapers, nothing that would have informed us about Stalingrad and the approaching disasters at the Eastern front. We rebelled because we were young and innocently stupid. Therefore, we were glad that we were told on one day in late January of 1945 in our last camp in Sulmierschütz to leave everything behind and march through snow and ice in order to reach the last train in Krotoschin, which would bring the remaining Germans of that region back to Berlin.

VI.

There is of course much more that could be told about my experiences in these three camps where I was more or less imprisoned during the Second World War. But this is an article on autobiographical storytelling and all the problems and effects connected with it. Let us therefore go back to the initial questions about method and memory. After finishing the necessary research on the topic, and after I had completed the first draft of my manuscript, including all the facts I remembered from these years, I realized that the Nazis' Program for Evacuating Children during the Second World War was not a topic of general interest, even among those historians who were known for their scholarly interest in German fascism. To be more precise, it was almost a taboo, as I found out when I looked through the secondary literature on the Nazi educational system that already existed. Who would therefore be interested in publishing such a book, I asked myself? In order to find that out, in the first week of October 1992 I went to the Frankfurt Book Fair, trying to find someone who would be interested in such a seemingly minor, perhaps even outlandish topic. Although I was already known to some of the publishers who specialized in contemporary German history, nobody seemed to be interested in bringing out a book on such a relatively unknown topic. But determined not to give up my search, I finally discovered on one of the tables of the Fischer Taschenbuch Verlag the series "The Era of National Socialism" (Die Zeit des Nationalsozialismus) where well-known historians such as Götz Aly, Wolfgang Benz, Sebastian Haffner, Raul Hilberg, Ernst Klee, Eugen Kogon, Alexander Mitscherlich, George L. Mosse, Fred K. Prieberg, and Gerhard Schönberner had published their books, and I was lucky enough to meet its editor, Walter H. Pehle. I told him about my project, but even he was not overly enthusiastic about publishing a book on the Nazis' Program for Evacuating Children during the Second World War, a phenomenon he had never heard of. After I had told him a little about it, he asked me bluntly how many children had actually been evacuated to these camps. When I told him, "Almost three million," he exclaimed: "What a potential readership! But what should the title be: Die Erweiterte Kinderlandverschickung, 1940–1945? That's not an attractive title for such a book. That should be the subtitle. Please come up with something more catchy." I had a sudden brainstorm and said: "How about *Als Pimpf in Polen*?" He replied: "That is brilliant! Please send me the manuscript as soon as possible."

VII.

I immediately went back to the drawing board, looked for typos in the manuscript, checked some of my facts, and found one of my former classmates in the Berlin telephone book. I called him up, and he even remembered me and sent me two photographs that I could use for my book. In one of them I recognized myself dressed in a Hitler Youth winter uniform with other camp inmates and a soldier of the German army on April 20, 1941, under a portrait of Adolf Hitler, whose birthday was celebrated on that day. My classmate even told me that our "camp leader" (Lagermannschaftsführer) in Groß-Ottingen, who had beaten us up all the time, was still alive and well, even receiving a special pension for his service in this function. I called up that man immediately, but he presented himself on the phone as an ardent enemy of the Nazi system and remembered the time in Groß-Ottingen only as a romantic episode in his younger years. Suddenly, after this conversation, I also began to mistrust my own memory. In my manuscript I had written that he was released from active duty as camp leader and sent as a soldier to the Eastern front in the summer of 1944, where I assumed that he was certainly killed in one of the last battles with the Red Army. Full of anger at all the hardships we had suffered under him, I had subconsciously sent him to his certain death. Finding out after fifty years that he was still alive and seemingly doing well, I changed his real name in the manuscript at the last minute into a pseudonym, in order to avoid a possible lawsuit. When I told the editor of my book about that change, he tried to persuade me to leave the man's real name in it. He even hoped that this would result in a court case, which would help to give the book more publicity. Fischer would even pay for all the legal expenses connected with such a trial, he assured me, but I refused in order to avoid being accused of libel.

VIII.

And there is one more story that is relevant in the context of how memory works. There was another factual error in my book, where my subconscious had also distorted my memory, and which I corrected at the last minute in an attached epilogue. In this case, my subconscious had worked in exactly the opposite direction. The only boy I befriended— although friendship was hardly allowed—was a young Georgian by the name of Shota Sagiraschwili, who, like myself, was one of the underdogs in the Groß-Ottingen camp. He was born in 1929 in Berlin and was the son of a leader of an independence movement in the Caucasian mountains who had been deported by Stalin in the mid-1920s to Germany; I found this out at the last minute in further research on the topic after I had finished the manuscript. Subconsciously, while writing the book, I had feared that his father had massacred himself and his entire family in May of 1945 when the Red Army finally marched into Berlin. While my subconscious had sent the camp leader to the Eastern front where he was killed, I had subliminally feared that my friend was dead, too. But I found out that the Sagiraschwilis had escaped from certain death by fleeing at the last minute from Berlin to Switzerland and then to Italy. I was relieved when I discovered that Shota was still alive, but I never heard from him again until I received an e-mail from him in the spring of 2015—after seventy years—from Saint Petersburg, which I assumed was in Russia, telling me that he was still alive and doing well. Since he gave me his telephone number, I called him up and learned that he did not return to Russia but was now living in Saint Petersburg in Florida and had found out as an eighty-six-year-old man interested in his early years that I had written a book on our camp experiences in Groß-Ottingen. So much for the sometimes mysterious ways the subconscious works in either one or the other direction.

IX.

The book *Als Pimpf in Polen: Erweiterte Kinderlandverschickung, 1940–1945* finally came out in June of 1993. Although no German newspapers reviewed it, the Fischer publishing house instantly sold two large editions of it. Why it was still a taboo at the time to talk about these camps is still unclear to me. But my book had an effect on another level I had not expected. In the following months, I received about fifty letters from people I had never heard of before. About 10 percent were from former camp leaders who tried to whitewash themselves, who attacked me for being someone who fouls his own nest (Nestbeschmutzer), and who presented the camps as Nazi "humanitarian" efforts to save innocent children from the evil British and American bombers rather than as efforts to strengthen the Aryan master race for future attempts at world domination. The next roughly 40 percent were from members of my generation who had suffered under the same brutalization and told me that they found my book—because of its autobiographical orientation—totally authentic and therefore a necessary attempt to bring to light the worst aspects of Nazi education under which they had suffered the same way as I had. The most interesting of these letters, I found, were those by the remaining 50 percent, written by much younger people, who told me either that they were now better able to understand their parents or even their grandparents who had been in similar evacuation camps, or that after reading my book they were now more enlightened about the radical Social Darwinism underlying Nazi ideology, which was not based on the often-proclaimed myth of a true national people's community but on the ruthless will toward the survival of the fittest, meaning the "Aryan" race.

X.

I got almost the same responses when I did readings from this book in West German bookstores, which the publisher and some of my friends arranged for me. Granted, there were also some hecklers who showed their misgivings in no uncertain terms, but the majority of those attending understood that the tendency of this book was to counteract the attempts of the neo-Nazi organizations in the 1990s to present German fascism as a "warm," people-oriented movement that stressed above all the solidarity of all Germans. And I was glad to hear that the book had this effect. After all, my intention from the beginning had been not to present myself as an unfortunate victim of Nazi fascism. Rather, by using autobiographical storytelling in the middle sections of the book I had intended to give it a more authentic character, instead of restricting myself to theoretical aspects that would interest scholars but would have bored the majority of less educated readers. And it was the latter group of readers I was mainly interested in, not the academic positivists who merely compile endless amounts of facts, or those scholars who only want to demonstrate their theoretical sophistication and therefore regard storytelling as an unworthy journalistic approach to academic endeavors.

XI.

Because of the continuing interest in German fascism in other countries, especially in the United States, it was easy for the Fischer publishing house to find an American press, namely the Northwestern University Press in Evanston, Illinois, that was interested in bringing the book out in English translation. I was notified about this in 1996 and was told that the Fischer agency in New York had found a translator who was willing to try her hand at this task. It was Margot Betthauer Dembo, a Jewish woman of my age, who, after attending a German school in Mannheim, had come to the United States with her family in the second half of the 1930s in order to escape Nazi persecution. I immediately got in contact with her after she sent me the first draft of her extremely precise, well-written translation. There was only one aspect that had to be changed a little bit. And that was the following one. Certain parts seemed almost like descriptions of American Boy Scout camps and sounded therefore a bit too harmless or innocuous. In order to change this, I went to New York and spent three days working with her—knowing all too well how difficult it is to translate Nazi jargon into English—to give the manuscript a more paramilitary character. She agreed wholeheartedly, and the book came out in this form in 1997.

XII.

The rest is—as the saying goes—history. I gave readings from the book in American bookstores, but the effect was different than in Germany. To be sure, audiences listened patiently, but they were not personally affected in the same way as people in Cologne, Frankfurt, or Berlin. Granted, American listeners had a human interest in my storytelling, but they did not perceive my book's underlying aim of counteracting the mythmaking about Nazi fascism among certain neo-fascist movements in Germany at that time. I therefore gave up these readings after some attempts to convey my message to a politically unresponsive or only superficially interested audience. One of the few gratifying experiences I had in this respect was when the American Kindertransport society had its biannual meeting in the spring of 2004 in Madison, Wisconsin and asked me to give them a report about my life as a boy in Nazi Germany. These were all people who had been allowed by the Nazi regime to leave Germany in 1938 to go to England, where they mostly grew up in foster families, and who later moved from there to the United States. They were really moved by my talk, and some of them even confessed that they had a somewhat better life in England than I had in Nazi Germany at the same time.

XIII.

Since then I have presented my experiences only in the course on "Nazi Culture" that I teach every spring with Marc Silberman and Pamela Potter in the German Department at the University of Wisconsin–Madison. In this context my storytelling still has an immediate effect. Here the audience consists mainly of about 100 students between eighteen and twenty-one years old, who are much more captivated by human-interest stories than by theoretical speculations about the underlying implications of Nazi ideology. They compare my stories mostly to their own experiences as youngsters in a so-called democratic society; they are glad that they spent their summers in Boy Scout or Girl Scout camps, where they were not forced to comply with a harsh daily routine aiming to turn them into representatives of a racist ideology. And so my storytelling goes on, trying to promote awareness of the differences between totalitarian and democratic forms of education. And the Fischer publishing house is also still supporting this attempt, having brought out my *Als Pimpf in Polen* in a new paperback edition in 2014.

Notes

[1] *Als Pimpf in Polen: Erweiterte Kinderlandverschickung, 1940–1945* (Frankfurt am Main: Fischer, 1993). In English, *A Hitler Youth in Poland: The Nazis' Program for Evacuating Children during World War II*, trans. Margot Bettauer Dembo (Evanston, IL: Northwestern University Press, 1998).

[2] Gerhard Dabel, *KLV: Die erweiterte Kinderlandverschickung, 1940–1945* (Freiburg: Schillinger, 1981); and Jutta Rüdiger, ed., *Die Hitler-Jugend und ihr Selbstverständnis im Spiegel ihrer Aufgabengebiete* (Lindhorst: Askania, 1983).

15: Too Near, Too Far: My GDR Story

Marc Silberman

I WANT TO TELL THE STORY of how I came to discover East Germany and to commit my professional life to the study of its culture. So this is an intellectual autobiography of sorts, not one that I claim to be representative but nonetheless one that might contribute to narrating the "story" of the German Democratic Republic (GDR), a state that has disappeared from the map, and one that also might reveal the challenges we face in making sense of postwar German history. It is not the first time I look back at the GDR; at the last count this seems to be the sixth time in the past twenty-five years that I am stepping back and assessing where we stand vis-à-vis what seems to be a closed book, whose tattered cover I keep reopening.[1] This repeated, perhaps even obsessive approach to the past has less to do with history than it does with the present, that is, how we see things now, retrospectively, at any given point in time. Thus I want to engage here in that double process of memory work: remembering and forgetting. For me to (re)construct the schemes and patterns that describe the changes, in particular the before and after of November 9, 1989, as I see them now, I need to locate myself, at the same time being aware that in order to tell a compelling story, I tend to erase the contingent and discontinuous quality of the past. So with this awareness, let me begin by reflecting on the GDR, which is situated for me somewhere between proximity and distance: at one and the same time too near and too far.

The story begins in late November 1989, when I received an airmail postcard from my dissertation advisor, who out of the blue wrote to ask what I thought about the collapse of the Berlin Wall and whether I would be changing careers as a result. The implication—that someone who studies and teaches about the GDR would have no future in German Studies, even if meant ironically—registered as a bad joke, that is, it did hit a nerve and reminded me of the struggle that had begun more than fifteen years earlier, in the mid-1970s, to make room for GDR studies within the study of German literature and culture, a time when I had embarked on writing one of the first dissertations in the United States on GDR literature. Of course, the collapse of East Germany because of its internal dysfunction was not the end of the GDR. My own conviction then was that more than ever it would become an interesting object of study, even if GDR research were to have only a marginal institutional future within North American German Studies. At the same time I was suddenly aware that GDR studies in North America had become historical, that it had a history of its own. In the meantime the GDR has no more disappeared as a cultural and historical reality with the passage of time than has medieval Germany or the Third Reich. Just as these eras of study and teaching are constantly reworked and refined, so does the GDR maintain its status as an object of interest informed by the critical approaches and questions of the respective present. Our task today is to problematize its culture, history, and politics in order to interrogate the assumptions we brought and continue to bring to our work, asking us to consider new perspectives and new instruments of analysis.

Let me step back much further beyond 1989. I am not a determinist and do not think my interest in the GDR was predestined. Quite to the contrary, I think life presents us with opportunities that we often do not even recognize as such and of which we sometimes have the good fortune to take advantage. Such was my situation in October, 1957, when the Soviet Union launched Sputnik, the first earth satellite. Sputnik surprised the American public and shattered the perception of the United States as the world's technological superpower, with the result that the space race began and government agencies began investing in all levels of education. I grew up in a suburb of Minneapolis and entered the fourth grade in fall 1957. I do remember vaguely the Suez Canal crisis of 1956, but I don't specifically recall searching the skies for Sputnik in 1957; nonetheless, it did have a fateful impact on my life, for within a few months of its launch, I was learning German in my fourth-grade class! This progressive school district decided that if the Russians were coming, the kids needed to know foreign languages, so each of the three fourth-grade classrooms was assigned a teacher once a week: mine was for German, next door was French, and the third was Spanish. Apparently there were no teachers available for Russian, but that wasn't the point. This was the Cold War and the beginning of the end of American isolationism after the Second World War, and it must have been one of the first attempts at what has now become known as FLES or Foreign Language in the Elementary School. For me, it meant that I continuously learned German through the rest of my public school education, and when I entered the University of Minnesota in 1965, I was able to transition right into the advanced German courses. The fact that my declared major at this point was French and that I began to learn French from scratch as a first-year student only shows what widening a kid's expectations at a young age can do.

My first real encounter with East Germany was in summer 1967 when I arrived as a nineteen-year-old undergraduate student for a year's study at the Freie Universität (Free University) in West Berlin, the lucky recipient of an exchange scholarship through the University of Minnesota's study abroad program. East Germany for me was a vague place behind the Wall, a tantalizing but risky attraction concealed by the "Iron Curtain." I am pretty certain that my studies in German up this point in the mid-1960s had never introduced literature from East Germany or even mentioned much more than the fact of Germany's postwar division. Indeed, I'm not sure I had read any literature in German that had been written after 1933 except texts by those Germans who had been exiled during the Third Reich, something I had in common with fellow students at the Freie Universität, I soon discovered. This in fact was one of the motivating factors for the student movement that took off in summer 1967 in West Berlin: school and university curricula scrupulously avoided any coverage of the recent and problematic German past, prompting young students to begin foraging into the past of their parents and professors, asking uncomfortable questions and getting some unpleasant answers about their complicity in the Third Reich. But that is a different story, one I won't pursue here, nor am I going to tell the one about the escalation of the student movement, with regular sit-ins, teach-ins, and street demonstrations. As an American citizen in West Berlin, I had border-crossing privileges to the other half of the city that West Berliners and West Germans could acquire only by jumping through a lot of hoops, and I took advantage of the situation. The first few casual acquaintances I made in the legendary East Berlin student pub Friedrichstrasse 116 snowballed, and as the anti-Vietnam war protests in West Berlin heated up and the Prague Spring began to unfold in Czechoslovakia in April 1968, followed by the eruption of violent student demonstrations in May 1968 in Paris, I became—as an outsider from the West—an object of desire and a center of attention among my East Berlin acquaintances as I had never before been in my life. This experience of intense exchanges with young people from East Berlin indelibly marked my relationship to the GDR, and in fact I still today have contact with a few of them.

Returning to the University of Minnesota after this extraordinary year of study abroad, I decided to double major in German and French and went off to graduate school to continue my studies of German in 1969, funded with a fellowship from the NDEA, which I mention only because this was a federal program that began in 1958 in response to that originary event in what would become my professional career—the launching of Sputnik! The National Defense Education Act, or NDEA, was authorized in 1958 with the specific goal of helping the US compete better with the Soviet Union in the fields of science and technology after the Sputnik scare. It also aimed to provide the country with defense-oriented personnel, including foreign-language scholars and area-studies experts, by funding graduate students at colleges and universities. I can not say that in 1969 my politics actually conformed to this NDEA agenda; I was doing my hardest to keep out of the Vietnam War, hanging on as best I could to my student deferment from the military draft. But that, too, is another story that does not belong here. In any case, I took the NDEA money and ran, becoming one of those foreign-language scholars with area-studies expertise. As a graduate student I returned to the Freie Universität in West Berlin for another year in 1970–71, participating in what I later discovered were some of the very first seminars offered on GDR literature at a West German university. By this time, the students on their own were organizing courses that their professors either refused or were unprepared to teach, and such was the case with the course on contemporary GDR drama (contemporary referring then to the 1950s and 1960s) as well as the other on recent GDR novels. This led in turn to my decision to write a dissertation on the East German industrial novel of the 1950s and 1960s, which I worked on in West Berlin for two years from 1972 until 1974. I would dearly have liked to live in the GDR while doing so, but it was literally impossible to find a way to do this at the time. Not until 1975, the year I defended my dissertation at Indiana University, was an official avenue opened for scholarly exchange between the United States and the GDR, when an NGO, the International Research and Exchanges Board (IREX), signed an agreement to promote such activities.[2]

Until the early 1970s West German and American literary scholars tended to see GDR literature exclusively as political propaganda produced by state scribes. This was just beginning to change for a number of reasons, and in the course of the 1970s increasingly attention turned toward the literary production of the East. One reason was that postwar literature more generally became an object of interest with the passage of time. If my own undergraduate education in the 1960s had focused exclusively on pre-1933 developments, by the 1970s both scholarship and the teaching of contemporary West German literature was on the agenda, and the interest in contemporary West German literature opened the door for a comparative glance at the postwar developments in the GDR as well. Moreover, the New Left cultural turn that had been initiated by the student movements in Berlin, Paris, Berkeley, and New York provided a seed bed for alternative literatures and approaches to cultural life, including that of East Germany. Finally, in 1972 the politics of détente or *Ostpolitik* for the first time led to the mutual recognition of East and West Germany as sovereign states, followed by the international community (including the United States) opening diplomatic relations with the GDR. That, together with the regime change in East Germany in 1971, when Walter Ulbricht stepped down and Erich Honecker became first Party Secretary, sparked considerable interest among scholars of Germany in the West about GDR culture and politics in general and literature more specifically.

The point of departure for my own study on literature about industrial labor was to examine novels about the working world as a form of poetic communication concerned with the postwar reconstruction of Germany, taking into consideration their status as popular literature. Perhaps motivated by a naïve American attitude of "fairness" but most certainly in reaction to the trendy discourse on the "death of literature" circulating in the late 1960s in West Germany, I sought to understand on its own terms how literature functioned in East German society. The idea that state policies would sacrifice the autonomy of literary production to cultural accessibility for all social strata fascinated me as a means to break the traditional class nature of educational privilege. By the time I had completed the study, however, I realized that the theme of the working world had actually migrated from the literary domain to film and television, in other words to a different popular medium; indeed, many of the novels I treated were adapted for visual media in the late 1960s and 1970s. Just to illustrate how quickly change can happen, let me point out that an important reason for not having covered this media shift in my dissertation was the fact that video recording only became possible in 1975 when the first Sony Betamax video recorders came onto the market. It was virtually impossible for a Western scholar to access GDR films and television before the early 1980s, and even then it was still very difficult.

My interests diversified after the mid-1970s, but I kept returning to Berlin, to East Berlin, and to East German topics, treating more recent novels, developments in the theater, and increasingly in the cinema, as access to movies became more convenient. And this brings me closer to November 9, 1989. I had spent a year and a half in Bonn and West Berlin researching a new project, a history of German cinema, from fall 1987 until December 1988. At the time I was buried in film archives and libraries, including in East Berlin, never even noticing what was going on right under my nose. In fact, when I looked back, this sojourn in Germany struck me—the scholar—as one of the calmest, even most boring periods I had spent there! Then, in summer 1989, I joined the faculty at the University of Wisconsin and began following with more and more trepidation the sequence of events: East German citizens making their way to West Germany via Hungary, which had opened its border a crack to Austria; hundreds and then thousands of East Germans crowding into the West German embassy in Prague and demanding to exit to the West; the Monday demonstrations in Leipzig attracting more and more participants chanting "Wir sind das Volk" (We are the people). Events were escalating as I began teaching during that fall semester in Madison. The fortieth anniversary of the founding of the GDR on October 7, 1989, was approaching like a fata morgana. The bloody confrontation in June 1989 on Tiananmen Square in Beijing was on everyone's mind as the largest Monday demonstration with more than 60,000 people unfolded in the streets of Leipzig on October 9. Was the gerontocracy at the head of the GDR political establishment going to opt for the Chinese solution? I first heard about the opening of the Wall on the morning news on Friday,

November 10. I couldn't believe it. How could this happen without me? There were television monitors set up in my department conference room and around the language lab with streamed coverage piped in from the rooftop satellite disk. Groups of us stood around, incredulous, also worried. I jetted back to Berlin over the winter break in December 1989 to see with my own eyes how the Wall was disintegrating; and in March 1990 I used the spring break to be in Berlin during the election that would lead ultimately to Germany's unification on October 3, 1990. And with that, the GDR disappeared.

So what has changed since 1989? To echo the title of this essay—too near, too far—I was both emotionally close but geographically distant, and the ones who could judge what was happening were those who were there. Does this mean that as an outsider I should reserve judgment? I do not think so, but my judgment approximates equivocation. Did East Germany disappear? Well, yes and no. It disappeared in the sense that the GDR as I knew it is gone, wiped off the map; but in another sense, it has become even more real as the process of figuring out "was bleibt" (what remains) has sharpened my sense of how it became what it was and why it failed. History and memory are two distinct but related concepts, both based on narratives and both subject to change as time passes and our attention shifts. Nothing illustrates better this dynamic process of narrativization than the consequences for German historiography and the politics of memory after the fall of the Wall. After decades of division and cold-war competition, something like a "German" identity was on the agenda. German unification was suddenly postulated not only on the level of political affiliation but also as a shared identity: for the first time since the end of the Second World War being German emerged as a "national" mission. There were attempts to rewrite the literary history of both East and West Germany; political theories of modernization and totalitarian governance were reconsidered; a wave of *Ostalgie* (nostalgia for East Germany) and sometimes even *Westalgie* (nostalgia for West Germany) washed over the cultural discourse of the newly united Germany; and perhaps most significantly the vanishing point of twentieth-century German history began to shift from 1933 to 1989, with normalization and united Germany's integration into a larger European Union the guarantee that "never again Auschwitz" would endure. I have also worked on Holocaust memory in Germany, which has taught me first that how Germans remember their past is an object of great scrutiny and second that the process of remembering is more important than the product, with competing views about the past rarely yielding satisfying results. I suspect a similar framework may emerge for our research on cold-war Germany.

In my opinion the single greatest change in our approach to East Germany concerns access to information and people. First and foremost I am referring to archives. Although it has taken years to sort things out, the

GDR was a bureaucratic state in the German tradition, which means that basically written documents were produced in multiple copies, filed away, and saved for posterity. Beyond the issues of data protection, privacy, and of course the Stasi files, this has produced a mountain of material that has gradually become accessible since 1990: party files, ministry files, files of academies and universities, files of companies, publishing houses, and organizations from the local to the district to the national level. While this access in itself does not produce a historical narrative and entails a lot of sifting and winnowing to identify relevant documents, it does allow insight into the often contradictory processes of decision-making that characterized all cultural (not to say political) activity in the GDR. I am reminded of a piece of advice that the East German writer Heiner Müller gave me in 1979, when I was working on a book about his dramas and wanted to know how he adapted to the changing cultural policies after the Berlin Wall was built in 1961: "Don't go near that," he said: as an outsider I would never be able to understand the dance-like give-and-take behind the scenes that characterized writers and cultural functionaries (he was talking about his expulsion from the official Writers Union and the bogus self-critique needed to save his skin). Since 1989 I have spent hours, days, and weeks combing through archives and libraries to be able to understand the intricacies of East German cultural life beyond the published party decisions and newspaper sources, which in themselves are often not reliable. As a result, the negotiations that characterized East German cultural life at all levels become ever clearer: straining against the National Socialist past, against the capitalist other of the omnipresent West, and against an increasingly ineffective party-state.

A second change I can identify is a gradual shift in the temporal focus of GDR research. Possibly because Western scholars only began to recognize GDR culture as a legitimate object of interest in the course of the 1970s, for reasons I detailed earlier, their engagement has been largely with the generation of writers, film makers, and intellectuals who came of age in the GDR, that is, those who emerged into prominence in the 1960s and thereafter. This focus reinforced a more general cold-war tendency to dismiss early East German culture as pre-modern, as simple propaganda mired in a didactic, socialist-realist mold, created in the spirit of a Stalinist dictatorship. While the idea that culture could be instrumentalized for the purposes of the five-year plan might have indeed been a fantasy of the Socialist Party elite in the early years of the GDR, to adopt this view as a critical approach neglects the actual complexity of East German culture and the real contradictions of the cultural scene in those early decades. Indeed, my own work on the literature and films of the 1950s, going all the way back to that dissertation on the industrial novel of the 1950s and 1960s, has convinced me that a careful analysis of the issues of social binding and integration, and of the attempts to remap personal interests onto collective interests that animated writers and artists at the time, already articulated both thematically and formally the tensions in East German society that would continue to be played out over the next decades.[3] In other words, this early period in the GDR is neither pre-modern nor simplistic but the very foundation whose cracks had become such serious fissures by 1989 that the entire edifice collapsed.

The fall of the Wall and the dissolution of the intra-German border meant not only mobility in both directions but also the possibility of spontaneous face-to-face communication with East Germans as our potential informants and witnesses. This is the third major change. During the 1980s both travel and communication had become easier between Eastern and Western Europe, but there were still palpable cold-war filter systems that regulated and discouraged the free exchange of ideas, including from the American side. With the end of the Cold War and what in shorthand we tend to call the Ossi/Wessi-mentality (Easterners vs. Westerners) that ensued, a new kind of privilege emerged for the American outsider. Suddenly we were interrogators and conversational partners whom the Ossis preferred precisely because we were not West Germans, possibly because we were seen as less prejudicial toward them. On the other hand, I have also encountered more recently the exact opposite, members of the older Ossi generation who resist sharing their knowledge and insights out of a fear, I surmise, that they are being exploited because of their identity as GDR "witnesses," in other words a "circle-the-wagons" defensiveness to protect the memory of "our GDR."

A corollary to this is a fourth change we are undergoing. We are beginning to witness a generational shift. Today's youth and young adults have few of their own memories of the GDR, and those mediated by their parents and grandparents are also going to become ever more remote. This is a global shift, not only among Eastern Germans. As the temporal and emotional distance to German unification increases, these historical events will become ever more dependent on cultural media and their interpretation. The exponential growth of media since the millennial turn, and I am referring not only to the old analog media of photography, film, and television, but also to the new digital formats that create a completely new kind of dynamic public sphere, will yield not only new forms but also new languages for treating the past. Globalization and migration have also led to a shift in social structures with attendant changes in historical consciousness: Germany is now an in-migration nation. Hyphenated Germans can no longer be pressed into a once-unquestioned national category, an achievement that the Berlin Republic has finally recognized at least formally with its constitutional changes in the citizenship laws. The heterogeneity of social structures and the plurality in the means of access to the GDR past are going to undermine any attempt to establish a master narrative of the Cold War and East and West Germany's role in it. A national approach to German unification, such as dominated discourse in the 1990s and to a large extent still does today, a view that sees unification as an exclusively German issue, ignores the European and global practices of power politics, economics, and culture. There are obviously national differences in the reconstruction of the past, but we will be encountering more and more parallel and overlapping accounts, which may bring about a paradigm change in the way we construct the postwar German narrative.

This brings me to a final comment on what changed after 1989, especially in terms of teaching: beyond the access to material and people that has enabled us to redefine and refine our research goals, we are now faced with the challenge to change our orientation if we want to enliven what I perceive to be an increasingly out-of-date agenda. GDR studies must overcome what I call its regionally or geopolitically defined focus and examine broader connections to German and European modernism, technology, socialism, and contemporary politics. It no longer suffices to center our attention exclusively on the GDR state and East German identity with its cold-war rubric; we need to integrate comparative and transnational perspectives. While most research on the GDR begins with the year 1945 and ends in 1989, and begins at the Elbe and ends at the Oder, because that is when and where the state begins and ends, I think it is time to conceive of the GDR as a "knot" with chronological ends reaching back to the nineteenth century and into the post-unification future, as well as geographically into Eastern and Western Europe and even the nonaligned world. GDR culture was not an island unto itself, and certainly since the end of the Second World War the idea of autonomous national cultures has been on the retreat. While the GDR may seem to be an exception, what with its boundaries having materialized into fences and the concrete of the Berlin Wall, it too was subject to dialogue, exchange, and competition both internally and externally.

Shifting attention from the national to the transnational suggests a counter strategy to the epistemology that established and has sustained GDR scholarship in North America since the 1970s. Tied to concepts of the nation, national culture, and national identity, discussions in both the East and the West have focused on defining the qualities and distinctiveness of East German culture, its difference being variously qualified as produced by postwar, socialist, and/or cold-war cultural policies. While I cannot ignore the national dimension of culture, I do insist that national specificity is a dialectical reference point of the larger international or transnational context. The very founding of the GDR, for example, harks back to the Soviet Union and the Comintern, and tension between national ambitions and international commitments surfaced in both politics and culture. As a result, many socialists who returned from exile to participate in building their vision of a "better Germany" in the East found their vision branded as incompatible and themselves vilified. Moreover, the GDR always struggled with the issue of whether it was committed to a modern, internationalist form of socialism or whether it was the true inheritor of a German tradition of culture and history. Of course, this had a special resonance because of Germany's history of nationalism and racism as well as its status as one of the birthplaces of socialism. Hence, I see the need to reposition East Germany and to identify blind spots of past approaches that have failed to contextualize it beyond the boundaries and temporality of the GDR. This is where I am now, looking back at the GDR: situated somewhere between proximity and distance: moving away, but getting closer as the very map itself is changing shape!

Notes

[1] See, for example, my brief report from a 1991 research stay in Berlin, "Whose Revolution Was It? Stalinism and the Stasi in the Former GDR," *GDR Bulletin*, 18, no. 1 (Spring 1992): 21–24; the introduction to the special section I edited on "German Studies and the GDR," *Monatshefte* 85, no. 3 (Fall 1993): 265–74; "Problematizing the Socialist Public Sphere: Concepts and Consequences," in *What Remains? East German Culture and the Postwar Public.* AICGS Research Report No. 5, ed. Marc Silberman, 1–37 (Washington, DC: American Institute for Contemporary German Studies, 1997); "Whose Story Is This? Rewriting the Literary History of the GDR," in *Contentious Memories: Looking Back at the GDR*, proceedings of the 28th Wisconsin Workshop, ed. Jost Hermand and Marc Silberman (New York: Peter Lang, 1998), 25–57; "Spuren der Zeitgeschichte in Zukunftsphantasien früher DDR-Gegenwartsromane," in *Keiner kommt davon: Zeitgeschichte in der Literatur nach 1945*, ed. Erhard Schütz and Wolfgang Hardtwig (Göttingen: Vandenhoeck & Ruprecht, 2008), 35–46; and the coauthored introduction "DEFA at the Crossroads: Remapping the Terrain," in *DEFA at the Crossroads of East German and International Film Culture: A Companion*, ed. Marc Silberman and Henning Wrage (Berlin: DeGruyter, 2014), 1–22.

[2] Marc Silberman, *Literature of the Working World: A Study of the Industrial Novel in East Germany* (Bern: H. Lang, 1976); see the earlier dissertation published by John Flores, *Poetry in East Germany* (New Haven, CT: Yale University Press, 1971). Other contemporaneous but unpublished dissertations include Alan Curtis Bedell's 1974 study entitled "Social Conflict and Its Literary Depiction in Eight Contemporary East German Novels" (University of Rochester), Charlotte Gebhardt's 1975 study "Bitterfeld and the GDR Novel" (Stanford University), and Vanessa White's 1980 study "A Comparative Study of Alienation, Identity, and the Development of the Self in Afro-American and East German Fiction of the German Democratic Republic from 1965 to 1972" (SUNY Binghamton). In addition, Irene Hedlin's dissertation was published under the title *The Individual in a New Society: A Study of Selected "Erzählungen" and "Kurzgeschichten"* (Bern: Peter

Lang, 1977), as was H. G. (Gunnar) Huettich's under the title *Theater in the Planned Society: Contemporary Drama in the German Democratic Republic in Its Historical, Political, and Cultural Context* (Chapel Hill: University of North Carolina Press, 1978).

[3] Beyond the articles mentioned in note 1, see as well these articles of mine that focus on the 1950s and 1960s: "Remembering History: The Filmmaker Konrad Wolf," *New German Critique* 49 (Winter 1990): 163–91; "Wolfgang Staudte: *Rotation* (Germany 1949)," in *Filmästhetik gegen Faschismus: Faschismus und Antifaschismus im Film*, ed. Joachim Schmitt-Sasse (Münster: Maks, 1993), 137–52; "'Family Troubles': A Generational View of Heiner Müller's Role in the GDR," in *Heiner Müller: ConTEXTS and HISTORY*, ed. Gerhard Fischer (Tübingen: Stauffenburg, 1995), 55–69; "Hauff-Verfilmungen der fünfziger Jahre: Märchen und postfaschistischer Medienwandel," in *Wilhelm Hauff oder die Virtuosität der Einbildungskraft*, ed. Ernst Osterkamp, Andrea Polaschegg, and Erhard Schütz (Göttingen: Wallstein, 2005), 238–62; "Learning from the Enemy: DEFA-French Co-productions of the 1950s," *Film History* 18, no. 1 (February 2006): 21–45; and "What's New? Allegorical Representations of Renewal in DEFA's Early Youth Films," in *German Postwar Films: Life and Love in the Ruins*, ed. Wilfried Wilms and William Rasch (New York: Palgrave Macmillan, 2008), 93–108.

16: Conflict without Resolution: Konrad Wolf and the Dilemma of Hatred

Andy Spencer

IN THE COURSE OF A 1981 public discussion with Wolfgang Kohlhaase and Stephan Hermlin, organized to mark the fortieth anniversary of the German invasion of the Soviet Union, former Red Army soldier Konrad Wolf fretted about the conflict-readiness of his nation's youth in this time of peace: "With [the consolidation of peace], however, goes the difficulty of making convincingly clear to succeeding generations that that which has been achieved must be defended."[1] To be sure, it should come as no surprise that conflict should have so colored Wolf's perspective: Although born in Germany in 1925, he spent ten formative years of his early life in Moscow, the Soviet Union having offered the entire Wolf family sanctuary after the National Socialists came to power in 1933. He went to school in Moscow and became a Soviet citizen in 1936, before enlisting in the Red Army at the tender age of seventeen and joining up with the political division of the 47th Army in March 1943. From just south of the Black Sea port of Novorossiysk in the Caucasus, the army's campaign took Wolf via Rostov on Don into the Ukraine and then Poland, on into Germany at the beginning of March 1945, and finally to Berlin.

For Wolf, conflict had played a crucial role in the formation of that principled standpoint that had proved decisive in the military defeat of Nazi Germany; it was in conflict that the roots of the very identity of the GDR were to be found. This view is hardly surprising, given that through his father Wolf knew many of the other political exiles in Moscow who had fought in the Spanish Civil War and then worked alongside the Red Army during the war years, and finally, beginning in April 1945, returned to Germany to start the work of creating the new socialist state. In his wartime diaries, which he wrote in Russian, he writes of visiting such future GDR luminaries as Willi Bredel, Walter Ulbricht, and Erich Weinert (entry of December 23, 1943).[2] Following the founding of the state, conflict remained just as decisive in preserving the gains made by the state in the face of constant provocation from the West. The danger represented by the enemies of socialism persisted as a topic of Wolf's public utterances until his death a mere nine months after the 1981 discussion, becoming something of an article of faith. Wolf remained convinced that the enemy would always work against the socialist state and would always look to undermine the latter's seeming security through, for example, the ruinous efficacy of its propaganda (something he had experienced firsthand during his time in the military), and therefore must be combated at all times. Logically, the continued existence of the state was contingent upon the youth of the nation being ready to defend that state, but impressing that upon young people who had been socialized in peacetime presented its own set of problems, which led rather to some particularly tortuous logic in his contribution to the 1981 discussion:

> Yes, how then, I ask, . . . can young people today be raised in the spirit of internationalism on the one hand, in the spirit of friendship between peoples, in the humanistic sense, in respect for human beings, their dignity and their lives, and then on the other hand, after more than thirty years of peace, how can these same young people get to know of the brutality of war from personal experience? Are we supposed to orchestrate some kind of war so that the young, as it were, get to experience it for themselves?

This veritable plea for the reactivation of an actual fighting enemy could, of course, be read simply as an overheated, frustrated acknowledgment of the changed political landscape, perhaps of the shortcomings of the SED-leadership in winning over the youth to its way of thinking, but at the very least it also speaks to the continued importance of that earlier conflict in Wolf's thinking, and it is for that reason that he would remain unable to ever publicly condemn any aspect of it, including its murderous excesses resulting from an inculcated hatred for the enemy; that he was, indeed, so shortly before his death, still seeking for ways to come to terms with those excesses. At that 1981 event he proffered the following:

> One of the greatest problems in the first weeks and months of the war was that the people in the Soviet Union, and especially the young people, had been raised in the spirit of political internationalism, that the Soviet people were possessed of a deep-seated belief in and high expectations for the German proletariat in particular and the millions of German Communists who had voted for Thälmann, for the KPD before Hitler. It was almost like a shock, it was almost a suicidal naïveté when in the first weeks of the war . . . many actually expected that now that Hitler had raised his weapons against the first country in which the working class had been victorious, all of these workers, who after all had stood with Thälmann only a few years before, would at least lay down their weapons, if not turn around. . . . Back then, one of the greatest shocks, traumas of the Soviet people was that their very deep trust in the effectivity of the proletarian internationalism of the German proletariat was betrayed and abused to such a degree that it then turned into pure hatred, and didn't only turn but was also purposefully and consciously steered in that direction, so that the

hatred would become an inner conviction of the people in order to save the country and the people.

In the present context it is not so much the merits or otherwise of Wolf's diagnosis of the causes of hatred that are of interest but rather the clear indication of his ongoing inner struggle. On the one hand he would seem to be arguing that the young people will only be won over once they have experienced for themselves the centrality of conflict, but on the other he is well aware of what is required to win that conflict: an instrumentalization of hatred. In her oral history of women who fought in the Red Army during the war, Svetlana Alexievich cites a commander of antiaircraft artillery: "You can't shoot unless you hate. It's a war, not a hunt. I remember at political classes they read us the article 'Kill Him!' by Ilya Ehrenburg. As many times as you meet a German, so many times you kill him. A famous article, everybody read it then, learned it by heart. It made a strong impression on me. I carried it in my bag all through the war."[3] In the 1981 discussion Wolf would himself reflect on Ehrenburg's call to hate, arguing that once hatred had become "an inner conviction of the people in order to save the country and the people," then he could, "understand, for example, Ehrenburg in his guiding mantra: 'Hate the German, kill the German, wherever you see him.' Perhaps it is exaggerated in its language or diction. After a certain time the headlines in the newspapers no longer read 'Death to the fascist occupiers' but rather 'Death to the German occupiers,' and Fritz became an insult." It is, I should like to argue in the following, worth looking back at Wolf's wartime experiences in order to shed light on just how little his views regarding conflict would change over the course of his life, even if those views gave him much to agonize over. In 1943 his inner struggle had been, understandably, less urgent, still very much outweighed as it was by feelings of attachment to the Soviet Union. Writing in his diary on March 18, 1945, Wolf explored his emotions now that he was back on German soil: Germany, as he now sees it, is his "fatherland," the Soviet Union his "homeland":

> It was, after all, eleven years ago that I came to the USSR. The Soviet country, the Soviet state, the Soviet people are indispensable for me, I could no more live without them than I could without air. Now that I am here in my fatherland there is nothing that would keep me here, quite the reverse, I'm drawn all the more to Moscow, to the USSR, my true homeland.

The fierce loyalty to the Soviet Union that comes through in the diaries is matched by Wolf's rejection of Germany and the Germans, having witnessed firsthand the misery that the German army had visited upon his "homeland": on April 11, 1943, at the beginning of his active duty, Wolf wrote of his impressions from the foothills of the Caucasian ridge where retreating German troops had left a trail of devastation in their wake:

> We drove through Beloretschenskaja, naturally everything is destroyed here. These animals systematically destroyed everything; every telegraph pole is torn down, every small bridge blown up. The houses by the stations are destroyed, burned out. The second track is ripped up, everywhere the debris of vehicles, train cars, locomotives and so on. The inhabitants tell terrible stories about the Germans. It is simply incredible that human beings are capable of such bestiality. The name German is used as a swear word by the people, is used to threaten the children. It is terrible, but true. (April 11, 1943)

Convinced of the Germans' inhumanity, he, like his fellow soldiers, adopts the dehumanizing term "Fritz" on April 14, 1943, and then again on July 7, but on August 29, while stationed near Kharkiv in the Ukraine, he goes beyond name-calling to recommend the most definitive of measures for a German air force lieutenant who had been shot down and captured: "Insolent to the last degree. I only had to look him in the face and already my hands started to twitch, he looked at one with such contempt. . . . A fascist to his marrow. Goebbels's propaganda has had such a profound effect upon him that the only thing, in my view, that one can do with him is to shoot him" (August 29, 1943). In searching for the cause for a worldview so deformed that the only response can be to "shoot him," Wolf often invokes the effectiveness of Nazi propaganda, as, for example, following an encounter with a captured first lieutenant three days later on September 1:

> A typical young German. Twenty years old, ten when Hitler came to power. He naturally went enthusiastically to the *Jungvolk*, where he could wear a uniform, carry a dagger, and participate in various war games. With that began his thoroughgoing indoctrination through fascist propaganda. Then he landed in the *Hitler Youth*, from there to the army, and everywhere the same thing was drummed into him: the genius of the Führer, and Goebbels's propaganda. As a result of that he developed into a well-heeled soldier for Hitler and a passionate fascist. He has understood that they have lost, but simply can not get into his head the thought that Hitler miscalculated. He hopes for something unreal, hopes that because the Führer has found a way out on more than one occasion he will manage it this time too. How deep within them this stupid, idiotic propaganda has penetrated. And how cleverly the leaders of fascist Germany handle them. (September 1, 1943)

The accumulated result of this indoctrination, Wolf believes, has been an extreme dulling of the senses. On October 1 he would ask, "How can these animals even dare to call themselves human!?" Three months later and still in the Ukraine, but now in Koselez, he writes a longer entry summing up his experiences of 1943, during the course of which he reflects, from a distance, on the news from inside Germany. His decidedly fatalistic view is that even though the Germans are aware that they have no hope at all of winning this particular war, this knowledge has not led to any soul-searching:

> The English bombed Berlin again yesterday. More than 2,000 tons of bombs were dropped within half an hour. I can't even imagine what happens during such raids. That is indeed a dreadful nightmare. And that every second, third day. The behavior of the Germans is a mystery to me. After all of these terrible bombardments, these military misadventures, there is no noticeable change in the thinking and actions of the Germans. The Devil may know what they are about, I almost believe that they have been rendered stupid by all this horror, these nightmares, this suffering; that they are incapable of seriously reflecting on the causes of the horror, and that they strive solely to evade, in whichever way they can, their present; strive solely to feed themselves, to survive this one day. They are already no longer capable of reflecting on tomorrow, the end of the war, the fate of Germany and the German people; that is beyond their strength and overtaxes their brains, strained to the limit as they are by the fascist demagoguery of fear and terror. (December 31, 1943)

Here Wolf seems to be at a loss, confident that Germany will be defeated but skeptical as to how a new society might be created by such weakened individuals. Yet some of the old certainty he showed following the encounters with members of the German armed forces returns, once he has experienced life in Germany for himself some fifteen months later:

> A few words on my impressions in Germany: I must say that the few inhabitants who have remained in our sector give the impression of being extremely frightened by the German propaganda, and so say what they think we want to hear just to be obliging to the Russians. They whine that Hitler and Germany are finished. One encounters a lot of fawning; sometimes it's simply loathsome! They have warned us that surprises await us here around every corner, such as a bullet in the back. I believe, however, that as a result of six years of war the German people have used up their last drop of strength and are so apathetic and dulled that they are prepared to do anything, are in agreement with whichever power, if only there might be peace and a cessation to the endless bombardments, shooting, and so on . . . The German people are of course now suffering unprecedented distress and there's probably hardly a German who could have imagined six years ago that he would ever find himself in a situation like this. But that is a lesson, a lesson such as the German people will never forget. It will spoil its appetite once and for all for "organizing" foreign living-space. (March 19, 1945)

The "unprecedented distress," as is clear from the lines that close the diary entry, includes also the actions of occupying Soviet troops:

All of the more or less big population centers have been heavily
destroyed, either as a result of the bitter fighting, or because of the
hatred vented by our soldiers. Many of my acquaintances, indeed
even friends, probably think that this grieves me, that I feel sorry for
the German cities, the population, and so on. I say quite candidly, no,
I will never feel sorry, for I have seen for myself what they did in
Russia, and I therefore understand that it is only in this way that they
will ever be dissuaded from going to war again. (March 19, 1945)

Here, in these later entries, we see a conflation of the German military with
the civilian population, and it is for this reason that we are taken aback by
the youthful Wolf's almost casual invocation of "the hatred vented" by the
Soviet troops, which, he seems to suggest, is an eminently comprehensible
response to the situation at hand. By the time he returned to his wartime
experiences in the film *I Was Nineteen* (1968), we can reasonably expect a
maturation process to have taken place in the meantime, and it is indeed
evident from the two scenes I will briefly discuss below, that he has added
nuance to his position. Nevertheless, the very choice of subject matter for
the film only underlies his belief that the experience of conflict is the cru-
cible in which convictions are formed. These two scenes are, I should like
to argue, also informed by his wartime experiences, but not those that one
might expect, rather by a March 1944 meeting in Pavursk, just east of
Kovel, with Lev Kopelev, who at the time was serving as Senior Political
Instructor for the Second Belorussian front. Kopelev had been seconded
briefly to Wolf's unit and the latter has only glowing praise for the older
man's abilities and commitment:

Major Kopelev makes a very pleasant impression. In the first place he
is a pleasant person and likable, and secondly, in my opinion, an outstanding expert. He has perfect command of the language and a great
deal of experience in our line of work. What's more, he conducts
himself entirely informally, without the superior attitude normally
cultivated by the people who come from higher up. Without a doubt
he is proving of great help to us both in the production of leaflets and
the interrogation of POWs. (March 28, 1944)

Ten days later Wolf writes of Kopelev's departure: "Major Kopelev left here
a short while ago. He proved to be of great help to us. We worked like
dogs. Leaflets, prisoners, broadcasts for the loudspeaker-system, and so on.
When he left it was at once more spacious and quieter. He is a very energetic and impassioned person and with these qualities he completely filled
our already quite cramped quarters" (April 7, 1944). Finally, on April 24,
Wolf looks back fondly on his time with Kopelev:

Once again it has been raining commanding officers from the front.
It's already been a few days since the Senior Instructor from the front
Major Sacharov, and First Lieutenant Gulowitsch arrived. Quite hon-

estly, Kopelev's visit was of greater help than that of these two. They literally sit there and don't know how to kill their time. Now and again they lose themselves in the files, making relevant and irrelevant remarks. But help—none at all. When I think of Kopelev and how cramped it was when he arrived: but the days were filled with work and activity, and there was no sitting around doing nothing. Here now it's the complete opposite, everything dies, any desire to do anything passes.

Such praise for Kopelev finds no echo after 1944. It is entirely possible that in the years immediately following the war Wolf would have been oblivious to Kopelev's fate: until December, 1946 Wolf had continued to serve as a member of the occupying forces in Berlin before being transferred to the House of Soviet Culture on Unter den Linden. In September 1949 he headed back to Moscow to study at the storied WGIK film school, completing his training in March 1955. Only then did he make the definitive move back to Germany to take up a director's contract at the DEFA film studios. However, after working at a furious pace and completing eight films Wolf was elected President of the GDR's Academy of the Arts in 1965, and it is hard to imagine that in that capacity he could have remained unaware of Kopelev's dissident status. Only a year after their 1944 meeting, Kopelev had been arrested while serving in the Political Department of the 50th Army in East Prussia and charged with "bourgeois humanitarianism" and "pity for the enemy" because of his criticism of and attempts to stop looting and raping by Soviet soldiers. He subsequently spent ten years in Stalin's camps.

It is equally difficult to imagine how Wolf countenanced that, given the fulsome praise he had heaped on Kopelev in the wartime diaries. Wolf's dilemma is compounded by the fact that his firmly held belief that the battle against opponents is one of life and death carries with it the corollary that the socialist camp must present a united front to the world. Problems and criticism must be dealt with "in-house" and not be allowed to provide fodder for enemy propaganda. In his public utterances Wolf never wavered from a fierce loyalty to the Soviet Union, even though we know from Aune Renk that he was devastated by his reading of Solzhenitsyn's "One Day in the Life of Ivan Denisovich" in 1962 and that he cancelled a proposed trip back to Moscow in the days following.[4] Did he know, one wonders, that Kopelev had met Solzhenitsyn while imprisoned, and that it had been at Kopelev's urging that Alexander Tvardovsky, the editor of *Novy Mir*, had published Solzhenitsyn's text?

As late as 1976 and the expatriation of Wolf Biermann, by which time Wolf had been functioning as President of the Academy of the Arts for a decade, we know from contemporaries that aside from penning the obligatory declaration of loyalty for *Neues Deutschland*,[5] Wolf's behind-the-scenes energies at the time were directed primarily at convincing the signatories of the open letter protesting the government's action to retract their signatures. It was not Biermann's critique that troubled Wolf so much as the public expression of support for him which, in Wolf's eyes, played into the hands of the GDR's enemies.

For this reason it is all the more intriguing that Wolf should have allowed himself a degree of leeway in the films that is absent from his public statements. Kopelev's shadow looms large in the two sequences of the film alluded to above. Both would appear to be entirely of Wolf's invention, which is to say there is no mention of either in "Homecoming 45," the initial treatment for the film, written in 1966 in the form of a reconstructed wartime diary—reconstructed because Wolf's actual diary breaks off on March 19, 1945. The first occurs when the youthful Gregor is made temporary commandant of Bernau, a small town some ten kilometers northeast of Berlin, where he meets a Pomeranian girl of roughly his age. The girl does indeed appear in "Homecoming 45," but the whole Bernau interlude is described almost lightheartedly. In the finished film, things play out very differently. Following their initial meeting in the afternoon, the girl returns to Wolf's command post in the evening with hopes of spending the night there, offering as her reason for wanting to do so, "Rather with one than with everyone."[6] The topic of rape at the hands of Red Army troops had ever been a taboo in both the Soviet Union and the GDR, and yet here that taboo is incontrovertibly broken, even though the exchange that follows between the girl and Gregor's female Red Army colleague of similar age offers, if not qualification, then at the very least context for a desire for revenge. Gregor explains to his colleague, who speaks no German, that the girl is scared "of our side," which prompts the response: "Then tell her the following, since you get along so well: I was scared too. Scared as an animal." Here the bestial imagery is employed to describe the victims of inhuman perpetrators. Hatred is the terrible leveler: "The Germans set our village ablaze in winter. It was thirty below zero. The people froze. I saw them lying there. All the old people, almost all the children. Tell her that, word for word." When the Pomeranian girl expresses doubt that German troops could have done such things the Russian screams back, "No understand? Scorched earth—no understand? You're a cow, a stupid, dirty cow, do you understand? . . . Why did you come to our country? Why did you bring us so much misery?" The last time that we see the girl is from Gregor's point of view as he leaves town on the back of a covered truck:

> Gregor sits down, he turns his head and suddenly sees the girl, the first person he met in this town. She stands some distance away, as though she had been waiting for him, and looks over to him. Her face comes closer and gets clearer, an open, questioning face. The truck starts up, and the girl remains behind and disappears of a sudden

because the truck takes a curve. Then she can be seen again, already smaller. Another curve and she disappears again and appears again, very small on the misty square.

It is a disquieting sequence, as the overwhelming impression is one of isolation and vulnerability: we fear what awaits her; the heated exchange between the two women from the preceding scene invites the viewer to understand the roots of Russian hatred while knowing full well what the consequences are going to be.

The second sequence takes place immediately before the visit to Sachsenhausen concentration camp in the Berlin suburb of Oranienburg. The treatment of Sachsenhausen in the film has attracted a good deal of attention because of Wolf's incorporation of documentary footage into his own film, but the sequence before Paul Sakowski's testimony from Richard Brandt's 1946 film *Todeslager Sachsenhausen* (*Deathcamp Sachsenhausen*), like the confrontation between the two women in Bernau, would appear to be invented. Gregor and his two crew members, Wadim and Sascha, arrive at an allotment garden on the outskirts of Oranienburg, and the viewer sees what they see, a group of six Soviet infantrymen leading a man out of a shed at gunpoint. Wadim runs over to them and demands to know what they have in mind. The soldiers tell him that the man is to be shot because he had hidden himself and obviously belonged to the camp. Wadim protests that the situation has to be "clarified" before any such action can be taken and addresses the captive, who, with the barest shake of his head, denies being a member of the camp guard. In the screenplay the man makes "the same shake of the head" when asked if he is a member of the SS, but in the film no such motion is made. The second soldier demands of Wadim:

> So what have you clarified?
> Wadim: He says that he doesn't belong to the camp.
> The third soldier: You believe a fascist?
> Wadim: No. But it has to be sorted out.
> A fourth soldier says emphatically: God will sort it out alright.
> Wadim says in a raised voice: You have no right . . .
> Off to one side the first soldier. He has not participated in the argument, for him everything is clear. He says not very loudly, in a voice that sounds thin with hatred: Have you seen the camp? What they did there with our people? You need only go a kilometer . . .

In a further deviation from the published screenplay, the officer who now appears from the shed brings with him an SS uniform and an automatic rifle, throwing them at Wadim's feet:

> He approaches Wadim. He says roughly: Enough of that, you angel of innocence. Where are you from then?

> Wadim cries excitedly: From Kiev.
> The officer says hostilely: And I'm a Leningrader.
> Wadim: You're lying. Leningraders aren't like this . . .
> The officer draws his pistol. He says threateningly: Get lost, quick . . .
> Sascha is suddenly there and grabs Wadim by the shoulders: Leave it, Wadim.
> In a commanding tone he says to the officer: And you put your toy away. Quickly.
> Wadim wants to tear himself away, but Sascha simply pushes him on: Come on, go . . .
> Very briefly the prisoner's face. He knows that he is going to die.
> Sascha leads Wadim out of the garden.
> Gregor stands by the truck and looks toward them.
> Sascha opens the door to the cab in order to push Wadim into the truck. As he climbs in Wadim turns his head toward Gregor, an expression full of reproach.
> Gregor's face, which is turned toward Wadim. He wants to say something, he doesn't know what.
> A shot rings out.

As with the earlier example from Bernau, the injustice of the trigger-happy Red Army troops is contextualized by the likelihood of the man's guilt, a likelihood that is actually strengthened between the writing of the script and actual filming, while the scenes that follow, including the footage from "Death Camp Sachsenhausen," serve to provide a moral underpinning to their righteous anger. Thus Wadim's doomed attempt to prevent lynch-mob justice represents a striking example of Wolf's raising of issues in his film that find no mention in his public statements, and perhaps most interesting here is the employment of Wadim as the searcher for truth and justice: in his diary entry of August 20, 1944, Wolf writes of his first impressions of Wladimir Gall, on whom the figure of Wadim is modeled: "I have a good relationship with Gall. He is a very cultivated and capable chap. He studied at the Moscow Institute of Philosophy, Literature and History, was a student of Kopelev's." Gall, in other words, acts in the film as Kopelev's surrogate and that "expression full of reproach" suddenly adds a lacerating level of self-reproach to Wolf's writing. The painful irony that 1968 proved to be not only the year in which *I Was Nineteen* appeared, but also the year in which Kopelev was expelled from the Communist Party for his advocacy on behalf of Soviet dissidents and his criticism of the Soviet invasion of Czechoslovakia could not have been lost on Wolf. He did not live long enough to see the censors excise Kopelev from Gall's 1988 memoir and rename him Dr. Pinski.[7]

The paths of Kopelev and Wolf diverged greatly after 1945 as Kopelev, the one-time mentor, paid dearly for his incorruptible refusal to excuse the inhumane treatment of the enemy as justifiable retribution, while Wolf, the former acolyte, on the other hand, remained quiet. Yet to ascribe Wolf's public silence on the matter to careerism or exoneration is to underestimate the importance of his abiding belief in the central role played by conflict and in the absolute and defining importance of the Second World War. He always returns to it. One might have expected, following *I Was Nineteen*, that Wolf would have continued to explore the issues raised in the two scenes outlined above, but he does not, choosing instead to maintain focus on the "good fight." After two films on the relationship of the artist to power, *Goya* (1971) and *The Naked Man on the Playing Field* (1973), he returns to it in *Mama, I'm Alive* (1976). After *Solo Sunny* (1979), Wolf's critically and commercially successful reckoning with the GDR state's inability to provide a space for the non-conformist, set very much in the present-day, he returns to it in *Busch Sings*, the six-part documentary he was still working on at the time of his death. Wolf's own coming-of-age in the Second World War, the conflict that represents the germination of the GDR forever defined the parameters of his tactical thinking, even as that state atrophied around him, alienating its own population and thereby discrediting its own founding myths. His sense of disillusion is palpable in the 1981 discussion, but his own sense of purpose remained unshakable. It is in the diaries, I believe, that we can see where that certainty originates.

Notes

[1] Konrad Wolf, "Krieg beginnt nicht mit dem ersten Schuß, Diskussionsbeitrag 24.6.1981," in *Direkt in Kopf und Herz: Aufzeichnungen, Reden, Interviews* (Berlin: Henschelverlag, 1989), 340–46. All translations in this chapter are my own.

[2] A German translation of Wolf's diaries is housed in the Berlin archive of the Akademie der Künste, catalogue no. 2029–31.

[3] Svetlana Alexievich, *The Unwomanly Face of War: An Oral History of Women in World War II* (New York: Random House, 2017), 105; first published in 1985. The journalistic output of Ehrenburg (1891–1967) during the Second World War has become synonymous with the anti-German attitudes of the time. The title of the piece cited here was actually "Kill" and it appeared in the Soviet military newspaper *Krasnaja Swesda* (*Red Star*) on June 24, 1942.

[4] Aune Renk, "Zur Position von Konrad Wolf" in *Kahlschlag: Das 11. Plenum des ZK der SED 1965; Studien und Dokumente*, ed. Günter Agde (Berlin: Aufbau, 1991), 201–12.

[5] Konrad Wolf, "Ein Mann, der einen anderen politischen Weg geht," *Neues Deutschland*, November 22, 1976, 3.

[6] This and all following citations are translated from the published screenplay to the film. See *Der Film Ich war neunzehn: Intention und Wirkung* (Berlin: Deutsche

Akademie der Künste, 1968), sequence 16, shot numbers 105–7 and 122, and sequence 26, shot numbers 137–57.

[7] Wladimir Gall, *Mein Weg nach Halle* (Berlin: Militärverlag der DDR, 1988). A later edition of the book restores Kopelev's name: *Moskau—Spandau—Halle: Etappen eines Lebensweges* (Schkeuditz: GNN-Verlag, 2000).

17: "Bleibt noch ein Lied zu singen": Autobiographical and Cultural Memory in Christa Wolf's Novel *Kindheitsmuster*

Luke Springman

CHRISTA WOLF'S NOVEL *Kindheitsmuster* (Patterns of Childhood, 1976) attained and maintains canonical status of autobiographical *Vergangenheitsbewältigung* (mastering the Nazi past).[1] Following its publication, psychological interpretations of *Kindheitsmuster* predominated, influenced by popular theories, such as those in Alexander and Margarete Mitscherlich's *Die Unfähigkeit zu trauern* (The Inability to Mourn, 1967) and Klaus Theweleit's *Männerphantasien* (Male Fantasies, 1977–78), and psychological approaches to the novel continue. After all, Wolf intensely probes the psyche of her child protagonist, Nelly, as a therapeutic process to uncover repressed memories through writing.[2] Analyses of remembering have referred to Christa Wolf's metaphor of the "Medaillon" in her 1968 essay "Lesen und Schreiben" (Reading and Writing), which uses the analogy of the cameo to describe distorted memories that have been stylized or aestheticized.[3] In the early 1990s *Kulturwissenschaftliche Gedächtnisforschung* (Memory Studies) emerged as a school of cultural studies in Germany. The tenets and methods suggest an approach to reading *Kindheitsmuster* that expands on the early psychological interpretations but will in the scope of the present essay remain mostly a suggestion for further development rather than a thorough and systematic analysis.[4] Memory Studies, as they have taken shape in the last quarter-century, often question the collective German understanding and regard for the Nazi past, which had become all the more urgent in light of German reunification and the reactionary politics responding to recent waves of immigration from the Middle East and Africa. Christa Wolf's reflections on memory and the process of remembering through writing in *Kindheitsmuster* invite further examination with respect to current events, particularly since they correspond to concepts of communicative and cultural memory. One must keep in mind that *Kindheitsmuster* is a canonical work of literature, and thus itself belongs to the store of cultural memory.[5] Moreover, *Vergangenheitsbewältigung* (a German word meaning coming to terms with the past) has not faded into the archive of forgotten scholarship, but rather continually evolves and expands its relevance. The present analysis concentrates on one discrete element that elucidates the processes of recollecting (and forgetting) in Wolf's novel and that has yet to be examined in detail: the mnemonic function of auditory signs and symbols through songs, which underscore the subtle power of everyday rituals to shape individual and collective memories and identities.

Scholarly and popular reception of *Kindheitsmuster* at the time of its publication was mixed, including negative reviews by prominent West German critics Fritz Raddatz and Marcel Reich-Ranicki, the latter of whom objected to the novel's narrative structure:[6] Wolf interpolates the story of her (the child character Nelly's) childhood coming-of-age under National Socialism, using scenes from a forty-six-hour family excursion in the summer of 1971 to the hometown that she has not seen since 1945. These scenes are also overlaid with reflections and commentary made during the process of writing in 1972–75. Compounded with the intersecting time frames, the narrative voice refers to the childhood figure in the third person and to her contemporary persona only in the second person, breaking from the traditional norm of the unifying (heroic) autobiographical perspective and instead using personal referents that challenge the veracity of memories and call the author's motives into question. Some passages of the novel appear to be random stream-of-consciousness commentary, with sudden temporal shifts and seemingly disjunctive narrative shreds, which, according to some critics, make for difficult reading. Yet, as Hans Mayer pointed out in his (mostly) appreciative review, the novel's structure is hardly unique. He cites as examples Thomas Mann and Uwe Johnson, and he points out that the course of events is not difficult to follow.[7] None of the narrative elements, including dreams and fantasies, are spontaneous or impulsive associations, and the songs do not serve merely as musical vignettes around a child's life. Everything in the novel intentionally contributes to constructing the pattern of a German childhood from earliest memories to 1947. In short, a girl grows up in a small German town in what is now Poland, is socialized according to the norms of the time under National Socialism, suffers a calamitous displacement before the advancing Soviet army, and finally begins to settle into a postwar world. Mayer particularly appreciated Wolf's courageous challenge to the two core elements of official GDR historiography, one that casts the Soviets as benevolent liberators and the other that asserted that most Germans did not support National Socialism but rather were victims of a fascist minority that has been overcome. On the other hand, others have argued that Wolf's literary "dissidence" in *Kindheitsmuster* does not directly challenge the state but is rather "soft" and "symbiotic," concluding in one case that "Wolf needed the state to allow her to point to its wrongdoings and the state needed Wolf to learn some truth about itself."[8]

Book reviews made little mention of the possible relevance of *Kindheitsmuster* to the West German discourse on confronting the Nazi past. Early scholarly reception of the novel, influenced by psychoanalytic theories, recognized in the child Nelly the development of coping mechanisms, such as disguising and repressing feelings and deceiving one's self and others. Under a universalized ideology that occupied all aspects of life, children learned to censor their speech, actions, and thinking, which over the course of time generated neuroses. According to Alexander and Margarete Mitscherlich, whose Freudian theories have been associated with Wolf's novel, Hitler embodied the narcissistic love-object through which Germans derived a sense of power and superiority within a racist ideology.[9] Consequently, moral responsibility for all who were "others" withered and the Führer became the nation's conscience, relieving people from the need to reflect on their motives and actions or those committed in their name; Nazi ideology supplanted all ethical and moral principles. With such a "turned-around consciousness," it became reprehensible not to participate in the eradication of Jews. After the war, reconstruction meant both economic renewal and appropriating new objects for Germans' collective "narcissism": "An die Stelle des Führers traten die USA" (The USA took the Führer's place.)[10] Accordingly, people dissociated themselves from their past by denying its reality (*Derealisierung*).[11] True to Freud's distinctions between remorse (*Trauer*) and melancholy, the Mitscherlichs proposed that Hitler had been the lost love-object that Germans did not properly regard as a lost part of themselves, and they failed to "mourn" its loss. As a result, memories of the Nazi past elicit melancholy and even self-hate or "the impoverishment of self" (*Ich-Verarmung*), leading to the development of neuroses, of whose origins the individual is unaware. According to the Mitscherlichs, Germany needed to collectively mourn their lost ego ideal through a process of empathy (*Einfühlung*) with its past. Still, the Mitscherlichs' interpretation of collective repression of the past cannot shed light on the more inscrutable workings of memory, which in *Kindheitsmuster* defy consistent patterns and mechanisms. In several ways, songs illustrate this point, such as when the narrator struggles to remember lines of a favorite poem but cannot get the old ditties from childhood out of her head,[12] or when despised Nazi songs keep springing to mind, despite conscious attempts to repress them (151, 179–181). Christa Wolf's meditative and at times seemingly mournful critical exploration of her childhood appeared at first to represent in many ways the very manifestation of *Vergangenheitsbewältigung* in literary form, although subsequent discussions of the novel have explored many other aspects of its rich and complex dimensions.[13]

While Freudian interpretations of Germans' repression of their Nazi past might seem passé (they are not), discussions about dealing with that past continue unabated and still refer to the Mitscherlichs' work, even in non-psychoanalytic discourse.[14] Events such as the *Historikerstreit* (historians' dispute, 1986–89), Martin Walser's speech in St. Paul's Church (1998), and recent reactionary movements against immigrants have aroused controversies and discussions that continually bring the Holocaust into public discourse.[15] Recurrences of the topic of German genocidal politics under Nazism have obviously become a concern in German memory studies. Cultural Memory Studies in Germany, a style of cultural historiography that emerged in part because of the influence of the Annales school, appropriated the concept of collective memory as developed by Maurice Halbwachs (1877–1945). It identifies the Nazi past as a period most urgently requiring active and careful integration into long-term German cultural memory. Aleida Assmann, a prominent representative of German cultural memory studies, declared in the introduction of her recent book:

> The reintegration of the country into the circle of civilized nations took place based on negative memory, which integrates its own criminal pre-history into a collective self-image and which is maintained through a ritualized acknowledgment of guilt. This guilt, however, is no longer a fictitious construct, in which a union of brothers kill an archaic progenitor. It is, rather, the murder of European Jews and other defenseless civilian minorities, which was conceived, assiduously planned, and thoroughly executed by Germans with transnational cooperation. Freud's notion of sacrificing the patriarch was an academic myth, yet the genocide of Jews is a surviving crime against humanity, meticulously documented by historical sources. Because this burden of guilt by far exceeds anything that can be emotionally endured or absolved, it affects future generations and is to be carried into the future. Memory culture, the focus of this book, is a response to this historical event.[16]

Thus cultural memory, generally defined as "the interplay of present and past in socio-cultural contexts,"[17] as the foundation of both cultural and individual identity, is the object to be investigated through enhanced interdisciplinary discourse. In *Kindheitsmuster*, with the genocide hovering over the entire narrative, the discursive narration returns frequently to "Gedächtnis" (the individual and collective mental site where memories lie) and "Erinnerung" (the latent and active memories of events), as well as to "Vergessen" (forgetting) and "Verdrängung" (repression) in the writer's commentaries during the process of tracing her own childhood.[18] In this regard, pervasive references to singing in the narrator's self-examination are neither accidental nor incidental but rather consciously illustrate the nexus of collective and individual memory.

Remembering and forgetting are foremost neurological functions, an aspect that Wolf does not neglect, and which contributes to the documentary layer of the narrator's memoir, with references to the cerebral cortex as the anatomical seat of memory (37) and the function of proteins in memory formation (140). However, external social interactions stimulate the biological processes that create memories, which in turn shape one's identity. Socially formed memory, designated as "communicative" memory (as opposed to "cultural" memory) according to Harald Welzer, denotes the intractable consensus among members of the group about what they regard as their own past in the interplay with the grand narratives of the "we-group" and what meaning they ascribe to it.[19] The narrator's self-analysis and deep probing into her past in fact correspond to several concepts in Welzer's synthesis of neuroscience and cultural studies, in which he analyzes communicative memory in terms of developmental psychology. It is the intractability of a collective, agreed-upon version of the German grand narrative with respect to the recent past that causes the frustration and consternation that shapes the central conflict of the novel.

According to Harald Welzer, remembering, which is the work of memory, is constantly active and evolving. Memory is not a storehouse in which some memories sit in plain view, while others reside in deeper recesses of the mind. Rather, recollecting the past sets into motion an interplay among vague, forgotten, and clear personal memories, which are also simultaneously influenced and shaped by an equally dynamic collective or cultural memory. In the research on *Kindheitsmuster*, a too-exclusive focus on physical locales as sites of memory overlooks the powerful associations resonating in the novel through music. Returning to an example mentioned above, the narrator realizes that she retains only fragments from among passages out of the grand literary heritage that she had once memorized, yet the "trivial" verses are permanently imprinted: "A test shows that she's right. Only fragments, even of the most popular Goethe poems. However [there is] an indestructible store of scullery-maid ditties and horror ballads from early childhood, and Spanish songs from old records that can't be played on the new turntable; also Morgenstern and Ringelnatz" (207).[20] Moreover, songs can even be equated with memories. Remembering songs was so important to Nelly at the end of the war that she kept a journal of first lines: "And she'll try to forget the songs in the green notebook, which has been lost, incidentally. It never works, overlapping eras of songs (385)." The green notebook and songs are emblematic for the failed censorship of the narrator's consciousness; the last sentence could indeed be read as "the layers of *memory* that overlie each other." Furthermore, by extension the tunes and lyrics integrate the autobiographical mind with the collective German consciousness, because these were the innocent children's games everyone played: "Kling, Glöckchen, klingelingeling" (98: Who's knocking there? Or literally, "Ring, little bells, ring-a-ding," 102); "Ziehe durch, ziehe durch, durch die goldne Brücke" (120: London Bridge is falling down, or literally "Go through, go through, through the golden bridge," 125). Along with these were classic songs such as Goethe's "Mignonlied" (88) and Matthias Claudius's "Abendlied" (281), as well as classic German soldier songs by Wilhelm Hauff (18) and Adelbert von Chamisso (60) that everyone sang. However, over time Nelly's world filled with popular marching and war songs from the nineteenth to early twentieth century, made popular by the former German Youth Movement and with Nazi propaganda music. Yet in the GDR, martial refrains such as "Ich hatt' einen Kameraden" (The Good Comrade) and "Der kleine Trompeter" (The Little Trumpeter) were over-layed, that is, rewritten to reflect Communist doctrine (355, 365). While these autobiographical memories, permeated with music and infused with powerful sentiments, played an important role in the narrator's socializa-tion, the traditions and rituals surrounding the music make it a special nexus of communicative and cultural memory.

Communicative memory always relates past and present inextricably with an orientation to the future and is essential for shaping future-ori-ented thinking and behavior. In Wolf's words: "In the age of universal loss of memory (a sentence which arrived in the mail the day before yesterday) we must realize that complete presence of mind can be achieved only when based on a clear past. The deeper our memory, the freer the space for the goal of all our hopes: the future (153)." In *Kindheitsmuster*, the loss of memories is connected to their alienation, that is, uncoupling images of the past from their emotional import. However, actual remembering as autobiographical memory of necessity involves emotions. Welzer, in light of his focus on developmental psychology, connects the future-directed work of memory to ineluctable emotional and physiological effects in the process of recalling previous experiences: "The memory of the emotion and the agitation in remembering meld seamlessly into a unified conscious experience of the 'moment' . . . This phenomenon is extremely significant for a theory of communicative memory, for in this way new memories of earlier memories arise time and again, which can always be emotionally shaded in the same or in a modified way."[21] Memories always elicit feel-ings, both corporal and affective, of some kind, even if those feelings include apathy or indifference. As a case in point, the child Nelly's memo-ries cling to powerful fears: "Has it been mentioned that this child's memory was preoccupied with eerie, frightening, and humiliating sub-jects?" (143). This passage continues with the narrator excavating the meaning of the dream image of the white ship, but the memory of this symbolic apparition actually represents the memory of emotions as events in themselves:

> The white ship is an eerie and frightening theme, but at the same time it's a shining, summery image in your fantasy-memory, which stores matters not really seen or experienced but only imagined, craved, or feared. It is true that the fantasy-memory is even less trustworthy than

the reality-memory, and therefore you were unable for a long time to interpret this image . . . The ship was sailing under a cloudless, blue sky in lightly agitated waters, also blue, with a white foaming wake, and it was very beautiful and meant war. (143)

Welzer in fact emphasizes that emotional memory, the "implicit" memory, proves less susceptible to "damage" than does the less sustainable "explicit" memory.[22] Moreover, emotions also reciprocally color or distort events, as demonstrated in the novel when the mental images of prisoners of war do not match with the ones caught on film: "A comparison of memories with films taken by Soviet cameramen shows the expected result: the memories have been distorted by emotion (shame, humiliation, compassion); they didn't allow the German prisoners to look as run-down as the enemy prisoners had" (329). In the end, Wolf summarizes cogently the spirit of the novel:

> Love and death, illness, health, fear and hope left a deep impression in your memory. Events that have been run through the filter of a consciousness that is not sure of itself—sieved, diluted, stripped of their reality—disappear almost without a trace. Years without memory which follow the beginning years. Years during which suspicion of sensory experience keeps growing. Only our contemporaries have had to forget so much in order to continue functioning. (387)

Here I disagree with the translation of the last sentence. I would interpret this rather as: "Never have a people had to forget so much in order to function in life as those with whom we live today." Forgetting in order to function, or in this case, the phenomenon of collective repression of the Holocaust, indicates that experiences lie latent in our minds. They can be recalled and superimposed on the documentary record. For example, the narrator conducts research on events of her childhood by gathering information from issues of the local newspaper, but the graphic memories brought to mind are of torch parades and bonfires (124). Visiting the sites of her childhood conjures up clear visions of people and places, until the catastrophic end of the war when, as she expresses it, her recollections are preserved the way amber preserves flies: dead (258). Writing her childhood while simultaneously recording the process is for the narrator an agonizing labor that connects the lifeless forms with emotions, allowing space for her to attach moral judgments to her memories: as Wolf expresses it, God and the Devil are in the catalogue of subjective experiences (310). Precisely the attachment of a moral dimension to the process of remembering salvages parts of the past that, through critical reflection, offer clearer focus on shaping the future. On the one hand, the narrator plumbs her *autobiographical* memory, implicating herself in the collective guilt of Germany's past as an act of personal confrontation. Wolf's novel, on the other hand, brings the conjuring of the past and German culpability into the contemporary public discourse, thereby injecting her story into *communicative* memory.

Agony and guilt associated with memory of the past in *Kindheitsmuster* have been amply discussed. My focus here concerns the transition of communicative memory to cultural memory and also their concurrency. Recollections can take place at the level of communicative memory, as in the personal narrative in *Kindheitsmuster*, and can also initiate a project of cultural memory, whereby a collective shift in the motives of a group lead to retrieval of texts (in a writing culture) from the repositories of records we call archives, and through them elevate new views of the past into the grand narrative of the social collective. There is also a simultaneity whereby aspects of cultural and communicative memory overlie and interact. In *Kindheitsmuster* the interplay of autobiographical and cultural elements surfaces in the auditory triggers of memory, specifically in songs. Christa Wolf's writings swarm with references to songs, from her *Moskauer Novelle* (Moscow Novella, 1961) to *Stadt der Engel oder The Overcoat of Dr. Freud* (City of Angels or The Overcoat of Dr. Freud, 2010).[23] *Kindheitsmuster* itself contains more than sixty references to specific songs and includes lines from many of those songs, yet studies focus on the physical sites and have not explored the mental sites encoded in lyrics and melodies. Sounds, music in particular, arouse associations with past experiences as much as or even more than visual stimuli. Common knowledge presumes that music strongly elicits a wide range of memory and emotions, and this assumption has been borne out in clinical studies.[24] Most of these songs belong to the popular cultural traditions, enshrined not with the same reverence as the canon of high literature, but nevertheless they are commonplaces woven in the tapestry of collective experiences. Songs are one form of archival and communicative media that along with rituals, texts, memorials, and museums add to the corpus of cultural memory, and as such they do not only function as vessels or vehicles of culture but rather shape and lend meaning to the cultural memory of a social group and thereby substantially influence cultural identity.[25]

Were some of these songs not merely the background or incidental music of the narrator's childhood? Certainly, the mood of songs generally shifts with time, from the children's ditties to martial choruses and finally at the end of the war to the melancholy strains of songs such as "Lili Marleen" (226), and to sentimental tunes from escapist comedies and revue films. Simply as impressions that activate feelings and recollections and as cultural artifacts, songs in the novel provide critical thematic elements. However, some arresting juxtapositions suggest a more trenchant commentary. For example, the narrator comments early on that there were some songs in her childhood that no one needed to learn, in this case traditional songs from the eighteenth and nineteenth centuries, because they just "hung in the air": "Maikäfer, flieg," "Ri-ra-rutsch, wir fahren in der Kutsch" and "Ein Jäger aus Kurpfalz." In contrast to the traumatic memories that artifacts and records elicit in the author, many of the tunes summon nostalgia and therefore should actually impede memory. Yet the one song Nelly sings loudly as the ubiquitous song that everyone automatically knew is a vicious and gory anti-Semitic hate song: "Jew-heads are rolling, Jew-heads are rolling, / Jew-heads are rolling across the street. / Blood, blood, blooood, / blood must be flowing thick as can be. / I don't care a crap about / the Soviet liberty" (136). The disconcerting incongruity between the comparatively innocuous traditional songs and the vile lyrics is intended to convey the depth to which Nazi barbarity had penetrated the collective consciousness and as such adds a stylistically effective ploy to illustrate the core distortion of values. In this respect Aleksandr Stević identifies nostalgia as constitutive of the Nazi discursive economy and claims that it is later used to repress memories of the Holocaust. In *Kindheitsmuster*, according to Stević, Christa Wolf debunks sentimental longing through the excruciating exhumation of "dead" memories.[26] The disturbing image of a young girl singing such a monstrous air certainly jars readers and makes them think about the abuses of sentimentality. In another case late in the novel, a juxtaposition of song titles foreshadows Nelly's transition to the GDR: "She continued to write first lines of songs into her green imitation-leather notebook, but they were different songs. ('A drum can be heard in Germany,' 'When everyone deserts the cause' . . .). Another two or three years, walking in the streets of a town whose name she hadn't even heard in 1945, she'll be singing: 'Rebuild, rebuild.'"[27] The title of the first song is "Der Führer," the other is a popular patriotic folksong written by Max von Schenkendorf in 1814. The third, "Jugend erwach!" (Youth Awaken!) rose to become one of the most commonly sung songs of the Free German Youth in the GDR. Nelly cannot eradicate the old songs from her consciousness; by listing the Nazi lines with that of the socialist anthem the narrator again stresses the endurance of the past, which one cannot fully repress and certainly cannot forget. Stević admits that "the abandonment of nostalgia is a desirable, if not critical goal, but one whose attainment is neither fully possible nor without paradoxical implications."[28]

In conclusion, the radical and violent historical rifts of 1933 and 1945 ushered in the extinction of fundamental norms and values that induced a kind of punctuated equilibrium in German society, supplanting in a sense former ideological "species" with those of a new order. Simply that such historical cataclysms took place only twelve years apart already made the shifts traumatic. The fact that Germany committed monstrous atrocities during those twelve years, atrocities that cannot be rectified, magnifies the trauma immensely. With her novel *Kindheitsmuster*, Christa Wolf illustrates the failures of the culture of forgetting by narrating her quest for autobiographical memory. Autobiographical or communicative memory (Welzer often uses the term interchangeably), encompasses contemporary history for a span of time in which people can share their biographical memories, a period covering three to four generations. Cultural memory is the past preserved in symbolic forms and institutions: rituals, traditions, commemorations, museums, memorials, canonical texts, icons. Cultural memories include what a group determines should not be forgotten and *how* past events should be understood. Communicative memory has a fluid, malleable quality, while cultural memory becomes largely fixed as foundational stories or myths. In *Kindheitsmuster*, the narrator refers to the transience of the contemporary age as opposed to the rigid preservation of the past:

> You suspect that we're living in times that are forgotten more quickly than those resilient good old days. (Throwaway times.) Different times that pass at a different speed. The present time, which seems to expand, which is measured by minutes, whose hours drag but whose years fly, taking life along with them on their flight. And compared to that, the time of the past, compact, vehement, concentrated, as though melted into time ingots. It is describable. Whereas the naked everyday time of the present cannot be described, it can only be filled in. (384)

The preservation of events as "ingots of time" can also begin co-terminously with autobiographical memories, as the cultural and communicative memories of the Holocaust most clearly demonstrate. For example, Yad Vashem opened back in 1953; the United States Holocaust Memorial Museum was dedicated forty years later and in 2008 still retained the services of over seventy Holocaust survivors. In Germany, the controversial Memorial to the Murdered Jews of Europe was inaugurated two decades after German President Richard von Weizsäcker delivered his famous memorial speech, to which Aleida Assmann and others point as the true beginning of West Germany's memory culture with respect to the Holocaust.[29] In all cases, as James E. Young has noted regarding Holocaust memorials, cultural memory in general ". . . is never shaped in a vacuum, and the motives for such memory are never pure."[30] And as Hans Mayer emphasized, *Kindheitsmuster* challenged the cultural memory of East Germany; the novel also indicted West Germany's culture of forgetting. Wolf's dialogic, communicative remembering in a conversation across three generations, with no closure or firm conclusions, constitutes a pattern or model for "never forgetting." What could be seen as a fruitful paradox, however, is that Wolf's novel as a canonical text belongs now to the stock of German cultural memory as a dynamic memorial to remembering. Songs in *Kindheitsmuster* illustrate the theme of conflict between nostalgia and memory, compellingly exemplified in the passage that posits a rousing march song against the realities of history: "A song follows, the song of the Hitler Youth: 'Onward, onward, fanfares are joyfully blaring. Onward, onward, youth must be fearless and daring. Germany, your light shines true, even if we die for you . . .' (These songs proved to be right, at least in part: many of those who sang them are dead. 'Our flag will lead us to eternity, our flag means more to us than death'" (193).

Notes

[1] Christa Wolf, *Kindheitsmuster* (Darmstadt: Luchterhand, 1979), 207; in English, *Patterns of Childhood*, trans. Ursule Molinaro and Hedwig Rappolt (New York: Farrar, Straus & Giroux, 1980). Robert Holub, "Fact, Fantasy, and Female Subjectivity: Vergangenheitsbewaltigung in Christa Wolf's Patterns of Childhood," in *Facing Fascism and Confronting the Past: German Women Writers from Weimar to the Present*, ed. Elke Frederiksen and Martha Kaarsberg Wallach (Albany: State University of New York Press, 2000), 217–234; here, 217.

[2] Alexander Mitscherlich and Margarete Mitscherlich, *Die Unfähigkeit zu trauern: Grundlagen kollektiven Verhaltens* (Munich: R. Piper, 1967); Klaus Theweleit, *Männerphantasien*, 2 vols. (Basel: Roter Stern/Stroemfeld, 1977–78); Lorna Martens, "Gender, Psychoanalysis, and Childhood Autobiography: Christa Wolf's *Kindheitsmuster*," in *From Kafka to Sebald: Modernism and Narrative Form*, ed. Sabine Wilke (New York: Continuum, 2012), 145–65.

[3] Lutz Köpnick, "Rettung und Destruktion: Erinnerungsverfahren und Geschichtsbewußtsein in Christa Wolfs *Kindheitsmuster* und Walter Benjamins Spätwerk," *Monatshefte* 84, no. 1 (1992): 74–90; here, 77–79; Caroline Schaumann, *Memory Matters: Generational Responses to Germany's Nazi Past in Recent Women's Literature* (Berlin: De Gruyter, 2008), 75–82.

[4] Schaumann, *Memory Matters*; Brangwen Stone, "Visiting the Hometown, Revisiting the Past: Christa Wolf's *Kindheitsmuster*," *Neophilologus* 96 (2012): 593–609; Kristin Felsner, *Perspektiven literarischer Geschichtsschreibung: Christa Wolf and Uwe Johnson* (Göttingen: V&R, 2010).

[5] Martens, "Gender," 149.

[6] Felsner, *Perspektiven*, 173; Björn Schaal, *Jenseits von Oder und Lethe: Flucht, Vertreibung und Heimatverlust in Erzähltexten nach 1945 (Günter Grass—Siegfried Lenz—Christa Wolf)* (Trier: Wissenschaftlicher Verlag, 2006), 194–97.

[7] Hans Mayer, "Der Mut zur Unaufrichtigkeit," *Der Spiegel*, April 11, 1977, 188–90.

[8] Anke Pinkert, "Pleasures of Fear: Antifascist Myth, Holocaust, and Soft Dissidence in Christa Wolf's *Kindheitsmuster*," *German Quarterly* 76, no. 1 (2003): 25–37; here, 25, 34.

[9] Wolfgang Emmerich, *Kleine Literaturgeschichte der DDR* (Darmstadt: Luchterhand, 1981), 211; Wolfgang Emmerich, "Der Kampf um die Erinnerung," in *Christa Wolf: Materialienbuch*, ed. Klaus Sauer (Darmstadt: Luchterhand, 1981), 111–17.

[10] Alexander Mitscherlich and Margarete Mitscherlich, *Eine deutsche Art zu lieben* (Munich: Piper, 1970), 78.

[11] Mitscherlich and Mitscherlich, *Die Unfähigkeit*, 43.

[12] Wolf, *Kindheitsmuster*, 207. Further references are given in the text using page numbers alone.

[13] Margarete Mitscherlich, "Die Frage der Selbstdarstellung: Überlegungen zu den Autobiographien von Helene Deutsch, Margaret Mead und Christa Wolf," *Neue Rundschau* 91 (1980): 291–316; Bernhard Greiner, "Die Schwierigkeit, 'ich' zu sagen: Christa Wolfs psychologische Orientierung des Erzählens," *Deutsche Vierteljahresschrift* 55 (1981): 323–42; Tiina Kirss, "On Weighing the Past: Vergangenheitsbewältigung and the Prose of Ene Mihkelson and Christa Wolf," *Interlitteraria* 10, no. 10 (2005): 196–216.

[14] Sabine Wilke, "'Dieser fatale Hang der Geschichte zu Wiederholungen': Geschichtskonstruktionen in Christa Wolf's 'Kindheitsmuster,'" *German Studies Review* 13, no. 3 (1990): 499–512.

[15] Sabine Wilke, "'Worüber man nicht sprechen kann, darüber muss man allmählich zu schweigen aufhören': Vergangenheitsbeziehungen in Christa Wolfs *Kindheitsmuster*," *Germanic Review* 66, no. 4 (1991): 169–76.

[16] Aleida Assmann, *Das neue Unbehagen an der Erinnerungskultur: Eine Intervention* (Munich: C. H. Beck, 2013), 9–10. My translation.

[17] Astrid Erll, "Cultural Memory Studies: An Introduction," in *A Companion to Cultural Memory Studies*, ed. Astrid Erll and Ansgar Nünning (Berlin: De Gruyter, 2010), 1–15; here, 2.

[18] Sabine Moller, "Erinnerung und Gedächtnis," *Docupedia-Zeitgeschichte*, April 12, 2010, http://docupedia.de/zg/moller_erinnerung_gedaechtnis_v1_de_2010.

[19] Harald Welzer, *Das kommunikative Gedächtnis: Eine Theorie der Erinnerung*, 3rd ed. (Munich: Beck, 2011), 15. First published in 2002.

[20] Wolf, *Patterns of Childhood*, 222. Further references are given in in the text using page numbers alone.

[21] Welzer, *Das kommunikative Gedächtnis*, 148. Cited in the quote: Joseph LeDoux, *Das Netz der Gefühle: Wie Emotionen entstehen* (Munich: Hanser, 1998), 218. My translation.

[22] Welzer, *Das kommunikative Gedächtnis*, 149.

[23] Withold Bonner, "Die Gegenwart der Vergangenheit oder Die Grenzen des Sagbaren: Briefe, Tagebücher und fiktionale Texte von DDR-Autoren um 1970," *Interlitteraria* 18, no. 2 (2013): 425–43; here, 426. Stone, "Visiting," 597.

[24] For an article accessible to lay readers, see Lutz Jäncke, "Music, Memory and Emotion," *Journal of Biology* 7, no. 6 (August 8, 2008), http://www.ncbi.nlm.nih.gov/pmc/articles/PMC2776393/.

[25] Jan Assmann, *Das kulturelle Gedächtnis: Schrift, Erinnerung und politische Identität in frühen Hochkulturen* (Munich: Beck, 1992), 89.

[26] Aleksandr Stević, "Intimations of the Holocaust from the Recollections of Early Childhood: Childhood Memories, Holocaust Representation, and the Uses of

Nostalgia in Danilo Kiš and Christa Wolf," *Comparative Literature Studies* 51, no. 3 (2014): 439–65.

[27] *Kindheitsmuster*, 356; my own translation.

[28] Stević, "Intimations," 463.

[29] Aleida Assman, *Das neue Unbehagen*, 57 and *passim*.

[30] James E. Young, "The Texture of Memory: Holocaust Memorials in History," in Erll and Nünning, *Companion*, 357–65; here, 365.

18: Narrating Germany's Past: A Story of Exile and the Return Home— A Translation of the Chapter "Above the Lake" from Ursula Krechel's Novel *Landgericht*

Amy Kepple Strawser

URSULA KRECHEL (born 1947 in Trier) first gained renown primarily as a poet in West Germany during the 1970s, although her first major creative work, the play *Erika* (1973), met with success and was translated into five languages. *Erika* established Krechel early on as a writer focused on women-centered themes, but also initially limited her access to grants and fellowships for precisely that reason. An independent author from the start, Krechel built on this early achievement by spending much of her time in the following years concentrating on her principal genre, poetry, whose volumes yielded a measure of critical acclaim though little in the way of monetary reward or earned income. She experienced firsthand the difficulties of attempting to make a living from writing poetry. Thus throughout her career she has also always published in other genres: non-fiction, such as an early handbook about the women's movement, writing and authors' guides, and reviews of others' literary works, as well as essays in newspapers and periodicals; mostly short-form fiction; and radio plays. However, her recent success has come from two lengthy novels, *Shanghai fern von wo* (Shanghai Far from Where, 2008) and *Landgericht* (State Justice, 2012), which have garnered respected literary awards, the Joseph Breitbach Prize and the German Book Prize respectively. These two works are based on years of meticulous historical research that the author conducted in China and Europe, and on the lived experiences of German and Austrian Jews during the Nazi period, the Holocaust, and the postwar years in the Federal Republic.

Krechel's poetry has itself often tended toward the narrative strand of the genre, although she has also published frequently esoteric as well as occasionally linguistically experimental verse. While not a writer of ballads like her contemporary and acquaintance Helga M. Novak (1935–2013), in several of her early poems Krechel relates real or imagined experiences, as in, for example, the elegiac "Meine Mutter" (My Mother) and in the dream-sequence "Nach Mainz!" (To Mainz!), both from the collection named for the latter piece (1977). More recently, Krechel's long poem *Stimmen aus dem harten Kern* (2005; *Voices from the Bitter Core*, 2010) speaks from the soldier's perspective from battlefields around the globe and across centuries. The cacophony it provides brings the all-pervasiveness of war to our senses by way of those who live and die on the front lines. Their stories are banal while simultaneously horrifying.

What follows is a translation of the first chapter of Ursula Krechel's most recent novel, *Landgericht*.[1] In this chapter we experience the return home in 1947 of former judge Richard Kornitzer from his state-imposed exile in Cuba during the Second World War. This extract clearly demonstrates Krechel's lyrical as well as narrative expertise in play, in particular with descriptions of the hamlet of Bettnang in Baden-Württemberg near Lake Constance; the depiction of incongruent emotions aroused by the reunion of Kornitzer with his wife Claire; and stories from wartime that Claire relates to her ten-years-estranged husband once they are reunited there. My goal was, and my hope is, to convey the lyricism as well as the historical significance of Krechel's story.

Ursula Krechel, *District Court*
Chapter 1: Above the Lake

He had arrived. Yes, he had, but where? The train station was at the end of the line, the platforms unremarkable, a dozen or so tracks, but then he entered the station hall. It was a magnificent artifact, a cathedral of a rail station, traversed by coffered barrel vaults, the windows flooded by a bright, flowing blue light, a light born anew after his long journey. The towering walls were overlaid with dark marble, "Reich Chancellery dark," thus had he named this hue before he emigrated, now he simply thought it grand and stately, maybe even intimidating. But the marble hadn't just been put onto the walls as cladding; it was also precisely graduated, the walls forming a geometrical arrangement. The floor was bare, behind every counter a neatly uniformed official, staring through a small round window, before him lines of people who were not so shabbily dressed. (When he considered that these people were those defeated in the war, beaten-down folks, he found they were holding their heads amazingly high.) He also took note of the French guards in the alcoves of the hall who were unobtrusively keeping an eye on the train station goings-on. The officials wore olive-green uniforms and were armed. As he seized hold of the stately hall with one sweeping glance, he could not imagine any possible occasion for intervening in this scene, and that's exactly how it remained. A quiet, admonishing present moment, and with it, a forcible certainty.

He could feel the soothing civility, the timelessness of this station hall, he looked at the tall swinging doors, surely three meters high and completely encased in sheets of brass. The word "Push" had been engraved onto the surface of the metal with a fancy script at about breast height. Cathedral doors that robbed the traveler of any affectations, the atmosphere of the rail station was grave and meaningful, and each individual traveler would surely arrive safely and on time at his destination. Kornitzer's destination had been in limbo for so long, he hadn't even thought up a vaguely defined dream location for himself, such that this contradiction felt especially poignant to him. His transitory existence had become for him a certainty. Everything was at once lofty and genuinely uplifting in this hall, he looked around, he found his wife, whom he'd notified of his arrival time, nowhere in sight. (Or could he be overlooking her after ten years?) No, Claire was not here. To his surprise, however, he saw many day travelers, skis over their shoulders, who had come from nearby resorts, in high spirits and with tanned faces.

He pushed one of the tall doors open and was bedazzled. There was the lake, a giant blue mirror, just a few steps from the pier, water gently swashing against it, not a ripple on the surface. Of course his arrival had been delayed, by a good two hours, but the delay seemed to him an overextension, the joy of arriving and being reunited with his wife had been deferred for an indefinite period. In front of him was the lighthouse ranging up from the water, to the side the Bavarian lion keeping watch on the harbor with a serene gesture of sovereignty, and over there the mountains, at once faraway and close at hand, a backdrop of white and gray and alpine pink, their boulders, their archaic force, irrevocable, incredibly lovely. Then he heard his name being called.

The reuniting of a man and a woman who have not seen each other for so long, who must have believed they had lost one another forever. The breathless freezing of time, the inability to speak, the eyes searching for the other's glance, eyes that grow big, drinking it all in, then lowering and turning away in relief, tired by the effort of recognition, yes, it's you, it really is you after all this time. One's entire face pressed into the collar of the other's coat, lifting it up again quickly, the trembling agitation of not being able to bear the eyes of the other, the eyes not seen for ten years. The bright, watery eyes of the man behind his wire-rimmed glasses, the green eyes of the woman whose pupils contain a dark ring. It is the eyes that orchestrate this reunion, but the ones who must endure it, those who must bear its duration, have changed, they are now getting on in years, of roughly the same height, at the same eye level. They smile, they smile at each other, the skin around their eyes crinkles, no blinking, nothing, nothing but the gaze, the long-held gaze, their pupils fixed. Then one hand breaks free, is it the man's hand or the woman's?, in any case it is a brave hand or more likely only the tip of the right middle finger that provides the courage and also the instinct and grazes the high cheekbone of the long-lost partner. A trusted finger, a nerve impulse quite distinct from any emotion. It is rather the sensitive, tightly drawn skin of the cheekbone that responds, that signals "alarm" to the whole body. A uniting of nerve cells, not those of this married couple, this one lasts much, much longer, it is a sensation that shakes up the entire neuroplexus, an "it's you, yes, it really is you." The instinctive recovering of the beloved, familiar skin was a marvel that the Kornitzers often spoke of later, much later, with each other, they couldn't communicate this to the children. It wasn't the "caressed" part of the body (man or woman) that sent the alarm to the entire body, it was the actively "caressing" one, and half a second later it was no longer clear who had done the caressing and who had been caressed. This hand, still lonesome, having done without the spouse for just over ten years, was still moving, twitching, stroking, even embracing and not wanting to let go again.

So went his arrival. This signaling of the nerve cells prepared the way for the whole person. A walk from the train station in the city of Constance to the inn at the harbor that Kornitzer hardly noticed, where he sat across from his wife and spooned soup into his mouth, luggage stacked high around him. He now saw his wife more like a silhouette, she'd grown thin, her shoulders raised from the cold, he saw her large mouth, now open to take in one or another spoonful of soup she shoveled in, he saw her teeth, the gold point that patched the tip of one of her cuspids that she'd once broken off in a fall, he saw that her hands had become coarser and rougher since their departure from Berlin. His own hands he hid in his lap. He'd swallowed up the soup swiftly and matter-of-factly. He looked at his wife, layer upon layer he tried to align the present image of the woman sitting across from him with that of his wife that he'd visualized all these years. It wasn't possible. Even the photo in his briefcase that he'd stared at so often until he thought he knew every detail—if this is even possible with a picture—was of no help. Claire was now someone who swallowed soup and apparently wasn't afraid of sitting across from someone who was practically a stranger. For a moment he thought: What is it that she has learned to be afraid of so that she is not afraid now? He refrained from asking: Claire, how have you been? This question presupposed a greater intimacy, a question that required time for a long, drawn-out answer, and above all time for listening, a calm, relaxed: Tell me all about it. And she didn't ask him either: Richard, how have you been? He would have had to shrug his shoulders, at a sped-up tempo, a quick beginning and a slowed-down ending and where to begin?, for his wife had finally scraped out the last of the soup from her bowl and dropped her spoon with a clank onto the porcelain (maybe her hand was trembling?) and asked: How many days were you traveling? To this, a brief answer was possible: Fourteen by ship and three days from Hamburg to Lake Constance. That didn't seem incredibly long to her, she didn't give the impression that she pitied him that. She took him along to her village, this was not according to plan. The relief agency that paid for his trip, that transported him to Lake Constance, had instructed him to report immediately upon his arrival to the appropriate location in his future place of residence. He told Claire this but she didn't want to hear anything about it. The relief agency isn't going anywhere, you can just as easily go there tomorrow. Kornitzer's luggage would be sent along after them by carriage, Claire had arranged something with a sturdy-looking man at the station, he was supposed to come back in about an hour, and then he appeared at the inn. Kornitzer and his wife helped him load up the pieces of luggage. Together bending and stretching, lifting and shoving, this was their first shared act that gave reason for an air of intimacy. A curtain that appeared before the couple when they retreated to Claire's flowery little room in apartment 6 of a hamlet called Bettnang, where the only rescued treasures were her record player and a typewriter. He thought he could still remember the typewriter from Berlin, she called it "Erika" and its lever action had made it through the entire war and evacuation without a scratch. Hats off to "Erika," and one of the first triumphant remarks that Claire said to her returning husband was: I hoarded a whole lot of ribbons, apparently typewriter ribbons weren't considered essential to the war effort, or someone forgot to declare them as such. And they take up very little space in the bag of someone on the run. So we can type up applications and letters that will look presentable. To this he was at a loss for words, only nodded, he saw how she had planned ahead. He had also considered what he should bring with him from the long journey. Coffee? Tobacco? Sweets? Tropical fruit? Proof of his activities? But the regulations changed from day to day about what was currently allowed, what was suddenly prohibited for reasons political or hygienic (or for practical reasons hiding behind ideological or fully inexplicable ones, perhaps for reasons of the customs officials). No one had any idea. What was wrong with a small sack of sugar? What about perfume and tobacco in the amounts allowed just a month ago? One stood there like an idiot, and maybe that was exactly the explanation for these perpetually contradictory restrictions.

Here's the washbasin, said Claire, I don't have running water. He looked at the wardrobe, at the bed as well, narrow, it looked almost virginal, the wobbly chairs. He read in Claire's expression a kind of shame, akin to humiliation. And he noticed her gesture, somewhat nonchalant, and recalled her former self-confidence: Please, that's how it is now, we've come to this, he looked at the light from the little lamp on the nightstand, and the incredibly thin ribbon to switch it off and on. And the couple who had to relearn what it meant to be a couple switched it off. Then it was dark and the darkness was a fumbling around, a school for the blind of the emotions, a small private school, yes actually only fumbling around and breathing. So on this first day they really didn't make it past that first sensation of "Is it you, is it really you?" and as reassurance: "Yes, it is you." Maybe in this lay a quiet overextension. There was no way to determine how and when this family could ever come together again. There was still the matter of two individuals set free who knew next to nothing about their own children.

The next day he made his way into town along the winding road, past meadows and farmyards set off from the road, mountain ridges ever in view, the puckered masses of rocks, bands of clouds, tightly bound above them. When he had been walking for a good half an hour, cumulus clouds rose up, snow-white heaps moving into each other, a malleable, haptic skirmish of clouds with no clear outcome in sight. Vehicles passed by him as did the postal van, but he wanted to walk, wanted to walk for a stretch until the lake appeared before him at a turn in the road. The gray in the air spread out over the surface of the water like a gentle veil. He walked six kilometers down the mountain, the backs of his knees pressing down, a very unusual feeling that pleased him, like that of a traveling journeyman. And yet he was a man in his mid-forties who had been through so much, too much.

The central part of town was an island, a fact that he hadn't paid much attention to upon his arrival, an island connected to the mainland, the countryside, by a long bridge. Along the shore were villas, community gardens, a splendid area. He also noticed right away that many of the villas were now occupied by French officers and their posts, sentries stood in front of them. Then on the other side of the bridge, houses made of wooden shingles, overhanging upper levels, overhanging roofs with dovetailed dormers. The town of Lindau was putting on the appearance of existing outside of time and space. The thought of this appealed to him, but he couldn't continue this line of reasoning nor could he draw any conclusions from it. Something about it was soothing to him, while at the same time it (but what was it?) was vexing him as well. He caught sight of gazebos, stone balconies, gabled structures and the steep staircases leading to the wine taverns, where presumably nothing had changed for sixty years, old-German stolid *Gemütlichkeit,* only the waitresses, standing in front of the wine taverns chatting with arms folded, were younger now, and Kornitzer regarded them with delight. And he saw something else and didn't know what to make of it. He had read of the devastation of the cities and towns in Germany, of vast wastelands of rubble, of conflagrations. In this town he didn't see a single ruin of a house, not even a solitary shingle seemed to have fallen from a roof. He had to ask Claire about this when he got back to Bettnang.

He made his way to UNRRA, the relief agency of the United Nations that was responsible for him, with no problem. The agency was housed in the second story of a sprawling building with an alcove on the side of the island facing the mainland on 20th Street. Some young men were sitting, actually slouching, Kornitzer thought, on chairs in the corridor; they spoke a melodic language among themselves, glancing up briefly when he sat down with them as if to say: What's he doing here? They might have been Poles or Ukrainians, forced laborers or freed inmates from a concentration or work camp who'd ended up stranded in this beautiful town and who needed or wanted to be taken somewhere to surviving family members or friends who were expecting them, just as Claire had been expecting him, or to a completely, unfathomably new life that they'd chosen for lack of the one that had been obliterated, just as he had wanted to be brought here for lack of his previous life in Berlin which now lay in ruins. (Claire had alluded to it in this way.) The door opened, and a young woman with a thick accent which he could not place whispered, perhaps defensively: The next person, please. Two of the men rose. Only one person, the woman said, and put up her right thumb by way of confirming her statement. Friend speaks German bad, explained one of those who'd leaped up and pushed his way into the room. The woman left the door open, it seemed she didn't want to be in a closed room with two needy foreigners. It took quite some time until the two of them left the room with a paper form, the door stayed open for the following supplicants as well. Then came a long while when the door remained closed. At this point Kornitzer sat with a young man who was missing an upper incisor and who pressed his tongue nervously into the space between his teeth. He said—more accurately, hissed through the gap in his teeth—he was simply taken, taken away from his parents, his village had been dislocated, all church members were rounded up, everyone who was young, he made a violent gesture over his shoulder, it was a gesture of contempt, everyone off to Germany. That had been very hard for the parents. With no son, with no help in the fields. And then he sank into a bleak silence that Kornitzer didn't dare penetrate with an inappropriate question.

When it was finally Kornitzer's turn, the woman closed the door behind him, which seemed proof of her trust in him. Kornitzer said what he needed to, a litany accompanied by the rustling of the appropriate documents, he reported that he had arrived here yesterday as a *Displaced Person*, that he expected assistance upon his return. His fear that she would take him to task for not seeking out the aid office *without delay* proved to be unfounded. He had also feared that as a *Displaced Person* he would be brought to a shelter for refugees. His being taken back in by his "Aryan" wife was not provided for in the paperwork. Presumably his case was extremely rare. The woman filled out a form with three carbon copies, sent him into the next room, where upon presenting one of the copies he received ration coupons. He was then instructed to take the remaining papers back to the first office, have a seat in the hallway, and wait for his exit interview. So now here he sat in the hallway again, this time with two young women who were hardly more than girls and who were winking at him in a strangely comical manner, as if their only possible way of making contact were an innocent, or supposedly innocent, but in reality artful game of the eyes. It was a winking game that felt like being stripped naked, and he had to drop his gaze, which seemed to offend the young women. Back in the first room, the female employee wanted to send him off politely yet at the same time swiftly, but he stayed put as if rooted in place. I'm a lawyer, I'm a judge, I would like to return to work as soon as possible. You're a DP, the woman said, you lost your German citizenship. I'm responsible for you as a DP, but not for you as a job applicant. Go to the courthouse, it's connected to an employment office. A very good man presides there. He saw to it that thirty-three were let go and forty-five were rehired as if it were nothing. Call on him. Glaziers are needed, masons and farmhands too, I don't know about judges. And with that she sent him off with a quick nod of the head meant to be friendly but which struck him as dismissive.

He wanted to discuss this piece of information first with his wife, just as he had once discussed so many things with her, business deals, plans for the future, daydreams that were not at all far-fetched. So he set out on his way back to Bettnang, up the winding road, the return trip took longer because the road was very steep, a world made of snowdrifts and already-blooming apple trees spread out between the lakeshore and the steeply ascending Allgau incline, everything was slowing and cooling down. And on the climb up he kept looking back at the lake, at the tall mountains, at the blessed landscape of the peaks and at the flouncing of snow along the side of the road. The moment was now one for empirical knowledge. Walking increased his cache of knowledge as an applicant and separated this from his knowledge as an unsettled married man, and the time that he spent waiting in Claire's room until she returned from the dairy barn where she had found work was composed of many timeless moments. Then she arrived with the postal van, she had rosy cheeks, but she was also tired from the workday in the office there, a type of work she was hardly familiar with, because in Berlin (back then, before they'd been separated) she'd of course had her own secretary. And what he had to tell her about his first encounter at the relief agency on German soil he related quickly, it melted like snow in the springtime sun. Get some rest after the long journey, Claire said, don't go to the employment office for a few days.

Many things had been truncated, had decayed away, but fortunately not his cognitive ability, nor his ability to feel joy, an excessive amount of joy. And for the fact that he could experience that, yes, that even his tentative arrival had given him joy, for this he was indebted solely to his wife. He hesitated to still call her "his wife" after ten years of separation. Yet she had overwhelmed him by the certainty with which she wanted him again as "her husband," which she had officially put into writing, and thus had he read the words. And to have him again, she had taken the most practical measures.

He looked out the window, saw the onion-shaped church steeple, behind it a mighty sun was setting, a plump, blazing fruit, tropical fruit, the mountains aglow, and something glowed within him. Yes, it was good to be here, to be with Claire. He was aglow, inspired to find work fit for him. An occupation that fulfilled and nourished him and Claire and the children too. The hamlet of Bettnang with its six, seven farmsteads didn't have an inn, the inhabitants sat on benches in front of the farmhouses, sometimes a neighbor would stop by. They drank cider and looked into the blue air, for Kornitzer this was an unfamiliar blue air. For this reason Kornitzer had no desire to join them. The hamlet had a one-room schoolhouse, a shoemaker, an alpine dairy, and a small store (that the people called the "little shop") where one could buy the most essential everyday items, zwieback for every occasion, sauerkraut in a barrel, matches and rubber bands and sewing needles and safety pins and twine. Most groceries, dairy products and fruit, came from the farm or garden, there was no need for them in the store.

Kornitzer liked to slip into the small church, altars in gold brocade to the left and the right and a pulpit fastened to the wall high up like a swallow's nest. The saints in gold on both sides of the main altar dreamy-eyed beneath their bishop's caps, St. Sebastian on the side altar to the right, arrows protruding in a regular pattern from his beautifully carved and painted flesh and smiling down sweetly at the supplicants. Everything had been completed in a comforting manner, in practice for centuries and never abandoned. The self-assurance of an agrarian culture that asks no questions and that itself won't be questioned. Claire perceived her husband's brief stops at the church as ironic, she was Protestant through and through, the extravagance, everything dipped in gold, the stucco garlands were unfamiliar to her, the enraptured faces of the saints did not move her. But whenever Kornitzer sat for a short respite in the little church next to the gold-brocaded saints, he liked it as well or maybe even better among the Catholics. (Claire went to the Protestant church occasionally and didn't make much fuss about it.)

The small village church with its accompanying field of meaning ruled the hamlet, from the steps of the church door looking out there was a marvelous view. The church was wreathed by burial plots leaning toward the wall of the cemetery. The tombstones gazed with big eyes, armed against death, into the mountainous terrain, warming their backsides on the cemetery wall for one or more generations until the next set of the dead needed the space. Kornitzer looked at the unbelievably broad puckering of the mountains, the icy cold made of granite, it wasn't surprising that in earlier times travelers found the Alps sinister, even hideous, and drew the curtains of their carriage closed whenever the groundmass came into view. And then his eyes drifted back to the village. The church, the cemetery, the rectory with its faded red windowsills, the firehouse and a handful of courtyards, settled in far and wide, the barns in the foreground, behind them in the right-hand corner the built-in cowsheds. Occasionally there was sufficient space from there to the road for a patch of flowers. Between the shanks of the farmhouse and the stable, the warm dung heap held sway. It was the center of the yard, the chickens scratched around in it, searching for worms and maggots, turning their necks around as if they owned the place, the rooster keeping watch on them. Kornitzer had never spent any length of time in the country, perhaps at most on hikes or when passing through a particular region on the way to someplace else. Bettnang with its charmingly picturesque location above the lake made an impression on him, the cobbler was pounding away at a horseshoe, cows were mooing, chickens cackling, the postal van came twice a day, and otherwise it was so quiet that he could achingly feel his own lack of calm for the first time since arriving at Lake Constance.

Claire made it clear to him that the village was now empty and back to its formerly calm state. About the same time that she arrived in the village, in January of 1944, a class of schoolchildren from the Ruhr Valley also arrived. The village, in a panicked uproar, was paralyzed by the horde of those seeking shelter. And the teacher, barely more than a skeleton himself, a man on the verge of retirement, took the children, whose names were compiled and numbered on a list and who wore their numbers on a sign around their neck, from the train station to the highest point in the village. Whether the town right next to the lake also had to take in so many children Claire did not know, most likely not, likely the children belonged in the villages, nobody knew the fate of the towns, that was the opinion going around, and it hadn't proven to be false. At the postal van stop, the teacher had arranged the children from the Ruhr Valley, she'd forgotten what town they were from, one after the other in rank and file, children with backpacks and little suitcases and flushed faces. The farmers' wives came out of their houses and each picked out one or two of the children. Her own farmer's wife, Frau Pfempfle, took on some girls, besides her own sturdy boys she wanted to have some girls on the farm, young city girls who gawked at the cows as if they were magical beasts und drank warm milk right there in the barn and were left trembling afterwards. The farm also had a Polish farmhand, she said. So, a forced laborer, he broke in and thought of the young man with the missing incisor whom he'd met up with at the agency. Claire ignored his objection: Not a soul said a word about forced labor, the farms wouldn't have been able to go on without farmhands. Their farmhand had sat at the table with the family until the chairman of the local farmers' association came for an inspection and advised the wife that this was not acceptable. The Pole was to eat in the barn. The next day, the woman again showed him his place at the table. Then, after the war, there were Frenchmen in the village, at least fifty of them, a billeting that made the farmhouses look as if they were as filled to the brim as hatboxes. Claire liked to tell these stories, and he liked listening to her. It had been like this before too. And then he at last had a chance to ask the question that had been troubling him since he'd walked down into town: Why hadn't the town been destroyed? The town had, with the help of Swiss diplomacy, been declared a site of the International Red Cross, Claire explained. For that reason, no bridges had been blown up either. On April 22, 1945, the town of Lindau had been put on alert. On a day-to-day basis, more refugees had come to the city. The few trains that were still running were already jam-packed. In the old town hall, an SS-headquarters had already settled in, that had seemed to be a safe place, and a military staff had moved into the district committee of the Nazi party. Rumors buzzing around town were in direct contradiction of each other. But Claire Kornitzer was able to remember the 30th of April, 1945, very clearly. It was a bright, radiant spring day, the day Hitler killed himself. At 8 o'clock in the morning, an enemy alarm sounded. It was said that the owner of an inn by the name of "Idyll" had driven up to the advancing Frenchmen and had pleaded with the officer in the first tank to protect his hometown. They said he had taken the lead for the tank and two motorized vehicles carrying troops coming in from Wasserburg. Shortly after 9:00 a.m. the first French tank proceeded across the Lake Bridge. On the tower of the Catholic Church flew a white flag. The detachment of combat troops and the police force were quickly disarmed by the French. Then more and more troops swooshed into the city, troops that just one day before had still been labeled the enemy, while the tanks stayed behind in Aeschach or continued on in the direction of Bregenz. Streams of people were everywhere, no one knew what might happen next. And there was so little trust among those gaping from the bridge that arguing the point would not have been worth the effort. One simply had to wait it out to see what would come of it.

The conditions for the surrender were made public in short order: curfew from 8 o'clock in the evening until 6:30 in the morning. A van with a loud speaker drove through town and the surrounding villages and ordered the delivery of all weapons, munitions, radio devices, binoculars. The few military personnel still remaining in the city were to report as prisoners. Without the slightest incident, then, the town had been occupied. The French had set up artillery on pasture gables, on railway embankments, and at other places throughout the city, and they soon fired them too. In Bregenz, SS troops had withdrawn and put up resistance. On the following day, then, Bregenz was shot up, there was pandemonium that was unheard of in the neighboring town. The ground shook, the sky was blackened by smoke, a cloud in the form of an anvil took shape, the town was ablaze in many places. It was the definitive defeat of the facts. There was nothing more to say about it, in the city and on the hills beyond it, no one wanted to even think about it anymore. Lots of people had stood on the Lake Bridge and had looked on at the drama in silence as the neighboring town burned—in horror yet with the secret satisfaction that one's own roof, gables, windowsills hadn't been hit nor had one's own head, which couldn't stop from being amazed at all this. The confederation of Allied airmen attacked for three hours, while shots from the heavy artillery flew overhead without pause. On Tuesday, May 1, Bregenz fell, the massive flood of combat troops moved on, the electricity was cut off, the newspaper was no longer being printed. A ghostly calm prevailed, streaming spring light spanning above it. God was asleep, God was resting after allowing so much chaos. The chaos (while speaking, Claire frowned) had more likely been a matter of beginning anew, before the creation of the world, and now no more thought should be given to any system of order, of systematization, since the origin of human history. Especially herself, a native of Berlin, a Prussian, a Protestant, she needed a mundane style of order, and to do without one was a special kind of punishment that she didn't deserve. Kornitzer had to smile at this calm outburst by his wife. About 150 Nazis had been arrested, she continued, even the local group leaders of three communities. The Nazi district leader had preferred to escape with a few members of his staff. But he was shot to death a few days later by a Pole, it was reported, and that's how Claire relayed it to her husband.

The innkeeper at the "Idyll" who had made such a big deal out of having welcomed the French was later accused of making up the story and left town. Claire Kornitzer could no longer think of his name, but that didn't matter. Now the details went like this: he had encountered the first French tank, and the officer asked him to show them the way into town, nothing more. And the revelation of this shamefully unspectacular heroic deed was so disillusioning that the man would have been completely forgotten, had he not been mentioned in the official gazette of the district. But Claire had thrown out this edition of the district paper, others she had kept, she didn't even know why. Erase any trace of the man, erase the "Idyll," she didn't know whether the inn with the funny-sounding name even still existed. And it didn't interest her, no, not in the least, she told her spouse, who was developing a patient attentiveness to anything related to local history.

Compulsory labor, compulsory labor ran through his mind at night while he was trying to sleep. I've forced my wife to recognize the concept of compulsory labor when she, like presumably all Germans, wanted to talk about the Polish farmhand. But he, Kornitzer, was German too! He had been expatriated, so therefore he had to limit himself half asleep to such a commonplace term as "all the Germans in the land." Or should he perhaps in this case go so far as to think of "all Germans who were infected by the ruling National Socialism"? That would include his wife, whom he would have rather left out, whom he had to exclude from this. The question irritated him, he saw himself as a conqueror with good intentions, but that didn't make him feel any better, so he took hold of his wife's arm that lay right next to him and kneaded it, even though he had actually wanted to simply caress it, but the inner tension of having treated Claire unjustly likely made him grab on with even more intensity, and Claire let out a sound that she likely wouldn't have uttered while awake, a deep, snorting sigh like that of a horse, and then he noticed too from her arm which he still held in his hand: Claire had fallen asleep a while ago. And Kornitzer, lying awake for a long time, told himself: I've treated her unfairly. That sounded good, even liberating, but again it was not a juridical concept. He reflected on this a bit more, wondering whether he could follow this up with a term that really fit; later, it was an inner constitutional complaint against himself. He could find no appropriate term other than "compulsory agreement"—that would be the most appropriate. But this compulsion could have been conceived of with approval, like an invitation to a legal contract that he had already entered into with his wife anyhow. He realized that he had not made himself culpable with respect to his wife, even as drowsy as he was. But there was a shadow hovering that could not be assessed morally or ethically, but rather was based solely on a particular niveau in the area of his specific branch of expertise.

After he had been tossing and turning in bed for at least an hour, he took hold of his wife's arm lying right next to him for a second time, full of trust, embracing it completely, as if it were a bolster, something that he could unconditionally latch on to, and that he did, and his wife gave the impression in the morning that she hadn't the slightest notion of all this commotion in his mind and in his emotional state, which was a relief, but also a bit hard to fathom.

How had Claire Kornitzer been able to find her husband? That was a long story. In the official gazette she'd seen a proclamation that sent chills down her spine:

> Germans of the Jewish Faith
> In preparation for the reparation for the moral and material injustices inflicted upon German citizens of the Jewish faith or ancestry, the registration of the category of people in question will be conducted. All German citizens of the Jewish faith or ancestry residing in the district of Lindau are hereby summoned to notify the appropriate mayor in writing by no later than January 20, 1946, according to the following guidelines:

Last and first names
Whether fully Jewish (at least three Jewish grandparents, as set forth
in the Nuremberg laws, or whether of mixed lineage to the 1st or 2nd
degree)
Birthplace and birth date
Last place of residence
Marital status
Previous occupation
Current occupation
Health issues incurred
Loss of assets

The mayors will present the collected notifications to the District
Court by February 1, 1946, at the latest.
District Administrator: sgd. Dr. Eberth

The announcement didn't apply to Claire Kornitzer, yet it seemed to her
a support handle, a life preserver, a certainty that she would be listened to
and that she could ensure that her husband, to whom it did apply, could
make his voice heard. Only she had no idea what means would help her
husband locate her and she him. She also had no idea how many people in
this rural administrative district would respond to this summons. The registration period was very brief, one had to buckle down to get pen to paper
in an effort to bring all the documents together and carefully enumerate
them. Was the deadline so soon since it was suddenly—a good half a year
after the end of the war—hurtful that until now no one had concerned
themselves with the Jews (as if the "Jewish problem" had been taken care
of in Auschwitz, in Majdanek), or was the deadline set so soon in order
that only the few returning home or those creeping out of hiding could
register? Claire puzzled over this, came to no conclusion.

She had no way of knowing that only 681 Jews had survived the war
in the French occupation zone, and if she had known that, she would have
merely been sick at heart, not astonished.

Soon after the appeal went out she'd seen this ad: *Large backpack with
leather straps about one meter long made of fir or beech wood wanted for
trade.* Yes, firewood was in demand, but means of transport were also
sought after. There was not enough space in a backpack to carry wood.
Maybe some towns had packs that they took on weekend hikes to the
mountains, and those with gardens often didn't hesitate to chop down
their trees, firs, beeches. The Pfempfles, the farmers she lived with,
wouldn't have even considered cutting down their fruit trees, the trees
were the foundation of the farm, they had always belonged to the family
like the dairy cattle. On the opposite page she read: *To my students, zither
lessons resume on Tuesday, January 22, 1946. The lesson room is 27/III
Main Street with Secretary of Customs Merkl. New students should apply in*

person. And she then saw the urgent *search for a bass player (slap bass) as well as a cellist and trombone player*, in addition *an experienced female pop (backup) singer* was needed. *Interested parties* should apply *to the Otti Weber-Helmschmidt Concert and Dance Orchestra*.

She read all of this very painstakingly, and she tried to get into the same spirit as the people who had placed these ads. And she also tried to imagine other people in her (not exactly willingly chosen) surroundings empathizing with her, Claire Kornitzer's, situation: the children sent away so that they would survive, their father sent much farther away so that he would survive. And the start of the war, the senseless machinations of the war that became a global conflagration, prevented her from emigrating, prevented the joining of the father with the children, prevented her from joining up with her husband on another continent. All of that left behind scars, tremors, casualties that could hardly be made known to a stranger. Backpacks, firewood, and a zither emerged from the fog; trombonists and bassists turned up as well and then receded back into the fog. And thus she had to meticulously and without all too much emotional baggage fill in the appropriate spaces on the forms, not overly much, by no means too wordy, but still compellingly and not tentatively. And so she wrote:

> Re: Registration of German citizens of Jewish faith or ancestry.
>
> On the basis of the proclamation in the official gazette (no. 4 of 1/15/1946), I am providing the following information:
> Last name: Kornitzer
> First name: Claire Marie née Pahl
> I am a full-blooded Aryan, however (in the sense of the Nuremberg laws) have been married to a full-blooded Jew since 1930. We are not divorced.

She underlined the word "not" twice: <u>not</u>, and again <u>not</u> divorced. In this way it stood out prominently from the rest of the page. And so she filled out the remainder of the questionnaire as follows:

> Husband: Dr. Richard Karl Kornitzer (former judicial member of the Patent and Copyright Association of the District Court I in Berlin)
> On 4/1/1933 dismissed without notice and without salary or pension because of his race.
> In February 1939 emigrated to Cuba and since February 1942 I have received no word from my husband.
> Children: Georg born 1/22/1932
>   Selma born 3/30/1935
> Both children were taken from me at the beginning of January 1939 and transported to be raised in England. Also concerning the whereabouts of my children I have received only contradictory information.

The entire set of issues about the restitution of assets, health status, all that doesn't concern her much right now, she only mentions it in passing, maybe she's hoping her jurist-husband will help her with these questions. At the moment she has other concerns, existential concerns, and she informs the administrative district office of these.

As to the question of reparations: I respectfully request your help to the best of your ability in both of the following matters:

1. To locate the current whereabouts of my husband and to support his poss. return.
2. To most kindly support my own efforts to obtain an entry permit for a brief visit to my children in England. In addition to visiting the children, without whom I have had to live for seven years, this short trip to England will serve the purpose of aiding in reuniting our family."

She writes without a complimentary closing, very self-confidently, she has suffered and sacrificed enough. She signs her name in large, sweeping letters: Claire Kornitzer, the letter e at the end of her first name is shaky, a bit tangled up in itself. Doesn't matter what handwriting experts might say about that (do they even still exist?), perhaps the excitement of anticipating a good outcome, perhaps even an optical correlation to the kidney stones that have been plaguing her for some time, as if she were passing something sharp, something extremely, inappropriately pointed, a hope, a self-assurance, the energy from this corner of Lake Constance to take up the reins into her own hands again, to get the family carriage that had veered off course for reasons well known back onto the right track. Claire Kornitzer set to work with a vengeance. And since she'd sent in her report, the relief agencies had become active, lists were compared, the cogs of a social machinery in high gear, things were abuzz, countless names of the missing in all kinds of papers and proclamations, lists of names were telegraphed over continents, the lists of the seekers and those of the ones being sought copied on top of each other again and again until they found the perfect match.

Kornitzer had found his wife again, and on top of that he had been granted a panorama that he'd never before seen. The green meadows with the cud-chewing dairy cows in the foreground, then a patch of woods, the broadly spreading groves of fruit trees, fruit plantations to be more accurate, since he had spent time in the Tropics, apples and pears in such abundance that he had never seen the likes of. And then added to that the backdrop of the mountains, peak by peak across a wide range. Cold and white, the first row chalky, the next with a bluish hue and those farthest back of a violet tinge, they scratched blood red into the blue sky. Like a schoolchild he memorized their names. He was embedded in a landscape that he could never have dreamed up, fresh air so plentiful that it verged on anesthetizing him. The sky at sunrise, whenever he saw it out of the window, had a fluff of hair covering it. The sky at sunset, with a long chain of waxy clouds, gave the impression of a model, coiffed up, models of clouds in a grand folksy display, creating the effect of a palace made of glass. Magnificent days followed by sheets of rain during which the mountain range receded into a mousy gray. The next day a feather bed in the sky, the air biting and paschal, still some snow in the ditches, drizzling, smudging, melting. Yes, here one had to be a farmer, one couldn't be anything else but a farmer with a rosy-cheeked wife wearing a headscarf in the barn, and a flock of children, pink and healthy with skin like milk and blood, and honey flowed, dripping over slices of bread spread thick with butter, in the kitchen a cross hung in a corner over the table at which they all gathered, and the children dipped the bobbles that fastened their cardigans at the top into the honey, and the farmer's wife watched over this with grace, she had plenty to do in the barn, in the house, the children were thriving, eating apples, the apples rosy-cheeked and the children too. (Maybe he was fooling himself. Maybe he was idealizing something unknown to him. This thin slice of life, the rigor of it, being forbidden to break ranks from within the community wherever their thoughts, actions, repressed feelings may have taken them, being forbidden to get carried away, to strike out on one's own—this was unknown to him.) A cow was calving in the barn, the dramatic movements within the animal's abdomen gave cause for close observation, and the children still sat at the breakfast table.

Yes, Richard Kornitzer was fond of the hamlet of Bettnang. Or did he simply like it so well because this is where he had rediscovered Claire, because in this farmhouse, *just a stone's throw from the main road*, there was an air of certainty that he had done without such a long time? On the ground floor lived the Pfempfles, the owners of the farm, husband and wife the same age as he and Claire, composed in the face of history—where and how the fruit grower had managed to survive the war Kornitzer didn't dare to ask, after all he was a guest here. On the second floor were refugees from the Egerland, sisters or sisters-in-law with three children and a husband who had managed to start up a shoe-polish business. Shoe polish was not an essential product, more of a luxury really, but still an affordable one. Thus there were cardboard boxes of shoe-polish tins towering up in the stairwell, wherever the man had got his stockpile from remained a mystery. The other woman's husband was missing, she knew nothing about his whereabouts or his likely death.

The Pfempfles milked and fed the cows, sprayed the orchards seven times a year as the District Orchard Inspector recommended, Kornitzer was made to understand it as follows: The winter spraying by mid-March, the first pre-bloom spraying shortly after budding, the second pre-bloom spraying shortly before the blossoms opened, the first post-bloom spraying immediately after the petals fell, the second post-bloom spraying approximately two weeks after the first post-bloom spraying, the third post-bloom spraying approximately two to three weeks after the second post-bloom spraying, earlier in case of rainy weather, later if it was dry and the late slough spraying from the beginning of August till the beginning of September. The greatest threat to the fruit was the apple blossom weevil, but aphids, slough, silkworm moths and codling moths could also threaten the harvest. The winter spraying fended off the larvae of various pests. The Pfempfles carefully recorded the preventive sprayings, nothing could be left to chance. At the first sign of any disease on the leaves or fruit, it would already be too late. On the sites of disease the spray made of copper chalk and lime sulfur could even cause damage. It was also important to spray early in the morning or late in the evening and never onto the open blossoms since the bees that pollinated the blooms had to be protected. And if possible when the wind was calm.

As fastidiously as the Pfempfles handled their apple trees, they allowed their sons the freedom to do as they pleased as long as the work on the farm was done. They had two sons, the elder one was the same age as Georg, the Kornitzer son, he was a tall boy with flaxen hair who exuded a quiet self-assurance as if he could take over the farm tomorrow: the cows, the apple trees, the parents now grown old—he had, after all, worked the farm on his own with only his mother and the Polish forced laborer—and a smaller boy who liked to fool around who Claire waved to when she returned to Bettnang in the evening with the postal van. A child who liked to hang around her room and who begged her to turn on the record player. She did it to please him, but she also took pleasure in his delight, that he longed for something that was not an everyday occurrence with the farmers, listening to music. Would you like to dance? she would occasionally ask him, but he waved her off. He said he didn't know how to dance. You can learn if you just try, she encouraged him. And she laid her hands on his shoulders, listen, she urged him and smiled her winningest smile, put your arms around me. Then they were off, swinging and stomping, lilting along with the melody from the record player, she put up with his stumbling and doubling over without a word. See, she said, you can too! And when the record was over, she burst out laughing, and her youthful dance partner drew himself up a bit taller, as if the shared adventure with the big-city tenant had made him worldlier and more grown up, at least a little bit. Let's do it again sometime, said Claire and then pushed the boy out the door before he could become firmly planted on the edge of her bed to hear another record. She said to her husband: The little one has so much fun with that. Her own pleasure could be seen just by looking at her. And the Pfempfles on the lower level sometimes whispered: Isn't it amazing that Frau Kornitzer, after all she's been through, hasn't lost her fun-loving spirit?

Translated by Amy Kepple Strawser

Note

[1] Ursula Krechel, *Landgericht* (Salzburg: Jung & Jung, 2012), 7–33.

19:   Storytelling in the GDR: An Interview with Eberhard Aurich and Christa Streiber-Aurich

Sylvia Fischer

STORYTELLING IS A MEANS of preserving the way of life from a given time and place: everyday-life details, cultural practices, social values, and political agendas. Furthermore, stories gesture beyond their immediate context and communicate particular views and ideas to the readers. Storytelling and literature in the GDR served both purposes. In the postwar years the promotion of literature focused on a distinct political and social program that was fueled by the need for communicating conceptualizations and practices of the new society to readers. Literature served as an instrument for educating the reader socially and politically. Through literature, values and practices of the new socialist country were addressed, and they were intended to move readers to participate in the process of building socialism in the GDR. In the 1970s and 1980s, after the GDR had been successful in establishing itself and consolidating as a state, literature as well as film, which had become an important cultural product by then, had changed their perspective. The stories now concentrated on introspection into the current state of the socialist society. The forward-looking view of the 1950s and 1960s, the verve and enthusiasm that the stories breathed—depicting the rebuilding of factories, acts of creating and growing, model-type workers and symbolic construction sites—had turned into a mode of reflection and discussion in the 1970s and 1980s.

Preservation through storytelling started out in the GDR in the 1950s and 1960s, with the goal of establishing a particular East German national identity. Literature and film did so through their choice of particular storylines and their discussion of social, political, and work-related issues on the one hand, their choice of scene and their depiction of certain character types on the other. Hence the numerous literary and cinematic images of factories, construction sites, workers, and Communist role models, as well as strong female figures and urban and heavily industrialized landscapes, had synthesized into a distinct East German identity by the mid-1960s. Later, in the 1970s and 1980s, a discussion of the generational gap between the prewar generation and the younger generations in the GDR, a discontent with social and political structures, and changed views on socialist ideals were added to the storylines of cultural products. Books and films formed a major part of the public sphere of the GDR and thus established a quasi-open discussion of the aforementioned topics and discourses.

Finally, GDR films and literature offer a primary source for studying the social and cultural history of the GDR. They preserve details of everyday life and topics of public discourse; throughout the decades, they documented political and social developments and changes in people's lifestyle within their stories, and thus provide invaluable material today for scholars and readers alike.

As a cultural official, a politician, and a member of the government of the GDR, Eberhard Aurich is an expert in cultural politics and the public sphere of the GDR. Born in 1946 and trained as a high-school teacher for German Studies and *Staatsbürgerkunde* (civil studies), Aurich served as the chairman of the GDR's youth organization, the FDJ (*Freie Deutsche Jugend*, Free German Youth) from 1983 to 1989. As a government official, he was a member of its several institutions: the Zentralkomitee der SED (Central Committee of the Socialist Unity Party), the Volkskammer (People's Chamber), and the Staatsrat (Head-of-State Council). By virtue of his appointment as chairman of the FDJ in the 1980s, Aurich worked closely with the GDR's highest ranked politicians and was engaged in decisions about youth politics and cultural politics geared toward young people in the GDR. I interviewed Aurich in July of 2015. Having been a witness to the cultural and political developments mentioned above, he is an excellent conversation partner with whom to discuss them. Aurich reflects critically and with great insight on the literary and cultural sphere in the GDR and his own political work in the FDJ. The interview is complemented by the contributions of Christa Streiber-Aurich, who worked for a TV station in the GDR and is currently with the *mdr* (Mitteldeutscher Rundfunk) TV station. After the political changes in the GDR and the German reunification in 1990, Aurich withdrew from politics. He currently lives in Berlin as a freelance writer.

Sylvia Fischer: Mr. Aurich, let us start at the beginning, with the first decades of the GDR. The literature published in the 1950s and 1960s aimed at winning over readers, and in particular young readers, for the building of the socialist society. The stories written during this time depicted individuals or groups that served as role models for the readers. The literary characters achieved the intended goal in the narrative: socialism and the new and better German state. In sum, literature was significant during the founding decades of the GDR. Please describe the situation from your point of view.

Eberhard Aurich: I agree with your statement. In those years, enormous importance was attached to literature, reading, and education, and in particular for young people, who were supposed to become the face of the socialist society. Child and youth literature in the GDR was always integrated into a great variety of cultural and artistic activities oriented toward young people and children. It was essential to bring humanistic values to life for them in light of the preceding Nazi era.

Fischer: So, you would consider literature an instrument of political and social education?

Aurich: Yes, that is correct. The intention was to associate education with a high degree of political and ideological formation. Young people were intentionally geared toward the values of the new society, and the literature published during this time was therefore carefully selected by cultural officials. The first publications during the postwar years, of course, were classic works of world literature. For example, many translations of Soviet literature were published and many of those works were taken as an orientation point for GDR literature.

Fischer: This orientation point refers to the aesthetic concept of socialist realism, which includes a strong preference for particular plots and storylines, and characters.

Aurich: Yes, that is right. You would find new topics and stories in the literature, mostly conflicts and phenomena of the new society, as well as stories about historical developments that had led to the emergence of this society. Historical knowledge was imparted, for instance, on the realization of the socialist vision after the Russian Revolution in 1917. Another important storyline was the fight against National Socialism, especially the fight led by German Communists and antifascists, who were portrayed as role models and father figures in literature. They personified and exemplified the values that literature was supposed to convey, such as courage, strength, empathy, and the commitment to a higher political cause. Another plot was the rebuilding of factories during the postwar years, thus intertwining manual labor and the political and social education of the workers. Anna Seghers said once that during the postwar years there were ruins inside and outside, meaning inside the people, and outside, in the landscape. Ruins had to be cleared away, after all, and something new had to be built.

Fischer: Can you speak a little more about specific storylines, discourses, and developments in the GDR's cultural sphere that were important during this time?

Aurich: When I was young, I read the children's book *Timur and His Squad* (1940) by the Soviet author Arkadi Gaidar. The book portrays a group of children who get together and turn a rubble landscape into a home of their own. The book conveyed the idea of a productive social community, which we found to be a very appealing worldview; it excited us. The book's first publication in the GDR was in 1950, and the topic was something new and genuine. Literature at that time was intended to set an example in the hope of motivating people to behave in a different social manner. That is, literature turned from heroic war epics to promoting a new society, with a new sense of community and peace.

Furthermore, there was a lot of literature about village life and agriculture in the 1950s and 1960s. The changes that happened there occurred over centuries. Feudalism was abolished and many people, for the first time, received their own plots of land during the land reform in 1946. It was no coincidence that the most important children's book published in those days—*Tinko* by Erwin Strittmatter in 1954—was set in the countryside, which was odd, given the fact that the focal point of a socialist society and its literature was usually the proletariat, the working class living in urban areas.

In sum, there was more at stake than literature alone. The intention was to exert influence on young people in several ways. Besides portraying particular characters, favoring particular storylines, and repeating topics and tropes, a lot of material resources were invested with that aim. Although there was never enough paper available during the postwar years, numerous copies of books were still printed and published. Apart from Aufbau Verlag (1945) and Verlag Volk und Welt (1947), the first publishing houses established were geared toward children's and youth literature, namely Verlag Neues Leben (1946) and Kinderbuchverlag Berlin (1949). In order to make literature accessible to young people, they provided a range of special issues, book series, and reduced prices. I personally got my books from the series Buchclub 65. Public libraries were created, and books required for school were free. Later on there was also a whole variety of children's and youth magazines such as *ABC-Zeitung* (ABC Magazine)[1] for kids starting school, or *Frösi* (Fun and Singing) for kids around the age of nine to twelve. Another interesting point is that famous and well-established authors were also considering children as the audience for their books. All this was aimed at fostering humanistic ideas and communicating new social values: peace, friendship, and solidarity.

Fischer: Did the intent of the literature remain unchanged until the 1980s, or did you recognize changes in topics and stories, or did certain discourses become altered at some point?

Aurich: Well, of course, the style of early GDR literature was bold and simple; social values were communicated in a direct manner. Things changed in the 1960s, when stories about individual figures emerged in literature as well as in film. These stories illustrated how individuals could contribute to the new society; they were setting examples for commitment to the newly created society, paired with a critical assessment thereof. Similarly, at this time, the GDR had become established and consolidated, and then the Berlin Wall was built in 1961 . . . and, as one result, literature dealt more with developments within GDR society, instead of focusing on the past or on the outside. In this period, some of the most instrumental novels ever written by GDR authors were published: *Die Aula* (The Great Hall, 1965) by Hermann Kant, *Der geteilte Himmel* (Divided Heaven, 1963) by Christa Wolf, *Spur der Steine* (Trace of Stones, 1964) by Erik Neutsch, and *Ole Bienkopp* (1963) by Erwin Strittmatter. All these works followed the same principal intention: to be in alignment with the socialist development within the GDR and to describe personal and social conflicts within the socialist society. That is, their goal was not fundamental political change, or a different society altogether, but—and I think most importantly—the discussion of conflicts within the existing socialist society in order to ensure social progress. These books, however, did not overemphasize those conflicts; rather, the conflicts were presented as a natural part of society, and the books were all well received. With regard to cultural politics, it is interesting to note that the novel *Spur der Steine*, for example, did not provoke any wide-ranging criticism by cultural officials, but some years later, the film version by DEFA director Frank Beyer (1966) became a subject of public debate. As a result, the film was eventually banned. We all know this story. There appears to be more power in pictures than there is in words.

Fischer: Literature in the GDR addressed certain target groups, and, as earlier stated, young people in particular. Storytelling was an educational tool. Can you speak more about the political and social influences of literature?

Aurich: Literature in the GDR had a certain mass impact. Compared with the situation today, a relatively small number of books were read by a great number of people. And there were a few books that were favorably received by many GDR citizens. Among them are the books I have already mentioned: *Tinko, Der geteilte Himmel, Spur der Steine*, and so on. The same refers to Soviet literature, for example, *How the Steel Was Tempered* by Nikolai Ostrovsky (1932–34), which was published by Verlag Neues Leben in 1947 as one of the first works of world literature that came out in the Soviet occupation zone. Many people of that generation were deeply impressed by the novel's depiction of the political struggles and construction efforts of protagonist Pavel Korchagin during the Russian Civil War (1918–21). People were also impacted by books such as *Nackt unter Wölfen* (Naked among Wolves, 1958) by Bruno Apitz, which portrays a group of Communists (prisoners) hiding a child in the Buchenwald concentration camp, or *Die Abenteuer des Werner Holt* (The Adventures of Werner Holt, 1960–63) by Dieter Noll, which portrays a young soldier becoming disillusioned with National Socialist Germany during the last stages of the Second World War. In the 1970s Ulrich Plenzdorf's book *Die neuen Leiden des jungen W.* (The New Sorrows of Young W., 1973) made a great impact among young people aged 16 to 26. The book was difficult to obtain, so it was heavily circulated among students. *Die neuen Leiden des jungen W.* was the story of a failure and a suicide. A book with a plot of this sort, or even with plot elements of this sort, was completely new. The book broke taboos, in writing as well as in social thought, as the protagonist dropped out of society.

Another interesting point is the publication of books that are not related to the GDR or socialism, for example books set in 1850s America that dealt with the fate of American Indians. *Die Söhne der Großen Bärin* (The Sons of Great Bear, 6 volumes, 1951–63) by Liselotte Welskopf-Henrich is a popular example; it was probably read by 80 percent of young people during the 1950s through the 1980s. The stories told in these books were not about the GDR: they told stories about a strong, resistant community fighting an overbearing enemy. This storyline provided points of identification with a socialist, antifascist society that sought to separate itself from the past, as well as to overcome capitalism.

Fischer: I can confirm your point about the mass impact of literature. Being born in the 1970s, I too have read all the books that you mention, including *Die Söhne der Großen Bärin*, just like my parents, who were born in the 1950s. This shows that literature, and certain stories in particular, have been transferred through all generations of the GDR. One can therefore claim that those books and their stories form a significant part of the cultural history and collective memory of the GDR.

Aurich: Yes, you are right; they are part of the GDR's cultural heritage. However, the transfer of certain books and stories also revealed a crucial issue that emerged in GDR society: the generation gap. For example, Irma Gabel-Thälmann's recollections of her father, Ernst Thälmann,[2] the political father figure for the GDR, *Erinnerungen an meinen Vater* (Recollections of My Father, 1951), was a book that saw numerous editions. Gabel-Thälmann's recollections were republished again and again, with a particular political aim. The aim was to develop respect for the efforts and ideological struggles of the prewar generations—that of socialist and Communist role models such as Ernst Thälmann—among young people of the 1950s, 1960s, 1970s, and 1980s. All this served an educational purpose, and offered points for identification, but later on it turned into a problem. Why? Politicians and officials in the GDR did not bear in mind that each generation has to find its own ways and role models, and has to develop its own views about past generations. Young people want to develop their own ideas, insights, and perspectives; they seek to prove themselves. However, such considerations were of minor importance to the party officials. They feared that critical thinking might provoke conflicts. Irma Gabel-Thälmann worked as a representative for the Socialist Unity Party of the GDR and the Young Pioneers' organization "Ernst Thälmann." When she read from her memories in public, for example in front of a work brigade or a school class, in the earlier years she gave a lively narrative about her father. She continued with these readings and public appearances well into the 1980s. Your own experience, Ms. Fischer, confirms this, as you have described to me how Gabel-Thälmann visited your elementary school for a reading in the 1980s. However, as she grew older, her performance became less and less convincing. It had transformed into a kind of antifascist routine by then, and her message was not reaching young people anymore. Clearly, it was problematic to stick to such educational activities, or at least to stick to the same format to present certain stories and topics throughout the decades.

Fischer: Please elaborate on which stories and books incited criticism from cultural and party officials.

Aurich: In the 1980s we were concerned about the story *Insel der Schwäne* (Swan Island, 1980), originally a youth novel by Benno Pludra. Strangely enough, nobody had got worked up about the book, much as with *Spur der Steine* in 1964; excitement was only caused by the subsequent film version, which was directed by Herrmann Zschoche (1983). I remember everything about this controversy because I had to supervise the film review that was to be published in *Junge Welt*.[3] The author of the review was assigned to discredit the film because it addressed the emergence of subcultures in a new housing district in Berlin. According to official cultural politics this development was regarded as highly inappropriate, as subcultures did not exist in a socialist society. Hence the book as well as the film portrayed the opposite of what we originally wanted and imagined—namely a homogenous socialist community—, instead clearly showing that some developments had turned out differently.

And that was actually the truth. The mere truth always aroused suspicions. The same controversy happened with *Erscheinen Pflicht* (Your Attendance is Imperative, 1981). Again, nobody was concerned about the story by author Gerhard Holtz-Baumert. In fact, hardly anyone had taken any notice of it. Later, when I was already chairman of the Free German

Youth, we saw the film version, directed by Helmut Dziuba. That was in spring 1984 and we had a very interesting discussion about the film. We planned to show it on the occasion of the Youth Festival in Berlin in June 1984, and I made the proposal that the première of the film should take place there, but this was not permitted. In May 1984, the première was brought to the National Film Festival in Karl-Marx-Stadt.[4] However, the film was withdrawn immediately afterwards, and was not shown again until after 1989.

Fischer: Were any specific reasons given?

Aurich: The story in the film is about a high-school class that is required to attend a political demonstration in honor of May 1st, which is Labor Day. They have to wear their Free German Youth uniform, bring a GDR flag, and listen to a speech by a politician. Most of the young people find this just boring and meaningless, and eventually sneak away from the demonstration. Hence the film is about how to deal with rituals in society. The fourteen-year-old young protagonist of the story is an honest character who is willing to follow her ideals, and she eventually collides with the formalism of rituals . . .

Fischer: . . . and she challenges the rituals and wonders about their meaning.

Aurich: Yes, and she also questions the background and attitudes of the older generations: her father, grandfather, teachers, and other role models. For the highest cultural officials, it did not seem appropriate to have this kind of debate in connection with another ritual, namely the Youth Festival. It was deemed too dangerous to question such activities, but I held a completely different opinion; I thought these were exactly the debates that were necessary in our society. Those debates could have convinced people to participate again in such rituals, and reverted the rituals into something that was not a routinized action, but something genuine, something that was positively internalized.

I recently read an article about a shift of debates in the 1980s, which sparked my memory of the film. The article stated that the socialist ideal was originally embodied by the society itself, but then it changed into an ideal that was embodied by individuals, and mostly by young people and children. And they, holding onto the ideal, came into conflict with the society, or perhaps reality. They could not relate their ideals anymore to what they experienced in their daily lives and eventually challenged this contradiction. The result was that young people became the true idealists, but they also got stuck in the contradiction between upholding an ideal and not finding it echoed within and by their environment. To write a book or make a film with such a storyline was new and different, and a drastic change from the 1950s and 1960s.

Fischer: This also means that young people in the GDR in the 1980s, represented for example by the girl in the film, asked their parents' and grandparents' generations—who lived through the Weimar years and the time of National Socialism—these important questions: What is the meaning of your political ideals for my life today, and how can I relate my 1980s reality to the story of your life? As you explained, Mr. Aurich, Irma Gabel-Thälmann eventually failed at establishing such a relation, and so did others.

Christa Streiber-Aurich: Yes, in the film *Erscheinen Pflicht* the girl asks her father, a party functionary, this question. After his death she continues to question her godfather, who is a functionary as well. She tells the latter: "You do not know what we want." He replies: "Well, what do you want then?" But this question remains open, as if she does not know the answer. Those young people did not want all that stuff dished up by the old folks, but they also could not clearly define what they wanted.

Fischer: What was the reason for that?

Aurich and Streiber-Aurich (in unison): Society in the 1980s had nothing to offer young people, or at best, it could only offer things within the old structures or ideologies.

Aurich: A young person who is always required to honor and appreciate achievements of former generations will eventually ask herself: What can I accomplish in this society today besides complying with the request to do my work well? Of course, there were some social offers, we as Free German Youth organized the so-called youth projects, which also included an air of romance—let me mention the building of a natural gas pipeline in Soviet Siberia—but those were exceptional cases. As soon as young people wanted to do something on their own, such as gathering freely or listening to foreign music, they immediately came into conflict with—and this is my deliberate choice of words—the old folks who could not understand them or even did not want to. They completely ignored the generation gap, the gap between their life story and the story of the younger generation of the 1970s and 1980s.

Moreover, in the 1970s, the Socialist Unity Party proposed that the Communist education of the youth be intensified. However, the meaning of Communist education in that society and at that time had never been defined. In the end, it meant to entrust your own life completely to society: individual life was to be absorbed into the collective. But this was an *illusion* [emphasis Aurich]. Probably the ideal of entrusting one's life to a collective is illusory or utopian altogether, and can never be achieved by humankind; however, at that moment in time, in the 1970s and 1980s, it was no longer the ideal of the young people of the GDR. They wanted just the opposite—they demanded more individualism and the realization of their own ideas.

Fischer: Is it possible to influence or change a society through literary works? In the 1950s and 1960s, as we stated, literature and the stories put forth an educational agenda pertaining to a political and ideological program, and it was successful in those decades. For the 1970s and 1980s, we discussed stories that highlighted generational gaps and other issues. Did these stories instigate social and political changes? Did they offer any solutions?

Aurich: In my opinion, literature alone cannot produce changes. . . . Changes can only happen in concurrence with the social conditions. Provided that literature and daily life—in the sense of how society treats its individual members—move into the same direction, literature can achieve its contribution to such a development. If they diverge, we are faced with the problem of what literature is really able to achieve. Can it really initiate change in social conditions? Did *Insel der Schwäne* or *Erscheinen Pflicht* cause any change in social structures? Not in any way. They certainly provoked some discussion—a few people might have thought some things over—but books and films cannot alter state-established institutions. On the other hand, it is correct to assume that literature had made a contribution to achieving social stability in the 1950s and 1960s. However, when that stability did not exist any longer because it could not be maintained economically and, additionally, when it was called into question by world politics, literature was unable to maintain its former intentions and was forced to take a different direction.

Streiber-Aurich: I think that literature, especially in the 1970s and 1980s, tried to describe problems and contradictions within the socialist society, but it could not offer any solutions or ways out of the contradictions. The stories got stuck in their own problematic world, if you will. There was an ideological dogma that contradictions were non-antagonistic, that they could be resolved *within* the socialist society [emphasis Streiber-Aurich]. . . . However, by 1989 at the latest, people had become aware that contradictions existed within the socialist society that *by no means* [emphasis Streiber-Aurich] were of a non-antagonistic nature, and the avant-garde literature of that time, and the public sphere in general, started to acknowledge that. However, it seems that it was too late, that it had become impossible to resolve the contradictions between ideal and reality, between the individual and society.

Aurich: Nevertheless, literature will always embody some critical potential. However, another question remains, and I shared this with some of my colleagues on the Central Committee of the Socialist Unity Party, with writers Hermann Kant, Gerhard Holtz-Baumert, and with a couple of actors who were party members: why did we not do anything to discuss or to solve the contradictions that we had become well aware of? We did not protest and only shared our concerns among close friends. One major reason for our reluctance was that the structures of GDR society were fixed as a matter of principle. Anyone who gave an opposing view, or just made a proposal that did not correspond to the current wishes of the political leadership, was suspected of striving for fundamental, political changes. When Soviet Chairman and leader Mikhail Gorbachev actually initiated such fundamental changes in the mid-1980s, the GDR party leaders quickly distanced themselves from them, since they recognized where such changes might lead. That is, they were always afraid to consider any proposal for changes, such as meeting the desires of young people by allowing them to travel, listen to music, gather in clubs, to let them do their own thing. What would have been the result of such activities? It may have led to the realization that the desires, wishes, and aspirations of young people in the GDR, and maybe of most people in the GDR, no longer corresponded with the current political and ideological agenda of the party, and that what the GDR had to offer its people was no longer wanted.

Fischer: It was a stalemate situation. What would have been a way out?

Aurich: Let me explain it in this way: we have learned an important lesson from the whole story. As a precondition of social progress and development, there must exist the possibility for changes within society. But this possibility was an illusion, which we only recognized after the demise of the GDR. As long as you can anticipate the possibility of change, people will join in and try. One joins by writing a book, another by making a film, and yet another by educating his students in a sensible manner. But then one faces more conflicts. I was constantly faced with conflicts, as the influence of our youth organization was declining among the majority of young people. The main problem was to figure out how to keep the citizens volunteering for state sponsored activities in addition to raising their motivation and willingness to participate. Again, as the film *Erscheinen Pflicht* showed very insightfully, the involvement of young people in cultural-political events was declining drastically, and for obvious reasons. However, we wanted young people to join as volunteers, and to take part in cultural-political activities as representatives and faces of the GDR society.

Everybody, in any official political position, in all governmental organizations, we all faced these conflicts in our respective places, insofar as we were still willing to intervene in social problems. By resolving these conflicts we would have created a rare opportunity to change the GDR considerably.

Fischer: Toward the end of the GDR, however, communication and renewed attempts toward mutual understanding took place in the public sphere as well as in cultural products.

Aurich: Yes, you are correct. Toward the end of the GDR, a tendency had developed to pursue an idealistic approach of creating harmony. One example from the cultural sphere is the film *Einer Trage des Anderen Last* (Bear Ye One Another's Burden, 1988), directed by Lothar Warneke. It was met with immense response in the GDR—what was the reason? The film portrays two people who hold different ideological views, yet enjoy one another. One protagonist is a pastor and the other is a Marxist. Suddenly even the troubles with the GDR churches in the 1980s were set aside.[5] People did not want confrontation and disagreement; they preferred an ideal of mutual understanding and dialogue. At the same time that the film came out, the GDR Minister of Culture, Hans-Joachim Hoffmann, published an article in a Swiss periodical. He propagated the idea that the two systems were no longer strictly contrary to each other but might coexist, an idea derived from Mikhail Gorbachev's efforts toward détente.[6]

Fischer: By "the two systems," you are referring to capitalism and socialism?

Aurich: Yes, capitalism and socialism and the political blocs of the Cold War. Hoffmann in his article had pondered upon what would happen if the two blocs agreed to mutually coexist in harmony with one another. As a result, I was charged by government officials with the "great" task of contradicting him and his views at a plenary session of the Central Committee of the Socialist Unity Party. Later, I apologized to Hoffmann for complying with this order. It would have been perfectly possible to hold a normal discussion about the whole matter, with Hoffmann supporting his opinion and I contrasting, but the intention was to condemn and demonize Hoffmann's views, completely neglecting the fact that the world had altered course. At this time Gorbachev was giving in more and more; he gave up one after another position of authoritarian power over the other Eastern bloc countries. Therefore, Hoffmann was not wrong in his conclusion that peaceful coexistence might be possible by simply getting along and cooperating with each other.

Fischer: Let us return to literature for the last part of our conversation. One of the roles of literature is to narrate people's lives, in fictitious or authentic versions that vary again and again. Literature is our collective diary and therefore contributes to our collective memory—a statement that is particularly applicable to the GDR. Why is it so important for people to narrate their lives and to tell their stories to one another?

Aurich: Everybody has their own self and personality, which exist in relation to their social environment and social interlocutors. Depending on what place people have found in society, they are either satisfied with themselves or not, they are proud of themselves, or maybe not. People actually like to talk about themselves, and if they find a partner who listens, they will be willing to tell their stories. Some people write down their stories, and if one takes heart, one's stories will be published and printed. What I mean to say is that our conception of the world is not only defined by our own story but is composed of all those other stories and of other people's experiences. We are not only shaped by the genes of our parents; we have our own impressions and experiences, and some of them are immediate, and some of them are indirect. These are the stories and experiences that parents and grandparents related to us in our childhood.

Fischer: GDR literature and film, and in fact the majority of cultural products, constitute a very homogeneous corpus as far as themes, motifs, and storylines are concerned. We discussed them today. Hence the GDR as a whole could be seen as a narrative that is continuously and meticulously recorded in its cultural products. I would claim therefore that the literary and filmic corpus of the GDR serves as a social and cultural history of the country. Do you agree?

Aurich: Yes, I would absolutely agree, and that is due to the originality of the GDR. After all, it had come into existence through separation from the other part of Germany. There was the idea of building a new and different Germany that defined itself as the better German state. This starting point propelled the emergence of a particular national identity in the GDR. Starting in the late 1950s, and ending after the building of the Wall in 1961, when the idea of a reunified postwar Germany had been shelved, the GDR leadership promoted an intensified identification with the GDR among the population. And this development of a particular GDR identity did take place, particularly through its cultural products, through the books and films. The GDR, in all its enclosure and provinciality, was a very small entity, mostly occupied with its own affairs, always looking inward. Only a small percentage of GDR literature dealt with the West—for instance, Christa Wolf's *Der geteilte Himmel* or the books of Anna Seghers. They cast a glance at the other part of the world.

Fischer: In your view, what significance does GDR literature have for readers today? Can it make an impact? How can these stories that we discussed relate to present-day readers and present-day Germany?

Streiber-Aurich: I think fewer people are actually interested in reading original GDR literature today. Nevertheless, people are interested in the topic, and read contemporary books about the GDR. Those are books written with a retrospective view, by authors such as Eugen Ruge or Monika Maron. I personally struggle with these books. When I read them, with their criticism and their attitude of knowing better, I can hardly believe that I kept living in the GDR—in this awful country that they describe—and that I did not leave it. I mean this ironically, of course. I don't like the negative and sometimes ridiculing attitude in these books, but I think it is this kind of literature that young people today prefer. They want to acquire knowledge about the GDR, or they want to inform themselves about the past, but they don't really want to understand. They may think: "Why should I read books by Christa Wolf? After all, they were written under political pressure and therefore do not tell the whole truth. When I want to find out something about the GDR, I am going to read today's literature because it is written in freedom and therefore tells the truth." I believe most of the younger people share this viewpoint.

Aurich: Yes, indeed. That is why I think that GDR literature will not be read by many people today and in the future. I think the stories don't connect anymore; they are maybe too specific to an earlier time with different ideologies.

Fischer: What about novels such as *Das siebte Kreuz* (The Seventh Cross, 1942) by Anna Seghers, which is a book about anti-fascism and the dire conditions of living in Nazi Germany?

Aurich: At present, there is certainly cause for us to reconsider that book and make it a topic for public discussion, because neo-fascistic developments are becoming evident in present-day Germany. However, I am afraid young people today who are concerned about these developments cannot make the connection to the book, or maybe not to the book alone. The things discussed in there are just not the same to them. Moreover, they are unable to imagine the Third Reich as the incarnation of inhumanity itself, and they do not fully realize that there is a connection to the people who organize fascistic actions in the streets today. Books like *Das siebte Kreuz* can help people to strengthen their powers of argumentation against neo-fascists, but the debates with these groups must also be fought with today's arguments.

Notes

[1] All translations are my own, unless otherwise noted.

[2] Ernst Thälmann (1886–1944), leader of the Communist Party of Germany from 1925. He was arrested by the fascist regime in 1933 and held in solitary confinement for eleven years. In 1944 he was murdered in the Buchenwald concentration camp. The GDR Pioneer Organization as well as numerous governmental and other public entities, including schools, streets, factories, work brigades, and buildings were named after him.

[3] *Young World*, daily newspaper of the GDR Free German Youth Organization.

[4] Today known as Chemnitz.

[5] Churches were the origin of reforms, opposition, and protest movements in 1980s GDR society.

[6] "Glasnost im DDR-Theater: 'Das Sicherste ist die Veränderung.' THEATER HEUTE-Gespräch mit dem DDR-Kulturminister Hans-Joachim Hoffmann," in *Theater 1988: Das Jahrbuch der Zeitschrift 'Theater Heute'* (Zurich: Orell Füssli & Friedrich, 1988), 10–20.

Contributors

PETER BEICKEN (PhD, Stanford University, 1971) is professor of German studies at the University of Maryland, College Park. He has published widely on Kafka, Ingeborg Bachmann, and film. He edited the early stories (1924–32) in the Anna Seghers *Werkausgabe* (2014) and has published several articles on Seghers.

HUNTER BIVENS (PhD, University of Chicago, 2006) is associate professor of literature and German studies at the University of California, Santa Cruz. He is the author of *Epic and Exile: Novels of The German Popular Front* (2015). He has also published widely on the literature and film of the former German Democratic Republic.

KRISTY R. BONEY (PhD, Ohio State University, 2006) is associate professor of German at the University of Central Missouri, where she also serves as coordinator of modern languages and teaches in gender and women's studies. She has published articles on Anna Seghers and Franz Kafka.

UTE BRANDES (PhD, Harvard University, 1982) is Georges Lurcy Professor of German at Amherst College in Massachusetts. Her early work was on German writers since the seventeenth century, but more recently she has specialized in Anna Seghers. She has published a monograph, articles, and two volumes in the Seghers *Werkausgabe*. Her work on Seghers's narratives about the 1960s and 1950s led her back into the time of Seghers's exile in Paris and Mexico City. Currently Brandes is focusing on Seghers's novel *Der Kopflohn*.

STEPHEN BROCKMANN (PhD, University of Wisconsin–Madison, 1989) is professor of German at Carnegie Mellon University. Since 2013 he has served as president of the International Brecht Society. He is the author of *The Writers' State: Constructing East German Literature 1945–1959* (2015); *A Critical History of German Film* (2010), *Nuremberg: The Imaginary Capital* (2006); *German Literary Culture at the Zero Hour* (2004); and *Literature and German Reunification* (1999). In 2007 he won the DAAD/AICGS Prize for Distinguished Scholarship in German and European Studies/Humanities, a prize that is awarded every three years. In 2011–12 he served as president of the German Studies Association.

Sylvia Fischer (PhD, Ohio State University, 2014) has taught German at St. Olaf College in Minnesota and the University of West Florida. Fischer's expertise is in GDR literature, film, and history; in 2014 she published a monography on the concept of *Heimat* in GDR literature and film of the 1950s and 1960s, and articles on Anna Seghers and Kurt Maetzig. She is a board member of the International Brecht Society and lives in Berlin.

Jost Hermand (PhD, University of Marburg, 1955) is Vilas Research Professor Emeritus at the University of Wisconsin–Madison and an honorary professor at the Humboldt University in Berlin, Germany. He has published extensively, including *Deutsche Kulturgeschichte des 20. Jahrhunderts* (2006), *A Hitler Youth in Poland: The Nazi Children's Evacuation Program in World War II* (1997), and *Old Dreams of a New Reich: Volkish Utopias and National Socialism* (1992).

Kristen Hetrick (PhD, Ohio State University, 2012) is associate professor of German at Doane University in Crete, Nebraska, where she also serves as chair of the Modern Languages Department and National Fellowships Advisor. Hetrick remains actively engaged in German literary studies, German-American studies, and the world language teaching community.

Robert C. Holub (PhD, University of Wisconsin–Madison, 1979) is Ohio Eminent Scholar of German and professor and chair of the Department of Germanic Languages and Literatures at Ohio State University. He taught at the University of California at Berkeley for twenty-seven years, where he was also dean of the undergraduate division, then served as provost at the University of Tennessee, Knoxville, from 2006 to 2008; and from 2008 to 2012 as chancellor at the University of Massachusetts Amherst. His scholarly work has focused on nineteenth- and twentieth-century cultural and literary history, with special interest in Heinrich Heine, German realism, Friedrich Nietzsche, literary and aesthetic theory, Jürgen Habermas, and *Vergangenheitsbewältigung*.

Weijia Li (PhD, Ohio State University, 2009) is assistant professor of German at the University of Wisconsin–Madison where he also serves as director of the Global Higher Education Master's Degree Program. His research and teaching interests include Chinese-German cultural encounters reflected in German literature, press, and art history. In 2010 he published a book on Anna Seghers's encounter with China in her life and works. He is currently working on a new book project that examines German and Yiddish writings on China by European Jewish refugees in Shanghai during the Second World War.

Elizabeth Loentz (PhD, Ohio State University, 1999) is associate professor of German and member of the Religious Studies faculty at the

University of Illinois, Chicago. She has published numerous articles as well as the book *Let Me Continue to Speak the Truth: Bertha Pappenheim as Author and Activist* (2007). She also currently serves as book review editor for the *German Quarterly*. She is writing a second book, "The Meaning of Yiddish in Twentieth-Century Germany."

MICHAELA PEROUTKOVÁ (PhD, Ohio State University, 2005) is associate professor of German at the Czech University of Life Sciences in Prague, Czech Republic. Her research interests include German-Czech-Jewish relationships and questions of identity in German and Czech postwar literature. Her recent book, *Jewish Identities in Czechoslovakia before and after World War II* (2016), deals with Jewish representations in Czech collective memory. She is currently working on a project that focuses on East German collective memory of the communist past.

BENJAMIN ROBINSON (PhD, Stanford University, 1997) is associate professor of Germanic studies at Indiana University in Bloomington and affiliated faculty in labor studies, cultural studies and European studies. His book *The Skin of the System: On Germany's Socialist Modernity* (2009) focuses on the philosophical dilemmas of real socialism as crystallized in the work of East German author Franz Fühmann. Recent publications include essays on the concepts of simplicity/complexity, Ernst Niekisch, Anna Seghers, and the Peircean phenomenology of "secondness." His current book project, "On the Magnitude of the Present: A Theory and History of Indexicality," explores the concept of radical indicators in philosophy, economics, and literature.

CHRISTIANE ZEHL ROMERO (PhD, University of Vienna, 1973) is professor of German and international literary and cultural studies and Goldthwaite Professor Emerita at Tufts University. She is the author of two monographs, on Simone de Beauvoir and Anna Seghers, and a two-volume biography of Anna Seghers (2000 and 2003) and she is the editor (with Almut Giesecke) of the letters of Anna Seghers in the *Werkausgabe* volumes *Briefe 1924–1952* (2008) and *Briefe 1953–1983* (2010). She has written numerous articles, focusing particularly on women writers, the literature of the German Democratic Republic, Austrian literature, exile, and migration. Currently she is working on a project concerning women in Viennese modernism.

MARC SILBERMAN (PhD, Indiana University, 1975) is emeritus professor of German at the University of Wisconsin–Madison. His research, teaching, and publications have focused on GDR literature, political theater in Germany (especially Bertolt Brecht and Heiner Müller), and German film history. He has edited numerous volumes of proceedings of conferences he helped organize, themed anthologies and journal issues, and *The Brecht Yearbook*, as well as translated Brecht, Müller, and other German authors.

Andy Spencer (PhD, Ohio State University, 1992) completed his dissertation under Helen Fehervary's guidance in 1992. A former editor of *Communications of the International Brecht Society*, he has published on topics ranging from the destruction of Dresden to Einstürzende Neubauten. For the past twenty years he has served as the resident director for Ohio State University's summer study in Dresden Program.

Luke Springman (PhD, Ohio State University, 1988) is professor of German at Bloomsburg University of Pennsylvania. His dissertation, "Comrades, Friends, and Companions: Utopian Projections and Social Action in German Literature for Young People, 1926–1934," was advised by Helen Fehervary. Much of his scholarship has dealt with youth culture of the Weimar Republic. In 2018–19 he was awarded a research stipend from the Staatsbibliothek zu Berlin. His current book project is on the propagation of imperialism to German youth in the Weimar Republic.

Amy Kepple Strawser (PhD, Ohio State University, 1991) teaches German and integrative studies at Otterbein University. Her dissertation, "Imaging the Body in Contemporary German and American Women's Poetry: Helga Novak, Ursula Krechel, Carolyn Forché, Nikki Giovanni," was advised by Helen Fehervary. In 2010, she published a bilingual translation of Ursula Krechel's *Voices from the Bitter Core* with Host Publications. In 2017, she and Helen Fehervary published translations of three stories by Anna Seghers including "The Excursion of the Dead Girls" in *American Imago*. Other of her poetry translations have appeared in *International Poetry Review* and *PEN International*.

Jennifer Marston William (PhD, Ohio State University, 2002) is professor of German and head of the School of Languages and Cultures at Purdue University. She has authored two monographs, *Killing Time: Waiting Hierarchies in the Twentieth-Century German Novel* (2010) and *Cognitive Approaches to German Historical Film: Seeing is Not Believing* (2017), and coedited the volume *Theory of Mind and Literature* (2011). She has worked with Helen Fehervary on editing two volumes of the Anna Seghers *Werkausgabe*, *Aufstand der Fischer von St. Barbara* (2003), and the forthcoming critical edition of *Die Gefährten*.

Index